EXECUTIVE MANSIONS and CAPITOLS OF AMERICA

EXECUTIVE MANSIONS and

By Jean Houston Daniel
and Price Daniel

CAPITOLS OF AMERICA

Published by Country Beautiful, Waukesha, Wisconsin
Distributed by G. P. Putnam's Sons, New York

 Distributed in the Dominion of Canada by Longmans Canada Limited, Toronto. Manufactured in the United States of America. Book design by Wilbur Howe. Color separations, Mueller Color Plate Company.

CONTENTS

Preface . . . . by Mrs. Lyndon B. Johnson 8

Introduction . . . . by Jean Houston Daniel 10

I. EXECUTIVE MANSIONS 12

History of Executive Mansions . . . . by Jean Houston Daniel 14

The White House 17

State Governors' Mansions 24

Commonwealth and Territorial Governors' Mansions 122

States without Executive Mansions 130

II. CAPITOLS 134

History of Capitols . . . . by Price Daniel 135

The Nation's Capitol 139

State Capitols 144

Commonwealth and Territorial Capitols 244

III. CHIEF EXECUTIVES 250

Presidents of the United States 250

Governors of the States 250

Governors of the Commonwealth and Territories 279

IV. APPENDIX 282

Present Executive Mansions: Original Cost and Architectural Style 282

Present State Capitols: Original Cost and Architectural Style 283

Historical List of Capital Cities 284

Bibliography 286

Acknowledgments and Credits 288

Index 290

Preface

By Mrs. Lyndon B. Johnson

No one who has moved into an Executive Mansion can read the vivid letters of Abigail Adams to her daughter back in Massachusetts, written shortly after her arrival at the unfinished White House in November 1800, without a pang of sympathy:

> *This House is twice as large as our meeting House* [she wrote]. *I believe the great Hall is as big—but this House is built for ages to come. Not one room or chamber is finished of the whole . . . To assist us in this great castle, and render less attendance necessary, bells are wholly wanting—promises are all you can obtain.*

The wives of our Governors who each two or four years step across the thresholds of their Executive Mansions do so in a mixed state of anxiety and awe. The task is to make an instant home, a pleasant place from which to govern, with the architecture and equipment that goes with the job. Their success is determined by their own ingenuity and their Legislatures.

Several of the Mansions which house our Chief Executives were built before the White House. Kentucky's handsome Georgian Mansion at Frankfort was built for $12,000 in 1797 for the Governor and is still in use by the Lieutenant Governor.

The newest Mansion is in Harrisburg, Pennsylvania. Built at a cost of $2,000,000, it was ready for occupancy in December 1968.

Several States have acquired real historic landmarks, handsome mansions built before the American Revolution for some leading family, and now occupied by the Governor of the State. Seven States have no Executive Mansion.

But a house is far more than brick and mortar, and ghosts of the past. It is the home of the family of a man who has been chosen by the people to chart that State's destiny for a period of time.

You feel the presence of those who have gone before, but the house becomes part of the daily life of the State. The work and the hospitality, the weddings and births and deaths, which occur within those walls are part of the contemporary history.

I am delighted that Jean Houston Daniel, one of the most gracious and history-minded First Ladies to occupy an Executive Mansion, has compiled the stories of the official residences and their Capitols.

No one could be more ideally equipped for such a task—by heritage, association and experience. Jean Daniel began assembling historic material on the Executive Mansions of our Nation in 1962 while she was First Lady of Texas. Living in that magnificent Greek Revival house of 1856, her interest was partially stimulated by the fact that her great-great-grandfather, General Sam Houston, served as Governor of two States—Tennessee and Texas, as well as in the halls of Congress from both States.

In her own right, Jean shared the responsibilities of a distinguished husband whose official duties required two years of residence in the Speaker's Apartment of the Texas State Capitol, while he was Speaker of the House; four years of work in the National Capitol as U.S. Senator; six years of residence in the Texas Governor's Mansion; and now, since 1967, constant work at the White House and in Governors' Mansions and State Capitols as Assistant to the President for Federal-State Relations and chief liaison with the Governors.

My husband is a strong believer in the working partnership of the States and the Federal Government as the best path to good government. Price Daniel has been a builder and unifier in that mission.

I believe this book will bring all of us closer in this delightful demonstration of the historical, architectural, political and spiritual ties which bind us together in "a more perfect Union."

Introduction

This book pictures and describes 117 houses and buildings which span more than 350 years of American history—from the Governor's Palace of New Mexico built in 1610 to the newest State Capitol being completed in Hawaii in 1969.

Buildings reflect the heritage and achievements of a people as effectively as histories, plaques and monuments. This is particularly true of the Executive Mansions and Capitols of America, for they are owned by the people and are occupied by those whom the people have chosen to write successive chapters of their history.

These Executive Mansions and Capitols are living symbols of the sovereignty of the American people, the stability and continuity of their governments, and the ability of the people to govern themselves through elected representatives. They serve as links to a glorious past and as inspiration for a challenging future.

When the British burned the White House and the U.S. Capitol in 1814, reconstruction was begun immediately, because even in those early years of the Republic, these two buildings had become symbols of the stability and strength of the new Nation.

The same reasoning prevailed in an older country when Winston Churchill advocated the prompt reconstruction of the House of Commons after it had been shattered by Nazi bombs in World War II. In a memorable speech citing the heritage and influence of the building and urging restoration "on its old foundations," Mr. Churchill said: "We shape our buildings and afterward our buildings shape us."

I subscribe to the theory that persons privileged to serve in these magnificent Capitols and to live in these historic houses are inspired by the buildings themselves with a keener sense of responsibility to the people whom they represent. Further, I believe that those who are so honored have a responsibility to record the history and preserve the character of these structures.

It was with this in mind that in 1957, while my husband was Governor of Texas, I began research and writing on the Texas Governor's Mansion. By 1962 this had led to research on residences other States provide for their Governors and more recently to the enlistment of my husband in this joint project, which covers not only the Executive Mansions but also the Capitols and a roster of Chief Executives.

Part I is devoted to the Executive Mansions—the White House and the State Houses in which the Presidents and the Governors live, work and entertain. Part II depicts the Capitols in which both executives and legislators serve. Part III lists the names and terms of all who have served as Chief Executives of the Nation, States, Commonwealths and Territories.

I am grateful to Mrs. Lyndon B. Johnson for taking the time, while still First Lady of the Nation, to write the Preface. No one has shown more interest in preserving the heritage and beauty of our land, particularly the Nation's capital city and the White House. Mrs. Johnson has indicated some of the reasons for my interest in Mansions and Capitols. It is true that I lived in the Texas State Capitol Building while my husband, Price Daniel, was Speaker of the House in 1943. Then, after a tour of duty in World War II, he served in the same State Capitol for six years as Attorney General.

My first experience with the Nation's Capitol and the White House was when my husband served as a member of the United States Senate from 1953 to 1957, after which we spent six years in the Texas Governor's Mansion. More recently, we returned to Washington where he served in the Executive Office of the President as Assistant to the President for Federal-State Relations and Director of the Office of Emergency Preparedness. Thus, many years of our lives have been spent and shaped within the walls of four of the buildings pictured and described in this book. In appreciation, we have given our time to this book as a public service without monetary compensation. The same is true of all other contributing writers. Although many State and Federal officials have cooperated in its content, the publication is financed not by governmental funds but solely by the private publishers, whom we thank for making it available to the public.

Aside from the history and architecture, I hope this book will remind us of the importance of the States in our Federal system and the need for continued cooperation at both levels of government. The States still have primary responsibilities in many areas affecting the lives of the American people, including a vital role in many joint Federal-State programs. It is the improvement of the Federal-State partnership that President Johnson stressed during his administration, a program in which my husband served as the President's liaison with the Governors. A measure of its success and nonpartisan conduct was indicated at the 1968 National Governors' Conference when a Republican Governor introduced, and the Conference unanimously passed, a resolution honoring the President and the program that resulted in "... the best working relationship that has ever existed between the State and Federal Governments."

Except for this excellent and nonpartisan cooperation between the State Houses and the White House, this book would never have become a reality. All Governors and First Ladies have contributed photographs or articles, or both. Each Governor's wife has either furnished or personally written the description and history of her State's Mansion. Thanks to them, my task has been mainly one of comparison with earlier research, compiling and editing.

My appreciation goes also to the Federal-State Relations staff and Regional Directors in the Executive Office of the President who have assisted in so many ways. A list of personal acknowledgments to them and others is contained on pages 288-289. I sincerely thank all of them, especially my husband and coauthor, Price Daniel, and Margaret Legath, whose advice and assistance have been of immeasurable help on the entire book, and Donald J. Carbone and Mary Pearl Williams for their excellent assistance in the research and editing of Parts II and III.

Jean Houston Daniel

I

EXECUTIVE MANSIONS

I Pray Heaven To Bestow
THE BEST OF BLESSINGS ON
THIS HOUSE
And All that shall hereafter Inhabit it
May none but Honest and Wise Men ever rule
under This Roof.
From a Letter of
JOHN ADAMS
November
MDCCC

History of Executive Mansions

By Jean Houston Daniel

Our Nation, forty-three of the fifty States, and all of our Territories furnish Executive Mansions for their Chief Executives. This perquisite of the office existed in some of the States and Territories before the formation of the Union, having originated in many of the former colonies of England and Spain. In colonial days, the name of "Governor's Palace" was more often used.

Outstanding examples inherited from Spain are the Palace of the Governors built in Santa Fe, New Mexico, in 1610, which, after housing the heads of six different governments, still stands as the oldest surviving public building in the continental United States; and the Spanish Governor's Palace built in San Antonio, Texas, in 1749. Both now serve as museums.

Still in use in the Commonwealth of Puerto Rico is La Fortaleza, or Santa Catalina Palace, originally completed as a fort in 1540, and occupied as the Governor's residence since about 1640. It is said to be the oldest Executive Mansion that is used as such in the Western Hemisphere.

At one time or another at least seven of the original thirteen English Colonies had official "Palaces" for their Governors, with the New England Colonies being among the exceptions. Those which survived the Revolution to become occupied by State Governors were the Virginia Governor's Palace at Williamsburg built in 1720 and Tryon Palace in New Bern, North Carolina, completed in 1770. These magnificent Georgian buildings have been reconstructed and are open to the public.

In those States where Governors appointed by the King or by Colonial Proprietors had been housed at public expense, the Legislatures apparently believed that Governors chosen by them or by the vote of the people should be treated with no less dignity. However, having severed themselves from the Crown and everything symbolic of kings, lords and palaces, the colonists soon began calling these official residences by more democratic terms. "Executive Mansion" or "Governor's Mansion" became the more acceptable name, although North Carolina called a later official residence in Raleigh the "Governor's Palace" from 1816 to 1865.

The word *mansion* sounded less royal and more meaningful. It has a Latin origin, from *mansio*, which means a staying, a dwelling, a remaining. It connotes an impressive structure that symbolizes stability and leadership. An Executive Mansion houses that leader in whom the people have put their trust. Formerly that leadership was inherited or awarded by royalty, but in the new American elective system, the Executive Mansion became a symbol of the sovereign power of the people—a power to be exercised by their Chief Executive in accordance with laws enacted by their elected legislators. Elected officials come and go, but the Executive Mansion remains, representing the continuity, importance and dignity of the office.

Thus, today, thirty-two States use the term "Executive Mansion" or "Governor's Mansion." Since 1872, Congress has referred to the White House as the Executive Mansion, although President Abraham Lincoln previously used the name on his official correspondence from 1861 to 1865.

However, the word *mansion* was not and is not now universally acceptable to all legislative bodies. Prior to 1872 Congress officially referred to the White House as "The President's House." Three States (Alaska,

The Palace of the Governors in New Mexico, built in 1610, is the oldest surviving public building in the continental United States.

Delaware and Idaho) call their residences the "Governor's House," and seven (Connecticut, Minnesota, New Jersey, North Dakota, Pennsylvania, Utah and Wisconsin) use the term "Executive Residence" or "Governor's Residence."

Maryland and the three Territories (American Samoa, Guam and the Virgin Islands) use the term "Government House." The Commonwealth of Puerto Rico uses "Executive Mansion" in officially referring to the more often used name of La Fortaleza.

Whatever the official name may be, there is an interchange in usage of the various terms, and some are better known by the historic names of the houses, such as La Fortaleza; Washington Place, Hawaii; Cedar Crest, Kansas; Blaine House, Maine; and Morven in New Jersey. Collectively these historic houses are referred to in this book as "Executive Mansions," meaning any dwelling furnished to a Chief Executive as an official residence designed to care both for his family and the affairs of State.

Most of the States provide Executive Mansions as a matter of necessity in order that the Governor may reside at the seat of government and discharge his official duties in a manner befitting the dignity and responsibilities of the office. Twenty-three States, either by constitution or statute, specifically require that their Governors "shall reside" at the seat of government. The requirement is inferred in nine other States whose constitutions or laws call for the establishment of official residences at the seat of government.

All of these thirty-two States, except Arizona and Michigan, provide official residences for their Governors. Arizona is the only State whose Constitution requires that the Governor "shall reside at the seat of government" but whose Legislature does not supply either a residence or a housing allowance. Oregon has no official residence but provides the Governor a rental allowance.

In addition to Arizona, Michigan and Oregon, the only others without Executive Mansions are the New England States of Massachusetts, New Hampshire, Rhode Island and Vermont. These are discussed under "States without Executive Mansions," pages 130-133.

After the Revolution, two Virginia Governors, Patrick Henry and Thomas Jefferson, used the old Governor's Palace at Williamsburg until the capital was moved to Richmond in 1780. In 1781 Virginia purchased a frame house on the site of its present Governor's Mansion, which served until 1810.

North Carolina's Governors continued to use Tryon Palace at New Bern until 1794 when the capital was moved to Raleigh, where a two-story frame residence was bought by the State in 1797 and served until the Greek Revival Governor's Palace was completed in 1816.

The first State to construct a Mansion after the Revolution was Kentucky in 1797. It served as the official residence of thirty-three Governors from 1798 to 1914, when the present Mansion was completed. The old one is now used as the official residence of the Lieutenant Governor.

By 1792 Thomas Jefferson was busy planning a new Governor's Mansion for Virginia and a President's House for the newly surveyed "Federal City" of Wash-

Virginia's Governor's Palace (circa 1720) was reconstructed at Colonial Williamsburg

North Carolina's restored Tryon Palace was originally built in 1770.

Kentucky's old Governor's Mansion (circa 1797) is older than the White House.

The classic lines of the "White House" of the Confederacy, now a Confederate museum, recall the charm of the Old South.

ington. In his own words, Jefferson had "reverence for the Graecian and Roman style of architecture." Vigorously converting his reverence to action, this man who had the greatest influence on American democracy soon came to have the greatest influence on the style of American architecture—an influence still visible in a majority of the buildings pictured in this book. James Hoban's design of the White House, later modified by Jefferson, was completed for partial occupancy in 1800.

Virginia in 1813 became the second State to construct a Governor's Mansion. This stately Georgian house with added classic porticos is the oldest State Mansion still being used for its original purpose. The Virginia Commissioners of Public Buildings were highly successful in their purpose of designing a home of distinction, "considering as well the honor and dignity of the State, as the conveniency of the Chief Magistrate. . . ."

North Carolina's Governor's Palace of 1816, mentioned earlier, was a two-story Greek Revival brick structure that housed twenty Governors and then Union General Sherman, who took possession on his "march to the sea" in 1865.

Georgia built its first Governor's Mansion at the early capital of Milledgeville in 1839. Patterned after Palladio's Foscari Villa, it is one of the most imposing examples of Greek Revival architecture in existence and is now used on the Georgia College campus.

Mississippi also followed the Greek Revival style in constructing its impressive Mansion in 1841, and it is still in use. In addition to Virginia and Mississippi, the States of Illinois, Texas, South Carolina and Maryland, and Puerto Rico and the Virgin Islands have Mansions which have been in use as such for more than one hundred years. To this age list should be added those of New Jersey (1701), Delaware (1790), Maine (1830), Hawaii (1846), and New York (1856), which were constructed more than a hundred years ago but which were acquired for Mansion purposes at later dates.

At least eight other States had Mansions prior to 1900 which are no longer in use as such. They include Indiana, Iowa, Missouri, Nebraska, New Jersey, North Dakota, Pennsylvania and West Virginia.

Another Greek classical structure of historical note was the "White House" of The Confederacy in Richmond, Virginia, built in 1818 and occupied by President Jefferson Davis from 1861 to 1865. It is now a Confederate Museum.

In the Appendix is a table (page 282) of all Mansions presently used as such, and giving the original cost and general style of architecture. It should be remembered that this does not include the earlier residences which once served but are no longer in use.

On the following pages, after the chapter on The White House, the Mansions of the States are presented in alphabetical order, followed by Puerto Rico and the Territories, American Samoa, Guam and the Virgin Islands.

The White House

The White House is the oldest public building in Washington and the most famous Executive Mansion in the world. Although enhanced by the dignity and charm of its classic architecture, its fame results more from the leadership which has been exercised within its walls in the human struggle for peace, progress, justice and liberty under law.

As the official residence of all but one of the thirty-six Presidents of the United States, it has become both a symbol and an integral part of the heritage of the American people. It is visited by more people than any other house in the Nation, with an average of 1.6 million annually during the past four years.

Both citizens and occupants recognize and are inspired by the fact that the White House really belongs to the people. President Franklin D. Roosevelt said, "I never forget that I live in a house owned by all the American people. . . ." President Theodore Roosevelt earlier expressed the same thought and added: ". . . It is a good thing to preserve such buildings as historic monuments which keep alive our sense of continuity with the Nation's past. . . ."

That continuity ties in with the original States which formed the Union. Their official Seals are carved on the marble-faced opening of the stairway in the Main Lobby. Two of them, Virginia and Maryland, ceded the land which forms the Nation's Federal City and donated funds toward construction of the White House and the Capitol. Sixteen of the thirty-six Presidents previously served as Governors of States or Territories, and most of these lived in State Executive Mansions described in this book. All but four of the Presidents previously served in State Capitols or as representatives of their States in the Congress.

George Washington, the only President who did not live in the White House, played the principal role in selecting its site in 1791, gave close attention to its construction and successfully resisted all efforts to reduce the extent of its grounds. Writing Federal Commissioner David Stuart on March 8, 1792, about the President's House and general plans for the new city, he said: ". . . The doubts and opinions of others . . . have occasioned no change in my sentiments on the subject . . . the public buildings in size, form and elegance should look beyond the present day. . . ."

Thomas Jefferson, serving as Secretary of State, prepared the notice and details of a competition by which $500 or a medal would be awarded by the Federal Commissioners for the best design of a "President's House." The competition was won by James Hoban of South Carolina, a native of Dublin, Ireland, who had designed the Greek Revival South Carolina Statehouse of 1790 in Charleston. His plan featured four Greek columns as embellishments and three Palladian facades. The exterior was completed in time for the first occupancy by President and Mrs. John Adams in 1800.

Although Washington and Jefferson, along with architects Hoban and Benjamin Henry Latrobe, are justly credited for the vision which produced this magnificent house on its eighteen acres of landscaped beauty, every succeeding President has contributed something toward its structure, grounds and history. Surprisingly, the major structural contributions to the building's grandeur were not made by aristocratic Presidents, but by four of the more democratic occupants—Jefferson, Andrew Jackson, Theodore Roosevelt and Harry S. Truman.

Jefferson and his Surveyor of Public Buildings, Benjamin Henry Latrobe, constructed the elegant east and west terraces; redesigned Hoban's projected South Portico, which combined both plans when finally constructed by Hoban in 1824 under Monroe; and planned the dramatic Ionic-columned North Portico.

Jackson, inaugurated in 1829, immediately initiated construction of the North Portico as planned by Jefferson and Latrobe; added cut glass chandeliers and Brussels carpeting in the East Room; and purchased many other elegant furnishings.

Theodore Roosevelt sponsored a complete renovation and expansion in 1902, insisting that architects McKim, Mead and White restore it to follow the original design. His main addition was a West Wing designed for office space, thus for the first time completely removing office functions from the residence. The West Wing was rebuilt in 1910; restored after a fire in 1930 and rebuilt and expanded in 1934. The East Wing was added for offices in 1942 under President Franklin D. Roosevelt.

President Truman, having added the balcony midway of the South Portico in 1947, sponsored the complete rebuilding of the interior of the Mansion in 1948. This was after a commission of experts found that the originally sound basic structure had been dangerously weakened and was unsafe due to the heavy stresses placed on the original supports and beams by years of remodeling, cutting of holes and sections for the addition of electrical wiring, piping for water, gas and air conditioning, and the addition of a steel roof in 1927. In 1949, Congress appropriated $5.4 million for the reconstruction, and President and Mrs. Truman resided across Pennsylvania Avenue at Blair House until the

Overleaf: Bright reds and blues form a lively contrast to the White House.

work was completed in 1952.

The first occupants, President and Mrs. John Adams, were unable to make many improvements during their brief stay in the unfinished building, but Mrs. Adams' letters to her daughter about the inconvenience of the place and how she used the barren East Room for hanging out the laundry form a part of its interesting history. They also left a heritage of spiritual faith and moral integrity, evidence of which is now displayed on the mantel of the State Dining Room. Taken from a letter written to his wife on the night of November 2, 1800, President Adams' second night in the White House, are the following words which President Franklin D. Roosevelt inscribed on the mantel:

I Pray Heaven to Bestow
The Best of Blessings on
THIS HOUSE
and All that shall hereafter Inhabit it.
May none but Honest and Wise Men ever rule
under This Roof.

James Madison suffered through the War of 1812 and innumerable formal receptions planned by his wife, Dolley. They added many furnishings, practically all of which were burned when the British set fire to the house in 1814. Dolley Madison is best remembered for saving from the flames the valuable portrait of Washington painted by Gilbert Stuart. It now hangs in the

The White House, which is the oldest and most famous public building in Washington, D.C., has been visited by an average of 1.6 million persons yearly for the past four years.

East Room as the only object in the Mansion which has survived from Adams' first occupancy.

James Monroe moved into the White House after Hoban's reconstruction in 1817. Having served as Minister to France, he and Mrs. Monroe used French firms to acquire many exquisite furnishings, and while he was praised for his pronouncement of the Monroe Doctrine, he was severely criticized for his lavish spending on foreign furnishings. A gilt pier table, a silver trunk, silver tableware and centerpiece, and an American purchase of marble busts of Columbus, Americus Vespucius and Washington remain today. In spite of the criticism over interior furnishings during Monroe's administration, Congress appropriated funds for construction of the Ionic-columned South Portico in 1824. Except for the additions and restorations already described as having occurred during the Jackson, Theodore Roosevelt, Franklin D. Roosevelt and Harry S. Truman administrations, there were no other major structural changes affecting the exterior. However, practically every President or his First Lady made interior changes as running water, gas, and electricity were introduced, and other comforts, decorations and furnishings were added to suit their tastes.

All of the Presidents are represented in the White House by items used by them or presented by their families or friends in their honor, or by their own distinguished portraits.

A Fine Arts Committee on the White House was created during the John F. Kennedy administration to assist in acquiring authentic historic furnishings. Mrs. Kennedy did research on the house and its furnishings. She restored many of the fine pieces which had been in storage and acquired many items which once were in the house. According to a survey, her television tour of the White House in 1962 was viewed by one-third of the people of the Nation.

In 1964, President Lyndon B. Johnson established a Curator of the White House and a Committee for the Preservation of the White House, and Mrs. Johnson has continued the work of beautifying the Mansion and the grounds. It is the Curator's task to advise the President on furnishings of historic interest, preservation thereof and placement of them in the public rooms.

Within the original Mansion walls, designed in 1792 (when the total Federal establishment had only 128 employees), there are now 132 rooms. There are seven additional rooms in the terraces, including a flower room and swimming pool in the West Terrace, and a theatre in the East Terrace. The West Wing has 73 rooms, including the President's Office and Cabinet Room, offices of the Presidential Assistants and secretaries, and the White House Mess. The East Wing has 32 rooms which provide offices for the First Lady's staff, the military aide, the White House Police and the personnel and disbursing staffs.

The entire complex is referred to as the White House, a name which originated from the popular designation given to the original residence on account of its light sandstone walls. Hoban's reports indicate that it was painted white both during construction in 1798 and upon his reconstruction in 1817, after the British had put it to the torch and burned out the interior in 1814.

Officially, however, from the time Major Pierre Charles L'Enfant placed the designation, "President's House," on Reservation 1 of his plan for the proposed capital city in 1791 until 1871, Congress referred to the structure as the President's House. Since 1872, in its Appropriation Acts, Congress has referred to the house as the Executive Mansion, with an occasional general statute referring to the entire complex as the White House. For instance, in 1961, Congress provided that "all that portion of reservation numbered 1 in the City of Washington . . . within the President's park enclosure . . . shall continue to be known as the White House. . . ."

President Theodore Roosevelt, in 1901, began using the name "White House" on his official stationery and advised the Secretary of State and other officials "to change the headings, or date lines, of all official papers and documents" requiring his signature "from 'Executive Mansion' to 'White House.' " This custom is still followed. When distinguishing between the residence and the office wings, both Congress and the President refer to the residence as the Executive Mansion.

Principal rooms of interest on the ground floor are the Library, Diplomatic Reception Room, China Room and Vermeil Room; and on the first or State Floor are the entrance hall, the main hallway, the East Room, the Green Room, the Blue Room, the Red Room and the State Dining Room.

The second and third floors are devoted to the family and their guests. Famous rooms there include the Rose Guest Room, in which Queens Elizabeth and Elizabeth II of Great Britain, Wilhelmina and Juliana of The Netherlands, and Frederika of Greece have stayed; the Victorian-furnished Lincoln Bedroom, which is associated with President Lincoln because it once served as his Cabinet Room and in it he signed the Emancipation Proclamation; and the Treaty Room, which also served as a Cabinet Room and in which the treaty of peace with Spain was signed ending the Spanish-American War.

The White House is open to visitors Tuesdays through Saturdays from 10 a.m. to 12 noon.

Opposite: The elegant Red Room of the White House has been decorated in the Empire style popular in the early nineteenth century. Walls are hung in gold-bordered cerise silk.

Below: The graceful South Portico of the White House, designed principally by Thomas Jefferson, was added in 1824 during the Presidency of James Monroe.

ALABAMA

THE GOVERNOR'S MANSION By Mrs. Albert P. Brewer, *First Lady of Alabama**

The Governor's Mansion of Alabama is an impressive Greek Revival structure featuring towering Corinthian columns, a recessed second-story balcony with an ornate balustrade, a stately porte-cochere and sprawling, beautiful grounds. It is located in the capital city of Montgomery.

General Robert F. Ligon, Jr., built the Mansion as a private home in 1907. This prominent Alabamian was an attorney, the Mayor of Tuskegee, Clerk of the State Supreme Court, and Adjutant General of Alabama during the Spanish-American War.

General Ligon built his palatial home on land deeded from the United States Government to "Rachel Hatchett and husband" on October 10, 1818, the year before the Alabama Territory gained statehood status. The Ligon heirs sold the home to the State of Alabama for $100,000 on October 13, 1950. The State spent an additional $130,000 renovating and refurnishing it for occupancy as the Governor's official residence.

Six Alabama Governors have lived in the home since the State purchased the imposing structure in 1950. They are former Governors Gordon Persons, James E. Folsom, John M. Patterson, George C. Wallace and Lurleen B. Wallace, and Governor Albert P. Brewer.

The Mansion has seventeen rooms and is maintained through State appropriations, with a normal staff of four employees. It is open for tourists from 10 a.m. to 2 p.m. on Monday, Wednesday and Friday of each week.

The handsome building is one of the most elaborate structures of the 1900-1920 era when many wealthy Alabama families resurrected the Greek Revival design which had dominated Alabama and Deep South architecture from 1840 to 1860. This architecture reincarnated the native monuments, motifs, impressions and sentiments of the great neo-classical architecture of the mid 1800's, a crowning era for Southern plantation mansions and town houses.

Four large columns with Corinthian capitals are the focal point of the massive white facade. Arched windows, window balconies and an ornate balustrade atop the beautiful south porte-cochere are other prominent features.

The spacious interior contains a pair of winding stairs which ascend from the landing of the grand staircase in the reception foyer and divide toward the private living area upstairs. Parquet floors and Alabama marble are indicative of the substantial building materials used to construct the home. The medallions and cornices are in accord with the Greek Revival style.

The full-length pier and mantel mirrors are among the original furnishings of the home. Collected items include: a silver candelabra, tray and punch bowl made for the *U.S.S. Alabama*, a famous battleship of World War II. The chandeliers over the grand staircase and in the dining room originally adorned an old hotel in New Orleans. Silver and crystal chandeliers, original furnishings of the Mansion, hang in the other rooms.

The furniture in the formal area is of the Victorian period constructed in Alabama especially for the Mansion. The dining room contains Queen Anne furnishings and antique silver appointments.

The paintings are fine representations of Confederate Alabama military heroes, General Joe Wheeler, Major John Pelham and Major Thomas Goode Jones, who was later Governor of the State. Portraits of William Lowndes Yancey, the fiery secessionist; Lieutenant Governor R. F. Ligon, Sr., father of the builder; and Confederate Generals J.E.B. Stuart and Robert E. Lee are also displayed. The scene paintings are by C. T. Phelan and Jan Both, the latter a noted Flemish artist.

At the rear of the Mansion, there is a large formal garden, one of the most beautifully landscaped gardens in Alabama. Prominent in the garden are lovely camellias, the State Flower. The garden extends through the block to Court Street and is surrounded by a high ornamental wall.

Alabama's first official Governor's Mansion was purchased for $45,500 in 1911. Moses Sabel built the home in Montgomery at 702 South Perry Street five years earlier. This structure was occupied by Governors Emmett O'Neal, Charles Henderson, Thomas Kilby, William Brandon, Bibb Graves, Benjamin Miller, Frank Dixon, Chauncey Sparks and James Folsom.

The Sabel Mansion was used for State offices until it was sold in 1959 to the Montgomery Academy, a private school. The State re-acquired the building in August 1962, and used it as offices for the State Military Department until the home was demolished in 1963 to make way for an interstate highway.

The State of Alabama had no official residence for its Chief Executive in Montgomery from 1847, when the city became the capital, until 1911. Neither Cahawba, Huntsville nor Tuscaloosa, capitals of the State from 1819 through 1846, had official residences for the Governor, nor did St. Stephens, the Territorial capital from 1817 to 1819.

*Assisted by the Alabama Historical Commission and the Alabama Department of Archives and History.

This palatial seventeen-room Mansion is the home of Alabama's Governors. Its Greek Revival design was popular in the South during the early nineteenth century.

Colorful mountain-ash berries accent the white Doric columns on the south side of the Alaska Governor's House.

ALASKA

THE GOVERNOR'S HOUSE By Mrs. Walter J. Hickel, *Former First Lady of Alaska*

For fifty-five years, the beautiful white house in Juneau at 716 Calhoun Avenue has been "home" to Alaska's First Families. The two-and-a-half story structure occupies its own little "island" surrounded by four busy streets. A pleasant south lawn is dotted with large mountain-ash trees bordered by a low, green hedge. The north lawn is enclosed by a white picket fence and boasts a small garden featuring roses and young evergreens.

The Mansion was authorized by the United States Congress in the Public Works Act of 1910, when Alaska was still a Territory. The appropriation of $40,000 covered the cost of construction and furnishings.

Construction began in 1912 under the direction of William N. Collier. The architecture has been called a liberal interpretation of New England colonial but, with a wide veranda and Doric pillars on the south side, the house can also be said to display a little influence of the antebellum South.

On January 3, 1913, the first official reception, hosted by Governor and Mrs. Walter F. Clark, was held. Since Governor Clark's time, the Mansion has been occupied by eight Territorial Governors and two Governors of the State of Alaska.

The Mansion faces south toward Gastineau Channel. Channel traffic ranges from huge freighters and the ferryliners of Alaska's marine highway fleet to sailboats, skiffs and kayaks. West of the channel, the snowcapped peaks of Douglas Island push toward the sky. Towering Mt. Roberts dominates the skyline to the east.

Against the east wall is a tall totem, the Governor's Totem, carved in 1939-40 by Tlingit Indians from Saxman and Klukwan as a gift to the Mansion.

The main door of the Mansion opens on the first of fifteen rooms. The color motif is muted green and old gold with highlights of bright yellow. Crystal chandeliers descend from the high ceilings. Alaska genre paintings, on loan to the Mansion from artists all over the State, decorate the antique white walls.

In addition to paintings, Alaska artists have loaned pottery artifacts and other art items. In this huge State, many of the works of art have traveled hundreds of miles to be on display for one year, and some of the artists live so far away they have never seen Juneau.

The four large downstairs rooms come into their own during official receptions and state dinners. They set a mood of warmth and elegance for evenings at the Mansion. The entire house was redecorated in 1967, shortly after Governor Hickel took office. At that time, third floor guest rooms were added and a portion of the basement was converted to a recreation room.

There are seven fireplaces in the Mansion. The largest and most attractive is in the first floor reception room. An American and an Alaskan flag flank the fireplace, and a brass American eagle spreads its wings above it.

Directly behind the reception room is the dining room. Here a table for twelve is surrounded by high-backed chairs with old gold seats. Austrian curtains are lowered on a large bay window across the west wall through the long hours of afternoon sunlight during Juneau's warm summers.

South of the reception room are a sitting room and music room. In the music room, many items of Alaskan memorabilia are displayed. Prominent among them is a large silver bowl commemorating the Harriman-Alaska expedition of 1899.

A large brass samovar bears testimony to Alaska's Russian heritage. The Brothers Mirimov made the samovar in Russia during the 1800's. Originally used to hold hot water for tea, a samovar today may be used to serve coffee or punch.

On the walls of the first floor halls are watercolors created in the 1930's under the sponsorship of the Federal Works Projects Administration. The largest painting in the Mansion is on the wall of the first landing of the stairs leading to the second floor. Framed in gold, the eight-foot-high painting depicts Czar Peter the Great. The painting originally occupied a place of honor in the Governor's House on Castle Hill in Sitka when Alaska was a Russian colony.

The official china of the State is off-white rimmed with gold and with a representation of the State Seal on the rim. The silver is monogrammed GH for Governor's House.

The family rooms are on the second floor. In addition to bedrooms and a living room, there is a corner room that served as the writer's office where a complete inventory of the Mansion's household items is compiled.

Of course, the Mansion is much more than a museum of art. It is the official residence of the Governor and as such serves for many state functions. Receptions for guests of the State, luncheons and annual legislative dinners are held here. Other visits and tours are arranged upon request.

The traditional event most looked forward to and most enjoyed is the annual Christmas Open House. All Juneau residents are invited to visit, and many hundreds stop by to share the season's greetings.

The stately Arkansas Governor's Mansion is set on six beautifully landscaped acres in Little Rock.

ARKANSAS

THE GOVERNOR'S MANSION By Mrs. Winthrop Rockefeller, *First Lady of Arkansas*

Arkansas' official Governor's Mansion is situated on six acres of land at West Eighteenth and Center Streets in Little Rock. The Arkansas General Assembly approved funds for the building of the Mansion in 1947, and it was completed in January of 1950. This first official Mansion of the State has housed the families of former Governors Sid McMath, Francis Cherry, Orval Faubus and Arkansas' present Governor, Winthrop Rockefeller.

The Mansion is of Georgian colonial architecture, with two stories and ten rooms, and is flanked on each side by high brick walls and with walkways leading to two guest houses. It is constructed of age-mellowed oversized brick that came from old State properties, among which was the State School for the Blind, formerly located on this site. The original cost was $100,000.

The building was redecorated in 1964 and completely renovated in 1967, at which time space in the basement area was utilized for additional storage, a laundry room and public facilities. Some of the other rooms in the house were re-floored and all were redecorated.

From the front, one enters the Mansion grounds through a double-iron-filigree gate, and walks along a circular graveled driveway. Stepping upon the veranda, one passes between massive white Doric columns to a large paneled door. The entire foyer is laid with marble, donated by the Batesville Marble Company, which sets off the spacious winding stairwell, above which is centered a crystal chandelier. Two centuries old, it was brought from France in small pieces and rechained in a process which took a period of three months.

Near the top of the first flight of stairs hangs a painting of Lady Willoughby by George Romney. This painting is loaned for use at the Mansion by the Rockefeller family. It is an especially fine painting and so rare that the Metropolitan Museum of Art has offered repeatedly to buy it. Other paintings used in the public rooms are loaned by the Arkansas Arts Center and feature the work of John Henry Byrd, who was Arkansas' first portrait painter of real recognition. Mr. Byrd moved to Little Rock from Camden in 1840 and his portraits hanging in the Mansion were done between 1850 and 1855.

A broken-front court table stands against the right-hand wall of the foyer. It holds a single boat-shaped silver bowl which is part of the sixty-two-piece set subscribed by the people of Arkansas and given in 1918 to the *U.S.S. Arkansas* and then bought back from the Navy for use in the Mansion. This bowl design features heads of eagles for handles and a latticework cover. Over the table hangs one of the paintings by Mr. Byrd, a portrait of Abbie Churchill, daughter of General Thomas Churchill, the thirteenth Governor of Arkansas.

The formal dining room is located to the right of the foyer. It, along with the other downstairs rooms, has off-white walls and oak-pegged flooring. Oriental rugs, now used in both the dining area and the living room across the foyer, were given to the Mansion by its present occupants.

The room's long Empire dining table is fashioned in four sections, each section resting on its own pillar and claw. On the table are two English Regency candelabra, dated 1810, which once belonged to a collection of Madam Balsan, a former Duchess of Marlborough. One section of the table has been removed and is being used as a separate piece in front of one of the dining room windows. It holds the great silver punch bowl, fashioned of three thousand silver dollars, one of the most magnificent pieces in the *U.S.S. Arkansas* collection.

Against the south wall stands a sideboard, crafted in England in 1778. Believed to be the oldest piece of furniture in the Mansion, it holds a variety of silver pieces. An 1800 French Empire clock graces the mantel-piece over the woodburning fireplace on the west wall.

Across the marble foyer to the east is the large living room. Both this room and the dining room have draperies made of Italian antique gold silk. They are tied with handmade silk tassels. The casement curtains are of white silk. On the mantel, over the massive wood-burning fireplace, is a pair of exquisite Waterford glass candelabra, gift of Mrs. Rockefeller. To the left of the mantel is a drum table supported by a turned column, resting on four concave legs. A Queen Anne candle slide table is featured in the room's center grouping of furniture. On the table is a jade box, a companion piece to the Ming horse which sits on the drum table.

These, and other rare and lovely pieces in the room, are part of the collection of Mr. and Mrs. John D. Rockefeller, Jr., parents of Governor Rockefeller, who is graciously sharing them with the people of Arkansas during his tenure in the Mansion.

On the north wall hang two Byrd portraits. One, to the right of the windows, is of Ann Sevier Churchill, wife of Thomas Churchill and daughter of Ambrose Sevier, the first United States Senator from Arkansas. The portrait to the left of the windows is of General Thomas Churchill. On the west wall, over a sofa, there is a Byrd portrait of Mrs. Weldon Wright, wife of Dr. Weldon Wright of Virginia, an early settler in Arkansas, and their daughter.

A grand piano, presented to the Mansion in 1954 by Mrs. Agnes Shinn of Harrison, stands in front of French doors which lead to a portico at the back. On the piano rests a great silver urn with a map of Arkansas etched on its side and naming various products of the State. To the left of the piano, on the south wall, is a portrait, also by Byrd, of Dr. Weldon Wright.

To the east of the living room is the den, where the walls are decorated in the same off-white as the formal rooms, but the carpet is a light green with an olive border. Colorful English crewel draperies hang at the windows, and two watercolors and an oil painting from the Arkansas Arts Center Celta Exhibition brighten the walls. The oil, "The Beach at Arabida," by Robert Bailey, hangs over a russet sofa against the inside wall.

A large antique English breakfront fills the end wall, and a heavy square game table with arm chairs is set up in the corner. On the south wall, a credenza with three sets of double doors holds a lamp made from a large brass coffee urn.

Sharing wall space with watercolors "Lobster Boat" by Fred Conway and "The River-Gold Home" by Townsend Wolfe, is an enlarged photograph of "Rose-wood," old home of William S. Fulton, Territorial Governor. This old home originally was situated just west of the present site of the Mansion.

The family breakfast room is on the south side of the formal dining area, and is a light and cheerful room with a parquet floor and a bay window. A round table, made from Arkansas pine, and featuring a large lazy susan for informal serving, sits in the center of the room. A maple buffet and hutch display fine old pieces of majolica, part of the Rockefeller family collection. An interesting fir branch, planted in a majolica tub of sand, stands against the wide. expanse of the window and looks very much like a bonsai tree. Another watercolor, "River Light," by Nadine Parker, hangs on one of the breakfast room walls.

The Mansion's kitchen completes the west wing of the house, and other family rooms, four bedrooms and a study, are on the second floor.

The Mansion staff consists of five persons. Tours are conducted on the first Friday of each month from 10 to 11:30 a.m. and from 4 to 5:30 p.m. and at other times by appointment.

CALIFORNIA

THE GOVERNOR'S MANSION By Mrs. Ronald Reagan, *First Lady of California*

Like the State of California, the history of the Governor's Mansion is rich and colorful.

The Mansion is an elaborate and handsome Victorian residence situated in the center of downtown Sacramento. When the Mansion was first constructed as a private home for Albert Gallatin in 1877, it was located on what was then the edge of town. Mr. Gallatin paid more than $75,000 for his home; the architect was Nathaniel D. Goodell of Massachusetts.

Ten years after the home was built, Mr. Gallatin sold it to Joseph Steffens whose son, Lincoln, gained fame as a writer. Then in 1903, the State purchased the home for $32,500 to use as its official Governor's Mansion. California's twenty-first Governor, George Cooper Pardee, was the first Governor to occupy it.

The home has three stories and twenty-three rooms, in addition to the basement, and above the third floor is a most interesting two-story cupola. A handsome carriage house lies adjacent to the residence.

There are eight fireplaces and mantels throughout the home, each made of a different variety of Italian marble.

Each First Lady of California has left her decorating mark in the home, but all have greatly admired the magnificent staircase, the gilt-edged ceilings and crystal chandeliers. One of the most interesting rooms is the third-floor ballroom with its handsome parquet floor.

In 1917, an attempt was made on Governor William D. Stephen's life by exploding eight pounds of dynamite in the area of the kitchen. Both the pantry and the kitchen were destroyed, but the Governor and his wife escaped unharmed. The responsibility for the blast was laid to a group nicknamed the "Wobblies," more formally known as the Industrial Workers of the World.

Thirteen Governors have resided in the Mansion over a period of sixty-four years, even though the building was declared unsuitable for occupancy for reasons of safety as long ago as 1941. In spite of this, no agreement was ever reached by the Legislature with regard to building a new Mansion. As a result, California's Governors and their families continued to live there until the first part of 1967 when Governor Reagan and I vacated the residence in favor of a leased home in the Sacramento suburbs.

Soon after we left, the Department of Parks and Recreation declared the home a State Historical Monument and opened it for public tours.

Early in 1967, a citizens' committee was formed to raise funds to build California a new Governor's Mansion. Approximately ten acres were purchased on a knoll overlooking the American River. Hopefully, additional funds can be raised to finance designing and building an adequate Governor's Mansion for all future California Governors.

It is my hope that the design of the Mansion will carry out the beautiful early California architectural style so long associated with the history of our State.

[*Editor's Note: Mrs. Adin D. Henderson, of Sacramento, a long-time State employee, wrote the following additional comments on the California Mansion:*]

The Victorian structure that today stands majestically at the corner of H and Sixteenth Streets in Sacramento was once described as resembling "a tall white wedding cake."

There are one hundred steps from basement to cupola. Lacy iron grillwork garnished the roof edges and cupola tower until the frenzy for scrap iron in 1942 caused Governor Culbert Olson to have the iron removed. The beautifully kept grounds are still surrounded, however, by the wrought-iron fence installed in 1878.

A great amount of the scroll work and "gingerbread" characteristic of the period is included in the construction. The elaborate moldings, carved door and window frames, and other complicated woodwork and fixtures would require a fortune to duplicate today. Its walls and high ceilings have extensive carved and sculptured ornamentation. All door knobs and hinges are of ornately carved brass.

It is open for tourists from 10 to 5 daily. Admission is fifty cents and children under 18 are admitted free.

Opposite: The former Governor's Mansion of California, an elaborate Victorian structure resembling "a tall, white wedding cake," was declared a State Historical Monument in 1967 by the Department of Parks.

COLORADO

THE GOVERNOR'S MANSION By Mrs. John A. Love, *First Lady of Colorado*

Until recently, Colorado did not provide a home for its Chief Executive. In 1960, the Boettcher Foundation, a philanthropic organization, offered the Boettcher Mansion and its contents to the State of Colorado "as a residence for present and future Governors." Being concerned with the Mansion's maintenance and operating costs, the Governor and the State Legislature were reluctant to accept the gift. However, much pressure from Colorado citizens and a cash grant of $45,000 from the foundation toward maintenance of the property for two years influenced the State officials to accept the gracious offer.

On April 21, 1960, the gift was officially accepted for the State by Governor Stephen L. R. McNichols, who became the Executive Mansion's first occupant the following August. Governor John A. Love, the thirty-seventh Chief Executive of Colorado, moved his family into the Mansion on January 11, 1963.

The three-story, twenty-seven room, red brick, colonial Mansion has white stone trim, two-story colonnades and ivy-covered walls. The house, surrounded by landscaped, terraced grounds, is located at 400 East Eighth Avenue, about eight blocks from the State Capitol in Denver. The grounds are enclosed within a six-foot iron fence.

Although relatively new as the Governor's residence, the Mansion is rich with the history of three of Colorado's pioneer families—Chessman, Evans and Boettcher—who lived in this palatial home during the past several decades. Walter Scott Chessman purchased the original site in 1904, planned the house and began its construction. He died before its completion in 1908. However, his widow and his daughter, Gladys, who married John Evans, grandson of Colorado's second Territorial Governor, in the residence, lived here for several years.

In 1926, the property was purchased by Claude K. Boettcher, Colorado's most successful developer of industries. Mr. and Mrs. Boettcher were world travelers, and the Mansion abounds with rare antiques, art treasures, and priceless pieces of furniture acquired during their travels. The lower floor of the Mansion has been kept very much as it was left by the Boettchers. The beautiful plaster relief ceilings represent a lost art and every attempt has been made to preserve them.

Among the other outstanding features of the house are the very large and beautiful chandeliers. The view from the front entrance down the long central hall to the sunroom gives a breathtaking glow of sparkling crystal and warm candlelights from three chandeliers. In the drawing room hangs a particularly lovely crystal chandelier of Waterford glass purported to have hung in the White House at one time. The dining room chandelier is Venetian with true color solid glass fruit adorning it.

The sunroom, a large, many-windowed room, has a white marble floor, Italian marble urns holding palms, and a fountain. The furnishings are white with accents of persimmon and reds. White Austrian shades hang on the curved, ceiling-to-floor windows.

Off of the main hall is a forty-by-twenty-eight-foot drawing room, luxuriously furnished but comfortable and inviting. The velvet and damask materials make the carved furniture most elegant. Among the fine furnishings are an armchair with an original Aubusson tapestry covering, a Louis XVI satinwood desk with ormolu mounts, two eighteenth-century Venetian chairs and antique French crystal wall brackets.

Opening into the drawing room is the library, where there are four seventeenth-century armchairs, a Louis XIV desk, and a lighted case displaying exquisite pieces of jade and quartz which date from the sixteenth and seventeenth centuries.

The State Dining Room is furnished with ornately carved Italian furniture and a pair of gilt and gesso Venetian consoles with mirrors. The table is ninety inches wide and can be extended in length to seat twenty-four persons.

The game room, which opens off a hall to a side entrance, originally had rather forbidding Oriental furniture, screens and paintings, until it was redecorated in 1965. The style of the present furnishings is reminiscent of the era in which the house was built, but this was accomplished with contemporary furnishings and modern comfort. The focal point of the room is a wall panel on which hang portraits of the Territorial and State Governors of Colorado. This is believed to be the only collection within the State of pictures of all Colorado Governors. Recently, a collection of pictures of the First Ladies of Colorado was assembled and hangs on either side of the doorway to the side entrance.

The modernized kitchen on the lower floor is a large unit with a long pantry between the kitchen and the

A lovely formal garden forms part of the setting for the beautiful Mansion of Colorado's Governors.

dining room. The upstairs is devoted to living quarters for the Governor and his family—four bedrooms, a den and a large central hall that has been made into a sitting room.

Early in 1968, the Boettcher Foundation again offered a gift to the State—money to be used with State funds for a major renovation of the Mansion. New plumbing, air conditioning and heating systems were installed and the electrical wiring was replaced and many changes were made on the second floor. Nothing was changed on the main floor and few changes were made on the third floor which is little used.

The spacious grounds complement the building and are particularly attractive during the summer months. A formal garden at the back of the house, below and beyond the yard, slopes down to a greenhouse and garage.

The approximately $40,000 annual allowance covers all expenses of maintenance, capital improvements and the staff of from four to six and a secretary.

The policy governing the use of the house is up to the family in residence. At the present time, it is used socially only for functions given by the Governor or his family. However, each Tuesday afternoon during the summer months there is open house from 2 to 4 when visitors are welcome. In the spring and fall and during the Christmas season, the Mansion is open longer hours (12:30 to 4:30 p.m.) to allow school groups to visit. Only the lower floor is open to the public at these times.

The elegant Residence provided for Connecticut Governors is a nineteen-room brick home well-suited to formal State occasions.

CONNECTICUT

THE GOVERNOR'S RESIDENCE By Mrs. John Dempsey, *First Lady of Connecticut*

The Connecticut Legislature first considered the question of providing an official residence for the State's Governors in 1943. Prior to that time, this had not been regarded as an urgent need in this small State. The most distant point from Hartford, the capital city, is less than one hundred miles. Commuting to the office posed no great hardship for a Governor. Furthermore, until 1931, Governors did not make a practice of going to the office in the Capitol every day. However, in the mid-war year of 1943, with a Governor in office whose home was fifty miles from Hartford, there was a general feeling among legislators and others that the time had come for Connecticut to provide their Chief Executive with an official residence.

The first task of the Connecticut legislative committee appointed to look into the matter was to decide whether to buy or build. Wartime construction problems were a major factor in the committee's decision to purchase an existing dwelling. The eventual choice was a nineteen room, five-story (including basement and attic) brick Georgian colonial residence, built in 1909, situated on six landscaped acres. The property at 990 Prospect Avenue, about three miles from the Capitol, is on a tree-lined avenue which forms the boundary between Hartford and West Hartford. The total cost of purchase, repair and alterations for the residence, officially opened in October 1945, was $170,000.

The Governor's Residence—the term preferred in Connecticut—is a well designed and beautifully furnished dwelling. With its 15,000 square feet of floor space, it serves both as a comfortable home for the Governor and his family and as an admirable place for formal dinners or receptions accommodating one hundred or more guests. Seven Governors, including Governor Dempsey, have occupied the Residence during its first twenty-three years.

The location and design of the house are not suited for making it a public building, with regularly conducted tours at stated hours. However, thousands of Connecticut citizens have been guests at the Residence since its first occupant, Governor Raymond E. Baldwin, opened it for public inspection on October 18, 1945.

The principal first floor rooms include: a reception hall, from which a graceful, white-bannistered stairway curves to the floor above, reception room, dining room with a table for twenty, breakfast room, library, spacious sunporch, kitchen, servants' dining room and butler's pantry. The second floor includes the master bedroom and Governor's sitting room, visiting Governor's room, French Provincial room and guest room.

The Residence, set back about two hundred feet from the street and partly screened by tall evergreens, is reached by a semi-circular drive. The house and the grounds are staffed and maintained by employees of the State Public Works Department.

Among the furnishings of the Residence are numerous reproductions of eighteenth-century period pieces and *objets d'art* on loan from the Yale University Art Gallery. A tall case clock made nearly two hundred years ago by Asahel Cheney of East Hartford, using curly maple inlaid with holly and sumac, is outstanding.

Two collections assembled by the writer attract much attention from guests in the reception room. One is an extensive collection of Waterford glass displayed in the heirloom credenza; the other, occupying the fireplace mantel, is a collection of donkeys, symbol of Governor Dempsey's party, which come from all over the world.

Pewter, ceramics and paintings from Yale's Mabel Brady Garvan collection add a colonial flavor to the décor. A statue in the reception room reminds visitors that Connecticut's great hero is Nathan Hale. It is the original model for the life-size Hale statue on the Yale campus in New Haven, executed by Bela Lyon Pratt.

In 1968, for the first time since the State acquired the Residence, the downstairs rooms were extensively redecorated. Darker hues were replaced by lighter shades, including an off-white in several rooms, giving a cheerful and more modern appearance to the Residence now approaching its sixtieth birthday.

DELAWARE

THE DELAWARE GOVERNOR'S HOUSE*

Until 1966, the State of Delaware did not have an official residence for its Chief Executives. In that year the General Assembly appropriated funds for the purchase, restoration, and furnishing of Woodburn, an historic house on King Street in Dover for that purpose. Governor and Mrs. Charles L. Terry were the first Governor's family to reside in it.

The large brick house was built circa 1790 by Charles Hillyard. It was then about a mile from town and was part of a tract of three thousand acres given by William Penn to John Hillyard in 1683. He was the great-grandfather of Charles.

Architectural historians have stated that this historic house is one of the finest Middle-Period Georgian houses in Delaware. Its well proportioned but large structure of three full floors, attic and cellar is impressive. The exterior brick work is Flemish bond at the north and south sides, with a belt course of five bricks in width between the first and second floors and with a water table topped with two courses of molded bricks.

At the north side of the house is the main entrance where the windows and doors are topped with flat or jack arches of cut stone. Everything about the house denotes spaciousness and ample proportions. The large windows with twenty-four panes and the sizes of the rooms themselves reflect this. The entrance from the north side through an interesting Dutch door with a semi-circular fan light leads to the entrance hall, a room measuring fifteen feet by forty feet, nine inches. Off this hall is the drawing room which is nineteen feet, eight inches, by nineteen feet, ten inches, and a dining room which also leads from the entrance hall is nineteen feet, eight inches, by eighteen feet, four inches. The rooms on the second and third floors follow the same general plan and are equally spacious and airy.

At the south end of the entrance hall is a staircase, with easy risers and wide treads of old heart pine, rising from the first floor to the third.

Notable among the features of this house is the distinctive woodwork of the Middle-Georgian Period. This is reflected in the window treatment, the dados around many of the walls, the chair rails and the fine moldings. The drawing room has particularly fine paneling in the chimney breast, terminating in dog-ears and with pediments over all the door openings. The cornices are different in each room and are well designed.

*Article furnished by Mrs. Charles L. Terry, Jr., former First Lady of Delaware, prepared by Mr. Leon de Valinger, Jr., Director, Public Archives Commission and State Archivist.

The furnishings are eighteenth- and early nineteenth-century antiques of Delaware, Delmarva Peninsula and southeastern Pennsylvania areas. The large paneled Dutch door at the entrance has original wrought-iron strap hinges and a large eighteenth-century handmade wrought-iron box lock. Among the notable pieces in this entrance room are a mahogany breakfront bookcase with desk compartment and leather writing bed; a Sheraton-style mahogany armchair of classical design; Philadelphia Chippendale-style antique mahogany side-chairs and armchairs; a fine Philadelphia Chippendale-style antique walnut serving table with Chester County marble top; and many other antiques. The lighting fixture is an antique brass twelve-light chandelier probably of eighteenth-century Dutch origin and later wired for electricity. The rugs in this room are a semi-antique Kerman and an antique Bijar Oriental.

The drawing room also has many fine antique furnishings. These include Chippendale and Philadelphia Chippendale-style sofas, Queen Anne-style tea table and burl walnut chest, Chippendale-style mahogany secretary and tilt-top table, Philadelphia Chippendale-style side chairs, fretwork looking glass, tea set of blue English Staffordshire transfer ware, and Baccarat crystal and bronze chandelier. The rug, with cartouches having Arabic inscriptions in ivory on a wine background, is signed by Castelli. The windows are hung with gold silk damask, tied with gold cords and tassels.

The dining room is more restrained than the neighboring drawing room and the marble-faced fireplace is less elaborate as is the cornice, but this room with its fine Middle-Georgian woodwork is equally impressive. A large Sheraton-style three-section mahogany breakfront china closet occupies the west wall. In it is kept the State of Delaware special pattern of china in colonial blue with gold embossed trim and the State coat of arms. A Sheraton-style, double-pedestal, extension, mahogany table occupies the center of the room. Around it are eight Chippendale-style mahogany side-chairs and two matching armchairs. There is a notable Philadelphia Chippendale-style walnut serving table with serpentine molded edge of Chester County marble and a Hepplewhite-style mahogany sideboard, which holds the State of Delaware sterling silver tea and coffee set as well as the flatware.

At the head of the stairs is the second floor hall which is a living area for the Governor's family. From it there is access to the main bed chamber suite and the

One of the finest examples of Middle-Period Georgian architecture is historic Woodburn, circa 1790, the Delaware Governor's House.

guest suite. The furnishings here include a Delaware Chippendale-style, mahogany slant-front desk which was owned by Governor Cornelius P. Comegys, who served from 1837-1841. The main bed chamber has fine woodwork also. There is the chimney breast and paneling detail and marble facing of the fireplace which are similar in many respects to the rooms below.

The spacious grounds of the Governor's House are well landscaped with numerous fine examples of old trees and specimen pieces of shrubbery. Among these are ancient pines, crepe myrtles, old English boxwood and, to the east of the house, a large boxwood maze in the formal garden.

The Governor's House is administered by the Public Archives Commission and the State Archivist serves as Director of it as well as of the other historic houses and buildings under the jurisdiction of this Commission. Governor and Mrs. Terry opened the Governor's House for public visitation on Tuesday afternoons during the hours of 2 p.m. to 5 p.m.

The Hermitage, Andrew Jackson's home in Tennessee, was the model for the Florida Governor's Mansion.

FLORIDA

THE GOVERNOR'S MANSION By Mrs. Claude R. Kirk, Jr., *First Lady of Florida*

The present Mansion of the Governor of Florida is located on Adams Street, north of the Tallahassee business district, almost in the exact center of a city block. It is surrounded by landscaped lawns and gardens. Large live oak trees, festooned with Spanish moss, frame the building itself. Azaleas, camellias and other flowering shrubs typical of the Old South border the broad sweep of front lawn.

The wide circular drive in front of the Mansion was made from old paving brick, a gift of the City of Tampa following the removal of old trolley tracks.

The brick building was erected and furnished in 1957 at a cost of $360,000. The architect was Marion Sims Wyeth, of Palm Beach, who modeled the building along the lines of Andrew Jackson's home, The Hermitage, at Nashville, Tennessee. The two-story center portion of the Mansion is faced with white Ionic columns and is balanced with symmetrical one-story wings on either side.

It is fitting that the Mansion bears a resemblance to General Jackson's home, for he was appointed the first American Governor of Florida shortly after the Territory was acquired from Spain in 1821. The Hermitage is considered one of the finest examples of Classical Revival architecture in this country, a style so often associated with the formative years of the young United States.

This is the second Governor's Mansion to occupy this site. The first was a white wooden structure surrounded by a colonnade of two-story high Corinthian columns. It was built in 1907 of slow-growth Florida pine but was razed after being found structurally unsound in 1953.

Prior to 1907, Florida's Chief Executives were responsible for their own living arrangements. Several of Tallahassee's fine old antebellum houses served as homes of the Governors during various administrations.

The Governor's Mansion not only serves as the residence of the Chief Executive but is also the setting for official entertaining. To fulfill this dual purpose, state rooms and family accommodations are separate. The state rooms occupy the first floor of the center section and the north wing, which contains a bedroom suite for official visitors.

The living quarters for Florida's First Family are located in the south wing and the top floor of the center section which is reached by a graceful circular staircase just off the marble foyer.

The furnishings and architectural detail, such as mantels, chandeliers and sconces, are typical of the period of the Mansion's exterior design. Many are original pieces, collected over a period of time by James L. Cogar, for many years curator of Williamsburg and a recognized authority on the décor of homes in colonial and Federalist America.

Original Chippendale and Queen Anne pieces blend with the best handcrafted reproductions. Cogar's search took him throughout the Eastern United States and the British Isles. He is particularly proud of a grandfather's clock which bears the name of its New England maker. Rugs for the State Reception Room were specially woven in India from designs popular during the early nineteenth century.

A feature of the State Dining Room is the silver service from the decommissioned battleship, *U.S.S. Florida*. The people of the State, notably school children with nickels and dimes, contributed $10,000 to purchase the ornate, custom-designed and made hollow ware, which displays a wide variety of Florida flora and fauna. When the battleship was retired in 1931, the silver was returned by Act of Congress, with the Governor designated as official custodian.

To insure that the Mansion will maintain the character and dignity befitting its purpose, a Governor's Mansion Commission was created by the Florida Legislature. This commission, traditionally composed of prominent Tallahasseans, works closely with the incumbent Governor and his family.

In addition to his main office in the Capitol, the Governor also has an office in the basement of the Mansion. An excellent collection of color prints of old Florida maps and Seminole Indian war chiefs, some of the latter by famed George Catlin, is a feature of this large paneled room.

Although the Mansion resembles an imposing nineteenth-century American home, the building is modern in all respects. All floors are served by an elevator. The Mansion also contains a large fallout shelter which is kept well-stocked and has extensive communications equipment. It could serve as a temporary seat of government during a disaster.

Just behind the north wing and adjoining the State Reception Room is a formal walled garden, which has been used for various occasions, from press conferences to formal entertaining.

A magnificent Greek Revival Mansion of rose-toned brick serves the private and public life of Georgia's Governor.

GEORGIA

THE GOVERNOR'S MANSION By Mrs. Lester G. Maddox, *First Lady of Geor*

At 391 West Paces Ferry Road, N.W., Atlanta, a winding driveway through the gateway of a wrought-iron fence leads past a guardhouse to the rose-toned brick Georgia Governor's Mansion. A lovely fountain adorns the front entrance of the huge three-story structure, which rises majestically atop a gently-sloped knoll nestled among a grove of oaks some three hundred feet from the street.

This classic example of Greek Revival architecture, which was so popular in Georgia and throughout the nation in the first half of the nineteenth century, comprises a total of 25,000 square feet in its three levels. Thirty white Doric columns, each reaching from veranda floor to roof, are on all four sides of the edifice. The structure is 91 feet across the front and back and the sides are 101 feet deep.

Known also as the Executive Center, it was completed in December 1967 at a cost of approximately $2.5 million. The first to occupy the Mansion was Governor Lester G. Maddox and his family.

The site, a beautiful eighteen-acre tract, was purchased by Georgia's State Office Building Authority, and the architectural and construction contracts were let to the Atlanta firms of Thomas Bradbury and

Associates and P. D. Christian Company, respectively, on July 1, 1965, under the administration of Governor Carl Sanders.

A dark mahogany front door, eight and a half feet tall is framed by leaded beveled plate glass and set in white handcarved molding. Panel windows, also eight and a half feet high, framed with blue-black shutters, are across the front, back and sides. A door, only slightly less magnificent than the front entrance, is on each side and in the back.

The front door opens into a marble-floored vestibule with a large bronze replica of the Seal of the State of Georgia embedded in the center of the floor. Just beyond the vestibule is a reception hall designed as a rotunda with a high dome above a circular stairway leading to the floor above. A gigantic gold and crystal chandelier of eighteenth-century Italian design hangs from the center of the dome. The State Reception Hall is furnished with an octagonal veneered pedestal-base table and two cane-seated armchairs, which are complemented by bronze busts of George Washington and Benjamin Franklin, by the noted French sculptor, Houdon.

The main stair hall has a pier table attributed to Lannuier, an American looking glass, an urn decorated with a rare portrait of Benjamin Franklin, and an early nineteenth-century gilt-wood and metal chandelier.

The vestibule to the right is a guards' room with numerous electronic devices connected with the security of the Mansion. Continuing to the right past this room is a small library with wall paneling, parquet floor and bookshelves of walnut. On one wall is the portrait of Georgia's first official historian, Hugh McCall. The library contains early nineteenth-century American-make pembroke and pier tables. All of the furniture in the library, as well as in the nearby State Drawing Room and the State Dining Room, is typical of the Federal Period from 1785 through 1840.

The molding in the State Drawing Room is designed in the pattern of the Greek honeysuckle bud and bloom, while the State Dining Room is embellished with an elliptical ceiling mold. Dominating the dining room is an eighteen-place Philadelphia table made about 1810, which can be opened to a length of fourteen feet. A marble-top side table of New York City origin stands along the east wall beneath a Federal-style glass. A handsome sideboard made in Philadelphia (circa 1815) is along the north wall, similar in design to a chest of drawers along the opposite wall, which is flanked by two New York Phyfe-style tripod base card tables with cloverleaf tops. The floor is covered by an Oriental rug. Another rarity in the State Dining Room is the fireplace mantel, one of the four antique marble mantels imported from England at a total cost of $9,500.

To the left of the front vestibule is a large coat closet and the only bedroom and bath on the main floor. This guest bedroom contains an American-made sleigh bed, an early nineteenth-century English needlework rug and a late nineteenth-century French wall panel depicting "Psyche Showing Her Jewels to Her Sisters."

The State Living Room measures approximately forty by twenty-five feet and is furnished with American-made pieces of the Federal period. Attributed to the workshop of Duncan Phyfe are two mahogany sofas whose red satin upholstery is like that in the Red Room of the White House. Two mahogany swivel-top tables are attributed to Charles Honoré Lannuier, a talented Frenchman working in New York at the same time as Phyfe in the early nineteenth century. A magnificent English double breakfront secretary-bookcase adds dignity to one wall, its highly polished surface reflecting in the two American-made eagle-top gilt mirrors on the opposite wall. Visible around an Aubusson rug is the handsome parquet floor.

The Mansion is admirably arranged so as to separate the public rooms described above from the private rooms occupied by the Governor and his family. Across the rear of the main floor, separated by double doors from the rotunda, are the private living quarters. Opening onto the rear veranda is the family living room with soft butternut paneling. Its furnishings include an American Federal sofa, a saber-leg drinking table of Baltimore origin, two American Federal tub chairs, a bull's-eye mirror and a secretary attributed to the Seymours, early nineteenth-century cabinet-makers in Salem, Massachusetts. An Austrian Savonnerie rug covers the floor.

The antiques in the family dining room include an early nineteenth-century chest of drawers, a dining table, two pine tables, six Phyfe-style sidechairs and a Chinese rug. Stairs lead from this area directly to the living quarters on the third floor.

Also at the rear of the main floor is the Mansion's well-equipped kitchen, which is outstanding. Particularly interesting is a walk-in cool room with permanent forty-five degree temperature. A door in the back leads into a freezer room large enough for a market.

On the third floor are six bedrooms, each having a private bath with gold-plated fixtures.

The President's Suite, the front central room on the second floor, serves as a guest room for visiting dignitaries. This impressive room displays a Pennsylvania-made four-poster bed dating from the 1870's. There is also an American Chippendale slant-top desk. Portraits of Thomas Jefferson and James Monroe hang on the South wall. The floor is richly covered by a nineteenth-century Ushak carpet.

A small guest lounge adjacent to the President's Suite again reflects the Federal period furnishings in the sofa and lady's writing desk, which are believed to be of Massachusetts origin.

West of the Presidential Suite is a guest bedroom. A reproduction English Chippendale four-poster canopy bed and an English chest of drawers are the noteworthy features of the room.

One next enters the Governor's oak-paneled study, which is furnished as an office. His private bedroom adjoins this study. The major items of interest are a tester bed and an English Regency gentleman's desk.

The central room at the northern end of the house is the First Lady's bedroom. Flanked by two tables from the old Governor's Mansion is a bed with an early nineteenth-century French headboard, an English satinwood table and a French trumeau. In the adjoining family sitting room are a sofa, an armchair and tables which were retained from the old Governor's Mansion, along with some antique English pieces, two card tables, a chest of drawers and a secretary-bookcase with églomisé paneled doors.

Toward the south front on the second floor are early nineteenth-century American and English pieces in the hall and two family bedrooms. Of particular notice is a handsome sideboard table. While most of the carpets used in these and other rooms on the second floor were made in Georgia, notable exceptions are an American needlework rug and a Turkish rug, each dating from the first half of the nineteenth century. The First Lady's office, at the southeast corner of the second floor, has eighteenth-century English and American antiques.

Curtains styled after fashions popular in England and America early in the nineteenth century hang in many of the Mansion rooms. Other articles reflecting the fashion of that era are elegant antique chandeliers and some distinctive Chinese and European porcelains.

The Mansion's art collection includes paintings by the distinguished American artists, Benjamin West, Ralph E. W. Earl, Thomas Doughty, John Neagle, Severin Roesen, Samuel King and Alvan Fisher.

Three sets of silver flatware are used in the Mansion. "Rochelle" by International Silver Company is used in the Banquet Room; "Francis I" by Reed and Barton is used in the State Dining Room; and "Savannah" by Reed and Barton is used in the family dining room.

There is a noteworthy collection of early nineteenth-century American antiques in the Federal and Empire styles. An important acquisition for this collection was a tea set made by the silversmith, Garrett Eoff, in New York City (circa 1815). This Empire-style tea set is decorated with meandering stylized leaves and flowers. It is on view in the State Dining Room.

Beneath the main floor and visible only from the rear of the Mansion is a lower level ground floor which includes a huge hall called the State Facilities Room or banquet room. It is one hundred by forty feet and will accommodate 350 people for luncheons, dinners and other affairs of the State or private organizations.

In the banquet room are exhibited several of the silver pieces used on board the *U.S.S. Georgia*. This elaborate set is decorated with the seals of the U.S. Navy, the State of Georgia and various Georgia cities.

A Fine Arts Committee supervised interior decorations and landscaping from July 1966 until June 1968, when supervision of the Executive Mansion, its furnishing and maintenance became the responsibility of a Mansion Committee comprised of the Secretary of State, State Auditor and State Budget Officer.

The Mansion is open for public tours each week Monday through Friday from 10 a.m. until 12 noon, and on Sundays from 3 to 5 p.m.

Editor's Note: Since 1839, Georgia has always provided for its Chief Executives on a grand scale "giving testimony to the quality and prosperity of the State." In 1835, when Milledgeville was the capital, the Legislature authorized construction of a $50,000 Governor's Mansion which was patterned after Palladio's Foscari Villa and still stands on the Georgia College campus as one of the most perfect and imposing examples of Greek Revival architecture. Ten Governors occupied this Mansion from 1839 to 1868, interrupted by General Sherman's use of the building as his headquarters during his "march to the sea" in 1864. After moving the capital to Atlanta, the Legislature purchased the John H. James mansion at Peachtree and Cain Streets in 1870, and this house served as the Governor's Mansion until it was declared unsafe in 1921. In 1925, Georgia purchased the Ansley Home designed by architect Anthony Ten Eyck Brown, on a six-acre site fronting on The Prado, built of solid Georgia granite on a natural rock foundation, with Cuban managua wood interiors. This Mansion, used by the Governors until the new Executive Mansion was completed had "seven bedrooms; five baths; large, wide verandas, and reception rooms that will care for three hundred to four hundred guests."

HAWAII

WASHINGTON PLACE*

Washington Place owes its origin to Captain John Dominis, who, after having made a number of voyages to the Islands, arrived at Honolulu from New York on April 23, 1837, accompanied by his wife and his son, John Owen Dominis, to take up his permanent residence in Hawaii.

In 1842, through the settlement of a longstanding lawsuit between Captain Dominis and the British Consul, Richard Charlton, the captain came into possession of the land on which the building now stands. In that same year the coral foundation was laid, but the building itself, of Greek Revival architecture, was not completed until 1846, being delayed from time to time by lack of funds. During this period Captain Dominis made several voyages, the profits from which were used to pay back debts and to resume building operations.

There were no regular architects in Honolulu in those days, but there were a few good mechanics. One of these, Isaac Adams, was selected by the captain to draw the plans and superintend the construction of the house, according to the ideas of Mrs. Dominis.

Shortly after moving into their new home, Captain Dominis sailed for China as a passenger in the brig *William Neilson* on a general trading voyage, but more especially to purchase handsome Chinese-made furniture for his new home. The *William Neilson* was never heard from after leaving port.

In the latter part of 1847, Mrs. Dominis rented a suite of rooms to the American Commissioner, Anthony TenEyck, whose wife had died some months previously. The United States Legation was established in the house, a flagpole was erected in the yard, and the American flag floated here as early as the end of 1847. It is to Commissioner TenEyck that Washington Place owes its name, as shown by the following letter from official correspondence, dated February 22, 1848, preserved in the Archives of Hawaii:

> I have much pleasure in making the following semi-official announcement to you:
>
> In honor of the day which gave birth to him, who was "first in war, first in peace, and first in the hearts of his countrymen," the great, the good, the illustrious Washington—the United States Commissioner, with the assent of its much esteemed and hospitable proprietress, has this day christened the beautiful, substantial and universally admired mansion of Mrs. Dominis, Washington Place.
>
> Thus let it be hereafter designated in Hawaiian Annals, and long may it remain in this distant isle of the Pacific, a memento of the eminent virtues of the "Father of his Country" and of the enterprise and the distinguished excellencies of its much lamented projector.

King Kamehameha III acknowledged this letter by having the following "Official Notice" issued:

> BY AUTHORITY
>
> Official Notice
>
> It has pleased His Majesty the King to approve of the name of Washington Place given this day by the Commissioner of the United States, to the House and Premises of Mrs. Dominis and to command that they retain that name in all time coming.
>
> KEONI ANA
>
> Home Office, Feb. 22, 1848.

John Owen Dominis, the only son of Captain and Mrs. Dominis, and the Honorable Lydia K. P. Kapaakea were married in 1862, and at once took up their residence with Mrs. Dominis at Washington Place. Mrs. Dominis died April 25, 1889, and the property descended to her son. During the intervening years his wife had been given the title of Princess Liliuokalani and named heir to the throne by her brother, King Kalakaua. On her accession to the throne on January 29, 1891, John Owen Dominis was titled Prince Consort. Washington Place became the property of Queen Liliuokalani on his death, August 27, 1891.

Iolani Palace was the official residence of the Sovereign, and so it was not until the overthrow of the Monarchy, January 17, 1893, that Queen Liliuokalani again became a resident of Washington Place. It was here that she was arrested for treason at the time of the 1895 Revolution, and it was to Washington Place that she returned after her nine months' imprisonment in the Palace. She continued to live here in semi-royal state, surrounded by her retainers. Her home was the rendezvous of the old "royal set" of Honolulu, a little kingdom where she was accorded all the honors that are the privileges of a monarch to receive. A well-educated woman, a composer of music and a writer, the Queen drew about her numerous friends. Washington Place became a mecca for distinguished travelers visiting in Honolulu. It was here that she died on November 11, 1917, at the age of 79.

The Hawaiian Islands became an integral part of the United States, June 14, 1900, as a full-fledged Territory.

*Material furnished by Mrs. John A. Burns, First Lady of Hawaii, from the State Archives of Hawaii.

Washington Place, the official home of the Governor of Hawaii, was once the rendezvous of the deposed Queen Liliuokalani's "royal set."

The Governor was an appointee of the President. Under the Republic and Territory, Iolani Palace became the Executive Building and no longer an official residence. No residence was provided for the Chief Executive.

Prince Jonah Kuhio Kalanianaole, one of the heirs to the estate of Queen Liliuokalani, suggested that the Territory acquire Washington Place as the Executive Mansion. The Legislatures of 1919 and 1920 appropriated funds for the purchase, and in May 1921, the property was acquired by the Territory at a cost of $55,000, including repairs and furnishings. In the meantime, Governor Charles J. McCarthy had leased it, and was using it unofficially as the Executive Mansion. Washington Place became the official home of the Governor of Hawaii when it was formally opened on April 21, 1922, by Governor Wallace Rider Farrington.

The Mansion has had several additions, each of which has followed the classical lines of the original structure. The largest of these were a large glazed lanai and an even larger open lanai added in 1953 to allow greater space for large receptions. There are seventeen rooms, including one lanai guest room.

The furnishings include many historic pieces such as Queen Liliuokalani's piano, bed, settee and numerous mementos. Still in use in the dining room is the silverware presented to King Kamehameha IV by Napoleon III in 1858.

Located in downtown Honolulu, the residence is visited annually by many school children and residents of the State, as well as dignitaries from all other States of the Union and from most of the nations of the world. Tours are arranged upon request.

This two-story frame house purchased in 1947 was the first official residence provided for Idaho's Governors. The ten-room house is primarily a private home for the Chief Executive and State functions are conducted elsewhere.

IDAHO

THE GOVERNOR'S HOUSE By Mrs. Don Samuelson, *First Lady of Idaho*

Idaho's Governor's House was built in 1914 by Mr. W. E. Pierce as a private residence. It was purchased by the State in 1947 at a cost of $25,000 and was the first provision the State had ever made for a residence for its Chief Executive.

The House, located at 1805 North Twenty-First Street in Boise, is a two-story frame structure with a portico over the circular drive and a fair-sized front porch at the main entrance. The grounds take up half a city block with most of the green area in the back lined with trees and shrubs.

On the first floor, a large reception-living room encompasses the entire width of the House with a fireplace at one end. The rest of the main floor consists of dining room, kitchen, sun porch, a hall leading to the side entrance, and the stairs. The second floor consists of two guest bedrooms, a master bedroom, two baths and a smaller room presently used as an office and study. A large family rumpus room, a bedroom, bath and several smaller utility rooms make up the basement.

Unpretentious though it is, the Governor's House had been modestly adequate until recent years. Increased activities of Idaho's First Family, paralleling the growth of the State, have placed a strain on its capacities, and plans are being formulated to build a new Governor's Mansion that will provide adequate facilities for family living and official State entertaining.

The 1967 Legislature set aside $200,000 for a new residence site. The appropriation says the money may be used for furnishings for the Governor's residence or diverted to other projects at the discretion of the Permanent Building Fund Advisory Council. Several sites are under consideration at the present time, but no plans for the new residence have been drawn up.

Idaho's present Governor's House was first occupied by Governor C. A. Robins in 1947. At that time, the legislative committee assigned to select the residence discussed the possibility of building a Governor's Mansion but dismissed the idea because of the cost. Governors prior to 1947 had to provide their own accommodations out of their salary, which sometimes proved rather costly, but necessary since an 1887 Idaho statute requires that the Governor live in Boise.

The Governor's House is not open to the public but each First Lady, at her own discretion, has allowed organizations and groups to use the residence. The State provides for a housekeeper-cook, but no provisions are made for other personnel.

The writer has created a Mansion Committee to assist and advise in the selection of many furnishings that are necessary for even the simplest official entertaining. Much of the furniture had been acquired over a period of many years and has been augmented by personal items from the First Family in residence. Under this committee's guidance, many items were restored and refurbished and new furniture was purchased as necessary. This has been done in such a way that the furnishings would be suitable for a new residence when it is built.

The State did not have official china, crystal or silver, and this was the next project undertaken by the committee. The response was overwhelming to the writer's expressed hope that, rather than have these items purchased with State funds, perhaps private contributions could be obtained. In the first six months, enough gifts and pledges were received to place the first order for twenty-four place settings of china. Hopefully, the crystal and silver can be ordered soon. The china pattern selected was Tuxedo by Lenox, the crystal pattern Bellmont by Lenox; and the silver pattern Reed & Barton's Burgundy. All will bear the Great Seal of the State of Idaho.

Another project of the Governor's Mansion Committee will be to acquire portraits of all of Idaho's First Ladies, to be uniformly framed and hung in the sun porch. Many Idaho heirlooms have been donated. The most notable of recent gifts was a collection of books by Idaho authors and books on Idaho history.

With the possibility of a new Governor's Mansion being built within the next few years, every decision of the committee regarding any item is based on its suitability for use in the present home and in a new residence. The ultimate goal of this committee, and of all Idahoans, is a Governor's House that will afford the gracious living that befits Idaho's First Family.

President Lincoln and his wife were frequent guests at this lovely Victorian Mansion, the home of Illinois Governors since 1855.

ILLINOIS

THE GOVERNOR'S MANSION

By Mrs. Samuel H. Shapiro,

Former First Lady of Illinois

Illinois' Governor's Mansion is a beautiful Victorian residence located on a landscaped knoll in downtown Springfield. It is three blocks to the southeast of the present State Capitol and three blocks south of the Old State Capitol, which was in use when the Mansion was built. It faces Jackson Street to the north, and its grounds are also bounded by Fourth, Fifth and Edwards Streets.

The twenty-eight room, white-painted brick Mansion is two stories tall and has a full ground floor or basement and an attic. When completed in 1855, it measured seventy-eight feet north to south and eighty feet east to west. Originally it had a fifteen-foot cupola above the center of the roof to light the spiral stairway that extended up from the first floor. The overall height of the building was sixty-four feet from the ground level.

There have been many architectural changes in the Mansion over the years, the most noticeable being the replacement of the cupola and the low gabled roof by a mansard roof and the remodeling of the stone entrance porch to provide stairs from the east and west with a driveway and state police guard's office beneath the porch. This last change had the effect of making the ground floor door the main entrance instead of the front door on the first floor.

Other alterations have involved the addition of a wing at the south for the kitchen, butler's pantry and food storage rooms, which were originally on the ground floor. The circular stairway has been replaced by L-shaped stairs, and porches that were open have been enclosed and converted into rooms. There does not seem to be a record of the year the red brick was painted white, but it was probably after the removal of the cupola in 1890.

The Mansion is the second Governor's House, as it was originally called, to be owned by the State of Illinois. Soon after the State capital was moved from Vandalia to Springfield in 1839, a house at the northwest corner of Capitol Avenue and Eighth Street was purchased as a home for the Governor and his family. It was a modest two-story brick building, a block north of Abraham Lincoln's home.

Three Chief Executives occupied this house before Joel A. Matteson was inaugurated as Illinois' tenth Governor on January 10, 1853. The new Governor and his wife had a family of six children and one of his first acts was to announce that he would hold open house each Thursday evening during the legislative session for members of the State Legislature, the Supreme Court and visitors to the city. Clearly, the Governor's House was too small for his family and for the entertaining he planned. On the following February 12, the Legislature created a commission and appropriated funds for building a new one. The sums appropriated were $18,000 for the house and furnishings, in addition to the proceeds from the sale of the old house.

The site the commissioners purchased was then a wooded slope at the foot of which was a small stream known as the Town Branch. They employed Chicago's first resident architect, John M. Van Osdel, to draw the plans, and the construction was begun in the summer of 1853. Van Osdel was the builder of two famous Chicago hotels—the Palmer House and the Tremont House, and other landmarks of early Chicago, as well as University Hall, the first building of the University of Illinois at Urbana.

The architect planned the Mansion to provide space for public functions as well as living quarters. The six rooms and the grand stair hall on the first floor were separated by sliding doors that could be pushed back to open the entire area for public affairs such as receptions or "promenading." Except for the dining room, the living quarters for the governor and his family were on the second floor.

Construction was completed in the fall of 1855, at a cost that was considerably more than the original appropriations. The commissioners had paid Nicholas H. Ridgley $4,500 for the two and three-quarters acres of land, and the total cost of the house, lot and furnishings was a little over $52,000. The old Governor's House was sold for $2,680 and the remainder of the deficit was made up from the Governor's contingency fund and additional appropriations.

The Matteson family moved into the Mansion on November 30, 1855, and on the following January 10, the Governor held a grand reception. Six hundred of the one thousand invitations he issued went to Springfield residents and, undoubtedly, Mr. and Mrs. Abraham Lincoln were among that number. There is no record of whether or not they attended. If so, they spent a chilly evening for the night was so cold that the heating system proved inadequate. Water froze in the pipes that provided gas for lighting, and the festivities had to be carried on by candlelight. Records of later events show that the Lincolns were frequent guests at the Mansion.

Governor Matteson was succeeded on January 12, 1857, by William H. Bissell, who was in such poor health that he was sworn into office at the Mansion rather than at the Capitol, as was the custom. He died in 1860, the only Governor to die in the Mansion. Abraham Lincoln was one of four friends who were allowed to visit him on the day before his death.

John Wood of Quincy, who succeeded Bissell, decided not to move into the Mansion and invited Mrs. Bissell and her family to stay there until the next Governor should be inaugurated. Thus, Wood was the only one of the State's twenty-four Governors since 1855 who did not live in the Mansion.

In addition to Abraham Lincoln, seven Presidents have been entertained at the Governor's Mansion in Springfield. They were Ulysses S. Grant, Rutherford B. Hayes, William Howard Taft, Theodore Roosevelt, Herbert Hoover, Franklin D. Roosevelt and Dwight D. Eisenhower. Other notable visitors have included poets Vachel Lindsay, whose home is still standing across Edwards Street, south of the Mansion, and Carl Sandburg.

Traditionally, the Governor holds a New Year's Day reception at the Mansion, and several other social events take place there every year, including a tea for the State's student historians each May. Also, the Mansion is open to tourists all day each Wednesday.

Beautiful old beech trees frame this attractive buff brick dwelling, the fifth Governor's Mansion of Indiana.

INDIANA

THE GOVERNOR'S MANSION

By Mrs. Roger D. Branigin,

Former First Lady of Indiana

The home which Indiana furnishes for its Governor is located at 4343 North Meridian Street, Indianapolis, about five miles from Monument Circle, the center of the city. This house was built in 1924 by the president of the Stutz Motor Car Company. Two years later it was sold to Mr. and Mrs. J. H. Trimble. In 1945, eight years after Mr. Trimble's death, Indiana bought the house, including some furnishings, from Mrs. Trimble for $72,500.

Meridian Street is one of the early thoroughfares of Indianapolis. The area on which the Mansion stands was formerly the summer home area of Indianapolis families and was called "Buchenheim" for the beautiful beech trees found there. The Mansion grounds still contain several of these lovely old trees.

The modified Georgian house has twelve rooms, five bedrooms and four baths, as well as a complete basement with a recreation room and an attic for ample storage. It is built of buff brick and is set about 130 feet back from the street. Originally, the tips of the wrought-iron fence which runs along the street side of the house were gold-plated but this was discontinued about 1963. A curved drive, with two entrances from the street, leads to the house and four-car garage.

This is the fifth home Indiana has provided its Governors. Although originally the State did not furnish its Governor's Mansion, now most of the furnishings belong to the State. One of the prized possessions is the piano, the cabinet of which is hand decorated. The State also has several paintings by Hoosier artists—deans of the Brown County Art Colony—which are now considered priceless. Among the many prized mementos of Indiana history in the Mansion is the silver from the battleship, *U.S.S. Indiana.*

Groups of fifteen or more persons, over twelve years of age may view the Mansion by appointment. Three persons serve on the Mansion staff.

The house has an air of friendliness and hospitality, as well as elegance. All Governors add their own touch by having their small home *objets d'art* around, for the house is—as Indiana intended—a home for its Governor.

IOWA

THE EXECUTIVE MANSION By Mrs. Harold E. Hughes, *Former First Lady of Iowa*

Iowa's Governors for some three-quarters of a century were wanderers living in unofficial residences, which was perhaps appropriate for a young prairie State with its rolling green lands, bordered on the east by the Mississippi and on the west by the mighty Missouri.

The first Territorial Governor, Robert Lucas, in the antebellum years of the 1840's, dwelt in lovely old Plum Grove (a house still preserved, named for the thicket of plum trees on its land), when Iowa City was the State's first capital. When statehood and progress moved the capital to Des Moines in 1857, Iowa's Governors continued—perhaps out of that rugged individualism which is one of their trademarks—to put roofs over their own heads.

The present Executive Mansion at 2900 Grand Avenue had but a single predecessor. In an old newspaper clipping of December 27, 1917, appeared the following: "After 70 years . . . Iowa's Chief Executive is housed in an edifice belonging to the State he serves." Governor William L. Harding and his First Lady and family lived in the modest white house, their official "mansion," which still stands on old Des Moines Street. His successors reverted, however, either to houses of their own choosing or Des Moines hotels.

Finally, in 1947, one hundred years after statehood, a permanent Governor's Mansion in Iowa became a reality. On Grand Avenue, the Nollen family of Dutch stock from Pella had built at the turn of the century a spacious home for gracious living. Omaha stagecoaches used to clip along a prairie road past the original eleven-acre site on which the rosy-cream Dutch Colonial house, with its lovely railed white portico, was erected in 1903. When Mrs. Nollen's father bought the site, Des Moines' Grand Avenue was still ankle-deep in mud or dust, according to the Hawkeye season. With the years, the elm-lined avenue came to represent the gracious manner of living which flourished in this growing capital city.

Purchased by the State in 1947 for $27,200, the Iowa Governor's Mansion today would be valued at well over $75,000. Five Iowa Governors and their families have lived in the three-story, twelve-room home, in its twenty years as an Executive Mansion.

Among the architectural charms of its interior are the colonial staircase and the beauty of the drawing room and library woodwork, once fumed-oak, later bleached to its natural color. Among the furnishings are many lovely period pieces, including a Haviland divan and a French eighteenth-century ebony-inlaid-with-ivory bric-a-brac cabinet.

Here and there some pieces are strictly Iowan, such as six rather stern-looking cane-bottomed chairs which antedate the Civil War; a beguiling little round table made a century ago in Pella; and the cherrywood breakfast set from the hands of distinguished craftsmen in the Amana colonies. A lovely breakfront contains a gift from the estate or the hand of each of Iowa's Governors, including Governor Beardsley's fountain pen; a Danish plate from the Hoeghs; a Prussian creamer and sugar bowl from the Lovelesses; a spode plate picturing the Liberty Bell from the Erbes; and from the Hughes, a sterling silver ashtray bearing the Iowa State Seal.

When the William S. Beardsleys, the home's first official family, moved into the Mansion in January 1949, the Mansion's staff numbered three people, which it still does. Much refurbishing and various improvements have altered the home within, but outwardly its rose-cream countenance still wears the same stately air, with a touch of southern hospitality in its architecture, and a hint of the Dutch perhaps, in its dormers and roof lines.

Charlotte Ellen Beardsley, its first official mistress, said there were no moving worries: "All you have to do is carry in your suitcase. . . . Everything is waiting for you—linens, utensils, silver and furniture!" So it has been with the families of each of the four Governors who have since occupied the Mansion: Leo A. Hoegh, Herschel C. Loveless, Norman Erbe and Harold E. Hughes. However, in her own very special way, each First Lady has made her contribution to this Mansion.

Warm and hospitable Mary Louise Hoegh sought to make the Governor's Mansion "more meaningful to the citizens of Iowa, to whom it belongs." To enhance it as a repository of the best, a small motto guided her:

The home of Iowa Governors, a Dutch Colonial Mansion featuring a railed white portico, stands along an avenue lined with stately old elms.

"To study and respect the past, to work in the present, to build for a meaningful future."

To all this heritage of the Mansion, the Hughes attempted to bring their awareness of other lands through objects of beauty from the Orient and other parts of the world where distant peoples have expressed friendship for this Midwest State. Also, we tried to show true prairie cordiality and hospitality through open houses, the first being held on the chill of an Iowa November day in 1965. Some 350 visitors paid their respects to the new occupants and to this executive residence which is their pride, too. Many expressed the thought, "It's nice to be able to come here. In a way, this house belongs to us all." Visitors' tours may be made by appointment.

In a sense, this home, its grounds, and its very existence span vast changes. Its citizens have moved from an age when a "thicket of plum trees" was the only security needed to an age when Capitol security police and pole lights must guard a State's executive. But this gracious house continues to warm First Families through the snowy Iowa winters and to offer them cool shade under its lovely trees during the warm summers.

KANSAS

THE EXECUTIVE MANSION By Mrs. Robert Docking, *First Lady of Kar*

Cedar Crest, the Executive Mansion of Kansas, is a Norman-style château made of native stone, brick and stucco, with casement windows.

The present Executive Mansion of Kansas, known as Cedar Crest, has been the property of the State since 1955. The house was actually built in 1928 and 1929 by Frank P. MacLennan, publisher of the *Topeka State Journal*, on an expanse of land about five miles west of the center of Topeka. The 244 acres belonged originally to the Pottawatomie Indians, then became known as "Martin's Hill." Mr. MacLennan bought the land for $61,000 from D. H. Forbes, who had farmed it for nearly fifty years, calling the place "Cedar Heights."

A contemporary newspaper account reports that for forty years Mr. MacLennan had owned a summer cottage, which he named "Cedarcrest," on sixty acres (now part of the Menninger Foundation grounds) adjoining the Forbes farm, and that it had been his idea to build a "modern colonial" year-round residence on the Forbes land if he could acquire it. This property is a long narrow rectangle sloping gently uphill through pastures from the south, then dropping off sharply through woods to the Kansas River on the north. The crest of the hill, overlooking the river valley on the north and the city of Topeka on the east, is a wonderful location for a home.

The land transaction was completed on February 28, 1928. Mr. and Mrs. MacLennan engaged William D. Wight, a Kansas City architect, and work on the house was begun after two farmhouses already on the site were demolished. Mr. Wight's design was, when completed, a plan for a Norman château rather than the colonial residence originally planned. The exterior walls are native stone, brick and stucco; the roof is Pennsylvania slate. Most of the windows are casements in harmony with the style of the house.

Mr. and Mrs. MacLennan worked closely with the architect in planning the interior. A central entrance hall opened on the left into the walnut-paneled twenty-by-forty-foot "library," its walls lined with bookshelves and its mantel faced in travertine marble. Mr. MacLennan's study, decorated with carvings of his family coat of arms and of fifteenth-century printers' marks, and with frescoes showing the bookplates used by many prominent writers, is at the back of the hall. On the right are the dining and breakfast rooms, the kitchen, pantry and a maid's room. An elaborate oak staircase leads to the second floor's five bedrooms, two baths, and maid's room and bath. On the third floor there is an enormous recreation room, a cedar room and attic. In the basement are the garage, laundry and furnace room. The mansion, reputed to have cost $60,000, was finished by October 1929, except for the final touches on the landscaping. The MacLennans lived here until Mr. MacLennan's death in November 1933, and his wife continued living in it until she died in November 1955.

In her will, Mrs. MacLennan bequeathed the house and land, her husband's 3,500-volume library, and a copy of the "Madonna of the Chair" to the State of Kansas, on the condition that the State would use it as the Executive Mansion, with twenty acres of the land to be used as a State park; the next regular session of the Legislature was to accept or decline the gift. The 1956 Legislature was a fiscal session, which had insufficient authority to accept definitively, and a final decision was deferred until the regular session of 1957.

In 1956, Governor Fred Hall expressed doubts about the suitability of Cedar Crest. Its distance from the Statehouse, five miles, and the fact that it was smaller by about 1,700 square feet than the house which then served as the Executive Mansion, would, Governor Hall feared, make Cedar Crest inadequate for the large receptions and State functions. Others felt that the existing Governor's Mansion, then seventy years old, was too costly to maintain; was obsolete; and located in a crowded neighborhood which was slipping downhill.

In January 1957, the State Architect submitted a report stating that it would cost between $55,000 and $90,000 to remodel Cedar Crest, and $35,000 more if the dining room were enlarged to banquet size and a terrace and servants' quarters added.

The Legislature, meeting in the early months of 1957, did not act at once. Governor George Docking, who had taken office in January, agreed in substance with Governor Hall's doubts about Cedar Crest, in spite of its beautiful grounds and spectacular view. Governor Docking pointed out that extra appropriations for staff and security would be needed and that maintenance of a house and grounds so large and (at that time) so far from town would be outrageously expensive; that in addition to the remodeling of the house, the twisting half-mile gravel driveway from Sixth Avenue (U.S. 40) to the house would have to be paved and a parking lot added for visitors' cars.

In spite of the reservations expressed by two Governors and other State officials, the 1957 Legislature did accept title to Cedar Crest as the Executive Mansion. Fearful of veto, the House and Senate at first accepted the gift by resolution in early April; a few days later, however, the Governor signed a Senate bill "with reluctance." Although the State of Kansas now owned the house and grounds, the 1957 Legislature failed to appropriate any money for the necessary remodeling, and Governor and Mrs. Docking continued to live in the downtown Mansion. A caretaker was appointed to live at Cedar Crest rent free in exchange for maintenance of grounds and house; he was there, as it turned out, until 1961. In 1959, the Governor tried to persuade the Legislature to relinquish title to Cedar Crest; this was not done, nor were any funds designated for remodeling.

Late in 1960, Governor-elect John Anderson expressed an interest in asking the Legislature to appropriate the money to remodel Cedar Crest. In the 1961 regular legislative session, $100,000 was appropriated to renovate the house, $94,000 already having been set aside for a new access road and a paved parking lot. A plan for central air conditioning, modernizing and enlarging of the kitchen, connection of the plumbing with the city sewer system, and refinishing paneling and wooden window frames was presented in June 1961. At that time, officials stated that the new Mansion should be ready to receive the Andersons by Christmas. Throughout the State, the Cedar Crest project was attacked because of its expense, and there were even some suggestions that the State did not really have a good title to the property.

In spite of these objections, bidding on the remodeling was opened early in August 1961. Work on the new driveway and access road, to be known as Kansas Highway 100, had begun. When the first bids on the remodeling were received, the lowest of them totaled $59,712 more than the appropriations. Changes were made in the plans and by September the bids came within the limits of the appropriations. Work began. In addition to the new paving, several changes were made: the basement one-stall garage was turned into a recreation room and a new two-stall garage was built to the north of the house under a cement-slab terrace; from the kitchen, pantry, and maid's room on the first floor emerged one long kitchen with work areas appropriate for preparing and serving of both small family and large party meals. On the second floor the maid's room became a small office; the big third-floor recreation room was divided into two bedrooms and a bath for the Governor's children or servants. Paneling was cleaned, walls painted or papered, and wiring modernized somewhat. New carpeting was laid and new curtains hung. Finally, in April 1962, the furniture, much of it reupholstered or refinished, was moved from the old Mansion to Cedar Crest, which then became the Governor's official residence.

The old Mansion was subsequently sold and razed, after serving the State for sixty-one years. Like Cedar Crest, it had been built as a private home in 1887, by Erasmus Bennett. It was a typically ornate Victorian brick house, painted white, standing on an oversized city lot about eight blocks west of the Statehouse. In 1901, the Bennetts sold the house to the State of Kansas for $26,000, and it became the first Executive Mansion. Governor William E. Stanley was its first Executive resident, after forty years of Kansas statehood during which Governors had to find their own lodgings in Topeka.

It is not known just how much of the furniture moved from the old Mansion to Cedar Crest has historical value. Because few or no records were kept before 1962, it is difficult to trace the history of many of the obviously old pieces in the Mansion, though the writer has initiated research on the subject. The dining room furniture, given to the State in 1945, was, according to the donor, carved by an artist who won a prize at a Philadelphia exposition in the eighties or nineties. A French ormolu clock now in the living room is said to have been ordered by Erasmus Bennett.

The staff at Cedar Crest varies according to the needs and preferences of each First Lady. The present domestic staff consists of five and a secretary to help with details and planning for entertainments. The writer personally supervises the housekeeping and the improvements to house and grounds. A grounds keeper on the staff, assisted by a trusty crew from the State Penitentiary, maintains the 244 acres of woods, pastures and gardens. Three ponds are stocked by the Forestry, Fish and Game Commission.

The Mansion is open to tourists and visitors Monday through Friday between the hours of 2 and 5 p.m. and by appointment for club and school groups.

Colorful gardens and landscaped grounds set off the impressive Mansion provided for the Governor of Kentucky. The French Renaissance building resembles Petit Trianon, the villa of Marie Antoinette near the Palace of Versailles in France.

KENTUCKY

THE GOVERNOR'S MANSION By Mrs. Louie B. Nunn, *First Lady of Kentucky*

Soon after Kentucky's new Capitol was built in 1910, interest was shown in providing a new home for the Governors. The old Governor's residence had begun to show the wear and tear of passing years, and a fire had seriously weakened its walls and destroyed floors and roofs.

The Legislature of 1912 appropriated $75,000 for the erection of a new home, and the Capitol Commission purchased the property that borders the eastern edge of the new Capitol grounds and furnishes an appropriate garden setting for the Mansion. The twenty-two room structure, which harmonizes in appearance and setting with the Capitol, was erected on a knoll overlooking the valley of the winding Kentucky River. It was ready for occupancy in 1914.

It is a fine example of classic architecture of the French Renaissance period and bears close resemblance to the Petit Trianon, Marie Antoinette's villa near the Palace of Versailles in France. It is elegantly proportioned, with a front portico graced with eight Ionic columns that rise three stories. A stone balustrade and terrace make an impressive entrance.

The formal living room, drawing room and ballroom all open off cross hallways and are furnished with lovely Louis XVI period antiques. The State Dining Room is a circular room with tall windows framing a picturesque view of the rolling hillsides in the distance. A small library-study, family dining room and powder room complete the first floor and public rooms. Double winding stairways lead to the family's private living quarters on the second and third floors. Tuesday and Thursday mornings are set aside for visitors to tour the first floor.

Paintings by noted Kentucky artists, on loan from the J. B. Speed Art Museum in Louisville, and several historical pieces of furniture owned by the Kentucky Historical Society, complement the Mansion's other lovely furnishings. A display of art and a collection of literature by Kentuckians will soon be added.

Imported crystal chandeliers and sculptured cornices reflect the atmosphere of elegance. The open cane mahogany furniture in the ballroom once graced the American Embassy in Panama. Some rare chests of applewood with inlay are mementos of the past. The huge breakfront in the family dining room is an antique of unusual quality. The family living areas mirror the individual taste of each Governor's family and are redecorated to fit their needs. The spacious grounds are carefully kept and landscaped. Greenhouses provide fresh bouquets all year round. Large areas of kitchen gardens yield fresh fruits and vegetables seasonally.

Under Kentucky law, a Mansion Committee of Frankfort citizens is appointed to give attention to the preservation and maintenance of the quiet elegance of the Governor's Mansion. At the present time, extensive repairs are necessary for the structural soundness of the residence, but no change of importance has ever taken place or is contemplated.

The household staff numbers twenty-eight. State police attend the safety of the Governor and the residence premises.

Editor's Note: Kentucky also provides an official residence for its Lieutenant Governor, and it is the oldest Governor's Mansion in the Nation still being used as an executive residence. This Georgian building, located at 420 High Street, Frankfort, was the first Governor's Mansion built by a State after the Revolution.

With a $12,000 appropriation by the Legislature, construction of this house began in 1797. Six years after statehood, in 1798, Governor James Garrard moved into this Mansion, and the home remained the official residence of thirty-three Governors until 1914, when the existing Governor's Mansion was built. In 1946, the Kentucky Historical Society acquired management of the then vacant old Governor's Mansion and, after extensive restoration and the addition of twentieth-century comforts to the interior, the house was designated the official residence of the Lieutenant Governor.

LOUISIANA

THE GOVERNOR'S MANSION*

The Louisiana Governor's Mansion, located east of the Capitol in Baton Rouge, is a four-level structure of Louisiana Greek Revival architecture, which was prominent in the State after 1830. The period marked a distinct departure from earlier Louisiana architecture and is considered by many to represent the finest architectural era in the State's history. William C. Gilmer of Shreveport was the architect for the Mansion built in 1963 at a cost of approximately $1 million.

Primary inspiration for the exterior design was Oak Alley, with a minor note of Georgian in the dormers, the fanlight of the doorway and the long window on the circular stair. The second floor veranda was omitted as being too informal.

The house is lined with white Doric columns on three and one-half sides. Exterior construction is of a hand-molded-type brick painted white, and the roof slate and paving on the porches is cleft-faced Vermont non-fading gray-green slate.

Ornamental planting areas are planned throughout the paved parking lot, and the lampposts there formerly were used on the streets of Plymouth, England. The copper lanterns atop the lampposts are also antique lanterns from Europe.

The Mansion contains 25,000 square feet of space. It was designed to incorporate the maximum of traditional beauty with an arrangement of interior space for maximum convenience to the family and efficient conduct of official functions of State. Family areas have been separated from areas reserved for State functions so that it is possible to transact State business in certain areas while the First Family carries on a normal living routine in other areas.

The unique element of the first floor plan is the inviting entrance to the family living quarters from the public rooms. The entrance can be closed off from the public rooms for complete privacy, and the formal areas or family quarters do not impede the free flow of traffic from one another.

The main entrance fanlight-paneled double door is typical of the period after which the Mansion was patterned, but was actually inspired by the main doorway of the late Senator Robert Taft's antebellum home in Ohio. The light fixture in the entrance vestibule with the Seal of the State etched on its crystal globes, together with the Adam lamp in the circular stairway, were removed from the former Mansion.

*Submitted by Mrs. John J. McKeithen, First Lady of Louisiana, from an article compiled by the Division of Administration, Office of the Governor.

The main reception hall and stair hall are paved with marble quarried and fabricated in Italy. A spectacular marble motif is found in the circular stair hall. The center of the hall has a six-foot-in-diameter marble slab containing the Seal of the State. This Seal is inlaid with approximately 2,500 pieces of marble incised into the marble cart wheel.

Flanking the reception area are the State Drawing Room (twenty-five by forty-five feet) and the State Dining Room (twenty-five by thirty-five feet). The matching five-foot, thirty-branch crystal chandeliers (circa 1830) hanging in the State rooms, together with a smaller crystal chandelier in the reception hall, were obtained in Europe and refashioned in New Orleans for the Mansion.

The furnishings in these public rooms are, with minor exception, reproductions of fine eighteenth-century pieces. The set of twenty-four upholstered armchairs in the State Dining Room are modified copies of eighteenth-century Hepplewhite chairs.

The door and window casings in the State rooms were inspired by similar trim used in Louisiana plantation homes of the same period. Other door and window trim is also similar to that of many of the finer old Louisiana

Inspiration for the Louisiana Governor's Mansion, built in 1963, was taken from Oak Alley, a famous Louisiana plantation, and from homes of New Orleans' Vieux Carré.

homes. The secondary doorways leading out from these rooms to the porches are found not only at the famous Louisiana plantation, Oak Alley, but also throughout the Vieux Carré and in many Louisiana houses.

The twenty-one-foot six-pedestal mahogany dining room banquet table is an eighteenth-century reproduction, which extends to twenty-five feet with added leaves. The top was made from an antique table obtained in England. It can be broken down into six individual tables, each of which seats six. Two large marble top serving consoles are from the East Room of the old Mansion, where they were provided with wood tops. The wood mantel is a copy of a mantel in Ormond plantation north of New Orleans. The woven documentary rug in the State Dining Room contains as its central motif the spread eagle with thirteen stars over it, with the border vignettes depicting persons and scenes from Louisiana history, such as the transfer of the Territory from France to the United States in 1803, and the battle of New Orleans.

The rug in the State Drawing Room contains the coats of arms of France and Spain in the field of the rug, with the border depicting even earlier scenes interwoven with the history of the State.

Adjacent to the formal dining room are the butlery and kitchen, which are designed to meet the needs of large receptions and dinners; next to the State Kitchen are the family butlery and kitchen. These are designed to meet the needs of the First Family when large meals are not required.

Separated by a foyer are the family breakfast room and family dining room. The family living room, which is located on the west side of the Mansion adjacent to the dining room, is paneled in tidewater cypress, one of Louisiana's fine native woods.

On the second floor are bedrooms for the family and guests. The First Lady's bedroom faces south and overlooks the front veranda. Immediately behind this room is the Governor's bedroom, which contains a wood-burning fireplace—Governor James H. Davis' sole request of the builders. The third floor contains a family recreation room, three supplementary guest bedrooms, an equipment room and storage rooms.

The ground floor contains the Governor's private entrance and garage; the security officers' lounge; locker rooms for servants; a fallout shelter equipped and supervised by State Civil Defense; and mechanical equipment.

MAINE

THE BLAINE HOUSE By Mrs. Kenneth M. Curtis, *First Lady of Maine*

The Blaine House, official residence of sixteen Maine Governors since 1919, and a National Historic Landmark since 1964, is a stately and imposing twenty-eight room mansion with nine baths, located opposite the State Capitol in the City of Augusta.

The history of the Blaine House is both interesting and colorful due in part to the fact that it was for many years the home of one of Maine's most renowned sons, the "Man from Maine," James G. Blaine. He was Speaker of the House, United States Senator, twice Secretary of State, and the unsuccessful Republican candidate for President in 1884.

The earliest records show that this lovely colonial structure was built by sea Captain James Hall soon after he acquired the property in August of 1830. The original structure consisted of a beautiful entrance hall with a front and back parlor to the left; a sitting room and dining room to the right, plus a small kitchen and pantry on the first floor; and four bedrooms on the second level. Captain Hall added an ell to the front portion of the building in 1833.

In November of 1862, James G. Blaine bought the property and presented the "old mansion house" to his wife as a birthday gift. The Blaine family made important additions to the structure of the house, building on to the west end of the ell practically a duplicate of the front part of the house as well as an adjoining carriage house which was later removed.

The Blaine addition, consisting of a study and a billiard room on the first floor, is perhaps the most historically significant part of the building for it remains today as it was in Blaine's day. At this time, Mr. Blaine combined the two front parlors into one long reception room and also combined the two rooms on the right of the entrance hall into one large dining room, referred to today as the State Dining Room.

No further additions to the structure were made until 1924 when the fourth section was added. This section, the final wing, was added at a right angle to the rest of the building in order to preserve, as nearly as possible, the original lines of the house. This addition on the northwest corner of the house added many necessary rooms to be utilized as the staff quarters and enlarged kitchen and laundry areas.

This addition was necessitated in 1919 when the house was given to the State by Harriet Blaine Beale, youngest daughter of James G. Blaine, as a memorial to her young son, Walker Blaine Beale, who fell in battle during World War I. The house was given to be used thereafter as the official residence of the Governor and family of the State of Maine. The State was in need of acquiring such a permanent residence due to the fact that the State Legislature had passed a resolve in 1915 making it mandatory for the Governor to reside in the Capital City of Augusta during his term of office.

A vast expenditure of close to $185,000 was recorded in 1919 for the purpose of renovating and furnishing the newly acquired Executive Mansion. At this time, the grounds were enlarged and several contiguous properties were purchased by the State.

Of significance was the fact that the roof was raised on the middle portion of the house to the height of the front and rear portions at this time. The color was also changed from a battleship grey to a more appropriate colonial white with green shutters, the same combination of colors found on the house today.

Because of Mrs. Beale's desire that the furnishings be in keeping with the architectural merits of the house, this matter was placed in the hands of the expert Boston firm of Pennell, Gibbs and Quiring. A few pieces were acquired from "Elmwood," the home of poet James Russell Lowell, a contemporary of Blaine.

It should be noted that outside of the Blaine study, which holds many of the original furnishings and belongings of Blaine, few of the pieces found in the house today were actual possessions of Mr. Blaine.

Mr. Blaine's desk from Washington is prominently displayed in the study as is his vast library of books which are enclosed in long, glassed-in bookshelves. The wallpaper is an exact replica of the paper chosen by Mr. Blaine himself, which hung in the room in the 1860's. It was the same print he had seen in President Lincoln's room in the White House. Of great value is the small pass on the desk which is carefully preserved and bears the signature of "A. Lincoln." It states: "Allow the bearer Hon. Mr. Blaine to pass from City Point to Richmond and return," and is dated April 7, 1865. A photo of this pass is recorded in the files of the Library of Congress.

The Blaine study is one of six rooms open to the public each weekday from 2 p.m. to 4 p.m. Except for the sunroom, located in the middle portion of the house, and the billiard room, the furnishings found in these rooms are all in keeping with the Federal Period.

The public rooms include the front reception room, the State Dining Room, the family dining room, the sunroom, the Blaine Study, and the billiard or pool room. A member of the permanent Mansion staff conducts the tours. Colorful brochures on the Blaine House as well as a recent pamphlet on James G. Blaine, published by the Maine Commission on the Arts and Humanities in cooperation with Governor and Mrs. Kenneth M. Curtis, are made available to all Blaine House visitors, who number in the thousands each year.

The sum of $20,000 was allocated by council order in 1962 for the purpose of further renovation and restoration of items in the Blaine House. Many fine period pieces were added or improved upon at that time.

The lovely Oriental rugs which are found in the reception room and the downstairs hallway were added at this time. They reflect the influence of the sea captains and the representative architectural period of the Blaine House, for the Mansion is but one of many such homes which belonged to early maritime travelers. Another example of this may be found in the beautiful hand-painted wallpaper with Japanese design in the family dining room, which distinctively reflects this Oriental influence.

Among the items which have remained unchanged since Mr. Blaine's time is the front staircase with antique balustrades. At the curve of the stairway stands a statue of Minerva, the Roman Goddess of Wisdom with torch in hand, who has remained in this niche since the Blaine family resided here.

The beautiful black marble fireplaces in the reception room remain intact. The marble for these was imported by Mr. Blaine from Italy. The ornate carved, gilt mirrors above the mantels were also original Blaine possessions. This room has two stately Corinthian columns which stand at the point of the division of the original two rooms.

The wood finish in the entire front part of the house is of plain oak, as are the floors. A tiled floor is in the sunroom, however. This room is unique in that it reflects a simple informality in contrast to the more formal rooms of the downstairs level. Sets of sash doors and two stationary doors form the outside wall of this room, with stone steps leading outside which are thirty-six feet in width, and make a separate entrance to the building. Between each two sets of doors are fluted columns which add much to the attractiveness of the design. The fireplaces here are of white stone. There are nine fireplaces in the Mansion.

Many handsome antiques are in the Blaine House. Among these are a pier table of Empire style with a New England slate top; an ornate hand-carved pie-crust design table; a beautiful French clock which dates back to 1825; lovely pineapple beds; and a handsome Pembroke table with two wide folding flaps. The beds and Pembroke table are said to have come from "Elmwood."

Many chairs in the reception room are Empire and Martha Washington, and a lovely Sheraton-style sofa, flanked by two Williamsburg tables holding antique colonial pewter lamps, is also located in this room.

In the State Dining Room are twelve original and rare Phyfe chairs; a Chippendale china closet and one in Sheraton design; a Sheraton serving table; and interesting knife boxes with urns.

Of historical interest to all visitors is the beautiful *Maine* silver service consisting of a large soup tureen, two covered vegetable dishes and a loving cup with moose-horn handles. This soup tureen and the vegetable dishes were presented to the battleship *Maine* at the time of her commissioning in 1895. The loving cup was presented to the captain by a group of Maine natives residing in New Orleans when the ship visited in port during Mardi Gras. The silver went down with the ship when the *Maine* was sunk in Havana Harbor in 1898, and although recovered six days later, it was not returned to the State for many years.

Also improved in 1962 were the Blaine House grounds. A large tennis court was built, which is flooded in the winter months to serve as an ice rink, and the areas of formal gardens were enlarged. A number of stately elms and maple trees grace the spacious grounds and enhance the beauty of the Mansion. The shrubbery and white picket fencing around the grounds help to maintain a note of privacy from the busy streets which flank the Blaine House on two sides.

The Bureau of Public Improvements, created in 1957, handles and oversees maintenance of the Blaine House and grounds as well as a large, fully equipped and furnished staff house and an ample, heated garage. Although each First Family has the right to alter the private living quarters to suit its own particular preferences, all changes in the public rooms must meet with the approval of this bureau.

The cost of maintenance of the Mansion and grounds was a mere $5,184.75 from the period of July 1921 to June 1922; whereas the appropriation total for the Fiscal Year 1967 was close to $48,000. Although the cost of maintaining the Executive Mansion has vastly increased over the years, the size of the staff has remained relatively small. The Blaine House has a permanent staff of five and a secretary.

It is an amazing accomplishment and a credit to the true Maine spirit of hard work and cooperation that relatively few "extras" are called in to help at the many teas, luncheons and formal dinner parties which are given on a regular basis by the Governor and First Lady. These many benefit teas are considered social obligations of all who occupy the role of First Lady of Maine.

In 1967, the Maine Commission on the Arts and Humanities, working with the writer, helped in selecting a number of fine and valuable paintings for loan to the Blaine House from various State museums. These paintings are changed each year and are in the public rooms as well as the private quarters on the second floor.

The private quarters consist of eight rooms: three bedrooms, a living room, a play room, a den, the Governor's study, the secretary's office, a small kitchenette and four baths. Two front bedrooms are used solely as guest rooms and are opened to guests during official functions. President Grant was among the notable Blaine House guests to occupy one of the guest rooms during a visit in 1873.

The Blaine House, which may be pointed to with pride by all Maine citizens, will undoubtedly continue for many years as the Executive Mansion. It stands today as one of the loveliest of all Governors' Mansions, rich in the proud heritage of the people and leaders of the Pine Tree State.

Overleaf: Summer foliage frames the Blaine House in this painting by Charles Klebe.

Gene Klebe

MARYLAND

GOVERNMENT HOUSE By Mrs. Spiro T. Agnew, *Former First Lady of Maryland*

Maryland's Government House, as the Governor's Mansion is known, echoes the many treasures of academic architecture which abound in the 320-year-old capital city of Annapolis.

Located between two significant landmarks and enhanced by a fountain and formal gardens, the Governor's Mansion holds appropriate prominence in the planned capital city. Francis Nicholson, colonial Governor from 1693 to 1698, having selected Annapolis for the Colony's new capital, reserved the highest ground for the site of the new "stadt" house, "the chief place and seat of Justice within the province for holding Assemblyes and Provinciall Courts. . . ." He also chose the adjacent land elevation for King William III's Anglican Church. Both sites retain their original function and circular setting although both now hold the third building to be erected on the original sites. The church has long been separated from government control and the Statehouse, which was built in 1772 and is still in use, had added structures. Yet these two important buildings, with Government House between, form an appropriate heart for old Annapolis.

Erected of brick in 1868-69, the House has undergone reverse metamorphosis from its original Victorian appearance to the present facade of five-part Georgian excellence. The central section is in grand proportions and supported by two wings with their adjoining hyphens. Of particular note are great chimneys, elaborate cornice and Palladian windows, a common trademark of architectural excellence in the 1700's and employed with superb skill in several pre-Revolutionary mansions throughout the city.

The fan-shaped windows of the hyphens add a repeat rhythm to the Palladian windows and bring harmonious balance to the exterior, while providing airiness and light to the interior.

Also deserving of notice is the residual "porch," an interruption in the facade by a forty-inch projection, defining building evolution from the true feudal style entrance (as found in the city's 1735 Old Treasury Building) to the late Georgian design, when this construction detail all but disappears. The Mansion's belt-course, a horizontal line of protruding bricks, adds further to the knowledgeable eighteenth-century design.

The rear of the building retains more nearly its Victorian origin and allows interior rooms to be of generous proportions.

The original cost of the building and land was over $100,000. Costs of additions and repairs have continued in varying amounts, the major alteration occurring in 1935 for the sum of $136,000. The most recent repairs to the interior, in 1967, required an expenditure of approximately $300,000 and provided primarily for functional safety and modern comfort.

Colonel R. Snowden Andrews of Baltimore was architect of the original building. The most significant architectural changes were made during Governor Harry Whinna Nice's administration, under the direction of architect Clyde M. Fry.

The home is opened on Tuesdays and Thursdays, by appointment, from September 1st through June 15th. The most important public festivity has occurred for several years on New Year's Day when all citizens of Maryland are invited to Open House and to exchange good wishes for the coming year with the Governor and his Lady.

Other special dates are Washington's Birthday, when members of the Maryland National Guard are honored guests, and Anne Arundel County day of the Maryland House and Garden Pilgrimage week, when the Governor's wife is hostess for tea to the thousands of visitors who arrive to view open homes in old Annapolis.

The Mansion is furnished to augment the classical grace of its architectural splendor. Three centuries of skilled furniture craftsmanship are represented, with some of the newest acquisitions being of the oldest design and executed in the original manner. The recent addition of an immense four-part banquet table complements an important Queen Anne highboy which graces one end of the State Banquet Room.

The State Seal, designed to depict Lord Baltimore's holdings in Nova Scotia and Maryland, and incorporating Baltimore armorial flags, enhances a set of handsome Wedgwood china.

While many of the furnishings are of massive Empire style, the State Reception Room is delicately furnished with exquisite Hepplewhite-design settees and chairs.

It is fitting that the oldest documented piece of importance is an eighteenth-century grandfather's clock, which originally belonged to the first elected Governor, Thomas Johnson, Jr., 1777-1779.

Twin mirrors of Sheraton design, bearing the ancient Seal of Maryland, reflect a grand sweeping staircase in the boldly proportioned entrance hall. The woodwork

Symmetrical chimneys and Palladian windows add to the dignity of Maryland's Government House in the heart of old Annapolis.

in the house is described as exceptionally beautiful, having monumental proportions and exquisite detail.

Typical of Maryland design at the turn of the nineteenth century are several mantelpieces decorated with plaster composition ornament characterizing Grecian divinities. Particularly lyrical is the family dining room mantel depicting a Dionysian merrymaking scene in the central medallion and incorporating bunches of grapes in turned supports.

Coalescent reminders of Annapolis' colonial heritage and continuing State administration are the Mansion's numerous imposing portraits. Among them is a Florence McCubbin copy of Van Dyck's "Queen Henrietta Maria," consort of King Charles I, for whom Maryland was named, which adorns the State Drawing Room. A handsome likeness of Sir Robert Eden, ancestor of Anthony Eden and last colonial Governor to serve Maryland, embellishes the overmantel of the State Drawing Room. This sovereign was so beloved by the Annapolitans, and their affection returned by him, that he came back after the Revolution to live out his life in this area.

Most first floor rooms boast fine Oriental rugs and handsome crystal chandeliers.

MINNESOTA

THE GOVERNOR'S RESIDENCE By Mrs. Harold LeVander, *First Lady of Minnesota*

In 1965, the State was given the former home of Horace Irvine, St. Paul attorney and lumberman, and his wife. The presentation was made by their daughters, Mrs. Olivia Irvine Dodge and Mrs. Clotilde Irvine Moles.

Built of stone and red brick in 1910, the English Tudor home is located at 1006 Summit Avenue, St. Paul, about one and a half miles from the State Capitol. The Residence has twenty rooms besides porches, pantries, closets, bathrooms and other service areas. It has high windows and vaulted ceilings, nine fireplaces and a solarium with a sunken marble floor and arched windows. The drawing room is paneled in African mahogany, the dining room in Circassian walnut.

It is Minnesota's first executive residence, and in accepting the gift in May 1965, the Legislature designated it as the "State ceremonial building" to be maintained by the Commissioner of Administration. In 1965, to make the house suitable for a First Family, money was set aside by the State Legislature for major remodeling and structural improvements, which took place over the following two years.

The family of Karl Rolvaag was the first Governor's family to live in the home after it became the State residence, followed in February 1967 by Governor Harold LeVander and his family.

The Building Commission of the 1967 Legislature prepared a budget for furnishings to replace those which had been loaned or rented to the State in 1965, and for improvements planned during the Rolvaag administration, such as an air conditioning and heating plant, restored floors in the lower level, a parking area, an ornamental iron fence across the front of the parking area, and landscaping. These improvements were completed in August 1968, three years after the State was given the house.

The designer, William Wiessner of St. Paul, has emphasized State colors of blue and yellow, along with shades of green, in accordance with the writer's endeavors to bring Minnesota lore and history into the setting. Truly representative is the area rug in the solarium designed from a plate of Red Wing pottery with the Star of the North in the center. The rug in the front hall carries another adaptation of the North Star. Furniture in both the drawing room and the dining room is eighteenth-century with draperies and upholstery fabrics giving the rooms a rich, formal tone.

The State has twenty-four place settings of formal china with the Seal of Minnesota. The dining room seats only twelve, so the solarium is used in case of a larger group for a seated dinner or luncheon. There are six persons on the staff.

A newly enlarged patio leads to the garden where Minnesota wild flowers and the Norway pine (Minnesota's State Tree) and other native trees will be planted. There will be a small pool in which the loon, the State Bird, and the walleye pike, Minnesota's State Fish, will be seen. The Minnesota Nurserymen's Association donated and cares for the plantings in the garden at the Governor's Residence.

There are plans for a Vietnam War Memorial in the garden. A sculpture, or possibly a fountain, done by a Minnesotan honoring the State's men who served in the Vietnam War, will be the focal point of the garden.

There is much interest in the newly acquired Governor's Residence because it is the first one owned by the State of Minnesota, but the size of the house does not lend itself to public tours.

The first Residence for the Governor of Minnesota, a stone and red brick home of English Tudor design, was acquired in 1965. The garden behind the Mansion is planted with trees and wild flowers which are native to the North Star State.

This palatial Mansion occupies an entire city block in Jackson, Mississippi

MISSISSIPPI

THE GOVERNOR'S MANSION By Mrs. John Bell Williams, *First Lady of Mississippi*

The Mississippi Governor's Mansion was completed in 1841 and was first occupied by Governor Tilghman M. Tucker and his family in 1842. Except for the Civil War years and the carpetbag era which followed, it has been the official residence of Mississippi Governors and their families ever since.

The seventeen-room Mansion, of Greek Revival architecture, occupies an entire city block in the busiest part of Jackson. Surrounded by tall office buildings, subjected day and night to the sounds of a busy city, open on four sides to the scrutiny of all who pass that way, the beautiful old building stands serene and gracious, the pride of all Mississippians.

The State of Mississippi made no effort during the first fifteen years of its existence to provide a residence for its Chief Executive. It was not until 1833 that the Legislature appropriated $10,000 for the construction of a "suitable house for the Governor, in the town of Jackson." The same law stipulated that such a house was to "adhere to plain republican simplicity."

Actual construction of the Governor's house was started in 1838, and it is quite obvious from the plans of State Architect William Nichols that his idea of "suitability" was quite different from that held by the Legislature. On February 21, 1840, he reported to the Legislature that the following progress had been made:

> The Mansion house for residence of the Governor is now being built agreeably with the plan approved by the last Legislature. . . .
>
> On the principal floor the main entrance is from a portico twenty-eight by twelve feet into an octagon vestibule, which communicates with a drawing room fifty by twenty-four feet, with a dining room, which by means of folding doors, may be made of the same size, and with the great staircase leading to the upper floor. . . .
>
> The portico on the principal front, will be supported by columns of the Corinthian order. In finishing the building, it is intended to avoid a profusion of ornament, and to adhere to a plain republican simplicity as best comporting with the dignity of the State.

At the time he made his report, he requested an additional $30,000 from the Legislature, and was given $20,000. Never one to let a reluctant Legislature deter him, he continued with his plans and when the Mansion was completed it had cost the State $50,094.93.

During the years that followed, the Mansion became the center of political and social life in the State's capital. Two blocks from the State House, it was a meeting place for "members of the Legislature, judges of the courts, strangers in town, and resident citizens generally."

After the outbreak of the Civil War, the Mansion was used for many important conferences by the military and political leaders of the State. On July 9, 1863, Union General William T. Sherman reached the Confederate trenches encircling the City of Jackson, and began a heavy bombardment of the city. After a week of continuous bombardment, the Confederate troops evacuated and Union Forces took possession. Since the Mansion was one of the few buildings left standing, Sherman moved in and made it his headquarters.

When the war was over, Governor Benjamin G. Humphreys moved into the Mansion with his family and was authorized by the Legislature to start the badly needed repairs on the building. Within a few years, however, the State came under carpetbag rule and, in keeping with the Federal policy of replacing Southern elected officials with Union appointees, General Adelbert Ames was appointed to supersede Governor Humphreys. Federal troops arrived in town, forcibly removed the Governor from his office at the Capitol, and then demanded that the Governor and his family vacate the Mansion. Mrs. Humphreys described their evacuation in a letter to her mother: "Mr. Humphreys came out and sent for a carriage for me, and wagons. He told me not to leave the house until I saw everything was put together ready to set in the wagons . . . and told me to put my box of silver on the carriage and take it with me. We had heard of Yankee raids before, and profited by the experience of others . . . I marched out with my children. . . . The file of soldiers was outside the gate. We walked out, got into the carriage and rode to Mrs. Barr's boarding house. Everybody on the street gazing at us as we rode through the streets."

Carpetbag rule finally came to an end in the early 1870's and the Mansion once again became the official home of Mississippi's duly elected Governor. For the next thirty-five years very little was spent on the Mansion. The people of Mississippi were too busy trying to rebuild their own homes and lives to take much interest in it. However, in 1908, when Governor Edmond Favor Noel was inaugurated, the decision had to be made whether to sell the Mansion or spend a great deal of money to repair, redecorate and add space to make it livable for that era. The Legislature decided it was too valuable to abandon, and appropriated $30,000 for renovation, erection of an annex, and grading, paving and ornamenting the Mansion grounds and walks. The two-story annex which was added to the back of the Mansion was designed to conform with the old building and seems a natural part of the whole.

Since 1908 other changes have been made in the Mansion. In the early 1940's Governor Paul B. Johnson, Sr., had the yellow brick exterior painted white; in 1944, the State Building Commission authorized funds to acquire permanent furnishings for the Mansion which are mostly historic period pieces; and in 1961 a major restoration of the Mansion was made. Today, Mississippians feel that they have one of the most beautiful official residences in the United States.

The Mansion has many visitors, but there are no daily tours. It is open on pilgrimage during March and April on Monday, Wednesday and Friday from 9:30 a.m. to 11:30 a.m. and on Tuesday and Thursday from 2:30 p.m. to 4:30 p.m. A hostess and a staff of nine assist in the care of the official residence.

This handsome French-Italian-style Mansion overlooking the Missouri River has been the home of Missouri's First Families since 1871.

MISSOURI

THE EXECUTIVE MANSION

By Mrs. Warren E. Hearnes, *First Lady of Missouri*

Five men, including a son of Daniel Boone, were dispatched from the provisional capital at St. Charles in 1821 to locate a site for the permanent capital for the State of Missouri. It was stated in the Missouri Constitution that it must be located approximately forty miles from the mouth of the Osage River and on the Missouri River. Of necessity, it must be located on high ground to prevent flooding; and as water was the main source of transportation then—there were but few roads—it must be located on the river. Thus, in 1822, the City of Jefferson was founded.

In that same year, the Missouri Legislature made provision for a home for the Governor and his family by appointing a Board of Trustees to select a site and set forth the specifications for the building. It was their plan to have this building serve a dual purpose, that is, to house both the State Legislature and the Governor's family. They chose the present site of the Governor's Mansion, a high bluff overlooking the majestic Missouri River. The first Mansion stood on the very same site that the present Mansion occupies today.

In all, there have been four "Mansions" since Jefferson City became the seat of government—the first, a temporary structure, followed by three permanent ones. It was at the urging of Governor B. Gratz Brown that the Legislature authorized the sum of $50,000 for a new Executive Mansion—one that was to be used solely as the Governor's home. The plans finally chosen were those of Barnett & Pinquenard, and the result is a residence that is considered one of the finest examples of French-Italian architecture still standing in the Nation.

In 1871, the family of Governor Brown—whom Missouri looks upon as its "building Governor," since he was responsible for several structures around the site of the Mansion—took up residence in the present Mansion as its first tenants. Located at 100 Madison Street, only eight hundred feet from the State Capitol, the building is currently valued at $1 million.

Ornate, hand-carved walnut doors, each weighing two thousand pounds, guard the front entrance. The winding staircase, also hand-carved and opening onto the entrance hall, is said to rival any other stairway in the United States in its beauty.

There are twenty-seven rooms, ten baths, and eight fireplaces, most of which are built of Carrara marble. All of the rooms of the Mansion are spacious, with unusually high ceilings. The ceilings are approximately nineteen feet high on the first and second floors. The basement is comprised of a garage, storage, laundry and servants' quarters.

The first floor, used mainly for State occasions, contains the great entrance hall, drawing room, sitting room, dining room, kitchen and a very ample butler's pantry. The second and third floors comprise the First Family's private living quarters, containing sitting rooms, bedrooms, a rumpus room and a television room.

The Mansion has, of course, been redecorated and renovated many times. However, there are some pieces of furniture which are of specific historical significance. For instance, the gold-leaf furniture in the drawing room on the first floor was brought from the Missouri Building at the St. Louis World's Fair of 1904. In a bedroom on the second floor is a massive canopied bed, which was used by the Prince of Wales (later King Edward VII of England) when he spent two days in St. Louis.

Governor and Mrs. B. Gratz Brown started a tradition that is still followed today, that of leaving a gift or memento to the Mansion upon the end of the administration. They left the beautiful pink granite pillars in front of the Mansion which were cut from the Governor's own quarries near Ironton, Missouri, and sent to Jefferson City in an unpolished state. There they were finished and set as a lasting memorial to Governor Brown. This is but one of the many traditions handed down as part of the Mansion's charm and history. Another lovely tradition, inaugurated with the Stephens' administration (1899-1903), is that of placing a portrait of each of Missouri's First Ladies in the Mansion. These are now hung on the walls of the entrance hall and the drawing room.

Governor Lloyd Stark had made extensive repairs during his administration in 1937-1941; and although the Mansion was very soundly constructed, the building fell into disrepair by 1956. Thus, it is to Governor Jim Blair that the people of Missouri owe a debt of gratitude for letting the people know the condition of the Mansion during his term of office. His active concern made possible a complete renovation of this lovely old home in order that it could be made safe and comfortable for Missouri's First Families and continue as a symbol of Missouri's achievements.

While many people had been privileged to see the Mansion as invited guests and during open house, it was not until the Hearnes' administration that the Mansion was opened to large groups for personal tours in order to acquaint the people of Missouri, as well as those from other areas, with the beautiful Mansion and its history. Tours are now arranged by appointment, except on weekends and holidays. The First Lady is assisted by a staff of five persons.

Each First Lady has had the opportunity to redecorate the Mansion in accordance with her own personal tastes and, of course, within a very limited budget. One of the first projects accomplished during the Hearnes Administration was the renovation of the eight fireplaces, which had previously been completely blocked with bricks. Although there are no records on this, perhaps it was done when steam heat was first installed in the Mansion. Now on a cold winter day, one can sit by a burning fire (gas logs), which adds a great deal of charm and warmth to the huge rooms.

During this same administration, the old flooring has been replaced in many of the rooms and the painted woodwork restored to its original state. A collection of antique lamps which blends with the furnishings of the Mansion has been started.

Perhaps most importantly, a new library was added to the Governor's Mansion in 1968. It was a gift from the Missouri Library Association and the Academy of Squires and was one of the ways we stressed the importance of good books in the everyday lives of people.

The present Executive Mansion has been the home of twenty-seven of Missouri's First Families. It has seen the joys and dreams along with the hopes and despairs of living. But most of all, this lovely old house overlooking the wide Missouri River has been their home as it has been home to all of Missouri's citizens.

MONTANA

THE GOVERNOR'S MANSION

By Mrs. Tim Babcock,
Former First Lady of Montana

They took the blue from her sky
The gold from the sunset
The green from her forests
And the tans from the prairies . . . .
This describes the Montana Governor's Mansion.

Finished in 1959, this $300,000 Mansion in Helena is located on a rise overlooking Montana's Capitol Building and commands a spectacular view of the Helena valley and surrounding mountain ranges. Modern in design, it is built in the likeness of a ship.

Chandler Cohagen of Billings, Montana, was the architect, and the Mansion was built by the Mel Buck Construction Company. It is constructed of concrete and steel and contains sixteen rooms and approximately 5,700 square feet of floor space on each of its two levels.

The Mansion is faced with vari-colored Norman-size brick, laid in a random pattern, and it is roofed with twenty-four-inch royal-type cedar shingles. The floors are concrete, supported by steel joists and then covered with vinyl tile, ceramic tile, slate and soft carpeting.

Plans for the Mansion began to take shape in 1953 when the Montana Legislature appropriated $125,000 for this purpose. Mr. C. F. Mueller, a civic-minded Helena resident who owned the property, donated the site for the new Mansion. Because he knew and loved Montana, he took the initiative in arousing support for the building of the present Mansion which, to date, has served three of Montana's Governors.

The main entrance is flanked by a circular driveway which opens into a large vestibule floored with flagstone. The building is 140 feet long, and the upper floor consists of eleven rooms, four large storage rooms, and a main entrance staircase leading to the lower level.

The upper level consists of reception room, living room, State Room, dining room, breakfast room, kitchen, three guest rooms with baths, the Governor's bedroom with bath, the east study room, a ladies' powder room and men's rooms.

The lower level of the Mansion has the same amount of space as the upper level. It contains two bedrooms and a sitting room and bath for the maid, a large recreation room, a men's room, ladies' powder room, furnace room, two large storerooms, utility room, and spacious lobby, with garage and tool room.

Shirley Kemp Gannon had charge of the original interior decorating and furnishing. She blended color, periods, tones and effects into a harmonious reflection of Montana's scenery and heritage. No single color or motif dominates the Mansion, yet each room contains some of the colors found throughout the dwelling—colors which have been taken from Montana's mountains, forests, streams and prairies—using them to create the individual character of the room.

Montana's Governor's Mansion is a modern concrete and steel structure faced with brick laid in a random pattern. The two-level house was designed to resemble a ship.

Each Governor's wife has added her personal touches. Room arrangements and color accessory changes are made with administrative changes. A staff of three help with the operation and maintenance of the home. Public tours may be arranged by appointment.

This Governor's Mansion replaced the one which had been in use since 1913, the former home of W. A. Chessman, one of Montana's wealthy founders. It was built in 1885, a twenty-room Victorian home of a bygone era, which served its Chief Executives well until the new Mansion was ready for occupancy.

NEBRASKA

THE EXECUTIVE MANSION

By Mrs. Norbert T. Tiemann,

First Lady of Nebraska

Nebraska's beautiful Georgian Mansion stands directly across the street from the State Capitol in Lincoln. It was completed in 1957 at a cost of $200,000 including furnishings.

During Nebraska's years as a Territory and from statehood in 1867 until 1901, no official residence was provided for the Governor and his family. Governors were said to live "all over town." None of the homes they occupied is in existence at the present time.

In 1899, the Legislature appropriated $25,000 for the purchase of a home, and shortly thereafter a large structure owned by D. E. Thompson, a division superintendent on the Burlington Railroad, was purchased. This home, located across the street from the Capitol to the south, cost the State $21,835.30 with furnishings. It served sixteen First Families, beginning with Governor William A. Poynter, who served from 1899 to 1901. Subsequent Governors, with two exceptions, lived in this "Old Mansion" until it was razed in 1956. Governor Samuel R. McKelvie (1919-1923) preferred to live in another home, and Governor Victor E. Anderson (1955-1959) lived in his own home in Havelock, Nebraska, until the new Mansion was completed.

The Old Mansion was considered a magnificent place, with its pillars, gables and verandas, but by the mid-1940's, it became obvious that the stately old structure could no longer serve the needs of Nebraska's Chief Executive. It was drafty, uncomfortable, had antiquated plumbing and was generally inadequate.

In 1945, 1947 and 1949, the Legislature appropriated money for a new executive residence, but the money went unused. At last, in 1955, the Legislature appropriated $200,000 for a new Executive Mansion to be built at approximately the same location as the old one. After the Building Commission had selected the architect and design, a rather heated controversy arose. Critics felt that the chosen design failed to complement the Capitol Building, affectionately known to Nebraskans as "the tower of the plains." However, the plans were finally approved and the razing of the old and beginning of the new proceeded.

Prior to demolition, the State Historical Society decorators selected items which were to be preserved. Then, nearly three hundred items (fireplaces, draperies, rugs, pots and pans, the front door, etc.) from the Old Mansion were sold at public auction.

This colonial Georgian Mansion is a fitting symbol of Nebraska's dign

Governor and Mrs. Anderson supervised the building and decorating of the new Mansion. The architect was Selmer Solheim; the builder, Walter J. Broer Construction Company; landscape designer, T. G. Welding; and interior decorator, John B. Peacock. Ground for the new Mansion was broken in September 1956. The following lines from Mr. Solheim best describe the new building:

> The design of the Executive Mansion for the State of Nebraska had to be planned for several separate functions and in such a manner that the

requirements of future Governors would, for the most part, be satisfied. Four separate functions were considered: Governor's residence; facilities for State receptions and State dining; accommodations for overnight guests; staff and service area.

The plan had to be functional and in this respect circulation of traffic was a primary consideration. A great deal of design study was given to the fact that each of the above areas had to be separate but contiguous, and become private within themselves, in the building. It seemed most effective to work from a central hub, or lower foyer.

The first floor of the Mansion is allocated to the public area and includes the State Drawing Room, the State Dining Room, Governor's library, and the Governor's private dining room, along with the service wing. On the second floor is the Governor's apartment, which includes the family room and three bedrooms, plus a snack kitchen. In addition there is a guest bedroom wing which houses three guest bedrooms, each with its own private bath. The basement area is designed to accommodate large groups for specific meetings and has quarters for the staff.

The selection of an exterior design for the Executive Mansion was not easily resolved. The Building Commission felt that the design . . . should have enough traditional character so that the aesthetic life of the building would be good for at least seventy-five years. Seven exterior design solutions were submitted; the choice narrowed to two, and a unanimous vote for the modified Georgian-colonial was cast.

The lower foyer with its elliptical staircase, hand-carved stair brackets, and wrought-iron rail is most unusual and dignified. The floor is white marble with a deep blue oval carpet. The ladies' powder room is enhanced with two oval Grecian lavatories with fourteen-carat gold-plated fixtures. The State Drawing Room is furnished in the Regency and Empire Periods. The hand-carved Georgian mantel is a distinctive feature of this room and the embossed cornice adds decorative value. The floor is carpeted in blue-green, the walls papered in white silk, and the curtains are changeable blue and green taffeta with swag valances. Above the mantel hangs a French barometer, circa 1800, approximately the same period as the décor.

The gallery of First Lady pictures runs from the drawing room to the State Dining Room. It seats twenty-two and is furnished in seventeenth-century mahogany, carpeted in soft beige, papered with brilliant yellow silk wallpaper and hung with yellow draperies. All of the woodwork, including door casings, built-in buffet, and punch bowl recesses, is hand carved. Two large silver punch bowls are from the battleship *Nebraska*.

The paneling in the Governor's library is from the Old Mansion and was refinished to blend in with the décor of the new library. The fireplace fireboxes, as well as the marble hearth, were also salvaged from the Old Mansion. The furniture is seventeenth-century English mahogany, very plain and massive. The colors are earth tones of beiges and brown.

In the Governor's private dining room, the carpet, walls and Williamsburg draperies are all in shades of blue. The corner cupboards hold antique and reproduction onion-skin Meissen. The furniture is Provincial.

On the second floor, the family room is decorated and furnished in the Provincial style with turquoise, gold and brown. The master bedroom is furnished in Louis XVI style with blues and creams, and the adjoining bath is entirely of white marble.

Light fixtures in the Mansion vary from luxurious crystal chandeliers in the formal rooms to bronze and pewter fixtures in other areas. The Sheldon Art Gallery loans art work, as desired by the First Lady.

On March 16, 1958, an open house was held to give the people of the State a chance to view their new executive residence. Despite the below-freezing weather, over 18,000 people toured the building during an eight-hour period, and many had to be turned away at closing time.

Tours are given on Tuesdays during the spring and summer, with occasional special tours for large groups. Nearly each week there is at least one tea, reception, meeting, luncheon, or dinner and sometimes many more. During the State's centennial year, 1967, 20,000 visitors were at the residence for various occasions.

The basic Mansion staff numbers six, and the State Building and Grounds Department takes care of major repairs and improvements.

NEVADA

THE GOVERNOR'S MANSION By Mrs. Paul Laxalt, *First Lady of Nevada*

The move to secure a permanent home for Nevada's Chief Executive and his family was initiated in 1907. Completed in 1909, under a $40,000 appropriation, it has been the official residence for twelve of Nevada's twenty-two State Governors.

Located in Carson City, the Georgian Mansion is the most impressive building in the city. It is ten blocks northwest of the Capitol, in an area renowned for majestic homes, many of which were constructed in the latter part of the nineteenth century.

The two-story, white frame structure, designed by George A. Ferris of Reno, has six large Ionic columns and rests on a sandstone brick base. Galleries extend around the structure on both the first and second floors in front, on the south side and in the rear.

No alterations were made to the Mansion during a fifty-six year period. However, in 1967, with an appropriation from the Legislature, incumbent Governor Paul Laxalt and the writer began the remodeling project. Dramatic changes were made both to the interior and exterior. Walls were removed, large windows were inserted, a modern kitchen was installed and a rumpus room was built in the basement.

The Mansion is opened to visitors and tours from 10 a.m. to noon each Wednesday, by appointments made through the Governor's office in the Capitol. It is also available to organizations for receptions and teas.

The music room, reception room, formal dining room, Governor's study, the luncheon room and the kitchen are on the first floor. The ground stairway, illuminated

Galleries extend along three sides of the two-story white frame Mansion, home of Nevada's First Families.

by a rheostatically controlled chandelier, leads to the second floor where the master bedroom suite, guest and family bedrooms are located.

Throughout the sixteen rooms of the Mansion are historical and rare furnishings. A 1782 Duncan Phyfe set graces the luncheon room; a grandfather's clock, manufactured in 1760 and still keeping accurate time, stands near the Governor's study; an antique secretary of the late eighteenth century, and an authentic French desk are among the many other interesting pieces.

The Nevada Governor is now required by State law to reside in the capital city. However, in the State Constitution of 1864, it was required only that the Governor maintain an office in the capital city. He was provided with nothing beyond his prescribed salary for a residence. A "Mansion fund" was appropriated after the executive residence was completed. Today, the State also provides a staff consisting of a housekeeper and a part-time maid. The State highway patrol provides protection for the Mansion.

The earliest section of Morven, New Jersey's Mansion, was built in 1701.

NEW JERSEY

EXECUTIVE RESIDENCE* (MORVEN)

Morven, the first official Executive Residence maintained by the State in more than one hundred years, has frequently been described as New Jersey's most historic building. Its story, covering more than two and one-half centuries, involves some of the great events of both pre-Revolutionary and post-Revolutionary America.

The earliest section of the house was built in 1701 by Richard Stockton on a tract purchased from William Penn in the wilderness of West Jersey, one of two colonies into which the present State of New Jersey was divided at the beginning of the eighteenth century. As the Stockton family grew in wealth and prominence, Morven was enlarged, and when the American Revolution began, its appearance was much the same as it is today. During the War for Independence the owner in residence was another Richard Stockton, grandson of the builder. He gave up his positions as a member of the Royal Governor's Council and of the Supreme Court of the Colony to support the Revolutionary movement and was one of the signers of the Declaration of Independence. He later served the American cause in various capacities until his health was impaired as a consequence of treatment received as a prisoner of the British, captured after the Stockton family had been forced to flee Princeton in the face of the enemy.

Meanwhile, the celebrated Princeton campaign was unfolding, and the British General Cornwallis seized Morven for use as his headquarters during this battle. As the invading troops withdrew, Morven was looted, defaced and partially burned.

With the triumph of Washington's army, Morven became closely associated with the first dramatic developments in the building of the new Nation. The Continental Congress met in Princeton in the summer of 1783 under the Presidency of Elias Boudinot, brother of Richard Stockton's wife, Annis Boudinot Stockton. Boudinot chose Morven for his official residence, and it was there that American leaders gathered to celebrate the signing of the peace treaty terminating the war. Washington, who was temporarily residing at nearby Rocky Hill, was a frequent guest, along with many other prominent political and military figures of the Revolution. Morven, in a sense, became the first "White House" of the newly independent United States.

Ownership of the house remained in the hands of the Stockton family until 1945, and long after the Revolution the Stocktons continued to play noteworthy parts in State and national affairs.

The house has borne its present name for almost two hundred years. It was selected by Annis Boudinot Stockton after her marriage to the grandson of the builder about 1755. Like many other Americans in the 1760's, she read the purported translation of the lays of Ossian, recounting the deeds of his father Fingal, king of the northwestern Caledonians. Fingal's home was known as Morven. Annis Stockton was so fascinated by the story that she decided to give the name of Morven to the Stockton homestead in Princeton, having in mind particularly the lines:

> Sons of Morven, spread the feast
> Send the night away with song.

Morven is an early Georgian house and reflects the classical influence of Italian Renaissance architecture that reached England in the seventeenth century. When the house was built, it represented a radical departure

*Adapted from pamphlets furnished by Mrs. Richard J. Hughes, First Lady of New Jersey, prepared by The Department of Conservation and Economic Development of New Jersey.

from the typical colonial dwelling of the period. What is especially unusual is that the early Georgian or Palladian style should appear in the distant, frontier-like settlement of West Jersey at a time when the style was relatively new in England itself.

How much the present-day Morven resembles the early eighteenth-century dwelling is a matter of conjecture. The rooms in the central portion of the house apparently have not been changed to any appreciable degree. Inevitably, however, over a period of 267 years the building must have undergone substantial alterations. The brick courses of the two wings, for example, vary from those in the main part of the house to such an extent that it is improbable that the wings and the central block were constructed simultaneously. In addition, the house was burned on at least two occasions—during the Revolution and again in 1821—and required extensive repairs. No important structural modifications were involved in the preparation of Morven for its present role. While a few architectural changes were made to meet the requirements of an official establishment, the principal purpose of the rehabilitation work authorized by the Legislature in 1955 was to place the house in the best possible condition for long-term use as an executive residence.

Morven, with its gardens and ancient trees, today covers some five acres. The quarters once occupied by slaves are still standing behind the main building, and a swimming pool with cabanas as well as tennis courts have been added.

On February 4, 1945, Governor Walter E. Edge purchased Morven with the intention of preserving the property and placing it permanently in the custody of the State. Governor and Mrs. Edge formally deeded the property to the State on January 18, 1954.

A committee of private citizens appointed by Governor Robert B. Meyner to determine ". . . whether Morven should be an historic site, an Executive Mansion, or a combination of these" and "what type of rehabilitation or repairs should be undertaken" unanimously recommended that the house be designated as the official Residence of the Governor.

The committee declared in its report:

> There is probably no other house in New Jersey that so strongly typifies the historic perspective of the State. Its five acres of gardens, lawns and ancient elms provide a setting in keeping with its long heritage and official dignity. . . . There is probably no State Executive Mansion in the country that more nearly combines these qualifications; and New Jersey could well claim a Governor's residence unique among the American States.

The decoration and furnishings of Morven follow those of an eighteenth-century country home as far as possible and practical. Some authentic antiques of the mid-eighteenth century are used. Other items are copies, gifts, and a few pieces of furniture from "Sea Girt," the summer home of former Governors.

In the entrance foyer or reception hall a case contains the 119-piece sterling silver dinner set from the battleship *U.S.S. New Jersey*. The late Victorian pattern includes the State and United States Seals. A portrait by Rembrandt Peale of Richard Stockton (1764-1828), lawyer and U.S. Senator, also hangs in the foyer.

A crystal chandelier, gold leaf Federal mirror and Regency settee in the main entrance hall were gifts of Mrs. Walter E. Edge. The settee and matching chairs are original Stockton pieces received from Citizen Genet, a French diplomat in the United States following the American Revolution, given in appreciation of his enjoyable visit at Morven.

In the dining room the eighteenth-century Regency dining table is authentic and typical of what was used here in earlier days. The chairs are copies of mid-eighteenth-century Chippendales. The sideboard is an original Adam piece. The mahogany "Beacon Hill" breakfront is a fine copy of the Hepplewhite 1785 English period.

Above the fireplace is a copy of a pastoral scene by Albert Cuyp. "Nancy Squire Dodd," holding spectacles and a book, was portrayed by James Mooney (American School, 1840). "Richard Stockton" is shown in typical Quaker dress.

The yellow wallpaper in the reception room or Gold Room is a copy of an eighteenth-century flock paper. Drapes, also copies, are hung in eighteenth-century drawing room style. The table to the right of the entrance is an original eighteenth-century gaming table; the troughs at the corner were for stake chips. The two settees are Sheraton and the breakfront, English Chippendale (circa 1800).

The portrait over the fireplace mantel of John Potter is by Thomas Sully (circa 1841). Over the gaming table is a picture of his wife, by the same artist. Between the windows is a portrait of Charles Woodruff Shields by James Morris (circa 1850).

In the drawing room is a handsome highboy once owned by Richard Stockton and used at Morven. A straight-backed chair was owned by Elias Boudinot. Mrs. Stockton, wife of "the old Duke," is portrayed by Charles Lawrence in a painting over the fireplace.

The library and solarium are also on the first floor. The upper floors contain the Governor's suite.

There is a Mansion staff of three persons. Tours are available by appointment on Tuesdays from 2 p.m. to 4 p.m., except during July, August and December.

NEW MEXICO

GOVERNOR'S MANSION*

The New Mexico Governor's Mansion, located in the piñon-covered hills on the outskirts of Santa Fe, slightly more than a mile north of the plaza, was completed in 1955. It has housed five Chief Executives and their families. While the Mansion is one of the youngest official State residences in the United States, it is only the third official home in more than 350 years of New Mexico's history.

The architecture of the Mansion is commonly known as Modified Territorial, a style which has its origins in the massive adobe communal dwellings of the Pueblo Indians and the equally massive, sprawling, single-story haciendas of the Spanish and Mexican settlers. To this basic structure, the Anglo-Americans added brick cornices, hard plaster exteriors, wide wooden window frames and deep portals.

The extensive, one-story fifteen-room Mansion is of brick and block construction, with the exterior painted earth color to simulate the adobe mud plaster of Indian and Spanish structures. The roof is flat and the thick walls are topped by brick cornices. The main entrance is through an impressive white door under the portal, which extends along the center of the northern portion, with wings jutting out on either side. The east wing and side contain five bedrooms, the Governor's study and a large family room.

The main entrance leads directly into the foyer, to the south of which lies the huge formal living room with its outside walls made largely of glass. The sitting room lies directly west of the foyer and opens into the large formal dining room.

Shortly after the Mansion was completed, it was apparent that it needed to be enlarged and modified for the convenience of the First Family. Fortunately, Southwestern architecture lends itself well to such adaptation. In 1957-1958, a covered terrace on the west was enclosed with glass and made into a formal dining room, with the original dining room converted into a sitting room. In 1965, the remainder of the west side was remodeled.

The only approach to the Mansion is from the west through a gate off Mansion Drive. A circular driveway leads around the front of the house, which faces north, and provides a spectacular view of the Sangre de Cristo Mountains. Deciduous trees and shrubs have been used in background landscaping of the area around the Mansion. Flowering crab apple, peach and plum trees, in addition to well-designed flower beds, give color to the grounds. Native piñon has been allowed to grow over much of the ten-acre site.

The convenience, beauty and privacy of the Governor's Mansion is far removed from the simplicity of the first structure built for that purpose.

The official residence of New Mexico Governors for nearly three hundred years was the Palace of the Governors, a massive, adobe, fortress-like structure built by order of Governor Pedro de Peralta in 1610 on

*Written by Dr. Myra Ellen Jenkins, New Mexico Archivist and State Historian at the request of Mrs. David F. Cargo, First Lady of New Mexico.

the north side of the plaza of the newly established Villa of Santa Fe. This famous structure, the oldest public building in the United States, served as the Capitol for the northernmost province of the Viceroyalty of New Spain (Mexico) until the establishment of Mexican independence in the late summer of 1821.† During the brief interlude of 1680-1692, the great Pueblo Revolt drove the Spaniards from New Mexico and the Indian oligarchy used the Palace as headquarters.

From 1821 to 1846, the Palace was home for Governors appointed by the Mexican national government. On August 18, 1846, Brigadier General Stephen Watts Kearny, commanding the "Army of the West," formally took possession of New Mexico in the name of the United States. Except for a few days in March 1862, when Confederate troops occupied the structure, Territorial Governors and their families lived in the Palace until the inauguration of L. Bradford Prince in 1889. Governor Prince used the historic building for receptions and other official occasions but lived in his own home.

Only one other Governor, George Curry, occupied the Palace briefly in 1908, while a new Mansion was being completed. Since 1909, the Palace has housed the Museum of New Mexico.

Realizing that the needs of the official family could no longer be met by the Palace, the Territorial Legislature in 1907 authorized construction of a new Governor's Mansion. The second residence, located on the northwest portion of the new Capitol grounds south of the plaza, was completed in 1909.

Sentiment for replacing the second residence with an Executive Mansion more in keeping with the historic architecture of the Southwest increased to such a point that in 1951 the Legislature allocated $100,000 for the construction of a new residence. The final cost of the original building, designed by architects W. C. Kruger and Associates, was $201,234.12.

Governors and their wives are often hosts at State receptions, dinners and other special functions. The Mansion was, however, designed primarily for the comfort and privacy of the official State family. There are, hence, no public tours or hours for public visitation.

†See picture, page 14.

The Modified Territorial style of the New Mexico Mansion is based on an architectural heritage received from the Pueblo Indians and the settlers of the Spanish colonial period.

NEW YORK

THE EXECUTIVE MANSION*

For the first hundred years of New York State's existence, its Governors were obliged to find living quarters for themselves. Although from time to time the Legislature considered the problem, the State remained without an Executive Mansion.

When Samuel J. Tilden became Governor in 1874, he rented a spacious private home on Eagle Street as his official residence in Albany. It had been built some twenty years earlier by Thomas Olcott.

The newspapers commended Tilden warmly for selecting this impressive Victorian house for a Governor's Mansion. They called it "large, handsome and well-appointed . . . an elegant residence." One New York City newspaper called it "perhaps the handsomest building in the City" of Albany. Everyone was pleased that finally a Governor of the Empire State lived in a dwelling befitting his office.

Governor Tilden's successor, Governor Lucius Robinson, continued to rent the house on Eagle Street, and in 1877 persuaded the State to purchase it for $45,000. It began its long and colorful history as the official residence of twenty-five Governors, three of whom became Presidents of the United States.

By the time Grover Cleveland was elected Governor in 1882, tastes had begun to change and there were second thoughts about the "elegant residence" which the State had purchased. "It is not a very imposing house," one of Cleveland's contemporary biographers wrote, "although there is some attempt at architectural beauty of a rather clumsy sort. . . ."

Governor David B. Hill, who succeeded Cleveland when he became President in 1885, was colorful, ambitious and controversial. Although a bachelor, he decided the Mansion was too small and persuaded the Legislature to remodel and expand it. The original Olcott house was then totally swallowed up, and the structure became a congeries of dormers, bays, balconies, turrets and gables, a prime example of what *The New Yorker*, years later, called "Hudson River helter-skelter."

The distinguished Governors Theodore Roosevelt and Charles Evans Hughes were followed in the Mansion in 1913 by Governor William Sulzer, who renamed the Mansion "the People's House" and ostentatiously reduced it to the status of a shabby political clubhouse before his impeachment. Alfred E. Smith, who was twice Governor (1919-1920, 1923-1928), converted the Mansion's backyard into a zoo where he kept dogs, donkeys, deer, raccoon, a bear, monkeys and a goat named Heliotrope.

The décor of the Mansion remained throughout these years stolidly Victorian. When the Franklin D. Roosevelts moved in (1929-1932), Governor Roosevelt decided to make it a museum of gubernatorial memorabilia. He wrote to former Governors and their families inviting them to send back to the Mansion some significant piece of furniture or *objet d'art* which had marked their occupancy. Little came out of the project, however.

Herbert H. Lehman was elected Governor in 1932, and his almost ten years in the Mansion were, for the most part, Depression years. Governor Lehman put the Mansion, like every other State facility, on lean rations. It was not until part of the ceiling fell, on the occasion of the Governor's annual dinner for members of the Court of Appeals, that he permitted any repairs or refurbishing to be done. However, they were held to a minimum with one notable exception: Mrs. Lehman persuaded the Governor to let her convert a poolroom on the first floor to a cloak room and powder room.

When Governor and Mrs. Thomas E. Dewey took over the Mansion during World War II few facilities were available for refurbishing, but they pulled the fading old rose brocade off the reception room walls. The oatmeal paper in the Governor's study fell off of its own accord. They took down the dingy blue velvet draperies with the gold trim, and replaced the stained glass windows with clear glass.

"My husband and I spent a Sunday mixing paint and finally came up with a soft green to cover the horrendous red walls," Mrs. Dewey recalls. "The lady with the lighted torch who held down the newel post was relieved of her duties. Chicken wire was installed over the chimney openings to keep out the bats. . . ." The furniture that was not falling apart was slipcovered in pleasant chintzes.

In more recent years, Governor and Mrs. Averell Harriman brought bright and attractive chintzes to the old house, plus a collection of historic paintings by Gilbert Stuart, Thomas Sully and the Innesses. Governor Nelson Rockefeller brought to the Mansion much of his own extensive collection of modern paintings and sculptures, including works by Pablo Picasso, Jackson Pollock, Paul Klee, Henri Matisse, Grace Hartigan, Franz Kline and many others.

On the night of March 2, 1961, a fire beginning in the basement of the Mansion engulfed the drawing room and swept up the stairs, reducing much of the house, including the valuable art collection, to a shambles.

All of the pent-up frustration which generations of New Yorkers had felt or sensed about their Executive Mansion now was released. Almost universally, across the State, editorial writers called for a new Mansion which would be a safe and fitting residence for the Governor. Many, of course, did not realize that sub-

*Adapted by Mrs. Isabelle K. Savell at the request of Mrs. Nelson A. Rockefeller, First Lady of New York, from the booklet, *The Governor's Mansion in Albany.*

This Victorian Mansion in Albany, New York, has had a rich, colorful history as the official residence of its Governors since 1874.

stantial individual efforts had gone into refurbishing the Mansion in recent years. Many were unaware that, however nondescript its Victorian architecture, the Mansion's interior, before the fire, was comfortable, gracious and handsome.

Governor Rockefeller pondered the choice between a new Mansion and a restoration. Then on March 22 he announced his decision to rebuild the old house. He said: "There is a great tradition in the Mansion on Eagle Street. Many great Americans have lived there. Many important events in the history of our State . . . have taken place there."

Accordingly, the house was restored. In the process, extensive reconstruction, not associated with the fire, was also undertaken. Most important, it was fireproofed.

Today it is staffed by sixteen persons, including keepers of the grounds. The result is that the Mansion today is sounder, safer, more functional, and more comfortable than it has ever been in all its history.

It is also re-emerging in a wholly new setting. When it was first built, more than one hundred years ago, it stood on a wooded hillside overlooking the Hudson valley. Gradually, the city crept up the hill and engulfed it, then, as cities will, deteriorated, leaving it in an area of urban blight.

Under Governor Rockefeller, the entire area between the Mansion and the Capitol, comprising approximately one hundred acres, is being converted into a great new complex of State buildings and public facilities. The Mansion, now formally designated as a place of historical significance by the New York State Historic Trust, will be part of the Capitol complex, a richly historic link to the past and an integral part of the unfolding future.

NORTH CAROLINA

THE EXECUTIVE MANSION By Mrs. Dan K. Moore, *Former First Lady of North Carolina*

The gracious City of Raleigh has been North Carolina's seat of government since 1788. Since that time, the State's Governors have been provided with three residences. The present one, located at 200 North Blount Street, was completed in 1890. It has been termed "the perfect example of Queen Anne Cottage style of architecture." While it was designed by the most renowned architects of its era, the men who crafted its bricks and shaped its timbers were inmates of the State's prison.

The three-story Mansion, consisting of thirty-six rooms, is constructed of North Carolina sandstone and hardwood. It has eight gables and numerous porches and balconies. The Mansion is open to the public Tuesday through Friday, from 10 a.m. to noon, September through May. Tours for the visiting public are conducted by docents supplied on a volunteer basis from civic organizations of Raleigh.

The first floor, a spacious and beautiful area, consists of a large entrance hall with sixteen-foot ceilings and Corinthian columns, two parlors, a ballroom, library, State Dining Room, kitchen and offices for the First Lady and for the patrolmen and security guards assigned to the Mansion. The second floor, with its seven bedrooms and baths, two family living rooms and dining area, provides gracious and comfortable living quarters for the First Family. It is not open to the public and thus can be visited only by invitation.

Less than two months after coming to live at the Executive Mansion, the writer felt the need for a knowledgeable and interested group to help preserve and enrich this beautiful old house. In March 1965, the writer called a press conference and announced the formation of the Executive Mansion Fine Arts Committee. Its purpose is to preserve and maintain the Executive Mansion as an historical asset of value to the State; improve the furnishings by encouraging gifts of objects of art, and furniture with historical or aesthetic value; serve as a screening committee to determine the suitability and use of each gift offered; review and approve any major renovations or changes in the Mansion or its furnishings, and, with the assistance of the State Department of Archives and History, to keep a complete list of gifts with their history and value for future reference; and to publicize the work of this committee so that the public would be aware at all times of what is being done.

This committee has secured in funds and value of gifts of furniture, from private sources, in excess of $125,000. In 1967, at the request of Governor Moore, it was made a statutory body by the General Assembly, and is now known as the Executive Mansion Fine Arts Commission. A landscape architect has been retained and plans have been drawn up for the improvement of the grounds. Funds were appropriated for this project by the 1967 General Assembly.

In addition to serving as a residence for North Carolina's Governor and his family, the Executive Mansion is the scene of hundreds of teas, dinners, luncheons, receptions and other social functions throughout the year. To assist the First Lady in these many duties, the Mansion is staffed with a hostess-housekeeper and some twenty employees.

A booklet has been published on the Mansion containing authenticated history as well as color photographs of both the first and second floors. A color slide program on the Mansion, with appropriate narration, has been prepared to be used by organizations and the public schools, and is also available through the Department of Archives and History.

Efforts are being made to have the Mansion designated as a historic landmark, thereby helping to insure its permanency, as this is a very important house in the life of a very important State. It is so because Governors and their families have lived and loved and worked here for more than seven decades. It is truly a house where history walks, where dreams are realized with elation and defeats accepted with resignation.

The massive North Carolina Mansion, which displays eight gables, is illustrative of the Queen Anne Cottage style of architecture.

NORTH DAKOTA

THE GOVERNOR'S RESIDENCE By Mrs. William L. Guy, *First Lady of North Dakota*

Bismarck, North Dakota, became the capital of the Dakota Territory in 1883. Since that time, there have been four Governor's Residences, including the present Residence located on the Capitol grounds.

The first was what is now known as the "Ordway House," so named for Territorial Governor Nehemiah G. Ordway, who moved here with the relocation of the capital in 1883 from Yankton, South Dakota, thus making Bismarck the Territorial capital of the Dakotas.

The second house, which at one time was the largest residence in Bismarck, served as the Governor's Mansion during the term of Gilbert A. Pierce. It was originally built to house the Northwest Express and Transportation Company during the years when it was common to see the long mule trains transporting freight down Main Street on their way to the Black Hills in South Dakota.

Louis K. Church followed Pierce as Governor and lived in the Ordway House. His two successors, Arthur C. Mellette and the first State Governor, John Miller, lived in private houses and in the Sheridan House Hotel.

The third house, built in 1884 and sold to the State in 1893 for $6,000, was first occupied by Governor Eli C. D. Shortridge. It served as the Residence for twenty-two Governors from 1893 to 1960. It had the distinction of being one of the few homes in the State that was finished on the interior with walnut. The second floor had three large bedrooms and two small ones, plus a bath and a large hall. The main floor had a dining room, living room, parlor, a large entryway, a kitchen and wash and store rooms. The huge attic was partially remodeled into a recreation room. There were tile fireplaces in the dining and living rooms. The mansion was considered to be drafty and difficult to heat, even after the walls received additional insulation. Little official entertaining was done due to lack of facilities and space. However, in the Dakota Territorial days, it served as the proper setting for glittering social functions.

The State's new Governor's Residence was completed March 30, 1960. Governor and Mrs. William L. Guy occupied the Residence December 31, 1960, with their five children. It is ideally located in a grove of trees on the southwest corner of the Capitol grounds. The home was designed, constructed and furnished by local firms and is considered a home more than a mansion.

North Dakota brick was used on the exterior of the building and on the fireplace located in the family living room. Perhaps because of the small windows which face the street, the house appears smaller than it is. It is set ten degrees off the compass to provide a view of the Capitol from the State Dining and Living Rooms. To many, this is the most impressive side of the building. Secluded in trees, it has one of the most interesting and well tended yards in the State. The flat roof over the family area includes white marble chips for color. It is said that considerable money was saved in the construction by substituting three-inch concrete slabs for hardwood floors and joists.

The Residence is open for visitors and tours, by appointment, from 10 to 11:30 a.m. and from 2 to 3:30 p.m., Monday through Friday, with the exception of a three-week period, usually in July, when it is closed during the annual major housecleaning and repair period. It is estimated that through the summer of 1968, over sixty thousand people toured the Governor's Residence. There are three permanent employees on the Residence staff.

The rambling functional house of brick, steel and glass was built at a cost of $250,000. The architecture is transitional, and there are eighteen rooms.

An interesting feature is that the Residence has two wings, the State and the Family wings, on a single floor separated by a central kitchen and folding door. Thus, it is possible to use the State wing for entertaining without disturbing the members of the family in the living room located at the opposite end of the house.

This functional home of brick, steel and glass, located on the North Dakota Capitol grounds, has eighteen rooms. The State and family wings are on the same floor, but are conveniently separated by a central kitchen and a folding door.

OHIO

THE GOVERNOR'S MANSION By Mrs. James A. Rhodes,* *First Lady of Ohio*

Ohio was a State for 117 years before a residence was provided for its Governor. During this period, forty-eight Chief Executives bought homes of their own, rented homes or lived in hotels. Governor William McKinley and his invalid wife, Ida, occupied rooms in the Neil House across the street from the State Capitol.

This frustrating situation finally ended when the General Assembly, after much debate and a number of pieces of legislation, authorized funds for the purchase and remodeling of the Charles H. Lindenberg home in Columbus. A product of the so-called "eclectic" period of architecture, the house is primarily Georgian.

The house was purchased in May 1919, and the remainder of that year was spent in altering parts of the Mansion and having new furniture made at the Mansfield State Reformatory. Governor James A. Cox, his wife and infant daughter moved in sometime in the spring of 1920. Ten first families occupied the Mansion between 1920 and 1957. Thereafter, the old Mansion, by action of the Legislature approved June 17, 1957, became the depository for State Archives.

On July 13, 1955, legislation was enacted by the Ohio General Assembly authorizing Governor Frank J. Lausche to accept from Mrs. Janet C. Harris and her husband, the Very Reverend Charles U. Harris of Highland Park, Illinois, the present Mansion, located at 358 North Parkview Avenue in Bexley, a Columbus suburb. The General Assembly also provided funds for necessary remodeling and for furniture.

This home was built in 1925 by Malcolm Jeffrey, son of the late Joseph A. Jeffrey, founder of Jeffrey Manufacturing Company. A magnificent Tudor-Norman Mansion of twenty-four rooms, it dominates a beautifully landscaped and shrubbed three acres in an area of gracious living, only four miles from the State Capitol. The massive proportions of the great stone and stucco Mansion include three floors, topped by a tiled roof. A gracefully curving drive, guarded by generation-old trees, leads into the grounds.

The main entrance, featuring richly stained hand-hewn ceiling beams and native limestone and Bedford stone, speaks of the richness of the interior. To the right of the entrance hall is a large sunken living room with a patterned ceiling, oak-paneled walls, large fireplace and comfortable contemporary furnishings. At the south end of the room, on each side of the fireplace, are inviting leaded glass doors leading to the music room.

Through another set of leaded glass doors, to the east of the living room, is a large stone-walled garden room which connects to a similar room, formerly a screened porch. The two rooms, overlooking the formal gardens and wide expanse of lawn, provide the needed space for entertaining the nearly one thousand people who attend functions at the Mansion each week. A vine-covered pergola of columns and heavy crossbeams leads from the garden rooms to the yard area, which is ideal for summer parties.

To the left of the entrance hall is the walnut-paneled dining room with its dazzling crystal chandelier. The McKinley silver service is often displayed here.

An intricately carved, walnut grand stairway leads from the entrance hall to the second floor. There, in the somewhat secluded South Wing, are the private rooms of the Governor and his family, including a book-lined study for the First Lady. One of the nine bedrooms on this floor contains a beautiful French suite which belonged to former Governor Cox when the first Mansion was furnished in 1919.

The Mansion is staffed by twelve trusties from the Ohio Penitentiary. The huge basement contains a paneled recreation room, in addition to the regular storage and laundry facilities.

Few pieces of historic value remain in the Mansion and records do not exist for most of these. Attempts made to trace their origin have been unsuccessful. Most of the furnishings in the Mansion belong to the Governor and his wife.

Under the supervision of the writer, extensive redecoration inside and alteration of the gardens outside have been completed.

The Mansion is not open to tourists, but is available upon request to groups for teas and meetings.

*Assisted by the Ohio Historical Society.

A massive stone and stucco Mansion, this three-story structure designed in the Tudor-Norman style, was presented to the State of Ohio in 1955.

OKLAHOMA

THE GOVERNOR'S MANSION By Mrs. Dewey F. Bartlett, *First Lady of Oklahoma*

The Governor's Mansion is a nineteen-room, modified Dutch Colonial, combination office and residence. Completed in 1928, the executive residence is of concrete construction faced with white Indiana limestone and a red tile roof. The building is sixty by fifty-five feet, with three stories and a basement.

Located a block from the State Capitol in Oklahoma City on a site selected by Governor Lee Cruce and the Oklahoma Legislature in 1912, the Mansion has been home for thirteen Oklahoma Governors. First to occupy it were Governor and Mrs. Henry S. Johnston.

Although authorized in March 1913, after the site selection had been approved in 1912, it was not until 1927 that the Legislature appropriated funds for construction of the Mansion. Architects were Layton, Hicks and Forsythe. The total cost was $100,000.

Governor Johnston's wife supervised furnishing of the residence, which at the time stood in the midst of a field of red Oklahoma clay. She is said to have commented on the absence of trees at the time, but today the Mansion's shuttered windows overlook well-kept, tree-shaded grounds, the trees and shrubs having been planted over a period of years.

The first floor contains a central main entry hall dominated by a winding walnut staircase, which extends to the third floor. At the foot of the staircase is a sculpture, "Buffalo," by Joe Taylor, professor of art at the University of Oklahoma. In the entrance hall and throughout the Mansion are works by Oklahoma artists. Among paintings in the hall are "Rebirth," a watercolor by Jack Vallee; "Silo," by June Phillips; "Dandelion," by Gene Hartsell and a landscape by Dick Goetz.

Off the hallway is the library, which is lined from floor to ceiling with bleached walnut bookshelves. A wood-burning fireplace is a focal point for the library. Recently, the Oklahoma Library Association undertook to furnish the library through private donations. Over the library fireplace is "Costa Brava," by Lorraine Moore; a metal sculpture of the Oklahoma State Bird, the scissor-tailed flycatcher, by Munk; "Abandoned Well, Stroud," a wood-carving by Billie K. Schafer; a bowl and vase by Montee Hoke; "Head," a study in wood by Clarke Bailey; and "Still Life," a work by Paul Maxwell.

Directly north of the library, across the hallway, is the Governor's study, a room thus selected because of its accessibility and privacy.

Also on the first floor is the dining room, which is furnished with table and chairs owned by the State of Oklahoma. A painting, "Washday," by Jay O'Malia, hangs in the room. A brass and crystal chandelier was purchased and placed here by Mrs. Henry Bellmon, wife of Oklahoma's eighteenth Governor, in 1963.

Since the dining room can seat only twelve guests, facilities have been expanded to include the garden room, which was formerly a sun porch adjacent to the dining room. A painting by J. Jay McVickers adds color to the garden room. Also on display are a bowl and vase by Montee Hoke and "Torso," by Jerold Graham.

The kitchen and family breakfast room also are on the first floor. The breakfast room has been designated as the Indian Room, since the art in it is by Indian artists. Displayed are "Hunters," by Acie Blue Eagle; "Plains Indian Camp," by Fred Beaver; "Dancer," by Carol Woodring; "Indian Ribbon Dancers," by Joan Hill, and "Indian Cook," by Terry Saul. Also on display are Indian headdresses and an Indian rug and basket.

The second floor, devoted to private quarters, includes four bedrooms, a sitting room and the writer's office, which has a fine view of the west Mansion grounds and the Capitol. The third floor is a twenty-eight by fifty-three-foot room, once used as a ballroom, but now used as a recreation room and meeting place for larger groups.

The interior of the Mansion has undergone periodic redecoration in keeping with the tastes and needs of the occupants. It was completely redecorated in 1959 during the administration of Governor J. Howard Edmondson, when $65,000 was spent in renovation and the addition of new furnishings. During Governor Bellmon's term of office, red carpeting was laid. Most of the art in the Governor's house is the Dewey Bartletts' personal collection.

Because the Mansion has lacked items of historical

interest, the writer has initiated a search to find one item representative of each of the former Governors, and it is hoped these will be on display soon. A collection of arrowhead rocks also will be displayed, as will an Oklahoma wheat harvest scene by Peter Hurd.

A sweeping, curved drive leads from the street to the Mansion portico, and the drive is lined in summer with red geraniums. On the grounds, generous use has been made of redbud trees, the Oklahoma State Tree, and other native trees and shrubs.

Visitors' tours may be made by appointment.

What was once a field of Oklahoma red clay is now the lovely wooded site of the State's Dutch Colonial Mansion. White Indiana limestone and red tile enhance the beauty of the home.

PENNSYLVANIA

THE GOVERNOR'S RESIDENCE By Mrs. Raymond P. Shafer, *First Lady of Pennsylvania*

Pennsylvania, one of the oldest States, has one of the newest Executive Mansions. On a three and one-half acre plot, with its ancient trees, the early Pennsylvania Georgian home of salmon-pink brick fronts on Harrisburg's historic Second Street and to the rear, across the expansive lawn on Front Street, commands a striking view of the broad Susquehanna River. Both in design and décor, it recognizes and provides for the executive, historical and social necessities which are part of a Governor's life. It was constructed at a cost of $2 million including furnishings. The George M. Ewing Company of Philadelphia served as architect and H. B. Alexander and Son as contractor. Governor Raymond P. Shafer's family were the first occupants in December 1968.

Thus, a three-century dream was culminated, for despite the Commonwealth's prominence in colonial and Federal affairs, the only previous Governor to have a residence specifically built for the purpose was Johann Printz (1643-1653). This Swedish colonial Governor erected a home of white cedar logs and yellow Stockholm brick on a small island in the Delaware River.

When William Penn became Provincial Governor in 1682, he built a superb manor house, "Pennsbury," since reconstructed, but it was essentially more private than public. His successors, including the colorful Benjamin Franklin, had their private homes in or near Philadelphia, which was then the capital. However, in 1812, by act of the Legislature, Harrisburg, one hundred miles to the west, was declared the seat of government to better serve an expanding population.

The Governors at Harrisburg, like their predecessors in the Quaker City, had to house-hunt because comparatively few lived within commuting distance of the new capital. Several private homes along the picturesque river bear small plaques marking the occupancy of Chief Executives during the nineteenth century.

An official residence for Pennsylvania's Governors first became a reality in 1858 when a property on South Second Street was purchased under Governor James Pollack. This first State-owned residence was short-lived, for its inadequacies were quickly recognized.

A second residence was purchased in 1864 on North Front Street. Through the years, many additions were made, including a matching and connecting house and, subsequently, an entire brownstone front on the "twins" to give a unified look.

Meanwhile, a summer home of farm-fieldstone at Indiantown Gap was acquired in 1941. In 1960, when legislation was approved to sell the house in town, the "Summer Mansion," despite its twenty-mile distance from Harrisburg, became the year-round Residence.

Construction of the new thirty-room Executive Mansion began in 1966 on a site within five minutes' drive of the Capitol Building. Its long, graceful lines are emphasized by two one-story wings which flank the main residential section of three stories. A black wrought-iron fence surrounds the property.

Entering by a circular drive, the visitor steps into a reception area dominated by a grand staircase, with a balcony landing, winding around three sides to the upper level, where private quarters are entered from an inner hall. The first floor of the main center structure embodies the entrance hall, drawing room, the grand hall, family dining room and family living room.

The South Wing is entered by a large hallway and includes an elevator to all floors, an office for the secretary to the First Lady, a walnut-paneled library, and the State entertaining facilities, consisting of an entrance hall, cloakroom, powder rooms, reception room, the State Dining Room, which can seat as many as 132 persons, and a kitchen.

The North Wing, entered by a somewhat narrower hallway, houses a powder room, breakfast room, family kitchen, service stairway and rooms used by the household staff and guards. The second floor comprises seven bedrooms, each with private bath, and two with dressing rooms and a utility room. The third floor houses two bedrooms and bath for domestic help. The basement includes a game room, Sauna bath, a paneled family room and storage areas.

The Commonwealth provides a housekeeping staff of seventeen persons and appropriations for entertaining at State functions. All furnishings are the property of the Pennsylvania State Museum and, consequently, are completely catalogued and will be restored and refurbished by its staff of experts when necessary.

In the spring of 1967, Governor Shafer appointed a committee of seventeen distinguished Pennsylvania women, headed by Mrs. Richard King Mellon of Pittsburgh, with the writer serving as honorary chairman, for the purpose of acquiring precious touchstones, both by gift and purchase. Through this committee's efforts, many outstanding antiques have been acquired. Among

One of the newest executive residences is this graceful salmon-pink Georgian Mansion completed for Pennsylvania's First Family in 1968. Two one-story wings flank the three-story main section.

them are a Philadelphia Hepplewhite tall-case clock; an antique hand-painted canvas wall covering, titled "Las Incas"; a pair of Hepplewhite George III breakfront cabinets; a selection of Tucker china, including a seven-piece tea set; a pair of Sheraton bowfront commodes; a Georgian pedestal desk; two Chippendale carved and gilded wall mirrors, and an antique hand-cut crystal chandelier of the Regency Period.

Wherever possible, materials and furnishings were drawn from Pennsylvania so that the Residence would symbolize the handiwork of the Keystone State.

The new Executive Mansion expresses the dignity and tradition of the Commonwealth and serves as a symbol of the sovereign power of the people. It is therefore appropriate that visitors are permitted to tour the public areas at certain intervals, and teas and receptions are held for State-oriented groups.

SOUTH CAROLINA

THE GOVERNOR'S MANSION*

Symbol of the grace and imperishable spirit of the antebellum South, the Governor's Mansion of South Carolina is a historic building which escaped the flames of war in 1865 when Union General Sherman's invading army devastated Columbia, the capital. Today it fulfills a vital role as the official home of the State's First Family and as the beautifully impressive setting for State social functions.

*Article furnished by Mrs. Robert E. McNair, First Lady of South Carolina; compiled by Everetta L. Blair, Ph.D. and Jack M. Scoville, A.I.D.

The 113-year-old edifice has, in effect, belonged to the people from its earliest days. Located upon a full city block in the heart of Columbia, it was one of a complex of buildings which comprised the Arsenal Academy, from which the area became known as "Arsenal Hill."

Converted from a State arsenal which housed one of the State's two military companies, the Academy was set up in 1842 to serve as a State-operated military academy of a secondary nature. When constructed in 1856 the Arsenal building, which was later to become

Opposite: Once part of the Arsenal Academy in Columbia, this home of classical Renaissance design is now the elegant South Carolina State Mansion.

the Governor's Mansion, cost $6,000 and was termed "a brick tenement building." A two-story double-house, detached from the main buildings and serving as the officers' quarters, it was untouched by the catastrophic fire during the Civil War which destroyed the Academy's center. It was the one remaining building.

In 1868, retiring Governor James L. Orr said in a statement to the General Assembly:

> The State owns a large, commodious and handsomely furnished building which commands a picturesque view of the city and the valleys of the Congaree, Board and Saluda rivers for many miles; a beautiful grove is in front of the house; the outbuildings are convenient and ample, and the adjacent grounds embracing some eight acres, will furnish a sufficient space for gardens, et cetera . . . I recommend that this edifice be set apart as the Executive Mansion of South Carolina.

After investigation and approval by a special committee, and the appropriating of $2,500 "to prepare said place," the simple but spacious Arsenal building was designated the Governor's Mansion.

Reconstruction Governor Robert K. Scott of Ohio was the first Governor to occupy the Mansion. Records show that the next two Governors during the Reconstruction lived in their own homes in the city and the building was rented to a Mrs. Sara Wright, "who conducted a boarding house there." In 1879 Governor W.D. Simpson made it his official residence and since then the Mansion has been occupied continuously by the Governors of South Carolina.

Through the years, the Mansion has undergone repairs and redecorating to keep it livable and to suit the individual tastes of the occupants. Drastic changes were made at one point in its history when its original design was altered by cutting arches in the walls that separated the two apartments of the original building.

Today, in its latest renovation, the Governor's Mansion combines the graciousness and opulence of the Old South décor with the functional beauty and comfort of the contemporary. Steel beams have reinforced sagging walls and two floors which had been declared unsafe have been replaced. The exterior is classical Renaissance. There are now twenty rooms and ten baths. A staff of fourteen is employed to care for the house and grounds, and the house is open for tours on Mondays through Fridays from 9 a.m. to 3 p.m.

Historic furnishings belonging to the State are highlighted in the soft refulgence of the first floor's antique crystal chandeliers, along with *objets d'art*.

In the formal dining room, interest is focused on the State's treasured silver, the magnificent silver service, comprising sixty-six pieces, from the battleship, *U.S.S. South Carolina*. In the dining room is displayed, also, the impressive State china, a Haviland pattern made in France in about 1919. It is bordered in gold and has the State Seal in the center.

Elegantly touched with gold, the State Seals gleam on the carved white mantel in the reception room. In an Empire secretary are exhibited the famed Doughty birds, the work of the noted English artist, Dorothy Doughty. The dainty birds have as a center figurine the South Carolina wren perched amidst a cluster of the State Flower, the yellow jessamine.

Another feature of this room is a portrait of Ann Pamela Cunningham, a native South Carolinian credited with the restoration of Mt. Vernon. Other paintings are of General Andrew Jackson by Ralph E. W. Earl; Angelica Kaughman by Thomas Sully and another by Jeremiah Theus. Over the fireplace is the portrait of Thomas Knox Gordon, last Royal Chief Justice of South Carolina, by Gilbert Stuart.

In the family dining room hangs a crystal chandelier which once belonged to Governor Francis W. Pickens. An English sideboard and a painting of Wade Hampton's ancestral home by Elizabeth O'Neill Verner also grace this room.

The small drawing room contains a linen press made in Charleston about 1795. On the mantel is a Sèvres porcelain Louis XVI clock with a pair of matching urns. A painting by Charles Fraser hangs beside the fireplace. Paintings by South Carolina artists Alfred H. Hutty and Ann Richardson also hang in this room.

Probably the most significant recent addition to the Mansion is the Arthur Middleton bed made in Charleston by Thomas Elke and acquired by Mrs. Robert E. McNair. This bed, together with a very handsome highboy, comprise the major furnishings of one of the two guest rooms.

A beautiful old cast-iron gate marks the entrance to the white-stuccoed Mansion, with its palmetto tree silhouette to the right of the main door and its Stars and Stripes and Palmetto State Flag flying. A cast-iron fence surrounds the handsomely landscaped grounds with their three-tiered fountain, trees and profusion of flowers. The gate and fence are symbols of the leisure and beauty of South Carolina's past which is preserved in the Governor's Mansion, an indestructible beauty which will be ever-present in the State's challenging, exciting future.

South Dakota provides this spacious residence on Capitol Lake.

SOUTH DAKOTA

THE GOVERNOR'S MANSION By Former Governor Nils A. Boe

The present residence of the Governors of South Dakota, located in Pierre, has witnessed the events of only the last thirty-two years. Much State history had occurred before its existence, for the surrounding area is rich in history and lore. The vast territory between the Mississippi River and the Rocky Mountains originally belonged to the Indians but in 1743 was claimed for the French King by the Verendrye Brothers' expedition. As a result of the Louisiana Purchase in 1803, the extensive lands became a part of the United States.

Statehood came in 1889. Upon admission to the Union, a fifteen-year controversy over a permanent location for the capital began. There were many contestants and much political maneuvering in the financially exhausting campaign, but one decisive factor in the final selection was that the citizens of Pierre had already built a Statehouse upon a twenty-acre site adjoining a small lake, all of which they had donated to the State.

The 1904 election outcome indicated that the voters had been convinced of the advantages and practicability of Pierre's site and facilities. To cement the victory, the citizens of Pierre immediately began to construct a permanent Statehouse just to the west of the existing two-story wooden structure. From this location, the new Capitol dominated the city and the surrounding Missouri River valley.

The man elected Governor in those days received an annual salary of $3,000 in addition to a $75.00 monthly housing allowance. He had to rent quarters wherever he could find them, thus several houses in Pierre can be singled out as having housed First Families.

The first State-owned residence was a modest yellow cottage situated opposite the Capitol on the eastern shoreline of Capitol Lake. It was sold and moved to another location in the city when the present Mansion was begun in 1936. Plans were prepared by Resettlement Administration architects and financed through the Works Progress Administration. The original construction cost of the fifty-seven by ninety-seven-foot structure was $24,500. It was built of native brick, lumber and concrete, typical of the early 1930 South Dakota trend to combine local materials with a rambling design whenever the allotted space permitted.

The resulting edifice is a spacious two-story, modified colonial residence which stands at 119 North Washington in the center of four and a half verdant acres. A gently curved driveway, bordered with shrubbery and colorful seasonal flowers, leads to the broad front doors. The gracious eighteen-room home contains two public areas. The pleasant décor of the large State Living Room generates a feeling of warmth and intimacy. The most unique features of the room include a fireplace made of petrified wood from the Badlands and an original oil painting entitled "Breaking Sod" by Harvey Dunn, a native South Dakotan well-known for his paintings of pioneer life. There are two other original Dunns in the Mansion. All three are on loan from the Dunn collection at South Dakota State University. "The Stoneboat," a second painting, is displayed in the State Dining Room.

The remaining rooms on the first floor comprise the family living quarters and include a comfortable living room containing the third Dunn painting, "After School," a dining room, den and large kitchen. Because the family and State rooms are in such close proximity, both are used on official occasions. Privacy is maintained on the second floor, where five bedrooms and three baths are located, in addition to the Governor's master bedroom with adjoining bath, dressing room and sleeping porch.

The basement of the Mansion is utilized for many purposes. A fascinating Indian Room filled with authentic artifacts of the State's original inhabitants is used by the family and also absorbs the overflow of guests at large receptions. A well-stocked fallout shelter was added in 1961.

As the number of permanent and historical furnishings in the Mansion is limited, the official occupants are at liberty to decorate the house with personal treasures, mementos and pictures.

The beautiful setting of the Mansion can best be appreciated from the secluded patio or screen-enclosed porch at the rear of the house. From there the lush lawn gradually slopes down to Capitol Lake, an artificial body of water fed by two continuously flowing warm artesian wells. One of these wells has been developed into a fountain whose bubbling water contains an abundance of natural gas. The phenomenon of this burning water is known as South Dakota's eternal flame. On the opposite side of the tree-lined lake, the Capitol and its dome rise nobly, an especially magnificent panorama when illuminated at night. This tranquil scene is interrupted only by the incoming and outgoing flights of the "Governor's Geese," huge flocks of mallard ducks and Canadian geese which use the lake as a year-round haven.

The Governor's Mansion is not open for regularly scheduled tours; however, all persons are welcome at the Governor's convenience or invitation. Organized groups may visit upon request and use the main floor to host their own teas or receptions. The resident staff is comprised of two in addition to grounds keepers.

TENNESSEE

THE GOVERNOR'S MANSION

By Mrs. Buford Ellington, *First Lady of Tennessee*

Tennessee was admitted to the Union in 1796, but it was not until 111 years later, in 1907, that the General Assembly established an official residence for its Chief Executive. No thought was given by early legislators to procuring a residence for the Governor so long as the State capital was shifted from town to town. For forty-seven years, from 1796 to 1843, the seat of government was determined by legislative resolution.

The Constitution of 1835 provided that, beginning in 1843, Nashville would become the permanent capital. The first legislation toward acquiring a Mansion for the Governor was introduced in 1850, but no positive action was taken. For the next half century, the matter came up before the General Assembly seven different times, but it failed to act.

Finally, in 1907, a three-man committee was authorized to "secure a suitable and appropriate Governor's Mansion, conveniently located to the Capitol of the State, and within the corporate limits of the City of Nashville." The home of Mr. and Mrs. John M. Gray, Jr., located at 314 North Vine Street, was purchased by the state for $31,000 and it became the first official Governor's Mansion.

The Gray home was situated on the east side of North Vine Street (now Seventh Avenue North) between Charlotte Avenue and Union Street, opposite the present-day Clarkston Hotel. This spacious, handsome home of dressed stone, with an enormous parlor, a conservatory, a stately staircase and a third-floor ballroom, was occupied by six Governors from 1907 to 1923.

With the end of World War I, the General Assembly decided to erect a suitable memorial for those Tennesseans who had served in that conflict. The War Memorial Building was to include the Mansion grounds and this meant the Governor's Mansion had to be relocated. In 1923, the General Assembly authorized a committee to find a suitable residence for the Governor, and after consideration of several sites, it recommended the purchase of the home of Mr. and Mrs. W. R. Tate, which was located at 2118 West End Avenue.

The Tate home, an imposing two-story structure, can best be characterized as Neo-Classic, a style which was quite popular during the first two decades of the twentieth century. On March 27, 1923, the State purchased this property for $27,500 and it became the second Governor's Mansion.

Between 1923 and 1949, a period of twenty-six years, this structure was the home of five Governors of Tennessee. However, by 1947, this building had become unsuitable due largely to the inconvenience of West End Avenue and the commercialization of most of the surrounding property.

In 1947, the General Assembly appointed a committee to locate other property deemed suitable for a Governor's Mansion. Three estates in Nashville, then available for sale, were considered by the committee. "Farhills," a home built in 1927 and occupied by Mr. and Mrs. Ridley Wills, was eventually selected.

"Farhills," located on Curtiswood Lane, is a handsome Georgian twenty-two room brick home of excellent proportions situated on a beautifully landscaped ten-acre lot. On January 7, 1949, the State purchased it along with certain furnishings in the house for a total cost of $120,350. Thus, in 1949, at the beginning of Governor Gordon Browning's term, this residence became the State's third official Governor's Mansion.

The Governor's Mansion has 15,000 square feet of floor space on two floors. The first floor is used primarily

The Mansion designated for Tennessee's Governors is a handsome Georgian brick house situated on a ten-acre site in Nashville. The twenty-two-room home became the third official Mansion in 1949.

for State functions. It includes a large formal drawing room, an adjoining sunroom, a library which serves as the Governor's office, a State Dining Room, a family dining room, kitchen, a small sitting room, and entrance hall in grand scale that includes an elliptical staircase. The second floor, containing five bedrooms, six baths and a living room, is the private living space of the Governor and his family. A staff of sixteen maintains the home. Tours are arranged by appointment.

This Mansion now properly enhances the "dignity and reputable honor of the Commonwealth," as the General Assembly intended. Its spacious and gracious rooms have welcomed two statesmen who became President of the United States, John F. Kennedy and Lyndon B. Johnson. In its drawing room was celebrated the first marriage within a Governor's immediate family to take place in the Executive Mansion—that of Robert N. Clement and Marilyn Wims, in 1966. It has come to be recognized as "a place where the dignity and honor of the State are lodged."

TEXAS

THE GOVERNOR'S MANSION

By the Author, Jean Houston Daniel

(With additions by Mrs. John Connally, Former First Lady of Texas)

The Texas Governor's Mansion, completed in 1856, has been the official residence of thirty-seven Governors and has witnessed 113 years of Texas history. Located in the City of Austin, it occupies an entire block on a hill across the street from the Capitol grounds, where it commands an excellent view of the State Capitol. It is the oldest building in the entire Capitol complex.

It is considered a fine example of Southern colonial or Greek Revival style, sometimes referred to as American Empire, typical of many of the antebellum homes of the nineteenth century.

The two-story white brick structure has six massive Ionic columns and dark green shutters. Galleries extend across the front on both floor levels. A spacious center hallway runs the entire depth of the building on the first floor, and it is graced by a beautiful winding stairway to the second floor.

Abner Cook was the master builder and contractor. The cost was $14,500, plus $2,500 for furnishings, appropriated by the Legislature in 1854, and financed by the sale of State-owned lots in the City of Austin.

The original structure had four State rooms on the first floor consisting of a large double parlor or formal reception rooms north of the hall and a library or drawing room and dining room south of the hall. On the second floor, there were originally four large bedrooms and a wide central hallway. The kitchen, carriage house and other complementary structures were detached and located to the rear of the house.

Throughout the years, many additions have been made, but all have preserved the original structure and architectural entity of the plans of Abner Cook. The additions included a family dining room, double kitchens, a guard's room and two powder rooms on the first floor, and a large family living room, small dining room and kitchen, extra bedroom, five baths, a small study and sleeping porch on the second floor, as well

This dignified white brick Mansion with dark green shutters occupies an entire city block across from the Texas State Capitol in Austin. It is the oldest building in the Capitol Complex.

as an elevator and back stairway. Thus, the building today has twenty rooms, the two spacious hallways, five baths and two powder rooms. It now measures 56 feet in width and 105 feet in length.

Although flanked on four sides by busy streets in the heart of the city, the Mansion appears secluded, dignified and yet hospitable. In 1967, Mrs. Connally, wife of Texas' thirty-sixth Governor, sponsored the construction of a white brick wall in the rear and along the back sides of the Mansion block and a rustic iron fence based in white brick across the front and front sides. This has added to the beauty and seclusion of the house, which sits in the center of the block. The rustic iron fence was part of the original fence which ran across the rear of the Capitol grounds.

In the same year, Mrs. Connally also sponsored a Mansion grounds landscaping and illumination program. The grounds were completely renovated, and improvements included gardens, reflecting pools, fountains, terraces and colonnades. The illumination gives a soft moonlight effect, with security lighting incorporated in the installation. All of this has added greatly to the beauty of the grounds and dignity of the building. Mrs. Connally was assisted by the Texas Fine Arts Mansion Subcommittee in supervising the project, and substantial contributions were made by the Texas Garden Clubs, Inc., other organizations and many public spirited citizens.

The Mansion is open for visitors and tours from 10 a.m. to noon on Mondays through Fridays. Thousands of tourists view the first-floor State rooms and the Sam Houston Room on the second floor each week.

All of the State rooms contain furniture and other items of historic interest, including large and priceless paintings by Gainsborough, Carle Van Loo and Sir Joshua Reynolds. In the first-floor hallway there is a large breakfront which houses a collection of mementos which once belonged to each of the First Families who lived in the Mansion. They include silver, china, crystal, books and even a Colt pistol which belonged to Texas' only bachelor Governor, Hardin Runnels, who served from 1857 to 1859. This display was assembled by the author in 1962.

On the second floor only one room is open to the public—the Sam Houston Bedroom. It contains the massive four-poster bed purchased by Governor Houston in 1860. Also in this room is the Stephen F. Austin desk, a bust of Houston by Elizabeth Ney, a rosewood chair which was originally in the French Embassy when Texas was a Republic and a coffee table made from a Confederate Civil War drum which was used at the Battle of Shiloh. This room also contains several framed documents and pictures, including pictures of General and Mrs. Houston, a framed letter written by him and an invitation to the first reception or "levee" which was given in the Mansion on August 20, 1856. This room often serves as a guest room for distinguished visitors, so long as they are up and out in time for the next day's tourists.

All other rooms are private and are used solely by the Governor and his family. Each family has added a personal touch or redecorated the private rooms to create as much of a home atmosphere as possible. Repairs have been frequent and costly.

A 104-page inventory, description and history of the furnishings of the residence was compiled by the author of this book in 1962 under the title "Furnishings of Historic Interest in the Governor's Mansion." This inventory is kept up to date by the First Lady and the State Auditor.

The Texas Governor is required by the Constitution of the State to reside in the capital city, and for this reason the State has always furnished him a house or compensation for rented quarters. This was true also concerning the Presidents of the Republic of Texas during the ten years when Texas was an independent nation. When Houston was the capital of the Republic, the Congress purchased the Main Street home of a future Governor, Frank R. Lubbock, for $6,000. When Austin was chosen as the new site for the capital in 1839, a white, two-story frame structure was completed as the President's House, but by 1841 it was in such disrepair that President Houston refused to occupy it. He and subsequent Presidents and Governors were furnished rented quarters or housing allowances until the present Mansion was completed in 1856.

For security and assistance with tourists, State highway patrolmen are on regular twenty-four hour duty. The State also provides a Mansion secretary and a housekeeping staff of from four to six persons.

The Mansion was once available to organizations for annual receptions, teas and the like, but this has long since been discontinued. Only social functions sponsored by the Governor and First Lady are now permitted. Appropriations for each biennium are made by the Legislature for maintenance, staff and repairs. However, each First Family is responsible for the expense of food and all entertaining, such as State receptions, dinners for visiting dignitaries and personal guests. Appropriations for staff and maintenance now

The Lone Star State is symbolized by the rustic iron fence set in a white brick base which complements the Mansion. The fence was added in 1967 to assure greater privacy for the Governor's family.

average approximately $40,000 annually.

In 1931, a three-member Board of Mansion Supervisors was created by the Legislature to advise and assist the Governor and First Lady on redecoration, maintenance, furnishings, acceptance of gifts and other matters concerning the Mansion. In 1966, this board was replaced by the Texas Fine Arts Commission, composed of eighteen members, and directed by the Legislature to advise State officials and agencies with respect to all State buildings.

Because of the cost and inconvenience of operating the Mansion both as a home and a public building attractive to tourists, there have been suggestions in recent years that a new Governor's residence be built for greater privacy to the First Family and that the present Mansion be converted into a museum. The Texas Fine Arts Commission and the State Building Commission joined in this recommendation in 1966. A consulting architect was employed, and the Building Commission requested an appropriation of $1 million for such purpose in the 1968-69 budget. Governor John Connally said that other items were of greater priority and no action was taken by the Legislature.

Thus, it appears that this stately house will continue yet awhile to serve as the residence for Texas Governors and that it will witness more of the aspirations, plans, romance and activities of those chosen by the people to preside over the destiny of the Lone Star State.

UTAH

THE GOVERNOR'S RESIDENCE

By Mrs. Calvin L. Rampton, *First Lady of Utah*

The present Utah Governor's Residence is a relatively new, contemporary home which was first occupied by a Governor and his family nine years ago. It is the second official residence which the State has provided for its Governors.

For forty years following statehood in 1896, Utah's Chief Executives lived in their own homes in Salt Lake City. In 1937, the widow of U.S. Senator Thomas Kearns deeded the historic family mansion to the State to be used as the Governor's Residence. The Kearns' mansion was one of a number of elaborate homes built at the turn of the century by Utah's silver barons. Thomas Kearns, the son of immigrant parents, came West to seek his fortune in the mines; he was twenty-eight years of age when he and two partners sank the shaft which became the fabulously rich Silver King Mine. The mansion which he subsequently built on East Brigham Street (now East South Temple) was completed in 1901. Modeled after a French chateau on the outside, its rooms were finished in various marbles, French and Flemish oak and Russian mahogany.

Governor Henry H. Blood moved into the Kearns' mansion in June 1937. Over the years, the mansion, while of great historic interest, became more and more of a maintenance problem for the State. It had been designed for service by a large staff, which was no longer available, and its heating and electrical systems were out of date. In 1951, the Utah State Historical Society developed an interest in acquiring the mansion as its headquarters, hoping that it would be able to maintain the building through private contributions. An unsuccessful bill was introduced in the 1953 session of the State Legislature, seeking to authorize transfer of the mansion to the society. The following session, in 1955, passed such a bill but made no provision for a substitute residence for the Governors.

The 1957 session saw a spirited but fruitless effort, mounted largely by various women's groups, to repeal the 1955 Act and retain the mansion for the Governors. It also produced an appropriation of $200,000 for the construction of a new Governor's Residence. Governor J. Bracken Lee moved out of the Kearns' mansion at the end of his second term, and the historical society moved in. However, hopes of private support have not

The Utah Residence, a Y-shaped home furnished in a contemporary style, was designed primarily for the privacy of the First Family.

been realized, and the State still maintains the building.

The location of the present Residence was determined in March of 1957 when the James A. Hogle family presented the State with two and one-half acres of land at Fairfax Road and Virginia Street. The site, in the foothills north of the University of Utah campus, has a magnificent view of the entire Salt Lake valley and its surrounding mountains.

A special committee was appointed to oversee the construction of the Residence. At Governor Clyde's express direction, the building was to be a "residence" rather than a "mansion"—that is, it was to be a home for the Governor and his family, with provision for small-scale entertaining and for the accommodation of State guests. William F. Thomas, the architect, was charged with constructing and furnishing the Residence and landscaping the grounds. Construction was begun on November 17, 1958, and Governor Clyde and his family moved in on September 1, 1959.

The completed Residence is a low-lying, contemporary home, built in the shape of a large Y. The

spacious kitchen is at the center of the Y; the stem contains a laundry room, two rooms and a bath for staff, a three-car garage and storage rooms for gardening equipment. The north-south arm of the Y (the family wing) contains a breakfast room which is used for family meals, a combined library and private living room, a master bedroom with dressing room and bath, and two other bedrooms and a bath. The east-west arm (the State wing) contains a dining room, a large sunken living room, and two guest bedrooms with baths. The arms of the Y enclose a large covered patio and a broad terrace which face south toward the valley and the mountains. A partially finished lower floor contains a recreation room, a small private study, and a number of storage and utility rooms. The grounds, which are extensive, are beautifully landscaped.

The house is completely furnished in contemporary style, including china, glassware, silver, linens and kitchen equipment. The Clydes, of course, brought some of their personal furnishings with them, including the organ which all of them enjoyed playing. Governor Rampton and his family are using their own library, some of their own paintings and furniture.

The Residence operates on a biennial budget appropriated by the State Legislature. There are few fixed regulations governing the expenditure of this budget, except that it must cover utilities, food, laundry services, staff salaries, and maintenance. The present staff consists of a housekeeper who lives in, a cleaning woman who comes five days a week, and a gardener. The gardener is assisted by a crew of four men from the County Welfare Department.

There are no regularly scheduled tours of the Residence, since it is intended primarily as a private home. Large receptions are scheduled in warm weather when we can utilize the patio and the terrace, and small dinners in cold weather when we can enjoy the big fireplace in the living room. In addition, the use of the Residence by outside groups for teas, receptions and special programs is permitted—preferably groups with State-wide or city-wide significance and, of course, they make all their own arrangements for each occasion.

VIRGINIA

THE EXECUTIVE MANSION By Mrs. Mills E. Godwin, Jr., *First Lady of Virginia*

Like many an ancestral home, the Governor's Mansion in Virginia's Capitol Square is the sum of contributions by a long and varied succession of occupants. Remarkably, it has retained the flavor of the office they held and of the State they served.

When the seat of government was moved to Richmond in 1779, as the British Army marched southward, the House of Burgesses talked of something along the lines of the Royal Governor's Palace in the old capital at Williamsburg, where Patrick Henry had lived as the first Chief Magistrate after statehood. But it was 1813 before the rigors of war and independence would permit a permanent new offiical residence. Meanwhile successive Chief Magistrates lived first in rented quarters and then in an unpretentious house on the present site.

In 1810, after bitter complaints from Governor John Tyler, father of the future President, the Legislature appropriated $12,000 and commissioned a Boston architect, Alexander Parris, to draw preliminary plans. But the Commissioners of Public Buildings were not satisfied that these properly reflected "the honor and dignity of the State," and added embellishments of their own, bringing the final construction cost to about $19,000 by 1813 when Chief Magistrate James Barbour moved in.

In turn, he was not satisfied with the stark, rectangular structure. He softened the austere lines of the hip roof with balustrades along the eaves, and railed in the four Georgian chimneys to form the Captain's Walk, which was removed after 1856 and restored a century later. In 1840, under Governor Gilmer, porticoes were added north and south to make these entrances more inviting. In 1846, under Governor William Smith, the separate kitchen, now a guest house, was connected to the basement by a covered passageway.

During the Civil War, volunteers with water buckets stationed on the roofs of the Mansion and the old kitchen saved both buildings from the evacuation fire that virtually destroyed Richmond's business section.

The Constitution of 1902 completed Virginia's legal emergence from the Reconstruction, and economic recovery was reflected in the new east and west wings added to the Capitol and by further refurbishing of the Mansion. Between 1902 and 1906, Governor A. J. Montague's wife scoured antique shops for the remnants of the original Mansion furniture. After one robust member of the House Finance Committee broke through a Mansion chair, her husband had little trouble obtaining the first major appropriation for improvements to the structure and furnishings. Among these, the tin roof was replaced with slate and the copper bathtubs with porcelain.

Governor and Mrs. Claude A. Swanson completed the transition to contemporary living, adding the oval dining room by Richmond architect, Duncan Lee, moving the outdoor kitchen into the basement, and throwing open the two back rooms on the first floor to form the present ballroom. In 1926, Governor Trinkle's son, Billy, ran under the Christmas tree with a lighted sparkler, and the resulting fire prevented Governor Harry Flood Byrd from moving in until the ballroom was rebuilt, the house rewired, and the interior redecorated. In the early 1930's, the John Garland Pollards rounded out the grounds by the addition of the north evergreen garden, redesigning the south gardens, and rescuing more discarded furnishings, including a set of Oriental rugs, which had been piled in the old stable.

Numerous additions and improvements were made during the next three decades by Governors James H. Price, Colgate Darden, John S. Battle, J. Lindsay Almond, Thomas B. Stanley, Albertis S. Harrison and Mills E. Godwin, Jr., including adding the circular drive with traditional brick and equipping and redecorating the east suite upstairs as private living quarters.

The south bedroom traditionally has been the Governor's bedroom, but more recent occupants have preferred the less formal atmosphere of the east suite. In a post-war visit to Richmond, Lafayette gave his name to the north bedroom and to its bed.

The Prince of Wales, who later became King Edward

VII, Marshall Foch, Charles A. Lindbergh, Admiral Richard E. Byrd, Winston Churchill, five Presidents of the United States and Queen Mother Elizabeth of England have been among the Mansion's honored guests.

Four future Presidents of the United States have lived on the site: Governors Jefferson, Monroe, Tyler, and young William Henry Harrison, while his father, Benjamin Harrison, was Governor. Patrick Henry lived here during one of his terms as Governor, as did Henry Lee, father of Robert E. Lee.

The Mansion has been both an official residence and a family home. Fitzhugh Lee's daughters, Virginia Lee and Nancy, scratched their names on the window panes of an upstairs bathroom. Young Gay Montague smashed bottles against the back wall, practicing for the christening of the battleship *U.S.S. Virginia.*

Mansion occupants have known, also, the extremes of sadness. One night in 1863 the body of Stonewall Jackson reportedly lay in state in what is now the ballroom. While her husband was in office, the first Mrs. John Garland Pollard suffered her final illness. In the summer of 1968, the body of fourteen-year-old Becky Godwin, struck by lightning at Virginia Beach, was brought for funeral rites to the great house where she had explored every cranny, and where her presence had brightened every room.

Tragically, for all of its own history and the historic figures who have occupied it, the Mansion has little, if any, of its original furniture and appointments. Outstanding among the exceptions are the cornices and woodwork in the entrance hall and front rooms, which survived the fire of 1926.

While it has often reflected contemporary tastes, recent occupants have gradually restored the Mansion to the Virginia fashion of colonial times. In the main hall, the old grandfather's clock, with the initials G. W. scratched inside, is an example, together with the Chippendale chests and the Pembroke and tripod tables. In the sitting room to the left, which was originally the Governor's office, Hepplewhite and Sheraton augment an old and very rare Kerman Oriental rug, and French generals on horseback in porcelain grace the mantel. In the drawing room to the right, Chippendale, Sheraton and an old spinet piano set the tone, and in this room is the eighteenth-century gilt mirror, said to be one of the original pieces Mrs. A. J. Montague rescued.

Similar well-known names in furniture round out the ballroom, which includes an ornate cabinet said to have been purchased by Thomas Jefferson and taken by him to the White House. Also in the ballroom are two old and valuable English fold-book tables. Eighteenth-century Meissen figurines occupy the mantel. The crystal chandeliers are reproductions of the original ones destroyed by the fire.

The fireplace in the State Dining Room has been closed, making room for a Hepplewhite sideboard to augment the imported Duncan Phyfe table which comfortably seats fifteen.

Some of the more valuable pieces are the paintings, some on loan from the Virginia Museum of Fine Arts, and including portraits of many former Governors of the State. In the drawing room hang an early nineteenth-century Corot, a rare St. Memin engraving and a Sully portrait. In the sitting room an old steel engraving pictures Washington with his generals. Paintings in the ballroom are dominated by former Governors, and in the State Dining Room, a large oil portrait of William Byrd II, founder of Richmond, presides from the east wall. At the turn of the north stairway hangs a portrait of Lady Doubleday by Sir Joshua Reynolds.

In specially lighted glass cases beside the two stairways, there is displayed the magnificent silver service from the battleship *U.S.S. Virginia,* a gift from the Commonwealth in 1906.

There are now a total of fifteen rooms and a guest house with two bedrooms. The staff consists of five persons. Despite renovations, restorations and rearrangements, the Mansion, which is open to visitors during Garden Week each spring, remains the very essence of Virginia.

Almost every Virginia Governor has contributed to the architecture of the Mansion. A Captain's Walk and balustrades along the eves are among the numerous additions made since 1813.

WASHINGTON

THE EXECUTIVE MANSION

By Mrs. Daniel J. Evans, *First Lady of Washington*

Standing atop Capitol Point, the Executive Mansion in Olympia overlooks the capital city, the Capitol grounds, the southernmost waters of Puget Sound and the Olympic Mountains. Surrounded by stately evergreen trees and flowering shrubs, the Mansion is of Georgian architecture, with a dark red brick facade and white pillars. A carriage drive and three large porches enhance the charm of the entrance.

A spacious entry hall lends itself to the circulation of many guests. Leading from this reception area, which is flanked on each side by a cloak room, is the thirty-five-foot ballroom, which was recently redecorated in white and gold. The exquisite chandeliers with Czechoslovakian prisms date from 1908 when the eighteen-room structure was completed.

During legislative sessions, the ballroom is used on many occasions. It is also used as an additional visiting area for the many guests who attend afternoon teas at the Mansion. Adjoining the ballroom is the State Dining Room, which is well-suited for formal dinners and buffets.

Leading from the right of the entrance hall is the drawing room, with a pink marble fireplace, and adjoining it is the Green Room, a family sitting room where guests may also be entertained. A recreation room is in the basement.

An authentic Georgian double staircase leads to the six bedrooms on the second floor. A part of the original furnishings is the grandfather's clock in the center of the stairway. The bedrooms are used as guest or family rooms, depending upon the size of the family in residence. Also on the second floor are a library and an office for the First Lady. Three bedrooms and a sitting room for the two full-time and two part-time members of the Mansion staff are on the third floor.

Much of the furniture acquired in 1908 by Governor Hay and his family, the first family to live in the Mansion, still remains. Many antique pieces have been acquired over the years, and antique paintings and *objets d'art* have been loaned for display in the Mansion by the State Capitol Museum.

A remodeling project in 1968 included the replacement of a frame front porch with a brick one, the redecoration of the ballroom, remodeling of part of the upstairs library and the First Lady's office, and modernizing of utilities. A three-member Capitol Committee must now decide whether to build a new Mansion in a different location, completely refurbish and remodel the present one with additions, or to carry out minor remodeling of the present structure until a decision regarding its future is reached.

Public sentiment seems to favor retaining the Man-

The residence of Washington's Governor is a charming eighteen-room Georgian Mansion located on Capitol Point in Olympia.

sion as an historic home in this relatively young State and establishing its worthiness for renovation and preservation. Plans have been drawn for extensive remodeling and the addition of 4,200 square feet. First-floor plans include the addition of a family living room, family dining room, maids' quarters, and public restrooms. The plans also include the enlargement of the entrance hall, cloak rooms, State Dining Room, and the complete renovation and enlargement of the kitchen and serving areas. On the second floor, four guest bedrooms and three bathrooms would be added along with the enlargement of the Governor's suite and the remodeling and rearrangement of the Governor's library.

These much needed changes would make it possible for the Mansion to assume its official role with greater distinction and to provide an atmosphere of comfort and hospitality for its guests and resident First Families.

A high portico supported by white Corinthian columns graces the front entrance of the red brick Mansion of West Virginia.

WEST VIRGINIA

THE GOVERNOR'S MANSION By Mrs. Hulett C. Smith, *Former First Lady of West Virginia*

The West Virginia Governor's Mansion is located on the Kanawha River at 1716 Kanawha Boulevard in Charleston, adjacent to the State Capitol and across the river from Morris Harvey College. The Mansion, completed in 1925 after the Legislature allocated $100,000 for its construction, was designed by a young Charleston architect, Walter Martens. It was first occupied by Governor E. F. Morgan.

This Georgian structure, built of red Harvard colonial brick, has a high portico supported by white Corinthian columns at the main entrance. The first floor formal areas, furnished in keeping with the architecture and history of the State, encompass a reception hall, ballroom, State Dining Room, drawing room, library, sunroom, family dining room and kitchen facilities. A magnificent double staircase ascends to the second floor, where eight bedrooms, a family room and four baths are located. The third floor has recreation rooms, two bedrooms and bath, sitting and study rooms.

Of special interest is the doorknocker, which was a gift to the Hulett Smiths for the Mansion, from Mr. C. F. Reininger, former President of the Powhatan Brass Company, Ranson, Jefferson County, West Virginia. Hand-sculptured and cast in solid brass, it portrays the Great Seal of the State of West Virginia, which includes the State Motto, *Montani Semper Liberi* "Mountaineers Always Free."

The floors of the reception hall are black Belgium and white Tennessee marble. The two Empire sofas and spread eagle tables were formerly used in the old Executive Mansion. Cut crystal newel posts emphasize the mahogany staircases.

The white marble mantel in the ballroom was designed for an old Irish castle over 125 years ago. The crystal chandeliers were originally used at Scott's Drug Store in Charleston. Four solid bronze Italian urns and a pair of andirons (circa 1700) are newly acquired. An engraving of Benjamin Franklin in Versailles has been cleaned and tinted in watercolors by Mr. E. E. Myers.

The room adjoining the ballroom was formerly a sunroom. It is now used as a small sitting room and contains gilded antique French furnishings. The Aubusson-designed rugs were made especially for the Mansion. The abbreviation for West Virginia is in the design for the ballroom rug and similarly designed rugs are in the State Dining Room and the small sitting room. The butternut-paneled library was recently redone to comply with the original architectural design. The wood is from Randolph County, West Virginia.

In the drawing room, the Federal blue carpeting has an acanthus-leaf design forming a border, and the same design is stenciled in blue with gold highlights on the off-white walls at the top of the moldings. Newly acquired for this room and the library are the crystal chandeliers which are from the crystal ballroom of the old Kanawha Hotel and the musical clock which was made over 275 years ago for The Hague by Jan Henkels in Amsterdam. The mantel was copied from an Adam mantel in the President's Cottage at the Greenbrier Hotel in White Sulphur Springs, West Virginia. The green and gold Sèvres urns (circa 1765) have been in the Mansion for many years. Placed in the drawing room in 1968 were two portraits—Anna Jarvis, founder of Mother's Day, from Grafton, Taylor County, West Virginia; and novelist Pearl S. Buck, of Hillsboro, Pocahontas County, West Virginia. Both are by Mr. Thomas P. Schmader of Charleston.

During the first two years of Governor Smith's administration, the Mansion was completely renovated and remodeled. After dry rot and damage to the underpinnings of the Mansion were discovered, the flooring on both sides of the marble hallway was removed in order to put in steel beams and joists with a concrete base, and new parquet flooring.

The kitchen was completely remodeled with natural cherry custom-made cabinets from Harrison County, West Virginia. This kitchen is equipped with sufficient work area and appliances to handle everyday family needs as well as large official functions. The informal family dining room faces a brick-walled garden on the Virginia Street side of the house.

A commission has been appointed to make regular inspections and recommendations to the Legislature for adequate upkeep and maintenance of the Mansion.

WISCONSIN

THE EXECUTIVE RESIDENCE

By Governor Warren P. Knowles

William Wollin

The Executive Residence, home of Wisconsin's Governor, is a Georgian house in a beautiful four-acre setting on the shore of Lake Mendota at 99 Cambridge Road in Madison. The house, which was finished in 1927, was built as a private residence and used as such until 1949, when the State purchased it for the sum of $47,500. Even at that time, the house had been appraised at over $200,000, and has, of course, increased in value during the ensuing years.

The exterior of the house is sandstone, painted white, with large white pillars. The grounds are entered through a gateway onto a curving drive ending in a circular drive at the entrance. A large tiered fountain circled with plantings of boxwood is in the center of the driveway at the front of the house. A slate terrace encircles the house, and on the lake side of the Residence comfortable outdoor furniture is placed. One of the beautiful views across the lake is of the State Capitol.

When the Residence was acquired in 1949, no provision was made for its maintenance. Consequently, through the years, though a certain amount of redecorating was done occasionally, the house was in need of repair, remodeling and complete redecorating when the writer was elected in 1964. The First Lady, who was an interior decorator, determined to make adequate restorations and improvements.

Toward this end the Wisconsin Executive Residence Foundation, Inc., was formed in 1965 for the purpose of receiving gifts of money, appropriate furniture and fine art objects for the refurnishing of the house. The State appropriated $240,000 which was to be used for such items as a new copper roof, new heating system, air conditioning, new electrical wiring and plumbing, remodeling of the kitchen and painting of the basement.

Funds raised by the foundation paid for complete redecorating, refurnishing, rugs and other fine items for the house. Antiques were acquired and used throughout the Residence where practical; rugs were custom woven; fine chandeliers and beautiful handmade draperies were installed. Furnishings consist largely of eighteenth-century antiques and reproductions.

There is a gatehouse at the entrance to the property where an employee and her husband reside.

To insure that the Residence will continue to be well maintained, that proper repairs are made, and that future redecoration will be in keeping with the design of the house, no renovation, repairs (except of emergency nature), or installation of equipment, furniture or furnishings for grounds and buildings of the Executive Residence may be performed until approved by the State Capitol and Executive Residence Board. A liaison

with the State Department of Administration, which is responsible for maintenance of the house, is provided by a special services assistant, who is responsible to the Department of Administration and to the Governor. The assistant is on the staff at the Residence to oversee management and use of the house and to provide continuity when there are administration changes.

The Mansion staff consists of six full-time and three part-time employees. Tourists are permitted every Tuesday from 1 to 3 p.m. during April through October.

A large, tiered fountain within the circular driveway is an attractive addition to the grounds of Wisconsin's Executive Residence.

WYOMING

THE EXECUTIVE MANSION By Mrs. Stanley K. Hathaway, *First Lady of Wyoming*

Wyoming had been a State for eleven years before the State Legislature appropriated funds for a Governor's Mansion, the gracious Georgian structure which still serves as the residence of Wyoming's First Family.

Completed in 1904, the Mansion was officially dedicated in January 1905 with a reception for Governor Bryant B. Brooks. According to a story in the *Wyoming Tribune:*

> [At this] first housewarming . . . the new and handsome Executive Mansion . . . was thronged with guests from Cheyenne and other portions of the State. The Mansion was brilliantly illuminated and presented a most striking appearance from every direction . . . Every part of the spacious house was radiant with electric lights and fragrant with ferns and flowers. The orchestra from Denver occupied a portion of the staircase landing, behind a bank of palms and furnished sweet music during the entire event. . . .

Since then, the Mansion has continued to provide the setting for innumerable State and social affairs, and has furnished hospitality to distinguished visitors from all over the United States. But perhaps the greatest distinction of the Wyoming Governor's Mansion is that it was the first in the Nation to have been occupied by a woman Governor. Mrs. Nellie Tayloe Ross was elected in 1924 to fill the unexpired term of her husband, Governor William B. Ross, who died in office.

A total expenditure of $37,000 was authorized for the Mansion by the 1901 Legislature. The large drawing room was decorated in French Provincial style and the dining room was in eighteenth-century décor. It is said that iron bedsteads and golden oak furniture comprised some of the bedroom furnishings in the first years of the Mansion's occupancy.

Outstanding furnishings from former years that are still in use include the beautiful Knabe grand piano acquired by Mrs. Brooks; the imposing grandfather's clock in the reception hall, chosen by Governor and Mrs. Leslie A. Miller; and the carved replica of the Great Seal of Wyoming, executed from native Wyoming cedar by the late Mrs. Nellie Hammond of Douglas, and presented to the State in 1937 on the occasion of Governor Miller's birthday.

A beautifully designed brass clock and brass candlesticks and bookends which depict an eagle in flight are frequently displayed in the library. They were selected from the "Merci Train," sent to the United States by the people of France after World War II in appreciation of this country's assistance to France. In the gallery just two steps above the level of the reception room, hung in harmonizing frames, are pictures of all of Wyoming's First Ladies, from Territorial days to the present time.

Nearly all of the Governors since 1905 have occupied the Mansion. However, Governor Joseph M. Carey, who was in office from 1911 to 1915, preferred to live in his own spacious home on Carey Avenue, and the Mansion stood vacant during those years. Governor Miller, who was in office from 1933 to 1939, lived in the Mansion for only the latter part of his six years in office, as the State headquarters of the WPA were located in the Mansion from the early 1930's until 1937.

After this use of the Mansion for offices, the first extensive renovation and modernization program was undertaken. The soiled and faded tapestries were removed from the bedroom walls and replaced with wallpaper, and major remodeling was done on the second floor. Extensive changes in the Mansion were again necessary in 1955 and 1956. New carpeting was installed throughout the first floor, with a striking replica of the State Seal woven into the carpeting in the large reception room. Grass cloth was placed on the walls of the library and new draperies were hung there and in the breakfast room. Governor and Mrs. Milward Simpson supervised the conversion of a storage room into a study furnished with unusual native wood furniture made in Cody, Wyoming. The upholstery fabric and the draperies in the room feature the Indian paintbrush, the State Flower, and pine cones in the design.

In 1958 a sun deck was added on the second floor which at the present time is being used as the writer's office. It is also an ideal spot to relax in complete privacy. Flowers bloom profusely in the sunny area.

The first floor of the Mansion includes the entrance foyer, the large reception hall, library, drawing room, study, formal dining room, breakfast room, kitchen, pantry, service port and the sitting room for the household staff.

The second floor originally had five bedrooms, but the 1937 remodeling program eliminated two of these to make possible additional bathrooms and dressing rooms. The third floor has three bedrooms and one bath. This floor has sometimes been used as servants' quarters and as overflow quarters for guests, depending upon the needs and wishes of the family in residence.

Establishment of a Governor's Mansion library was begun in 1967 by the writer. Nucleus of the collection was some sixty books by Wyoming authors presented by the Wyoming Press Women's Association. The project is a continuing one and it is hoped that the library will eventually reflect all phases of Wyoming's development from the frontier era to the present.

The twenty-three-room Mansion occupies unfenced grounds comprising a quarter of a city block at 300 E. 21st Street, within walking distance of the State Capitol. The household staff regularly includes two persons. Tours are arranged by appointment.

The home of Wyoming's First Families was the first Mansion in the Nation to be occupied by a woman Governor. Since 1905, all but two Chief Executives have chosen to live in the Mansion.

The Government House of American Samoa is a white clapboard home which was built of sturdy redwood beams and siding.

AMERICAN SAMOA

(Territory)

GOVERNMENT HOUSE

By Mrs. Wayne Aspinall,

First Lady of American Samoa

It is unlikely that any Governor's Mansion in the United States has a view equal to the one from Government House in American Samoa. It sits atop a hill named Mauga-O-Ali'i ("Mountain of the Chiefs") overlooking Pagó Pago Bay, recognized as one of the most beautiful natural harbors in the world. The rambling, eleven-room, two-story white frame home is surrounded by palm trees and heavy tropical foliage, but it can still be seen from all parts of the bay area below.

Government House was the second building constructed by the United States Navy after the chiefs of

Tutnila ceded their islands to the United States and the American flag was first raised just below Mauga-O-Ali'i on April 17, 1900. The first building was a coaling station warehouse at the main dock. Government House was then built in 1903 as the home for the Naval Governor at a cost of $18,651.

Through the years it served as the home of the Naval Governors, and, since civil government was established in 1951, it has been the official residence of the Territorial Governor.

It has been remodeled a number of times, mostly to replace termite-ridden wood and timber supports that deteriorate from the exposure to high tropical humidity. Nothing has been done, however, to alter its original charm as an imposing old home of the South Pacific, and it rivals in prestige the home of Robert Louis Stevenson at Vailima in Apia, Western Samoa. The staff consists of five persons. Tours are made by appointment.

[*Editor's Note: The following additional information on Government House was provided by Mrs. Rex Lee, First Lady of American Samoa, 1961-1967:*]

The open wall construction of the House gives a commanding view of fabled Rainmaker Mountain, over which the First Family can watch equally spectacular risings of sun and moon, and the full reaches of the bay along the shores of which are clustered the picturesque homes of the Samoans. The waters of the bay, aquamarine when the sea is calm, become deep purple-green as a sudden squall moves in to form a turbulent sea.

The House is built of sturdy redwood beams and siding, the basic structure of which has withstood the ravages of dry rot, termites and destructive tropical hurricanes. However, by 1961, because of deferred maintenance and the apparent lack of interest of those responsible for it, Government House had become a run-down, ill-equipped place that was not befitting America's only piece of soil in the Southern Hemisphere. Plans had been completed by the previous administration for a new, modern Government House. Its new occupants, Governor Lee and his First Lady, discussed the matter with the Island leaders and their wives, and decided there were more pressing needs for money that might become available. In addition, the basic structure of Government House was sound; it could be renovated. But even more important was the charm and meaning the building held for the Samoans. The importance of this can be seen in the fact that when the lights go on at Mauga-O-Ali'i the villagers turn on their own, for in Samoan custom it is the village chief's house whose lights are turned on first in the evening.

Governor Lee was persuaded that Government House was a symbol of America's presence in the South Pacific and that replacement would be a mistake. Consequently, the House was completely renovated and many of the worn-out furnishings that had been made by the Seabees during World War II were replaced by tropical-styled rattan furniture. Floors and sections of some of the walls were attractively decorated with Samoan pandanus matting. The characteristic and interesting tapa cloth served as decoration in the Samoan flavor.

The ground floor is designed for public purposes. Off the reception area is a large dining area that is used for both receptions and official dinners. On the other side, the reception area opens into a long glassed-in hall which accommodates several hundred people and is the center of official receptions. This in turn opens to the formal garden. The upper floor is reserved for the Governor and his family.

The House is completely surrounded by stately cocoanut palms, mango and breadfruit trees, with a generous sprinkling of other tropical trees and plants such as frangipane, aromatic ginger, hibiscus and bougainvillea. Since the top of Mauga-O-Ali'i presents a very limited yard area, the front part of the House faces a small formal garden of tropical plants, ti, ginger, croton and poinsettia. Bird of paradise plants form a border. A steep staircase leads down the mountainside to the bay where early day Governors had a boat dock.

Behind the House and in another small garden setting, the chiefs built a beautiful native ceremonial *fale* (house) in which they present to the Governor and his distinguished guests the traditional 'ava ceremony. The Samoans have been called the architects of the Pacific, and in erecting this thatched roof *fale*, they did not spare their skills. The perfectly executed ceiling of arched cocoanut trunks in uniform lengths woven together with sennit and the hand-carved hardwood columns attest to their skill. Many a dignitary, ranging from chiefs of state, premiers, ambassadors, high ranking military authorities, congressional and parliamentary leaders from faraway countries, to business leaders, writers and other professional people throughout the world have experienced the thrill of the 'ava ceremony in this fine addition to Government House.

For almost seven decades Government House has been America's symbol in the South Pacific. The Islands' hopes and aspirations have been centered there, and many decisions bearing vitally on their future have been made there. The big white clapboard house with its American flag floating in the tropical trade winds will continue to be a bond that binds Samoa to America for many decades to come.

Top: Guam's Government House (rear view) is a modern split-level concrete home.
Above: Lush foliage along the drive partially obscures the front of the House.

GUAM

(Territory)

GOVERNMENT HOUSE By Mrs. Manuel F. L. Guerrero, *First Lady of Guam*

Government House, official residence of Guam's Governor, is located on an Agaña Heights promontory with a sweeping view of Agaña Bay. Historic Plaza de España and the ruins of the Territory's pre-war Governor's Palace can be seen from the north portico of Government House. The present site was formerly that of a naval officers' club.

Construction was started in 1952 and completed in 1954 at a cost of $300,000, one-third of which was provided by Federal appropriation and the rest by the Territorial government.

The First Family's home, a split-level, one-story, ranch-type concrete structure, has three almost equal sections—an entrance hall and a multi-purpose living-dining area; a sleeping area with four bedrooms, three baths and a study; and a service area with a kitchen, staff quarters, laundry and a carport. A swimming pool, which had been part of the officers' club, was filled by former Governor Ford Q. Elvidge and has remained unused by succeeding Governors.

Government House serves not only as the official home of the Governor and his family, but it also has been the scene of many formal receptions over the years. Many prominent visitors, including members of the U.S. Congress and other Federal officials, have been guests at Government House. It also provided emergency shelter for many families during Typhoon Karen in 1962, when the island suffered great devastation.

The grounds of Government House provide a vantage point for professional and amateur photographers. About fifty yards northwest of Government House is Fort Soledad, built by the Spaniards over two hundred years ago to provide a lookout for the stockaded Spanish garrison in ancient Agaña. From the fort, photographers have a panoramic view of the capital city, including the Paseo de Susana which juts into Agaña Bay, and Marine Drive, the island's main thoroughfare running along or close to the shore from Apra Harbor to Andersen Air Force Base.

The staff for maintenance and operation of Government House consists of nine persons. Tours are arranged by appointment from 9 to 11 o'clock each morning.

PUERTO RICO

(Commonwealth)

LA FORTALEZA*

La Fortaleza, or Santa Catalina Palace, is the oldest building now used as an Executive Mansion in the Western Hemisphere. It was the first of a series of forts built in San Juan Harbor which, in time, made San Juan one of the strongest defense bastions of the Spanish Empire in America.

Its construction was started in 1533 and finished in 1540. At first it consisted of a circular tower and four walls enclosing a patio. This tower, still in existence and known as the Tower of Homage, has thick stone walls and two vaulted rooms, one of which is the chapel. The tower's name originated from the custom of the castle's Governors pledging loyalty and courage at the top of it in times of danger. Great interest in this tower and a second circular one called Torre Austral stems from the fact that they are among the few structures in the hemisphere that have the architectural style popular in Spain during the early days of America's history.

Only twice was this fortress taken by invaders. First, in 1598, when the Earl of Cumberland took San Juan; and second, in 1625, when the Dutch Commander Boudewyn Hendrick took control of the community and installed himself in La Fortaleza.

A raging fire marking the withdrawal of the Dutch caused great harm to the building, and its reconstruction began in 1640. Since then, it has been customary for the Governors to reside at La Fortaleza. During the reconstruction, the Santa Catalina hermitage outside the walls was destroyed but later integrated into the walls, thus giving rise to the name of Royal Fortress or Palace of Santa Catalina.

On November 27, 1822, it was officially decreed that La Fortaleza would be the residence of the Governors of Puerto Rico, formalizing a custom observed since the seventeenth century.

In 1846, the Count de Mirasol, then Governor, expanded La Fortaleza, reconstructing the building almost completely, except for the west side, to the palatial appearance that it has today. Under the Governor's reconstruction plan, which was carried out by Don Santiago Cortijo, lieutenant colonel of engineers, the austere wall of military architecture built in 1640 was replaced by the present neoclassic facade. The first floor has a massive pine door leading to the main staircase and the interior patio. The floor of the vestibule is paved with old stones called Canarias stones.

The main staircase, as remodeled, is tiled with Genoese marble and the steps are of Puerto Rican *ausubo* wood. The banisters are Tuscan-style and the risers are embellished with nineteenth-century Catalonian glazed tiles. There are three decorative stucco plaques, under crowns, with the emblems of Puerto Rico, Castilla and Leon. Further up are four windows of Arabian style. The dome is decorated with military standards and flags.

The reception hall is tiled with Genoese marble. Four paintings on the walls depict Luis Muñoz Rivera, Eugenio Maria de Hostos, two nineteenth-century Puerto Rican patriots, and George Washington and Simón Bolívar. Near this room stands an antique mahogany clock whose face was broken by the sword of the last Spanish Governor, marking the last minute of Spanish rule in the New World. Puerto Rico was occupied by Major General Nelson A. Miles in the Spanish-American war and was ceded to the United States by the Treaty of Paris on December 10, 1898.

On the State Dining Room entrance is a decorative Spanish rococo coat of arms dating from the eighteenth

*Adapted from *La Fortaleza* by Teodoro Vidal, furnished by Mrs. Roberto Sanchez-Vilella, former First Lady of Puerto Rico.

La Fortaleza, the Executive Mansion of Puerto Rico, was completed in 1540. It was the first of a series of forts which made San Juan one of the strongest defense bastions of the Spanish Empire in America.

century, surrounded by the chain of the Order of the Golden Fleece, whose grand master was the King of Spain. The fresco shows the Bourbonic *fleur-de-lis,* and the emblems of Castilla, Leon and other Spanish provinces. The eighteenth-century type ceiling has old *ausubo* wood beams. The floor is tiled with Genoese marble and the rug bears the Seal of the Commonwealth and the coat of arms of Juan Ponce de Leon, the first Governor. A set of beautiful crystal fruit bowls bearing the Seal of Spain is on the table. Tradition holds that the bowls were sent to La Fortaleza by Queen Isabella II.

The old kitchen in the upper room of the South Tower was discovered in 1956 when old boards were removed. It has since been restored and furnished with utensils similar to those used in the sixteenth century.

The principal décor of the Hall of Mirrors, which dates back to the remodeling of Count de Mirasol, consists of ten beautiful mirrors whose burnished gilt frames are topped by ribboned flower garlands. Twelve classic pilasters with Corinthian capitals from socle to frieze give the room an air of formality. Its floor is white and grey Genoese marble. A stucco rosette in high relief stands out from the center of the ceiling, bearing six coats of arms containing, by order of surname, the heraldic emblems of General Juan Prim y Prats, Count de Reus, who commissioned this work during his Governorship (1847-48).

Native furnishings are found in the tea chamber and the music room, adjacent to which is a gallery with classical columns.

Running along the east front is the Governor's office, a large room, formerly called the Throne or Court Room, dating back to the 1846 reconstruction. Inaugurated on November 19, 1848, with a sumptuous ball given by the Count de Cheste, Governor at the time, it was used for official functions. Of Isabelline décor, this spacious room has twelve Ionic pilasters rising from the floor to join countless putti in high relief and linked by flower garlands. At the center and ends of the ceiling are three neo-Renaissance rosettes from which hang three elaborate crystal chandeliers. Above twelve wooden doors, three of which have delicate latticework, are twelve stucco shells containing the coats of arms of Puerto Rico, Spain and Castille, and figures representing Minerva, Protectress of the Arts, Peace, Justice, Perseverance, Fidelity, Strength, Charity, Vigilance and Mars. The white and grey Genoese marble floor contains three marble ornaments corresponding to the ceiling rosettes.

The Fortaleza Chapel, measuring twenty feet in diameter and topped by a semi-circular vault, is in the upper room of the North Tower. It has a "chapel gallery," or window, where the Governor could hear Mass privately without being seen by other worshipers. This sixteenth-century chapel was redecorated in 1951 by the Dutch artist, Marcolino Maas. It contains a mosaic of opaque tiles representing Christ on the cross; a stained-glass window depicting Catherine of Alexandria, La Fortaleza's patron saint, and John the Baptist, patron saint of Puerto Rico's capital; the Seal of Puerto Rico; and the coat of arms of Ponce de Leon.

On the wall next to the Bastion of Santa Catalina is a two-ton cannon brought over from Vicques Island in 1954, bearing the crown, in relief, of the British monarch—the traditional monogram of G. R., Georgius Rex, with three linked symbols meaning that it was one of the cannons of George III (1738-1820), during whose reign the United States won its independence.

This magnificent twenty-two-room palace is open to the public Mondays through Fridays from 9 a.m. to 5 p.m.

THE VIRGIN ISLANDS

(Territory)

GOVERNMENT HOUSE (CHRISTIANSTED)

By Mrs. Ralph M. Paiewonsky, *Former First Lady of the Virgin Islands*

In executive residences the Virgin Islands stands unique among the States and Territories in two ways. The Governor's House is also the Capitol, where territorial business is conducted, and there are actually *two* Government Houses. Although that of St. Thomas is the official Government House (described under *Capitols*, page 249), the house in Christiansted, St. Croix, is lacking recognition as such only because the Chief Executive functions primarily in St. Thomas. When he visits St. Croix, however, Government House is his official residence.

At one period in history Christiansted was the main seat of government. From 1665, St. Thomas had been the center of the Islands' governmental activities and St. Croix was the home of the Vice Governors. Suddenly, in the middle of the nineteenth century, the social and economic life of the Islands shifted to St. Croix, propelled by the booming sugar and rum industries of that Island. Because of this, the Colonial Council of 1862 reasoned that St. Croix was the most likely place for administrative activities. However, the move was short-lived. In 1871, St. Thomas again became the center of governmental operations and has continued to be so to the present day.

Some have said this was a pity, because Government House in Christiansted is, indeed, a majestic structure, reputed to be one of the most imposingly beautiful in the West Indies. Of masonry construction and built in three sections, from 1774 to 1860, it is in the style of northern Renaissance. At the north end, a formal staircase of twenty-five steps flanked by two marble busts leads to a second-story gallery surrounded by archways and painted in classical details. Similarly, the street side is entered through a long arcade.

The first floor of the structure, which encompasses 37,200 square feet, houses the District Court and government offices.

On the second floor is the impressive ballroom. It is ninety-eight feet long and twenty-two feet wide. Set in the two long walls are a series of alcoved archways, between which are twenty-six gilt-framed mirrors reaching almost from floor to ceiling. At their feet are exquisite tabourets with gilded griffin legs and upholstered in red leather. Flanking each mirror is a bracketed wall chandelier with crystal globes. These match the four hanging overhead, which, incidentally, were donated to the Islands by the Danish Government in 1952—replicas of those removed at the time of the transfer of the Virgin Islands from Denmark to the United States in 1917. A life-size portrait of Frederick VI of Denmark dominates the far wall. The solid, pitched-pine floor gleams from decades of hand-rubbing.

A conference room, which doubles as State Dining Room, completes this floor. As its counterpart in St. Thomas, it is furnished with lovely hand-made mahogany pieces. On its walls are portraits of Peter Von Sholten, the Danish Governor who freed the slaves in the tumultuous period of 1848, and King Christian V.

The third story consists of the residence quarters of the Chief Executive. This also contains many fine antiques made by local artisans.

The people of the Virgin Islands are proud of their traditional closeness to their Governors. For example, the present Commissioner of Health, Dr. Roy Anduze, recalls how as a boy, an incurable truant, he was actually called to Government House by Governor Waldo Evans, a man appointed by the U.S. Navy, which had jurisdiction over the Islands at that time.

He was ordered to stop playing hooky and also to improve his grades. Should he show improvement, the Governor told him, he would be invited to go to St. Croix aboard a naval vessel at the end of the term. Disciplining himself, Roy never played hooky again. He improved his grades, graduating among the top three. Subsequently he became a foremost physician, the first native surgeon to emerge from the Islands. The doctor emphatically declares he would never have amounted to anything except for the Governor's guidance.

The Government House in Christiansted is an appropriately impressive symbol of the Islanders' relationship with their Governors. Designated a National Historic Site, it is open daily to the public.

A wide formal staircase leads to the second-story front entrance of the unofficial Government House of the Virgin Islands, located on St. Croix.

States without Executive Mansions

As stated in the Introduction, only seven States provide no Executive Mansion—Massachusetts, New Hampshire, Rhode Island and Vermont in the New England States, Michigan in the Midwest, and Arizona and Oregon in the West. There have been attempts in these States to provide a house for the First Family, but these have met with little success except that Michigan does provide a beautiful summer residence for the Governor at Mackinac Island. These States will be discussed individually under the regional groupings listed above.

NEW ENGLAND

It was more than 130 years after the formation of the Union before a New England State had an official residence, and only two, Maine and Connecticut, now have Executive Mansions. Maine was first, with the gift of Blaine House to the State in 1919, and then Connecticut, after 157 years of statehood, purchased its Mansion in 1945.

Many explanations have been suggested for New England's historical stance on this subject, including the original Puritan faith and frugal nature of a people who had not financed royal residences for colonial Governors and wanted no semblance of a palace for their elected Governors. They had the purest form of democracy in their town hall meetings. Even after statehood, the legislative assemblies moved about from town to town for many years before establishing permanent capitals.

Equally important is the fact that distances to the capitals of the smaller States are short enough to permit Governors to commute from their homes. No New England State requires its Governor to reside at the seat of government.

Massachusetts

In Massachusetts any citizen can present a bill to the Legislature as a result of the State's custom of "free petition." Over the years, the State Librarian and Archivist report that many bills for a residence have been filed by citizens, but no legislation resulted.

In 1957, Governor Christian Herter, as he was about to retire from office, recommended a Governor's Mansion to the Legislature. The result was no Mansion but an annual appropriation of $10,000 a year in order that the Governor may rent quarters in the capital city of Boston.

In 1963 and 1964, Governor Endicott Peabody advocated the establishment of an official residence. Bills were filed but none was passed.

Finally, in 1967, it appeared that Governor John A. Volpe would be more fortunate. The town of Dedham was willing to donate to the State for a Governor's Mansion the twenty-one acre site and twenty-four room house known as the Endicott Estate. The Legislature accepted but failed to provide sufficient funds for repairs and restoration.

Mrs. Volpe, while First Lady of Massachusetts, wrote in 1968 that the Mansion project was in "limbo," and detailed in chronological order the events concerning the proposed Mansion that "we have and do not have" as follows:

> On October 11, 1967, Governor Volpe approved legislation authorizing the Commissioner of Administration, on behalf of the Commonwealth, to acquire by gift for use as a Governor's Mansion, the land and buildings thereon located in the town of Dedham, known as the Endicott Estate.
>
> On November 18, 1967, Governor Volpe signed into law a bill establishing a Governor's Mansion Commission and appointed five members for terms of one to five years. . . . On December 1, 1967, in the town of Dedham, the five-member Commission was sworn in. On this same day, the Commonwealth accepted the deed to the Endicott Estate from the town of Dedham, for use as a Governor's residence. This is the first facility made available in Massachusetts for use as a Governor's Mansion.
>
> On January 5, 1968, an Act providing for a Special Capital Expenditure for the Governor's Mansion was passed in the amount of $300,000 for renovations, improvements, furnishings and equipment. However, evaluations made by the Mansion Commission concluded that a minimum of $650,000 would be required for necessary improvements to the interior, exterior and grounds before occupancy could take place.
>
> Additional funds were requested in the Supplementary Budget but, to date (September 6, 1968) they have not been appropriated. Without sufficient funds, the Governor's Mansion Commission has no idea if and when occupancy can be expected and what course of action they will take in their recommendations to the Governor as to whether or not the estate should be kept or returned. So as of this date, we do and we do not have a Governor's Mansion.

New Hampshire

Mrs. John W. King, former First Lady of New Hampshire, advised that there were no pending prospects for an Executive Mansion. She stated that several offers of private homes have been made through the years, but none has been accepted by the Legislature.

The diverse views on the subject were spoken at the 1956 Constitutional Convention, during consideration of Resolution No. 36, which would have authorized "a suitable residence for the Chief Executive." Here are some of the excerpts from the debate before the Resolution was killed as "inexpedient":

> "I do not feel that our State is in a financial condition at this time to finance a mansion. . . ."
>
> "We have held our dignity through all the years in many, many ways. I think it is past time that this State should have a Governor's home . . . And I think we should maintain the dignity of the State of New Hampshire, when we have visiting people here. . . ."
>
> "I have always considered the office of the Governor an honor to be passed around among those who could afford it. And all the Governors that I ever knew could build their own mansions, and they don't need any help. . . ."
>
> "I hate this word 'mansion' around so much, because it scares people. A decent suitable residence is satisfactory and that is what the resolution calls for. . . ."

If anyone ever prevails upon the New Hampshire Legislature to accept or build a Mansion, he will have to convince more members than in any other State legislative body. Its House has 400 members (for a population of 606,921), exceeded in size only by the 630-member British House of Commons and the 435-member U.S. House of Representatives.

Rhode Island

Rhode Island, founded by Roger Williams, was the only one of the original Colonies which never had a Royal Governor sent over from England. Because the people always elected one of their own residents as Governor, Mary T. Quinn, Assistant for Archives in 1962, expressed the opinion that this might be the reason "a residence for him was never considered." No housing allowance is provided for the Governor.

Mrs. John Chafee, former First Lady of Rhode Island, agreeing that a Mansion is unnecessary, writes:

> There is no Executive Mansion in Rhode Island It is my belief that it would not be an advantage to the people of this State to have one.
>
> Rhode Island is a very small State—fifty miles by forty miles. The capital, Providence, is within easy reach by fine roads from all four corners of the State. This means commuting to work is not a problem for any Governor. He can be home every night no matter where he travels in the State.
>
> For entertaining purposes, we are fortunate in having our beautiful State House, the famed Newport mansions owned by the Newport Preservation Society, and other fine facilities available. The absence of an Executive Mansion probably eliminates certain functions that otherwise might blossom unnecessarily. It also means that the Governor can separate his public life and his family life with more ease.
>
> The people of Rhode Island are best served now by not undertaking the expense of maintaining a residence for the Governor where unequaled facilities are at hand, and the short distances make him always available to the center of government.

However, in the 1968 Legislative Session, a Special House Commission was authorized to conduct a study of the feasibility of acquiring suitable property for use as a Governor's Mansion, including the Sprague Mansion in Cranston, former residence of the late Senator Theodore Francis Green. Its report to the General Assembly will be made in 1969.

Vermont

In Vermont the Legislature is a bit more generous with the Governors, appropriating sufficient funds to pay for their rented quarters in the capital city of Montpelier. Also, the General Assembly has appointed committees at least twice to study the feasibility of an Executive Mansion, but no favorable action was taken.

Mrs. Philip Hoff, former First Lady of Vermont, describes "the most serious consideration" given to the subject as follows:

> By Joint Resolution No. 27 of the Acts of 1953, a committee of four members from the General Assembly was set up to confer with the Building Council and to investigate the feasibility of buying or building a suitable residence for the Governor. This committee reported to the Legislature of 1955 as follows:
>
> a. It had investigated various residences, both privately-owned and State-owned. It also had investigated the feasibility of erecting on various parcels of State-owned land.
>
> b. It recommended acquisition of property located at 100 East State Street, Montpelier, then owned by Mr. and Mrs. George J. Bertrand, for a Governor's residence. It estimated total cost of the property, furnishings, and repairs at $43,375 and annual operating costs at $3,436.
>
> The Legislature rejected the special committee report. In 1967, a portion of House Bill No. 8 provided for $250,000 to build a government residence at the Redstone site. This site is State-owned, not far away from the State House, and is very lovely. The residence would have included not only living quarters, but would have provided for modest State occasions and working areas.
>
> This particular portion of the House Bill was deleted almost immediately. Undoubtedly, something similar will be offered again, if not in 1969, then at a subsequent session.

MIDWEST

Michigan

As early as 1871 at the dedication of the Capitol Building, Governor Austin Blair, who had served as Michigan Chief Executive during the Civil War, advocated a Governor's Mansion, saying:

> The Governor should live at the Capital of the State. . . . He needs a home here, and ought to have a mansion which is at least as respectable as the mansions of most private citizens. . . . I am a swift witness that the people of Michigan have dealt hardly with their Governors since this Constitution went into effect. . . . I think it has some tendency to degrade the office, although I know there will always be found gentlemen who are willing to risk almost anything for the honor of this great office. But the citizens themselves ought not to require this; and I really hope it is about to pass away. . . .

In spite of many efforts through the years and a provision in the Constitution of 1963 that "An Executive residence . . . shall be provided at the seat of government for the use of the Governor," the Legislature has progressed only to the planning stage. An excellent study and history of the issue in Michigan and other states was written by David S. Brown in 1961 for the Michigan Institute of Public Administration, entitled "A Governor's Residence in Michigan?"

Mrs. George Romney, former First Lady of Michigan, is optimistic and presents the following interesting account:

> Michigan is one of seven States which does not provide a Governor's residence in its capital city. The State periodically has been urged to provide such a residence, and on two occasions the Legislature appropriated funds for that purpose. Nevertheless, Michigan still is without an official residence.
>
> This presents an inconvenience as well as a financial burden on the Governor, who must rent or purchase a suitable home, furnish it and provide for its maintenance.
>
> The new Constitution of Michigan which was adopted in 1963 provides for the erection of a Governor's residence and its maintenance. At the present time, there are exciting plans for a complete new Capitol complex, whereby State offices will be grouped together and a new Capitol Building erected. There is to be a beautifully landscaped mall incorporating a dramatic fountain between the proposed new structure and the old Capitol Building. The latter is to be preserved as a museum and will house works of art as well. Those considering the location of the new Governor's residence believe that it should be in the general area of the new complex. However, no definite site has been selected and, so far, only general discussion has taken place concerning the architectural plans for the executive residence.
>
> Because of the unique situation of Lansing in the central part of our State, I believe it will be particularly important to citizens of Michigan to have a Governor's residence. Many functions, including State and legislative gatherings, would be centered in this area were there a beautiful and meaningful building.
>
> We are at a disadvantage without such a structure. The role of the Governor and his wife is made more difficult as far as personal relationships, State functions, hosting visiting officials and providing facilities for State organizations are concerned.
>
> The State does own a charming cottage for the Governor on Mackinac Island. One of the loveliest settings in our whole country is the view from this summer residence. The cottage stands high on a hilltop overlooking the picturesque little village which resembles the fishing towns along the Mediterranean Coast. Below are the bright blue waters of the straits, and the sparkling Mackinac Bridge which gracefully connects the upper peninsula with the lower one. Although the cottage is available only two months of the year, it provides a complete change of atmosphere and pace, especially since no automobiles are permitted on the island. There is a fresh, invigorating crispness in the air, and the cottage itself has a rambling informality that is homespun and inviting. This summer home was made available to the Governor in 1945.

WEST

Arizona

In Arizona there has been less sentiment expressed for an official residence than in any State outside of New England. In 1965 a bill was introduced which

A rambling summer cottage on Mackinac Island provides a change of pace for Michigan's Governor.

would have made an appropriation of $150,000 to the State Planning and Building Commission to "Purchase or Construct a Governor's Mansion . . . to Equip the same, and providing for the Maintenance thereof . . ." This bill was held in Committee and did not reach the floor for debate.

The Arizona Legislative Review, reporting the failure of the proposal, said: "Two Democratic and two Republican former Governors when interviewed, in effect dismissed the idea as an unnecessary expense at this time. . . ." This view is shared by the present First Lady of Arizona, Mrs. Jack Williams, who writes as follows:

> A Governor's Mansion for a State with many years of historical association makes sense, perhaps; but not so for a relatively new State to build an elaborate residence for its Governor. Arizona taxpayers would not look kindly upon the extravagance of staffing and maintaining such an institution. Even the wealthy in the West find that securing domestic help is out of the question. . . .
>
> . . . As it is today, there is very little problem of entertaining for the Governor's wife in Arizona. A Mansion would inevitably require its use for purposes of State dinners as well as tours and teas. All of these activities cost money, and today it is hard to justify the value of dollars spent for social affairs that could be better spent for welfare service.
>
> What entertaining is necessary can be done much more effectively and economically at one of the major hotels or private clubs. The tours for students and visitors are confined to the State Capitol, which is an old and historically interesting building.
>
> Should the citizens of this modern State ever wish to domicile their Governor, it might be more practical to engage a Governor's Penthouse or suite atop one of our high rise hotels or apartments, where security is provided and modern conveniences are available.

Oregon

An Executive Mansion for the Governor is a perennial subject in Oregon, with present and former Governors and many citizen groups favoring legislative action.

Every effort thus far has failed, although the Legislature in 1967 enacted an Executive Residence Statute authorizing the Capital Planning Commission to accept donations from public and private sources and authorizing the Department of General Services to construct, decorate, landscape and furnish a "State Executive Residence" if sufficient funds are contributed.

This action followed a very comprehensive study and report in 1966 entitled "Governor's Residence for Oregon," written by Leander Quiring, Director of the Department of Finance and Administration. He traces the history of action and inaction in Oregon and other States and makes a good case for the State furnishing a residence not alone for the Governor but for dignity and convenience in conducting the affairs of State.

Mrs. Tom McCall, First Lady of Oregon, writes:

> Oregon has no official residence, but I believe the State needs one and should have one that would incorporate the native woods and stone of our State.
>
> The City of Salem has no available house that is adequate for a Governor's needs. I would hope that plans for a mansion or residence could go ahead in the near future.
>
> There is not much more to be said. I provide my own china, silver, linen and furnishings. For a small family like mine, it is far beyond my ordinary needs. I do not have tours, but I do make my house available to groups whose interests are worthy.

An unusual situation in Oregon is that the State owns the house near the Capitol rented to the present and some of the former Governors on the same basis as any other citizen would be charged. He is given a general expense account but nothing specifically or sufficient to cover this monthly rental along with the other necessary expenses which are incurred.

Epilogue

This summary of views and events relating to the seven States without Executive Mansions indicates that some day they too will appreciate their desirability not alone for the Governors but for the dignity and heritage of the State and the more efficient conduct of their public responsibilities.

The people take pride in these Mansions, especially when they are permitted to visit them on tours.

Some constitute an additional burden to the First Family, but the conveniences far outweigh the trials and tribulations.

Those Governors who worry about the people's reaction to Mansion expenditures should take heart from a former First Lady of Texas who was about to install the first steam heat in the Texas Mansion. When told that it might defeat her husband for re-election, she replied that she would rather be warm for two years than freeze for four. The steam radiators were installed and the Governor was re-elected.

So, even without a Mansion, may there always be those, described by former Governor Austin Blair of Michigan, who "will risk anything for the honor of this great office."

And those with Mansions who have tribulations might remember President Calvin Coolidge's response when warned that the White House roof was dangerous and badly in need of repairs. He said, "I suppose there are plenty of others who would be willing to take the risk of living under that roof."

II.
CAPITOLS

History of Capitols

By Price Daniel

Churches preceded Capitols in North America just as religious faith preceded and influenced political pronouncements of independence from the Crown.

The principal purpose of the settlement of at least six of the original Colonies was to establish religious freedom, and the same objective was high on the agenda of the leaders in the other Colonies. Following closely was the desire for self-government through elected legislative assemblies, and until Capitols could be erected, many of the colonial Legislatures met in churches.

The first representative assembly in America met in the Episcopal Church in Jamestown, Virginia, in 1619. The church pictured here has the original tower, while the remainder was built on the original foundations. It was used by Virginia's elected assembly as late as 1632 and possibly until the first of Jamestown's four State Houses was provided in about 1635.

In 1630, the first Massachusetts Legislature convened in the Meeting House of the First Congregational Church in Boston. Its first State House, the oldest standing Capitol Building in America, served from 1713 to 1798, but during interruptions by the British in 1774 and 1775 the legislators met in Congregational Churches at Salem, Watertown and Cambridge.

When the people of Connecticut severed themselves from Massachusetts in 1637, their first elected legislative body (General Court) met in the First Congregational Church in Hartford, which was used until 1661.

New Jersey's first Legislature met in the First Presbyterian Church of Elizabeth, New Jersey, from 1668 to 1676, and Pennsylvania's early legislative sessions were held in Quaker Meeting Houses in Philadelphia from 1683 to 1695, and then again in the Quaker Friends Meeting House from 1703 to 1707.

New Hampshire, upon separation from Massachusetts in 1739, used the First Congregational Church in Exeter for its early legislative sessions; Vermonters met in the Congregational Church in Westminster in 1775 to proclaim their independence from New York, later meeting in churches located in Castleton, Bennington and Montpelier; and New York legislators met in the First Reformed Church in Fishkill in 1776, when the British were about to seize the Capitol in New York City.

Other meeting places, such as inns, courthouses and private homes, also preceded the building of State Houses, but the church buildings were more prominent and imposing in most of the Colonies. Thus, it is no coincidence that in 1775 Patrick Henry's famous "liberty or death" speech was made at the Virginia Convention assembled in St. John's Church at Richmond, nor that the signal for Paul Revere's alerting ride was given from the steeple of Old North Church in Boston.

Neither is it a coincidence that a people who early advocated separation of church and state should, after building their Capitols, continue to open their legislative sessions with prayer—a practice which still exists in the Houses of Congress and of every State Legislature.

Nor is it a coincidence that in wording the American Declaration of Independence in Pennsylvania's State House (Independence Hall) in 1776, the framers evoked the "Laws . . . of Nature's God"; declared that all men "are endowed by their Creator with certain unalienable Rights"; appealed to "the Supreme Judge of the world"; and asserted "a firm reliance on Divine Providence" in their mutual pledge to each other of "our Lives, our Fortunes and our sacred Honor."

Early Americans opposed government by Divine Right but not by Divine Guidance. This is evidenced in some manner in every Capitol Building in America.

For instance, in 1955, the Congress set aside a small Prayer Room in the National Capitol for the individual use of members of all faiths. Its stained-glass window depicts George Washington kneeling in prayer, and the main inscription above are words from Abraham Lincoln's immortal Gettysburg Address, *"This Nation Under God."* The names of all of the States are also inscribed along with the words *"E Pluribus Unum"* ("One out of Many").

The attitude of the first President has been shared by his successors. Washington said in 1789, ". . . while just government protects all in their religious rights, true religion affords to government its surest support."

When the provision of separate Capitols did commence, Virginia again led the way among the Colonies, with the first in Jamestown in 1635 and three others there before the seat of government was moved to Williamsburg. From 1700 to 1704 the Assembly met at the College of William and Mary until the present reconstructed building was originally built in 1704.

New York was next in 1699 with a Capitol Building which served the Colony, the State and the United States. It was remodeled with a classic-columned portico by Major Pierre Charles L'Enfant, later planner of the City of Washington, in time for the inauguration of George Washington in 1785. It served as both State and Federal Capitol until 1790, and thereafter as the State Capitol until 1797.

Massachusetts followed in 1713 with its old State House, which is now a museum; Delaware in 1722; and Pennsylvania in 1736 with what is now reverently known as Independence Hall. It served as the State House until 1812. Both the Declaration of Independence

The first representative assembly in America met in the Episcopal Church in Jamestown, Virginia, in 1619.

Left: Boston State House is the oldest Capitol building in the United States.
Below: The eighteenth-century Union Jack flies over the Colonial Williamsburg Capitol.

and the U.S. Constitution were signed in this building, and it also served as the National Capitol in 1777 and again from July 2, 1778, until June 21, 1783. Rhode Island's first Capitol was the Old Colony House from 1739 to 1900, with a co-Capitol at Providence from 1763 to 1900.

In 1751, South Carolina constructed its first State House in Charleston. It burned in 1788, and James Hoban (later architect for the White House) designed and constructed the first State House in Columbia, South Carolina, in 1790 along the same classical lines as L'Enfant used in remodeling the New York State House. It was destroyed by General Sherman in 1865, but the present South Carolina Capitol was under construction and ready for occupancy in 1866.

Maryland has the oldest continuously used Capitol, the beautiful Georgian State House at Annapolis constructed in 1772, which also served as the U.S. Capitol in 1783-1784. North Carolina built Tryon Palace in 1774, a magnificent combined State House and Governor's Palace at New Bern, which has been reconstructed and restored.

Thus, by the end of the War of Independence in 1783, there were known to the leaders of the Colonies at least nine elegant State Houses, all of which were Georgian style. After the War, Capitol architecture took a decided turn to the classical forms of Greece and Rome. A leader in the political revolution, Thomas Jefferson, was also the chief proponent of the architectural change.

Jefferson felt that the new American states had a kinship with the ancient republics of Greece and Rome and that the style of their ancient temples was expressive of the monumental dignity that should attach to American public buildings. He had assembled the most complete architectural library in the Colonies; was a devout reader of Palladio, who had revived the Greek classical architecture in Italy; had planned his first design for Monticello in 1774; drew plans for Greek columns to be added to the Governor's Palace in Williamsburg while Governor of Virginia in 1779; and studied French adaptations of classic architecture while Minister to France.

He had encouraged a young architect, Charles Bulfinch, to study the style in France and Rome, and by 1785 Bulfinch had planned the classical Capitol for Massachusetts. It was completed by him in Boston from 1795 to 1798 with a spherical dome and an arched and colonnaded portico reminiscent of the Garde-meuble in the Place de la Concorde in Paris. It still stands as the central portion of the State House.

In the meantime, Bulfinch had seen the classical front added to the New York State House by L'Enfant in 1785. Fiske Kimball relates that the young architect, James Hoban, also had a drawing of the remodeled structure and that it served as the model for the South Carolina Capitol completed by Hoban in 1790. Bulfinch followed a similar classical style in his design of the Connecticut Capitol in 1796, which served that State until 1879, and is now preserved as a museum.

In 1785, while still serving as Minister to France, Jefferson was requested by Virginia officials to consult an eminent architect for a design for the Virginia State Capitol. He accommodated them by making his own sketches patterned after the Maison Carrée in southern

France and consulted with Clérisseau, French architect and writer. A model was prepared, shipped along with the plans to Virginia, and the Greek-style temple was completed in Richmond in 1789. Architectural authorities give Jefferson the credit for being the first to thus adapt a classical temple to practical uses other than that of worship. The Virginia Capitol preceded the Madeleine in Paris, the first important classic temple church in Europe, by more than twenty years.

In 1794, New Jersey's State Capitol at Trenton followed a more Georgian style but was later altered with the addition of a dome and columns.

In the planning of the Federal City and National Capitol in 1791, L'Enfant sought plans of European cities collected by Jefferson as well as the plans of the Virginia State Capitol. As Secretary of State, Jefferson conducted most of the transactions with the Federal Commissioners appointed to supervise the capital city and its public buildings. Early he wrote L'Enfant, "When it is proposed to prepare plans for the Capitol, I should prefer the adoption of some one of the models of antiquity which have had the approbation of thousands of years. . . ." Later, Jefferson proposed and prepared for the commissioners a competition for the best design. He and President Washington approved the winning submission of a gifted amateur, Dr. William Thornton.

The Thornton plan, which has remained a basic part of subsequent plans and additions, called for a spherical Roman dome, a classic arched and colonnaded front, and Palladian facades. These features, together with the higher and larger dome added later, appear in many State Capitols throughout the Nation. Some of the ideas came from State Capitol planners such as Jefferson, L'Enfant, Bulfinch and Hoban, and were later followed by them and by their successors in many public buildings in Washington and in State capital cities.

Two of the typical classic-style successors which are now used as museums are the Kentucky State House built in 1830 and the old Illinois State Capitol constructed in Vandalia in 1838. Abraham Lincoln served in the latter and led the successful fight to move the capital to Springfield.

Both past and present Capitols are evidence in brick and stone of the ability of a free people to govern themselves through elected representatives. They serve as connections with the past, a knowledge of which is essential for wise decisions as to the future.

Further description and history of the U.S. Capitol follow this historical introduction, after which there are pictures and separate articles on each State Capitol in alphabetical order, and then those of the Commonwealth of Puerto Rico and the Territories.

The Governors and their staffs, State Archivists and Librarians, and the writer's official staff and Regional Directors, are responsible for the material on these individual capitol buildings. Further aid has been received from books listed in the Bibliography, but original sources have been sought in every instance possible, especially when conflicting information appeared in previous writings. The product is the result of joint Federal-State efforts, and it is hoped that this book will contribute to increased co-operation between the National and State Capitols and those who are chosen to work therein for the American people.

The Appendix carries special credits and acknowledgments to specific individuals, and the writer expresses appreciation to each of them and especially to Don Carbone for his compilation and editing of the articles on the individual Capitols.

Left: The most renowned Statehouse in America is Independence Ha
Above: The Illinois Capitol built in Vandalia in 1838 is now a museu

The United States Capitol

Nothing in America attests more vividly to the strength of the Nation and the foresight of its founders than the Capitol Building of the United States. At the time the site was chosen in the new Federal City of Washington in 1791, it was planned that the building should be both serviceable and monumental. Major L'Enfant viewed what was then known as Jenkins Hill as "a pedestal waiting for a monument." Washington insisted that "the public buildings in size, form and elegance should look beyond the present day," and Jefferson said that "embellished with Athenian taste" it would be "the first temple dedicated to the sovereignty of the people. . . ."

Construction of the building in five sections covered a period of seventy years, from the laying of the cornerstone by President Washington on September 18, 1793, to the placement of the Statue of Freedom atop the present dome on December 2, 1863. To further complement the monumental majesty of the structure, the terraces were added in 1884, and the east-central portion was extended, enlarged and reconstructed in 1957-1962.

The interior is a veritable gallery of beautiful works of art, some of which took seventy-six years for completion, and many of which were the result of more than twenty-five years of work by artist Constantino Brumidi.

Jefferson prepared the announcement of competition for the design of the building, which was published in 1792, with $500 and a city lot as the prize. None of the first proposals was accepted. Three months after the deadline a young physician and amateur architect, Dr. William Thornton, was granted permission to submit a belated plan. Both Washington and Jefferson commended the design, and it was accepted by the commissioners appointed to supervise planning and construction.

The first section to be constructed was the original Senate wing joining the Rotunda area on the north. Construction of this section began in 1793. President Washington officiated at the formal Masonic ceremony for laying of the cornerstone. Stephen Hallet, a professional architect who had emigrated from France, was employed as superintendent. He was succeeded by George Hadfield.

Despite many difficulties—disputes between Dr. Thornton and the professional architects; slow sales of lots in the new city, necessitating the borrowing of funds; and a shortage of skills, tools and materials—the north wing of "Congress House" was virtually complete by autumn 1800, when the Government was moved from Philadelphia. On November 22 in the Senate Chamber, President John Adams addressed the first Joint Session in the new Capitol.

This first section had to accommodate the 32 Senators, 106 Representatives, the Supreme and Circuit Courts, and the Library of Congress, for not even the foundations were complete for the rest of the Capitol. In 1801, the House moved into a temporary oval-shaped hall, on the south-wing site, disparagingly known as the "Oven," but returned to the north wing in 1804.

The second section was built so as to join the future central dome section on the south. Commenced in 1804, it was not completed until 1811, although the House of Representatives first occupied it in 1807. This wing was the work of Benjamin Henry Latrobe, a thoroughly trained professional architect, who collaborated closely with Thomas Jefferson after Jefferson became President in 1801. In 1803, Jefferson created the post of Surveyor of the Public Buildings of the United States and placed Latrobe in charge both of the Capitol and the White House. Together they modified some of Thornton's Capitol design and added "Athenian embellishments" of the Greek style.

These first two sections, the original Senate and House wings, were temporarily connected by a wooden arcade, and work had barely begun on the central section when, during the War of 1812, British troops set fire to the building on August 24, 1814. A small group of determined patriots and a rain storm were all that saved the Capitol from complete destruction. While the legislative halls were being restored, Congress met first at Blodgett's Hotel and then in the "Brick Capitol," a building hastily completed by Washington citizens in 1815 in order to discourage a proposal to move the seat of government to another city. This structure was located on the site now occupied by the Supreme Court.

Latrobe resumed work on the burned-out Capitol, which he called "a most magnificent ruin," in 1815. He restored the House and Senate wings, strengthening them with marble, brick, metal and sandstone. He redesigned a semicircular House Chamber and enlarged the Senate Chamber.

Resigning in 1817 after a dispute with the Commissioner of Public Buildings, Latrobe was succeeded by Charles Bulfinch, the Boston architect who had designed the Connecticut State House of 1796 and the Massachusetts State House of 1798. Bulfinch finished work on the wings in time for the Sixteenth Congress to occupy them on December 6, 1819. More notably, he completed the third and final section of the original Capitol—the central portion which joined the wings together. This included the magnificent classic-columned east and west central fronts, the Rotunda, and the low wooden copper-covered spherical dome. The entire original unit substantially as designed by Dr. Thornton was thus completed in 1829, and the Capitol Architect's position was then abolished.

In the score of years that followed, the Nation grew rapidly—and Congress with it. By 1850 it was obvious

Overleaf: The Nation's Capitol Building took seventy years to complete.

that Congress needed larger quarters, and it appropriated $100,000 to construct new chambers for both Houses as additions on the north and the south ends of the Capitol. In 1851 President Millard Fillmore chose as architect for the project Philadelphia's Thomas U. Walter, a pupil of William Strickland, who had been Latrobe's understudy and protégé. Strickland had designed the Tennessee Capitol in 1843, and Walter had designed the Ohio Capitol in 1838.

The cornerstone for the new north and south wings was laid by President Fillmore on July 4, 1851, and Secretary of State Daniel Webster deposited in the stone an epic manuscript, which ended with these words:

> . . . And all here assembled, whether belonging to public life, or to private life, with hearts devotedly thankful to Almighty God for the preservation of the liberty and happiness of the country, unite in sincere and fervent prayers that this deposit, and the walls and arches, the domes and towers, the columns and entablatures, now to be erected over it, may endure forever. God Save the United States of America.

The new south wing was completed sufficient for occupancy by the House in 1857 and the north or Senate wing in 1859. Work had not progressed far on these extensions before it was apparent that they were going to dwarf the central dome. So, in 1855, the original dome was removed to make way for the majestic dome of today. An engineering masterpiece for the times, it has a double cast-iron shell and weighs nearly nine million pounds.

The War Between the States broke out before the new dome was finished, but at President Lincoln's insistence the work continued. He said "If people see the Capitol going on it will be a sign to them that we intend the Union shall go on."

During the Civil War the Capitol served as a military barracks, hospital, and even as a bakery when Congress was not in session. Still the work proceeded on the porticos of the new wings, which were finished by 1863.

Except for the addition of the terraces beginning in 1884, no other substantial changes were made on the Capitol until the east front extension in 1957-1962, under Architect of the Capitol J. George Stewart. As Walter had recognized almost a century before, this addition to the center section was desirable to overcome the impression that the dome overhung the east portico. President Dwight D. Eisenhower laid the cornerstone for the new east front on July 4, 1959, and most of the work was completed in time for President John F. Kennedy's inauguration there in 1961. The project substituted marble for the crumbling sandstone front, part of which now can be seen as an inside wall along a new passage linking the two chambers. Two and a half acres of space, including 102 rooms, were thus added by the thirty-two and one-half-foot extension outward. In addition, the marble walls of the wings were cleaned and the dome repainted. The project cost $11,383,000.

The Capitol now has sixteen and one-half acres of floor space with 540 rooms on five floors, and covers four acres of land. The Capitol grounds now total 131 acres, including the nearby legislative office buildings. Th landscaping was largely the work of Frederick La Olmsted in the mid 1870's.

Interior

The interior of the Capitol is a treasurehouse c beautiful paintings, sculptures, and assorted Americana with over five hundred artistic items displayed on o within the halls, chambers, Rotunda and offices.

The most notable artistic display is in the Rotunda Entered from the east front, under Luigi Persico' pediment figures of America flanked by Justice an Hope (President John Quincy Adams' suggestion), pas Persico's statues of War and Peace, through the massiv ten-ton bronze doors by Randolph Rogers telling th story of Columbus, the Rotunda is nearly 100 feet i diameter and more than 180 feet high.

The Rotunda walls display eight huge paintings, eac about 14 by 20 feet, of early American history. "Th Landing of Columbus" by John Vanderlyn, "Th Baptism of Pocahontas" by John Chapman, "Discover of the Mississippi" by William H. Powell and "Em barkation of the Pilgrims" by Robert W. Weir, typif the days of discovery and colonization. The struggle fo independence is shown in John Trumbull's quartet "The Declaration of Independence," "The Surrende of General Burgoyne," "The Surrender of Lord Corn wallis," and "Washington Resigning His Commission."

Interspersed with these paintings are several statues including Washington (a bronze copy of Jean Houdon' great work in the Virginia State Capitol), Jefferson Hamilton, Andrew Jackson, Ulysses S. Grant and th toga-draped Senator Edward D. Baker. There are tw of Lincoln, a giant marble head by Gutzon Borglun and a full-length statue done from life by a seventeen year-old girl, Vinnie Ream.

The ceiling of the dome presents Constantin Brumidi's gigantic allegory, "Apotheosis of Washing ton." In the 4,464 square feet of fresco, the firs President, in general's uniform, sits between Liberty and Victory, with thirteen other figures for the origina States completing an inner chain. Below Washington in the outer circle, is Freedom, with other groupings o Greek deities and American heroes symbolizing arts an sciences, maritime progress, commerce, mechanics an agriculture. Brumidi, at age sixty, devoted eleve months to the dome painting, finishing it in 1865.

Beneath the dome is the Rotunda frieze, a panoram in fresco of the Nation's history. Brumidi began thi when he was seventy-two, but fell from the scaffold i 1879 after completing a third of the work. He died a few months later. From Brumidi's sketches, his pupi Filippo Costaggini continued on the eight other section of the fourteen planned, leaving a thirty-foot gap by 1888. Finally, in 1953, the remainder of the three hundred-foot expanse was filled by Allyn Cox, wh added three panels.

Many other examples of Brumidi's work, both paintings and decorations, are to be found in the Capitol, particularly, in the Senate Reception Room, the Hous and Senate Appropriations Committee Rooms, and along the Patent Corridor on the ground floor of the

Senate wing. Placed in this "Brumidi Corridor" in 1968, a Carrara marble bust of the artist by Jimilu Mason honors the "Michelangelo of the United States Capitol" —or, as he signed his work, "C. Brumidi, Artist, Citizen of the U.S."

South of the Rotunda is Statuary Hall, which was the House Chamber from 1807 to 1857. In 1864, Congress, evicting the peddlers who had put the vacated room to profitable use, authorized each State to contribute two statues of distinguished citizens from its history. Eventually, the sheer weight of all this sculpture endangered the floor; now each State is limited to one figure on display in the Hall, with the others placed in the Hall of Columns and elsewhere in the building.

A few feet west of the Rotunda is the small and simple nondenominational Prayer Room. There, members of both Houses can go for individual meditation and prayer, reminded of the words from the 16th Psalm on the stained-glass window: "Preserve me, O God, for in thee do I put my trust."

Other main-floor areas in the Capitol's center section are set aside for conference and committee rooms and for offices of the House and Senate leadership and other officials. A walnut-paneled House Reception Room links the center to the south wing and the Chamber of the House of Representatives. Along the Speaker's Lobby are portraits of forty-three former Speakers of the House.

The House Chamber itself, a rectangular area 139 by 93 feet, is paneled in walnut, with gray marble behind the rostrum on which is inscribed the national motto: "In God We Trust." State Seals border the ceiling, and portraits of Washington and Lafayette flank the dais. An encircling gallery looks down on the 435 Congressmen, seated where they wish, but with Democrats to the right of the Speaker and Republicans to his left. Here are held joint sessions of Congress, as when the President delivers his annual State of the Union message.

Outside the House Chamber, to the sides beyond the cloak rooms, are the Grand Staircase East, displaying Howard Chandler Christy's painting, "Scene at the Signing of the Constitution," and Grand Staircase West, with "Westward the Course of Empire Takes Its Way," by Emanuel Leutze.

The Senate side also has a pair of great stairways, complete with massive oils. On the east is "The Battle of Lake Erie," by William H. Powell, and on the west, Francis Bicknell Carpenter's painting of Lincoln reading the Emancipation Proclamation to his Cabinet.

Of the rooms around the Senate Chamber, the President's Room and the Marble Room are to the north of the private lobby, while the office of the Vice President is situated in the northeast corner beyond the Senate Reception Room.

In the Senate Chamber, special desks are assigned to the one hundred Senators, with Republicans and Democrats to the Vice President's left and right, respectively. Around the gallery above are marble busts of twenty former Vice Presidents.

From the Senate Chamber a long hallway leads past the Senate Conference Room and the Old Senate Chamber—occupied by the Supreme Court from 1860 to 1935—through Latrobe's small Senate Rotunda to the main Rotunda.

Below the Capitol Rotunda is the Crypt, intended originally as a memorial to Washington. Underneath it is a tomb meant for the first President's remains, but it never served that purpose. Here is kept Lincoln's catafalque, used since 1865 for all who have rested in state in the Rotunda. In the Crypt itself is a marble block depicting a trio of pioneer suffragettes.

The Capitol once also housed the Library of Congress, founded in 1800. Twice burned out—in 1814 and in 1851—the Library eventually outgrew its quarters and in 1897 moved to its own building east of the Capitol.

Less known and visited are the many other areas in the Capitol which serve every possible need of the building and its occupants; from post office to restaurants, from carpenter shop to barber shop, these make the Capitol a virtual city within a city.

More than all this, however, more than the grandeur of its art and architecture, the Capitol of the United States stands for the Nation's past achievements and its future aspirations, truly a "temple dedicated to the sovereignty of the people."

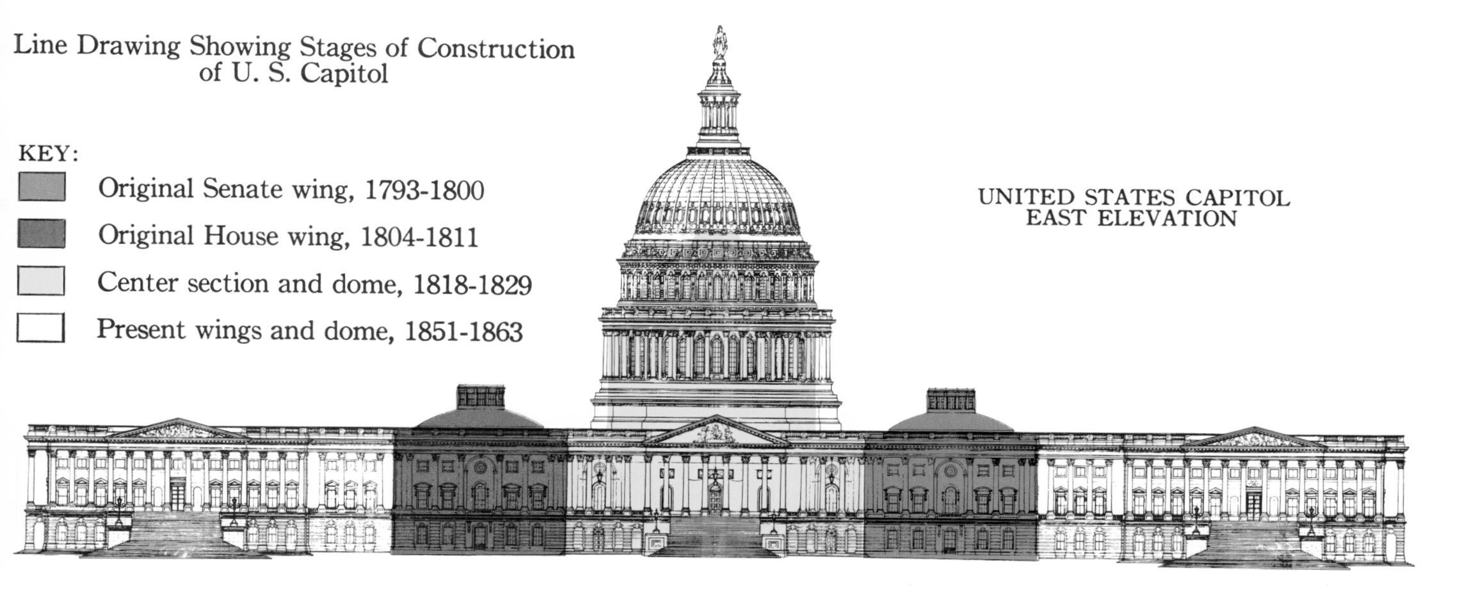

Line Drawing Showing Stages of Construction of U. S. Capitol

Jefferson Davis, President of the Confederacy, was inaugurated on the front portico of the impressive State Capitol of Alabama.

ALABAMA

THE STATE CAPITOL *Montgomery*

In 1820, one year after Alabama gained statehood, the capital was moved from Huntsville to Cahaba, where the first State Capitol building had been completed. Following a flood in 1825, the capital was moved to Tuscaloosa, where a new Capitol was completed in 1826.

In 1846, the Legislature selected Montgomery as the capital. The City of Montgomery donated a tract of land for the Capitol at the head of Dexter Avenue (then Market Street), which had been set aside for that purpose by the foresighted founder of Montgomery, Andrew Dexter. The city issued bonds and the Capitol was built at no expense to the State of Alabama. The structure, designed by Stephen Decatur Button of Philadelphia, was completed in late 1847, whereupon all records and offices were transferred to Montgomery.

On December 14, 1849, the thirtieth anniversary of Alabama statehood, a fire burned the roof of the House of Representatives. Most of the contents of the Statehouse were rescued, but the building was gutted within three hours. The Capitol was rebuilt on the foundations of the old one, of brick and plaster, and with some alterations in the original design, at a cost of $75,000. Additions, including a classic dome and stately columns, were completed in 1851.

Originally 200 feet long by 150 feet wide, the Capitol was first enlarged in 1885 by the addition of a $25,000 east wing to the rear of the building. This seventy-by-fifty-foot extension housed the Supreme Court and the State Library. Beginning in 1889, improvements were made on the Capitol Square, first with landscaping by Frederick Law Olmsted. Additional property was bought and, following an architectural competition won by Frank Lockwood, a design was adopted whereby the Capitol was to be enlarged by the addition of identical south and north wings measuring 130 by 150 feet. These were constructed in 1905 and 1911, respectively.

Included in the Lockwood additions to the Capitol was a stained glass skylight in the top of the dome. In 1937, murals painted by Roderick McKenzie depicting the history and life of Alabama were also placed in the dome.

The Lockwood design for the enlargement of the Capitol called for no alteration in the original structure, which remains as it was in 1851. The six columns on the portico are of the Corinthian style originated by Minard Lafever, while those supporting the dome are of orthodox Corinthian design. Atop the portico is the clock of the City of Montgomery, placed there in 1851.

The graceful twin spiral staircases, ascending from the entrance hall to the legislative chambers on the second floor and the visitors' gallery on the third floor, have no visible means of support. Portraits of Alabama Governors line the first floor corridors, the Governor's office, and reception rooms.

On the Capitol grounds is a handsome monument to the Confederate dead, erected by the Montgomery Ladies Memorial Association. There are also statues of Dr. J. Marion Sims, Dr. John Allen Wyeth, Jefferson Davis and Albert Patterson, and a memorial to the Marquis de Lafayette, who visited Montgomery in 1825.

At the invitation of the Alabama Secession Convention, representatives from the other seceding States met in the Senate Chamber of the State Capitol on February 4, 1861. The Confederate Congress continued to meet there until it adjourned to meet in Richmond in the summer of 1861. In the Senate Chamber the provisional and permanent Constitutions were drafted and approved and Jefferson Davis was elected President of the Provisional government of the Confederate States. He was inaugurated first President of the Confederacy on the front portico of the Capitol. Over the dome of the Capitol the first Confederate flag, the Stars and Bars, was raised by Letitia Tyler, granddaughter of President John Tyler, on March 4, 1861.

ALASKA

THE STATE CAPITOL *Juneau*

Until 1900, Sitka (Old Archangel) was the capital of Alaska. In that year, the United States Congress moved the seat of the Territorial government to Juneau. Executive offices, however, did not leave Sitka until 1906. When Alaska's first Territorial Legislature convened in March 1913, it used rented space in the Elks Lodge, a private building in Juneau.

Located on Fourth Street between Main and Seward Streets in Juneau, the present Alaska State Capitol originally was the Federal and Territorial Building but was ceded to the State by the 1958 Alaska Statehood Act. Alaska was formally admitted to the Union on January 3, 1959.

Approximately $1 million went into the site and the building. In 1911, Congress appropriated only half the amount needed to buy the site, but Alaskans were not to be denied their eventual Capitol. Afraid the building might be indefinitely delayed, the citizens of Juneau raised enough to purchase the rest of the area, which they then gave to the Federal Government.

Designed in the offices of James A. Wetmore, supervising architect for the Federal Government, the functional six-story building was constructed by the N. P. Severin Company of Chicago.

Completion of the building, on February 2, 1931, climaxed twenty years of effort by the citizens of the Territory. Frills were at a minimum. As Alaska's Delegate to Congress, Judge James Wickersham, said at the dedication, " . . . more attention is given to serviceable space and ease of access and use by a busy people . . ."

The building itself is of brick-faced reinforced concrete, with Indiana limestone used for the lower facade. The four columns of the portico, as well as the building's interior trim, are of light and dark Tokeen marble from the quarries of Alaska's Marble Island.

The Territorial Legislature thus had its first permanent chamber, and so it has remained through statehood. The second floor accommodates the State Senate and House of Representatives. The Governor's offices and the Supreme Court are on the third floor, the Superior Court on the fifth. Occupying the first floor is the Alaska Division of State Libraries. Formerly situated in the Capitol, the United States Post Office is now in the new Federal Building on Glacier Avenue.

Opposite: Tokeen Marble, a native stone, was used in the columns and interior of Alaska's Capitol. The functional six-story structure in Juneau was originally the Federal and Territorial Building.

ALASKA STATE CAPITOL BUILDING

ARIZONA

THE STATE HOUSE *Phoenix*

Situated in the center of State House Park are the Arizona State Capitol and other legislative halls of Arizona government. State House Park is located in the western section of Phoenix on 17th Avenue between Adams and Jefferson Streets.

Completed in 1900, the Capitol served Arizona during its late Territorial days and its transition to statehood in 1912. State growth increased demands on the government, necessitating the construction of an addition to the Capitol in 1918 and another in 1939. As the economy of the State surged forward after World War II, it became apparent that more space would be needed, and in 1960 new Senate and House buildings were added to the Capitol complex.

From January 22, 1864, to September 26, 1864, the Territorial Capitol was a small walled tent located at Camp Whipple in the Chino Valley near Prescott. On September 26, 1864, the Legislature convened in new quarters near the Governor's house in the town of Prescott, and it remained there until 1867, when it moved to an adobe building in Tucson. For the next ten years, most hectic in the history of the Territory, the "Old Pueblo" was the seat of government. On March 23, 1877, Prescott again became the site of the Territorial Capitol, and it remained there until February 4, 1889, when it was moved to Phoenix.

Part of the old City Hall served as the Capitol in Phoenix until occupation of the present Capitol in 1901. This building thus shows a blend of Spanish influences with modern classical Renaissance architecture.

Designed by James Riley Gordon, architect from San Antonio, Texas, the original building, now the east wing of the State House, is 182 feet long and has an extreme depth in the center of 84 feet. A dome, forty-four feet in diameter, surmounts the building, above which stands the winged "Victory Lady," sixteen feet in height. The distance from the floor to the tip of the torch is ninety-two feet, six inches.

The most striking interior architectural feature of the east wing is a central light shaft, twenty-two feet in diameter, which reaches to the dome. On each floor a railing encircles the great shaft and defines the inside border of a commodious Rotunda.

Although the main entrance is on the ground floor, the original plan, amended by reason of insufficient funds, called for an entrance by way of massive granite steps leading to the second floor.

Completed at a total cost of $135,774.29, including fixtures and incidental expenses, the original four-story structure is constructed almost entirely of Arizona materials. The first floor is of grey granite from the Salt River Mountains. The upper walls are tufa, a porous stone found in the mountains of Yavapai County. The foundation is made of malapai rock from the Camelback mountain area.

The second section of the State House, which now forms the connecting bar between the east and west wings, was designed by A. J. Gilford and erected in 1918 at a cost of $155,000. The west wing, known officially as the Department of Justice Building, was completed in 1939 at a cost of $658,441.35.

The Senate and House of Representatives wings are constructed of tufa stone, Ozark marble, Roman travertine marble and polished rainbow granite. The conforming lines of classical architecture and landscaping enhance the setting of modest, Southwestern atmosphere.

The sixteen-foot winged "Victory Lady" proudly stands on the
dome of the Arizona State House. Several additions have been
made to the building and the original section (center) now forms the east wing.

ARKANSAS

THE STATE CAPITOL *Little Rock*

The Arkansas Capitol, which resembles the National Capitol in Washington, became the seat of State government in 1911. Standing majestically amid beautifully landscaped grounds, it houses the Governor's office, the legislative chambers and other government offices.

The land on which the Capitol stands was originally acquired in 1840 for a consideration of $1,000 and consisted of approximately forty acres located on rolling land immediately west of the originally plotted portion of the city of Little Rock. Until 1901, when construction on the present Capitol began, the site was occupied by the first State Penitentiary.

Planning for the Capitol began in 1899. Actual construction on the foundation began in 1901 with the use of convict labor. In 1903, the Legislature appropriated $1 million for the building and a contract was awarded. Five years later, the funds were exhausted and the building was not completed. George W. Donaghey, who was elected Governor in 1908, promised to complete the Capitol. Under his leadership, the General Assembly appropriated additional money and employed Cass Gilbert, one of the foremost architects in America at the time, to replan and rebuild the upper part of the Capitol, including the dome.

The Legislature of 1911 was the first to convene in the new building, although the project was not entirely completed until 1914. It had cost $2.2 million and had taken fourteen years to complete.

From an architectural point of view, the Arkansas Capitol has been widely recognized as one of the finest in the country and has been used by many States as a model and guide for their Capitols. It is constructed of white native stone commonly called Batesville marble and of Indiana limestone. Its interior is of Alabama marble. The building is 420 feet long with an average width of 150 feet. The interior height of the dome from the first level is 185 feet while the top of the dome, covered in twenty-four-carat gold leaf, is 230 feet above the ground. Six magnificent bronze doors, made by Tiffany of New York, grace the entrance.

The first seat of government when Arkansas became a Territory in 1819 was at Arkansas Post, but the capital was moved to Little Rock the following year. During the Confederacy, the State Capitol was a two-story frame structure in Washington, Hempstead County.

Little Rock has had two earlier Capitols—the Territorial Capitol, where the last Territorial Legislature met in 1835, and the Old State House, which was the Capitol from 1836 to 1911. Both have been restored. Arkansas Post, the Old State House and the present

Arkansas' Capitol resembles the United States Capitol and is considered one of the Nation's finest examples of classical design.

State Capitol appeared on a 1936 U.S. postage stamp commemorating the centennial of Arkansas statehood.

The Old State House, center of almost a century of Arkansas history, is acclaimed as one of the finest examples of antebellum architecture in the South and is now used as a museum. It stands as a monument in the long road from that day of September 13, 1836, when James Conway stood in front of the Legislature and said, "Fellow citizens, the date of our existence as a free and independent State has commenced."

CALIFORNIA

THE STATE CAPITOL *Sacramento*

Set in a forty-acre park, magnificent with its wide stretches of green lawn and numerous native and exotic trees and plants, the State Capitol at Sacramento is one of the most beautiful and substantial Capitols in the United States. Within the park area, a visitor from any corner of the globe can find some species of plant life native to his homeland.

The original structure is of Roman-Corinthian design by Miner F. Butler, four stories in height and surmounted by a great dome of copper-covered wooden sheathing. At the apex of the dome is a "lantern" cupola with a small domed roof supported by twelve columns. The crowning ornament of the roof, which is covered with gold leaf, is a ball, thirty inches in diameter, made of copper and plated with gold coins. The length of the building is 320 feet, the depth 164 feet and the height (not including the dome) 94 feet. The ball on the dome is 220 feet above street level.

A most striking feature of the interior of the Capitol is the Rotunda with its domed ceiling. In the center of the Rotunda, and facing the main or west entrance of the building is a statue of Columbus making his last appeal to Queen Isabella of Spain. The walls are decorated with murals depicting historically significant periods of the State. These murals were provided for by the Legislature in 1913.

The portraits of thirty-two former Governors of the State of California are exhibited on walls of the first floor corridors. Also exhibited on these walls are the famous paintings of "The Last Spike" and "Crossing the Plains" and portraits of three of California's early-day pioneers. Replicas of the ten flags which have flown over California since 1542 are now displayed from the second floor of the Rotunda, forming a colorful circle directly under the dome.

The structure was first occupied by the Governor, State officers and the Legislature in the fall of 1869, but was not actually completed until 1874 at a cost of $2.6 million. The area covered by the original building was 52,480 square feet, and its brick foundations extend deep below the basement floor. These foundations were patterned after the ancient Spanish fortress in Panama, probably the strongest type of construction known. In 1951, a five-story addition to the Capitol was constructed at a cost of $7.6 million.

Beautification of the Capitol Park began in 1869, at about the time the Capitol was first occupied. In 1870, the grounds were graded with soil enriched with loads of river silt. During the winter of 1870-1871, some eight hundred trees and shrubs from all parts of the world were set out. This original planting consisted of some two hundred different kinds of rare plant life. Today, there are more than 40,000 trees, shrubs and flowers in the park. With more than eight hundred varieties of flora represented, ranging from subarctic to subtropical in origin, Capitol Park stands as one of the finest collections of plant life in the country.

California's first Capitol, under Spanish rule from 1770, Mexican after 1822 and American since 1846, was the famous Praesidio at Monterey. After the Constitutional Convention met in Monterey in September and October 1849, the first California Legislature convened in San Jose on December 15. A two-story adobe building there served the government when statehood was achieved in 1850. Vallejo was the next seat of government in 1852, but only for a few days. Because of poor accommodations there, the legislators moved to the Sacramento County Courthouse where they remained until the end of the session. In 1853, the Legislature convened again at Vallejo but moved the capital to Benecia after a month. Again in 1854, because of poor housing, the Legislature returned to Sacramento and a new courthouse. Except for part of 1862, when a flood forced temporary use of San Francisco's Exchange Building, the Sacramento County Courthouse served as the State Capitol until the present building was occupied in 1869.

Opposite: One significant feature of the Roman-Corinthian California Capitol is the "lantern" cupola at the apex of the copper-covered dome.

KEEP
RIGHT
STOP

COLORADO

THE STATE CAPITOL *Denver*

Colorado's State Capitol is located in Denver, the "Mile High City" with an elevation of 5,280 feet. With its great, gold-covered dome—42 feet in diameter and rising 272 feet above the ground—it stands on a ten-acre site donated in the late 1880's by Henry C. Brown. The Corinthian architectural plan of Elijah E. Myers was selected for the structure.

The cornerstone of the building was laid with appropriate ceremonies on July 4, 1890, by the Masonic Lodge, and the building was first occupied in 1895. The last wing of the building was not completed until 1907. The original cost of the building was $2.8 million; landscaping, furnishing and other work brought the total cost to $4 million.

Seventeen years were required to complete this granite building, which contains 160 beautifully appointed rooms. More than two hundred stonecutters from Maine, Vermont, California and Texas were employed. The outer walls measure five feet thick.

The cornerstone, located at the northeast corner of the building, weighed twenty tons in its rough state. In the cornerstone are to be found a Bible, an American flag, the Constitutions of the United States and Colorado, many State records, historical data, a collection of coins and a walking stick made from a piece of the keel of "Old Ironsides."

All material used in the building is native except the steel girders and trusses and the ornamental brass. The outer walls of the Capitol are of granite, quarried near Gunnison; the foundations and wall-backing are of Fort Collins sandstone; the wainscoting and many of the interior pilasters are of Colorado onyx. The pinkish-brown onyx is complemented by floors of snow-white Colorado Yule marble.

In 1908, the dome was covered with gold leaf at a cost of $14,680. In 1950, a complete regilding job was finished with double-weight gold leaf at a cost of approximately $22,000 to the State, with the Colorado Mining Association donating forty-eight ounces of gold leaf for the project.

Murals depicting the development of Colorado adorn the walls of the first-floor Rotunda. These were the gift of the Boettcher Foundation of Colorado in 1938, and were done by Allen True of Denver, a distinguished American painter. The lyrical inscriptions that accompany each panel were composed by the noted poet and writer, Thomas Nornsby Ferril of Denver.

The floor plan is designed in the form of a Greek cross measuring 383 feet by 315 feet. Each face of the structure is dominated by a high Corinthian portico. Broad corridors, paved with white marble, extend from each of the four entrances to the grand staircase in the Rotunda. Immediately above, a circular well pierces the structure to the tower beneath the dome, where the inside and outside observation galleries are located. In the dome, sixteen circular stained glass windows bear the portraits of outstanding Colorado pioneers.

Offices of the Governor and his staff occupy the southwest wing of the first floor of the Capitol. Offices of the Attorney General, Auditor, Treasurer and Secretary of State are also on the first floor. These offices have been remodeled and refurnished in recent years.

The Supreme Court Chambers and Law Library are located on the second floor of the Capitol, in the north

The granite walls of Colorado's State Capitol are five feet thick. Two hundred stone cutters from four States were employed in the construction of the building which took seventeen years to complete.

and east wings. The offices of the seven Justices of the Supreme Court are on the second and third floors of the north wing. The Senate Chamber is located in the south wing of the second floor. The State House of Representatives is located near the west side of the Rotunda, on the second floor.

The Capitol exterior was cleaned in 1966 and restored to its original light grey. Outside illumination of the Capitol, which sits on a commanding hill with attractively landscaped grounds facing the front range of the Rocky Mountains, provides an impressive sight at night. A long mall sweeps to the west and ends with the Denver Municipal Building, the Greek Theater, the Public Library and the new Denver Art Museum.

For thirty-four years Colorado had to house its Territorial and State government in temporary, scattered, rented quarters, first in Denver, then in Colorado City (now a part of Colorado Springs), back in Denver, then in Golden City. Finally, by vote of the people on November 8, 1881, Denver was made the permanent capital of the Centennial State.

Statues of Connecticut's colonial leaders and men of letters adorn all four exterior walls of the elaborate statehouse in Hartford. The building is the only Gothic-style Capitol in the United States.

CONNECTICUT

THE STATE CAPITOL *Hartford*

Hartford has been Connecticut's seat of government since it broke off from the Massachusetts Bay Colony and its first General Court convened in 1637, although the city was a joint capital with New Haven from 1701 until 1875. Of the Legislature's many previous homes in both cities, only Hartford's Old State House, designed by Charles Bulfinch and used from 1796 to 1879, is still preserved. It is now a museum.

The present Capitol, a Gothic-type structure capped by a golden dome and located adjacent to the beautiful forty-one acre Bushnell Park, became the official seat of Connecticut's State government in 1879, although the building was not actually completed until 1880. Its architect was Richard Marshall Upjohn.

The exterior is of marble from the old quarries at East Canaan, Connecticut, and granite from Westerly, Rhode Island. The interior columns are also of marble and granite quarried in Connecticut, Maine, Vermont and Rhode Island. The floor designs are famous for their beauty. The woodwork finish is oak, black walnut and ash.

The entire cost of the building was $2,532,524.43. The cost of the furniture was an additional $100,000.

Within the Capitol are the chambers and offices of the General Assembly, the headquarters of the State's elected officials and several commission offices. On the north and east sides of the exterior, historic scenes are depicted in bas-relief, while statues of colonial leaders and men of letters are found on all four exterior sides of the building at the second-and third-floor levels.

In addition to several statues, there are on the grounds "The Petersburg Express," a mortar relic of the Civil War, at the entrance to the southeast driveway, and on the north terrace, two nine-inch Dahlgren guns once used on the *Hartford*, Admiral Farragut's flagship in the famous Civil War naval battle at Mobile Bay. The figurehead and a model of the *Hartford* are in the north lobby.

The House of Representatives is on the second floor. The traditional system of unit representation, whereby each town sent either one or two representatives to the Connecticut House of Representatives, was abolished in favor of a plan creating 177 assembly districts with one representative each, effective with the 1966 State election. The House is equipped with an electronic roll call system and each desk has its own microphone. Particularly eye-catching are the beautiful, multihued, stained glass windows and the blue carpet colorfully emblazoned with the armorial bearings of the State.

The Senate Chamber is on the third floor. Visitors will be interested in the circular arrangement of the thirty-six Senators' desks in the chamber. By tradition, the Senators refer to themselves as members of "The Circle." In contrast to the blue of the House, the carpeting in the Senate is a deep red, which harmonizes with the wall paneling and desks.

The ornately carved chair on the rostrum from which the Lieutenant Governor of Connecticut presides over the State Senate was made from the celebrated "Charter Oak," the giant tree which once concealed the Charter of Connecticut from the British.

The Hall of Flags is on the first floor. On September 17, 1879, the battle flags of Connecticut's own Civil War regiments were moved from the Old State Arsenal to a permanent museum in the new State Capitol. Other mementos of the State's illustrious past are also located in the Hall of Flags.

A bronze statue of Nathan Hale stands in the first-floor corridor of the Capitol, facing the east entrance. Its marble base carries the immortal words uttered by the young patriot as he was about to be hanged: "I only regret that I have but one life to lose for my country."

DELAWARE

LEGISLATIVE HALL *Dover*

Delaware's present Capitol was completed in 1933, replacing the Old State House, which had served as the seat of State government since 1792. Known as Legislative Hall, the new building, designed by E. William Martin of Wilmington, emphasizes Georgian colonial architecture. It is constructed of handmade brick and follows the style of the old Capitol.

Legislative Hall is located east of The Green in Dover and is easily recognized by its formal beauty, highlighted with gables, chimneys and a three-tiered tower.

The interior of the building is reminiscent of the eighteenth century with the woodwork and other appointments following the theme of that era. This is particularly noticeable in the Governor's office suite, which is furnished in eighteenth-century décor. Two paintings by Thomas Sully hang in the Governor's office. Both are portraits of Delaware-born heroes of the War of 1812, Commodore Thomas MacDonough and Commodore Jacob Jones. The walls of the hallways of Legislative Hall hold other portraits of distinguished Delawarians, including many World War II heroes.

The House and Senate Chambers are on the first floor along with offices for members of the Legislature and meeting rooms for various committees. The Governor's offices as well as the office of the Lieutenant Governor and Secretary of State are on the second floor. The Legislative Reference Bureau is located temporarily in the basement.

Both the north and south ends of the building have been extended—new construction carefully preserving the colonial atmosphere of the building. The additional space is used for offices and conference rooms.

Partly because of its name, but primarily because of its long service, the Old State House remains to many Delaware citizens the State's "Capitol." It stands on the site of the first Kent County Courthouse, erected in 1722, which became the State Capitol in 1777. Originally built from 1787 to 1792, the Old State House was expanded several times until it was no longer possible to keep up with the space needs of the government. It is still used for some State offices but will eventually be restored as a landmark in the history of Delaware, first State to ratify the U.S. Constitution.

Legislative Hall replaced the Old State House which had served Delaware since 1792. The Capitol retains the colonial atmosphere appropriate to the heritage of the Nation's first State.

A. K. Pfister

319
27

FLORIDA

THE STATE CAPITOL *Tallahassee*

The offices of Florida State government are located in a beautiful landscaped section of Tallahassee known as Capitol Center—and the focal point is the Capitol building itself. A handsome, striking edifice, its architecture follows classic Greek styling, including six Doric columns. Also attractive is a high dome, with still another dome atop an arch-supported cupola.

Its cornerstone was laid in 1826, but because of financial difficulties the building was not completed until 1845, the year Florida was admitted to the Union. It was remodeled in 1901 and at that time the north and south ends were enlarged and the dome was erected. Twenty years later, the Capitol was enlarged a second time when the east and west wings were built. In 1938, a new north wing was completed, and a new south wing was added nine years later. However, the center is still the same brick building, dating back to 1845, which replaced the log cabins used originally by the Florida Territorial Legislature.

The Capitol has been the scene of historic moments in both State and American history. Here, in 1861, the Secession Convention declared Florida's withdrawal from the Federal Union and established the independent Republic of Florida. Later, Florida became a member of the Confederate States of America. It also housed three Constitutional Conventions—in 1865, 1868 and 1885. The last date was when the present State Constitution was adopted. In this same building, in 1876, the Florida Canvassing Board counted in the votes of four Republican electors, thus assuring the election of Rutherford B. Hayes as President of the United States.

Tallahassee, a tiny Indian village, was originally selected as the capital of the State because of its location. It was midway between St. Augustine, the capital in 1819, when the U.S. purchased the area from Spain, and Pensacola where the second session of the Territorial Legislature was held in 1822.

Although threatened once, Tallahassee was the only Southern capital east of the Mississippi not captured by Federal troops during the Civil War. In 1865, a Federal expedition set out against Tallahassee and came within sixteen miles of the city. But, at a point called Natural Bridge, a mixture of local citizens, a few Confederate troopers and cadets from what is now Florida State University halted the invaders. After Lee's surrender in April, and the end of the war, Federal military authorities occupied the town and the Stars and Bars were replaced with the Stars and Stripes.

Opposite: The focal point of Capitol Center in Tallahassee is this handsome building designed after the classic Greek style.
The Secession Convention met here in 1861 to declare Florida's withdrawal from the Union and establish the State as an independent republic.

DO NOT ENTER
ONE WAY

GEORGIA

THE STATE CAPITOL *Atlanta*

The present Georgia Capitol building in Atlanta was begun October 26, 1884; the cornerstone was laid September 2, 1885; and the massive building of Indiana limestone was finished and occupied June 15, 1889.

First home for the Georgia Legislature, both as a Colony and as a revolutionary State, was Savannah. The British capture of Savannah in 1778 forced successive moves to Augusta, Heard's Fort, Ebenezer and Augusta again. The government returned to Savannah in 1783, but during that session once more chose Augusta, where the U.S. Constitution was ratified January 2, 1788. After moving to the town of Louisville in 1796, the Legislature erected its first permanent Capitol. This served until the move in 1807 to the small middle-Georgia town of Milledgeville, capital for the next sixty years.

Construction of the Capitol in Atlanta followed a decision by the Legislature, confirmed by a popular election in 1877, to fix the seat of government in that city. The first Capitol in Atlanta, 1868-1889, was the Kimball Opera House.

Because of a shortage of funds, money for construction of the new Capitol in Atlanta was not provided until 1883, when the General Assembly appropriated $1 million for the project. The legislative act stipulated that the cost should not exceed that amount.

The five Capitol commissioners appointed to supervise the project selected a design submitted by the Chicago architectural firm of Edbrooke and Burnham. Counting the additional land, salaries, architects' fees, execution of the frescos in the halls and offices and other items, the cost of the entire project came to $999,881.57.

Ironically, because of the General Assembly's strict limitation on expenditures, the Capitol was built not of Georgia marble, which was in abundant supply in the State, but of less expensive Indiana limestone. Georgia marble was used, however, for the interior finish of walls, floors and steps, as well as for the cornerstone. Some 450,000 bricks from the old Atlanta City Hall, on the site of the Capitol, went into the new building, and the iron girders in the structure were produced in Pennsylvania from Georgia ore.

The style of architecture of the Capitol is classical Renaissance. Its greatest length, north and south, is 347 feet, and the greatest depth through the center is 272 feet. The open Rotunda extends upward 237 feet from the second floor.

The Byzantine dome of the Capitol is seventy-five feet in diameter and is surmounted by a fifteen-foot statue. As part of a renovation which took place in 1957 and 1958, forty-three ounces of native Georgia gold were donated by the citizens of Dahlonega and of Lumpkin County and were applied in the form of gold leaf to the dome. The gold dome of the Capitol is an impressive part of the burgeoning Atlanta skyline.

The Capitol is on a hill where Federal troops camped outside the Atlanta City Hall, during Sherman's occupation of the city in 1864. In recent years a number of handsome new State office buildings have been built around Capitol Hill, flanking the Capitol itself. From the Capitol dome the entire surrounding area may be viewed, including the beautiful Kennesaw and Stone Mountains in the distance.

Opposite: A fifteen-foot statue crowns the Byzantine dome of Georgia's Capitol, which is styled along classical Renaissance lines.

Above: Iolani Palace, the royal residence after 1882, remained the seat of government when Hawaii achieved Territorial status.

Below: The unique cultural and natural history of the Island State inspired the contemporary design of the new Capitol.

HAWAII

THE NEW CAPITOL *Honolulu*

One of the initial acts of the Legislature after Hawaii achieved statehood on March 18, 1959, was to appropriate funds for the design of a new Capitol to be erected opposite Iolani Palace, the existing Capitol. Begun in 1965, the legislative chambers and offices were used during the 1968 legislative session. The balance of the project is scheduled to be completed in the early summer of 1969.

The new Capitol, while highly functional in design, manifests symbolism of both the cultural and the natural aspects of Hawaii. From a distance, it suggests an ancient Hawaiian great house. At close range, it appears to rise out of a lovely moat—symbolic of the Pacific Ocean—on tall columns which resemble Royal Hawaiian palm trees. The exterior walls of the legislative chambers slope upward in the manner of a volcanic cone. The impression of the volcano, so characteristic of the origin and geology of Hawaii, is further enhanced by the upward view from the lobby. Here, one can look up at the sky through the huge conical opening, which exposes the lobby to the natural elements of Hawaii's tropical climate.

From the upper floors of the Capitol, especially from the Governor's offices, the full panorama of Oahu is visible: Iolani Palace, Pearl Harbor, downtown Honolulu, the mountains and the sea. This view will be enhanced as the total Capitol development is completed. The Palace will be restored and the grounds will be expanded to create broad green spaces throughout the seat of government.

Iolani Palace, the old Capitol, the only royal residence in the United States, was built by King Kalakaua. The cornerstone was laid on December 31, 1879, and on December 27, 1882, the King took up official residence. The first Iolani Palace, built in 1845 of coral blocks, occupied this same site—once a section of a Hawaiian temple which was destroyed in the early 1800's. It was used for royal receptions and other state occasions by Kings Kamehameha III, IV and V and Kings Lunalilo and Kalakaua.

The present Palace reflects the European influence brought back by Kalakaua from a trip around the world. Built of concrete block and brick with cement facing, it measures forty by one hundred feet. Its tower rises to seventy-six feet. The name "Iolani" may be translated "Bird of Heaven" and signifies to Hawaiians the Supreme Being above all gods. It was a sacred name in old Hawaii and was given to both Kamehameha II and Kamehameha IV.

Upon Kalakaua's death in 1891, his sister, Liliuokalani, became Queen and lived in the Palace until the overthrow of the monarchy in 1893. Two years later she spent nine months as a prisoner in the Palace, following an insurrection that attempted to restore her to the throne.

The Palace became the executive building of the republic and remained the seat of government after Territorial status was achieved in 1900. The House of Representatives met in the Throne Room and the Senate in the State Dining Room, while the Governor and Lieutenant Governor occupied what had been the royal bedrooms on the second floor.

The Governor's office and both houses of the Legislature retained use of the Palace's rooms while awaiting completion of the new Capitol. When restored as it was in the days of the monarchy, Iolani Palace will live on as a vivid representation of Hawaii's history and cultural preservation.

IDAHO

THE STATE CAPITOL *Boise*

Located in the heart of Boise in the center of two beautifully landscaped city blocks at the end of Capitol Boulevard, the Idaho State Capitol commands an impressive view of the capital city.

Idaho Territory was organized March 4, 1863, from what are now the States of Idaho and Montana and a large portion of the State of Wyoming. Lewiston was the capital until the second Legislature designated Boise in May 1865. Idaho was reduced to its present boundaries in 1868, and on July 3, 1890, it was admitted to the Union as the forty-third State.

A small frame building served the Territorial Legislature in Lewistown. In Boise, the Legislature occasionally met in such places as the Overland Hotel or at Hart's Exchange, later known as the Central Hotel. A more substantial building was used as the Capitol from late 1886 until 1912.

By act of March 3, 1905, provision was made for a Capitol Building Board. The Governor, Secretary of State, State Treasurer and two public-spirited citizens became the Capitol Building Commission. The original appropriation was only $250,000, because much of the cost of the building was to have been paid from the sale of public lands allowed to the State by the Idaho Admission Act. The Capitol Commission decided to serve as its own contractor. Work began on the first floor during the summer of 1906.

The problem of obtaining sandstone for the outside finish was solved when the Commission purchased a stone quarry at Tablerock in October of that year. The site was convenient for use of prison labor and the Commission regarded the land as a sound investment.

The original design for the State Capitol, following the same classical style of architecture as the National Capitol, was only for the central section and the dome. The construction of it took more than six years. In August 1912, a contract was awarded for the design of wings for the building. Actual construction of the wings was delayed until the Legislature authorized funds for completion in 1919. The entire structure was finished at the end of 1920.

When completed, the building cost $2,098,455, with another $130,833 for furnishings. It covers 50,646 square feet, with floor space totaling 201,720 square feet. The height of the building, including the bronze eagle atop the dome, is 208 feet.

Alaskan marble was used on the floors, staircases and interior ornamentation, while the inside walls are of

The magnificent Idaho Capitol located in the heart of Boise commands a sweeping view of the city and the surrounding mountains.

Vermont marble. The Rotunda proper has two circular promenades. The one on the fourth floor is sixty feet in diameter and the one on the third floor eighty feet. It is of unique construction in that it is supported by columns. The fourth floor features 301 life-like specimens of birds. On the main floor is a gilded statue of George Washington on horseback, carved from native yellow pine.

The House and Senate Chambers are located on the third floor on the east and west sides, respectively.

On the fiftieth anniversary of Idaho statehood in 1940, the Capitol building was honored by being depicted on a U.S. postage stamp.

ILLINOIS

THE STATE CAPITOL *Springfield*

The handsome domed building which is the State Capitol of Illinois is actually the sixth Capitol the State has had since it was welcomed into the Federal Union in 1818. Construction began in 1868 but was not completed until 1888, twenty years later, although the various departments of the government started occupying the structure in 1876. The cost skyrocketed far above the original figure of $3 million, winding up at approximately $4.5 million.

Occupying nine acres of land, the building, which measures 379 by 268 feet, is in the shape of a Latin cross. The focal point is a vast dome, which rises to a height of 361 feet, with still another forty-four feet to the tip of its flagstaff. It is topped with a red beacon as a warning light for approaching aircraft. The dome is supported by walls seventeen feet at the base. The foundation, ninety-two feet in diameter, sits on solid rock. Farther below this strata is a rich vein of coal.

The Rotunda walls and arches are solid stone, faced with Missouri red granite. This material also was used for the polished columns on the Rotunda's third floor. The bases of these columns are blue granite and Tuckahoe marble. Various kinds of marble are used extensively throughout the interior, including the grand stairway. The interior is very impressive with marble mosaics, historical murals, oil paintings and statuary.

As visitors enter the Rotunda their eyes go to a bronze statue of "Illinois Welcoming the World" which stands at the center of the Rotunda floor. The statue was first displayed at the Columbian Exposition in Chicago in 1893. Branching off from the Rotunda are two stories of executive offices in the four wings of the building.

The present Capitol building was preceded by five other such structures, with only its immediate predecessor being in Springfield. The others were located in Kaskaskia and Vandalia.

Kaskaskia served as the first capital when Illinois was organized as a Territory and continued until 1820, two years after Illinois became a State, when Vandalia was selected as the new capital. The first two Capitols are no longer in existence. Both the State House and the city of Kaskaskia have been swallowed up by the rampaging Mississippi, while the original building at Vandalia was destroyed by fire in 1823 and was replaced by a brick structure.

However, pressure for a more centrally located capital was growing. The General Assembly called for a popular vote to choose from six sites. The subsequent vote in 1834 was so close for three cities—Alton, Springfield and Vandalia—that the result was never announced, and Vandalia remained as the capital.

Some citizens, including Abraham Lincoln, mounted a heavy campaign to move the capital to Springfield. Finally in 1837 they were successful, despite the efforts of Vandalians who razed the old building and built a new $16,000 State House in the summer of 1836 while the Legislature was in recess.

The cornerstone for the first building in Springfield was laid on July 4, 1837, and operations began there in 1839, a year before the officially set date. It took sixteen years to complete and ended up costing twice as much as its orginally estimated $130,000. It remained as the Capitol until 1876 when the State government moved to the present structure. The old building was used as the Sangamon County Courthouse. Recently restored to its appearance in Lincoln's day, at a cost of $7 million, it was dedicated in 1968 as a Lincoln shrine.

Opposite: Illinois' General Assembly convenes in this handsome structure built in the shape of a Latin cross. The vast dome, rising to a height of 361 feet, is supported by walls 17 feet at the base.

INDIANA

THE STATE HOUSE *Indianapolis*

When Indiana became a State in 1816, Congress donated four square miles of land on which to build a capital city, the land to be selected from those sections of the public land remaining unsold. The grant further provided that proceeds from the sale of lots within the four square miles could be used to defray the costs of erecting the Capitol and other public buildings.

In 1820, a commission appointed by the Legislature selected a site at the juncture of the White River and Fall Creek for the new capital. The site was approved by the Legislature the next year and, after much debate, the proposed city was named Indianapolis, meaning Indiana City. In April 1821, the work of laying out the city began. One of the surveyors, Alexander Ralston, had been employed by the French engineer, Pierre L'Enfant, in mapping out Washington, D.C., and at his suggestion the city was to be one mile square, with streets crossing at right angles and four wide avenues pointing to a circle in the center.

The Capitol grounds, known as The State House Square and Governor's Circle, near the center of Indianapolis, are cited in the Constitution of Indiana and by that authority are never to be leased or sold. The latter plot is the site of the famous Indiana Soldiers' and Sailors' Monument. The second of two State Capitols occupies State House Square.

The State government moved from a small two-story stone structure in Corydon to a very similar building, the Marion County Court House, in Indianapolis in 1825. It occupied the first specially constructed Capitol in Indianapolis from 1835 to 1878.

The present State Capitol is a classic Corinthian-design four-story building of Indiana limestone with executive offices of the State government, including those of the Governor, Lieutenant Governor, Secretary of State, Treasurer, Auditor, Attorney General and government agencies. It also contains the chambers of the House of Representatives, the Senate, and the Supreme and Appellate Courts.

Construction on the present Capitol began on October 12, 1878, on the site of the former Capitol and was completed ten years later on October 2, 1888. Two architects were engaged in its building—Edwin May from 1878 to 1880 and Adolf Scherer from 1880 to 1888. The cost was $1,980,969, just under its $2 million appropriation.

The distinguishing feature of the Capitol is the massive dome, 72 feet in diameter and rising from the center to a height of 234 feet. The dome is constructed of stone and rests on eight great columns of Maine granite. Eight Italian Carrara marble statues of heroic size placed within the Rotunda at the third floor level represent Law, Oratory, Agriculture, Commerce, Justice, Liberty, History and Art. On each floor a corridor sixty-eight feet wide extends the entire length of the building and is illuminated from attic to basement by ample skylights. A double row of marble columns, piers and pilasters support the upper structure.

Memorials to many Hoosier heroes are placed inside the Capitol and on its nine acres of grounds. A statue of Oliver P. Morton, Governor of Indiana from 1861 to 1867, stands outside the east entrance to the building. On the southeast corner is a statue of Thomas A. Hendricks, Governor from 1873 to 1877 and Vice President of the United States in 1885. In front of the south entrance is a bust of Robert Dale Owen, author, statesman, philanthropist and active campaigner for the rights of women. Just west of the south wing of the building is a bust of Christopher Columbus. Portraits of Indiana's Governors line the fourth-floor corridor.

The massive stone dome rising from the center of the Hoosier Capitol building is supported by eight wide granite columns.

IOWA

THE STATE HOUSE *Des Moines*

Created as a separate Territory in 1838,.Iowa moved its capital from Burlington to Iowa City in 1842. Later that year, the Territorial Legislature occupied the first permanent Capitol—now the administration building of the University of Iowa—remaining there until 1857.

In 1854, the Fifth General Assembly of the State decreed a location "within two miles of the Raccoon forks of the Des Moines River" for its new Capitol in Des Moines. The exact spot was chosen when Wilson Alexander Scott gave the State nine and a half acres with a hilltop view of the countryside. A group of Des Moines citizens built a temporary Capitol (later bought by the State) near the present location of the Soldiers' and Sailors' Monument. In use from 1857, it was eventually destroyed by fire, but in the meantime the permanent Capitol was being planned and built. In 1870, the General Assembly established a Capitol Commission to employ an architect, choose a plan and proceed with work on the permanent Capitol. The frugal legislators, however, stipulated that the cost was not to exceed $1.5 million of available funds and that the tax rate was not to be increased. Unfortunately, this proved uneconomical, for soon after the cornerstone was laid in 1871, a hard winter caused the cheap materials of the foundation to crumble. Almost all of the stone work had to be redone. A new commission obtained adequate appropriations and a new cornerstone was placed in 1873. Work was finished in 1886 at a cost of $2,873,294.59.

The modified Romanesque building was dedicated in January 1884, with the General Assembly in session. The executive offices were occupied the next year, and the Supreme Court's chamber was dedicated in 1886.

In 1902, in order to modernize and repair the building, a third Capitol Commission was created. While work proceeded, a disastrous fire in the north wing, January 4, 1904, ruined the House Chamber and damaged other offices. The commission restored the building, purchased paintings and mosaics and redecorated almost all the interior. The original decorations are still in the Senate.

The commanding feature of the Capitol is the central towering dome. This was constructed of steel and stone and covered with gold. The gold leaf was replaced in recent years at a cost of $79,938. The dome is surmounted by a lookout lantern reached by long, winding stairs, and a finial 275 feet above the ground floor. The Rotunda beneath the dome is sixty-seven feet in diameter. Four smaller domes of simple design rise from the four corners of the Capitol. The pediment over the front entrance discloses a fine piece of allegorical sculpture. The building itself measures 364 by 247 feet.

Materials for the Statehouse came from Iowa and neighboring States: stone for the basement was quarried in Johnson County; stone for the main structure from Carroll County in Missouri; steps, columns and other parts from Anamosa, Iowa, Ohio, Minnesota and Illinois. Imported and domestic marble of twenty-nine kinds was used in the interior; and the wood used was nearly all from Iowa forests of black walnut, cherry, catalpa, butternut and oak.

A hilltop overlooking the Iowa countryside provides a lovely site for the Romanesque-style State House in Des Moines.

The Senate Hall is 58 feet long, 91 feet wide, and 41.9 feet high. It is finished in marble, white oak and scagliola. Furnishings are mahogany. The figures in the ceiling represent Industry, Law, Agriculture, Peace, History and Commerce. The Hall of the House of Representatives, finished in marble, scagliola, and black walnut, is 74 by 91.4 feet, and 47.9 feet in height.

Over the main stairway hangs "Westward," a large painting by Edwin H. Blaskfield, signifying the settling of Iowa. Above this are six Venetian mosaics representing Defense, Charities, Education and the Executive, Legislative and Judicial branches. The Rotunda features many battle flags and twelve statues of Art, History, Science, Law, Fame, Industry, Peace, Commerce, Agriculture, Victory, Truth and Justice.

KANSAS

THE STATE HOUSE *Topeka*

Kansas was admitted to the Union in 1861, and Topeka was selected as the capital city of the State in an election held that November. Several buildings served as meeting places for the House and Senate during the following eight years.

At the legislative session of 1866, a plan was adopted for a State House. The east wing, started that year, was completed in 1873, using stone from Geary County. The other three wings were built of stone from Cottonwood Falls. The first legislative session in the building was held in 1870, although work on the west wing did not begin until 1879.

By the summer of 1880, the west wing was practically enclosed. The House of Representatives of 1881 met in the unfinished new hall for that session, while State offices were occupied during the same years. The total cost of the west wing was only about $300,000 against $500,000 for the east wing, which was very much inferior to the former in material and workmanship.

Construction of the main building was authorized in 1881. In 1892, rooms were temporarily finished and used on the ground floor of the south wing. The completed building cost the State of Kansas $3,200,588.92, the last of which was paid by the State in March 1903.

The building measures 399 feet north and south, 386 feet east and west, and 304 feet to the top of the dome. There are 296 steps from the top of the building to the top of the dome.

At one time, some State offices had handsome porcelain bathtubs and washstands of pure white marble, put in during the Populist administration, which also added the Georgian marble in the third-floor Rotunda.

The wainscoting in the center of the building on the first floor is of Tennessee marble, in the west corridor of Mandual tile, and in the east corridor of Georgian marble. The large upper panels in wainscoting on the second floor are built of Siena and Lambertin marble from Italy. The Governor's offices are on this floor and are finished in white mahogany from Mexico.

The Senate Chamber and the House of Representatives are located on the third floor. The large panels on the wall of the Senate Chamber are Mexican onyx. All of the wood in the Senate is walnut, except for the solid cherry desks and chairs of the Senators. The material around all of the doors in the Senate Chamber is beautifully cut Tennessee marble. The marble in the House is from Tennessee, and the wainscoting on the east wall is made of various kinds of imported marble, trimmed with Italian Carrara, with panels of Brocelian marble and Belgian green marble in the base of the handsome columns.

The principal features of the dome interior are the four large mural paintings near the top. The east panel represents Religion, Knowledge and Temperance; the north panel, Plenty; west panel, Peace; and the south, Power.

There are sixteen acres of land inside the sidewalk line of the Capitol grounds.

The Kansas State House, built entirely of native stone in the popular classical style, is 304 feet high with 296 steps leading from the top of the building to the top of the dome.

KENTUCKY

THE STATE CAPITOL *Frankfort*

Kentucky's classic Capitol is the fourth erected in Frankfort. While a district of Virginia, Kentucky held nine conventions in Danville, finally drawing up a State Constitution there in 1792. The Constitutional Convention designated Lexington as the site of the first General Assembly, which, meeting in a log building in that town in June 1792, chose Frankfort as the permanent seat of government.

The first Capitol there, built in 1793-1794, burned in 1813; its replacement, completed in 1816, suffered a similar fate in 1824. The third, modeled in part after a Greek temple to Minerva, was finished in 1830. This Old State House is now the home of the Kentucky Historical Society and contains the State's archives, a museum of history and a library.

Impetus for a new Capitol came when it was determined that the Federal Government would give the State at least a million dollars for Civil War and Spanish-American War claims. The 1904 General Assembly matched the amount and appointed a Capitol Building Commission. At a special session the next year, the Legislature chose a thirty-four acre site in South Frankfort. Ground was broken that May and the cornerstone laid in June 1906.

Partially occupied in 1909 and dedicated on June 1, 1910, the new Capitol cost $1,820,000, which was widely regarded as a great bargain for a public building. That figure included land, construction, and furnishings. Remarkably, only one piece of power-driven machinery, a steam concrete mixer, was used; all other equipment, including a crane and steel bender, was hand operated.

Surrounded by a stone terrace, the three-story Capitol has oolitic limestone facing above a base of Vermont granite. The building is 403 feet from east to west, 180 feet north to south; its Rotunda measures fifty-seven feet in diameter. The outer walls are graced with seventy ornamental Ionic columns of Bedford stone.

Over the north entrance, the sculptured pediment shows Kentucky as a heroic woman, standing before the chair of State and attended by the personified figures of Progress, History, Plenty, Law, Art and Labor.

Inside, thirty-six Vermont granite columns flank the long nave, adorned with oil paintings in lunettes and at each end with a mural scene from the life of Daniel Boone. The east mural shows explorer Boone and his party first viewing the Bluegrass Region, while at the west end of the nave he is shown negotiating with the Indians for the purchase of Kentucky. The interior walls and stairway are of white Georgia marble, the floors of light Tennessee and dark Italian marble.

There is much French influence within. The Rotunda, dome and lantern are copied after the Hotel des Invalides, site of Napoleon's tomb in Paris. Stairways, balustrades and bannisters resemble those of the Paris Opera, while the State Reception Room was inspired by Marie Antoinette's drawing room in the Grand Trianon Palace at Versailles.

The House and Senate Chambers feature scagliola—ornamental plastering with a marble-like effect. Both the legislative halls and the Court of Appeals are rich in mahogany.

Bordering the Kentucky River, the well-landscaped Capitol grounds include the Governor's Mansion and the Capitol Annex.

Opposite: Seventy ornamental Ionic columns grace the exterior walls of the State Capitol in Frankfort, Kentucky.

STOP

LOUISIANA

THE STATE CAPITOL *Baton Rouge*

Louisiana's State Capitol at the time of construction was the tallest building in the South. Thirty-four stories, 450 feet in height, it was erected on the site of the old campus of Louisiana State University in Baton Rouge, which now is converted into twenty-seven acres of landscaped grounds. The Capitol was built in fourteen months, from January 1931 to March 1932, at a cost of $5 million. It was designed by Architects Weiss, Drefous and Seiferth of New Orleans.

The Capitol's elaborateness lies in intricate and costly artistic interpretations of the State itself. The story of Louisiana is the decorative theme of every detail and object that went into the edifice. Yet the building is efficiently designed and provides 249,000 square feet (nearly six acres) of floor space for governmental agencies.

In front of the building, broad steps of Minnesota granite are flanked by statuary groups called "The Patriots" and "The Pioneers." The forty-eight steps arranged in four groups are each inscribed with the name of a State, the thirteen of the lower groups representing the original colonies. The remaining steps are inscribed with the States' names in order of their admission to the Union, the State of Louisiana being the eighteenth in 1812.

The entrance door of the Capitol, fifty feet high, is decorated in architrave by Lee Lawrie. The molded bands depict the natural resources and industry of Louisiana, and over the door is the State Seal and Motto. On either side is carved a passage from the document of the Louisiana Purchase. Beneath these are friezes designed by Adolph Alexander Weinman, on the east, "The Spirit of Liberty and Peace," and on the west, "Government." Over the huge windows of the Senate and House of Representatives in the base of the building are carved the heads of twenty-two of the great men who have had a part in Louisiana history.

Around the fourth floor, from which the building rises to its towering height, is a frieze by Ulric Ellerhusen. On the south it portrays "Young Louisiana" and its early struggles and admission to the Union. On the west is "Louisiana at War"; on the north, "Louisiana Jurisprudence"; and on the east, "Louisiana at Peace."

This frieze is reproduced in bronze in the Memorial Hall around a ceiling that is a pictorial interpretation of Louisiana's history. On a field of golden oak leaves and red acorns is emblazoned the emblem of each nation to which Louisiana has belonged—Indian, Bourbon France, Napoleonic France, Spain, the Confederate States of America and the United States.

The Memorial Hall is the most magnificent chamber of the building. Of huge proportions, 35 by 120 feet, the hall has a floor of polished lava from Mount Vesuvius. In the center of the floor is a huge bronze plaque on which is outlined in relief a map of Louisiana. The plaque is ten feet in diameter and weighs 3,290 pounds. The names of Louisiana's sixty-four parishes (counties) are carved around the border. Leading resources and products of each parish are also depicted. Murals by Jules Guerin, a distinguished French painter, are at either end of the hall. Above the entrance to the Senate Chamber is "Abundance of the Earth" and over the House entrance is "Goddess of Time."

The Capitol contains more than thirty varieties of marble and stone from every producing State and several foreign countries. The walls of the Memorial Hall are of Italian marble, dark red, brecciated with white. The Senate Chamber is of French marble in violet, with panels of grey from Germany. The Senate lounge, leading off from a corridor, is walled in marble from the Pyrenees Mountains, black veined with white, with rose and yellow markings.

From the observation tower, almost 450 feet above the ground, it is possible on a clear day to see the surrounding country for a distance of twenty miles. The Mississippi River, winding out of the north, passes the Capitol near its base and disappears around a great bend into the south.

The skyscraper Statehouse sharply contrasts with Louisiana's Old Capitol, still standing in downtown Baton Rouge. A turreted blend of the Norman, Gothic and Moorish, its style has attracted praise and criticism since it was begun in 1847. Burned by Federal troops in 1862 and later rebuilt, it again became the Capitol in 1882. It is now used as a war memorial and museum.

Baton Rouge did not become Louisiana's capital city until 1849. The first seat of government under the State and its predecessor Territory of Orleans was New Orleans, where the Spanish regime's Government House was used until 1828. The capital was Donaldsonville from 1828 to 1831 but then reverted to New Orleans. During the Confederate and Reconstruction periods the government was situated in Opelousas, Shreveport and New Orleans before returning to Baton Rouge.

Opposite: Every decorative detail in the skyscraper Capitol at Baton Rouge illustrates an aspect of the Creole State's History.

The State House of Maine originally resembled the Boston State House. In 1909, it was redesigned in the Greek Rėnaissance style l now retains only the "Bulfinch Front" of the original structure.

MAINE

STATE HOUSE *Augusta*

Citizens of Portland built Maine's first State House there in 1820 when Maine was separated from Massachusetts and granted statehood. In 1827, Augusta was designated the capital, and in 1829, the cornerstone of the present State House was laid.

The State House, designed by the eminent Boston architect, Charles Bulfinch, and built of granite from nearby Hallowell, Maine, was completed in 1831. The Legislature first met there on January 4, 1832. Originally estimated to cost $80,000, the Capitol, after landscaping and furnishing, actually required $139,000.

Bulfinch's design for the Maine Capitol was similar to that for his earlier Boston State House. This is still evident in the columns-over-arches treatment of their front porticos. The architect did not settle for copying himself, for each design displays its own individuality.

In 1909-1910, the State House was redesigned by G. Henri Desmond in Greek Renaissance style and rebuilt almost completely. Hardly more than the "Bulfinch front" was retained from the original structure. Its length was doubled to three hundred feet. A 185-foot dome, crowned by W. Clark Noble's copper figure of Wisdom, covered with gold, gives the building imposing height. Spacious wings were constructed for the House of Representatives on the north and the Senate and executive chambers on the south.

The State Archives offices are located on the second floor of the Capitol. The State Library occupies the first two floors of the north wing, while the State Museum is on the first floor south.

The Museum features examples of the minerals, plants and animals found in Maine, as well as many items from the State's history. One display in particular is most unusual: Live land-locked salmon and brook trout swim in a stream, across which stretches a replica of an old-fashioned covered bridge.

Along the Capitol's corridors hang portraits of distinguished sons of Maine, and battle flags are exhibited in the Rotunda.

The State House's beautifully landscaped grounds, covering thirty-four acres, reach to the Kennebec River, an appropriate setting for this distinguished building.

MARYLAND

STATE HOUSE *Annapolis*

The Maryland State House in Annapolis is an imposing edifice with a prominent place in American history. This building, the third Capitol to occupy the commanding site of the town's highest point, was begun in 1772 at a cost of 7,500 pounds sterling. The large, unique wooden dome, made without nails and held together with wooden pegs, was added after the War of Independence.

Although the General Assembly no longer meets in the original section, it is the oldest State Capitol still fulfilling its original purpose. Since 1780 only one session of the Maryland Legislature has been held elsewhere; in 1861 the session was moved about seventy miles west to Frederick because of the strong Confederate sentiment of the people of southern Maryland.

In its earliest years the State House was the scene of events of major historical importance. Here, as the American Revolution was drawing to a close, the Continental Congress met, with Annapolis serving as the capital of the United States from late November 1783 until June 1784.

General George Washington came to Annapolis on December 23, 1783. In the room now on display as the Old Senate Chamber, he appeared before Congress and resigned his commission as Commander-in-Chief of the Continental Army. Thomas Jefferson, author of the Declaration of Independence, was there; so were signers Richard Lee, who had offered the resolution that the Declaration be adopted; Samuel Chase, future Justice of the United States Supreme Court; and James Monroe, future President.

Three weeks later in the same room the Treaty of Paris was approved by Congress, thus officially ending the American Revolution. On that January 14, 1784, in the Old Senate Chamber, the United States became one of the family of nations. And here, on September 14, 1786, the Annapolis Convention issued its call for the gathering which met in Philadelphia the following year to write the American Constitution.

Thus, it may rightly be said that this State House witnessed the final acts of the American Revolution as well as one of the major events leading to the formation of a sound government of the United States.

The State House is divided into two parts. The colonial or original building can be recognized by its beautiful architecture, using plaster walls and wooden columns, while the annex or new part uses matched marble walls and marble columns. A broad, black line in the floor separates the old from the new. Early in the twentieth century, the State House was redesigned in such a way as to preserve all of its original colonial features, while adding a $600,000 annex to the west. This annex contains the present meeting places of the Maryland Senate and House of Delegates.

The following features of historical interest are found in the State House: Old Senate Chamber, with the original Charles Willson Peale painting of Washington, Lafayette and Tench Tilghman at Yorktown; Edwin White's famous painting of Washington resigning his commission; the Flag Room with many historic banners, including one of the Revolutionary era; and many portraits of prominent Maryland figures, including the four Maryland signers of the Declaration of Independence.

Opposite: The distinguished State House of Maryland (circa 1772), where General Washington resigned as head of the Continental Army, is the oldest Capitol still fulfilling its original purpose.

MASSACHUSETTS

THE STATE HOUSE *Boston*

The choice of the site for the Massachusetts State House, at the summit of Boston's Beacon Hill, was made in 1795. The cornerstone was laid on the Fourth of July that year by Governor Samuel Adams, assisted by Paul Revere, Grand Master of the Grand Lodge of Masons. It was carried to the site by fifteen white horses, representing the number of States of the Union at that time.

Designed by the Boston architect, Charles Bulfinch, the Massachusetts State House was completed early in 1798. It replaced a smaller State House which had been, for more than sixty years before the American Revolution, the seat of Massachusetts' colonial government. The Old State House, topped by the British Lion and Unicorn, was built in 1713 at what is now Washington and State Streets. From its balcony was proclaimed the American Declaration of Independence. Within its walls the Constitutional Convention sat during the first three months of 1780, reviewing and revising John Adams' draft Constitution for the Commonwealth of Massachusetts. Said to be one of the oldest public buildings in America, it is now used as a historical museum.

Facing south, on a sunlit day the present State House is a colorful sight with the sun bringing out the warmth of the red brick walls, the gleam of the white pillars and trim, and the brilliant reflection of the gold-leaf dome.

The original building has a 172-foot front; the height, from base course to pinnacle, is 155 feet; and the foundation is about 106 feet above the waters of the bay. The dome is 53 feet in diameter and 35 feet high. The original cost of the building was approximately $134,000.

The dome, originally shingled and painted a lead color, was covered with copper by Paul Revere and Sons in 1802. In 1831, the roof was covered with new copper and painted grey. At a later date it was painted yellow and, since 1874, it has been covered with gold leaf. World War II brought a temporary transformation to battleship grey. The dome itself has been rebuilt twice, in 1859 and 1897, when an effort was made to reproduce the lines and proportions of the original.

Extensive improvements have been made since the original construction, including five additions. The first, in 1831, was expanded in 1853-1855 and replaced in 1889-1895. Wings of white Vermont marble and granite were added from 1914 to 1917 when the State House was painted white. Lastly, from 1958 to 1960, the underground Archives and Records Building was added in front of the west wing.

When the General Court (legislature) met in 1898, the Senate moved from its old chamber, now its reception room, to the former House Chamber in the Bulfinch building, and the House occupied new quarters in an addition designed by Charles E. Brigham. The House, however, refused to sit unless the "Sacred Cod" moved with it. The wooden replica of a codfish has since 1784 (and perhaps since 1742) always hung where the Speaker of the House can see it.

The interior of the building is most impressive. From the ten-columned Doric Hall, next to the entrance, the Senate staircase Hall leads to Memorial Hall—often called the Hall of Flags. Side stairs lead from the Senate Staircase Hall to the Senate Chamber on the east, and the Governor's office and the Council Chamber on the west. Beyond Memorial Hall, the House staircase branches to the House on the west, and on the east to the office of the Secretary of the Commonwealth. The building also includes the State Library.

At the summit of Beacon Hill in Boston stands the Massachusetts State House. Governor Samuel Adams, assisted by Paul Revere, laid the cornerstone of the building on the Fourth of July, 1795.

MICHIGAN

THE STATE CAPITOL *Lansing*

On a spacious landscaped site across from the Lansing City Hall stands Michigan's four-story Capitol, topped by a dome and spire rising sharply to 276 feet. Including its porticos and steps, the building measures 420 by 273 feet. Above a limestone foundation, its walls are faced with white Ohio sandstone.

The design, in later classical Renaissance, was the work of Elijah E. Myers. An allegorical bas-relief, symbolic of Michigan's development, decorates the pediment high above the east entrance.

On either side of the Rotunda, a grand staircase rises from the ground floor to the fourth. Balconies look down upon the Rotunda's display of battle flags and its floor of glass blocks set in iron. At the base of the dome are murals of Michigan Science, Astronomy, Justice, Industry, Navigation, Education, Art and Agriculture.

The ground floor and first floor house various historical exhibits, including facsimiles of the four State Constitutions. The House and Senate Chambers and the executive offices are on the second floor, the judicial chambers and the House and Senate galleries on the third.

The Capitol's granite cornerstone was laid on October 2, 1873, and the building was dedicated in January 1879. It cost $1,510,130.

Two previous State Capitols were destroyed by fire, but after they had completed their governmental function. The Capitol in Detroit from 1828 to 1848, later the city's first high school and public library, burned in 1893. The first Lansing Capitol, a frame building, was replaced by a brick structure in 1853 and was demolished by flames in 1884.

Lansing became the capital of Michigan in 1848, succeeding Detroit eleven years after the State was admitted to the Union. Detroit had been the seat of government during Territorial times. The 1835 Constitution called for selection of a permanent State capital by 1847. After weeks of debate, the Legislature chose Lansing as the most accessible site, even though there were few roads and no railroads to the town. Its industry consisted of one sawmill. There was dense forest and a single log house.

Both the city and the government have since grown greatly. A Capitol Development Program calls for construction of a new Capitol west of the present structure, as well as several other buildings nearby to house much of the executive and judicial branches of the government.

The stately white granite Capitol of Michigan
is situated on a spacious landscaped site in Lansing.
The four-story building follows the classical Renaissance style.

MINNESOTA

THE STATE CAPITOL *St. Paul*

The Minnesota Capitol in St. Paul, sitting atop a hill, can be seen for many miles in most directions and it is well worth viewing. One of its many outstanding features is its huge dome, said to be the world's largest unsupported marble dome. The remainder of the building is of Georgia marble, except for the foundation and steps of native grey granite.

The structure was designed by the renowned architect Cass Gilbert, who received the contract as a result of a design he submitted in competition sponsored by a legislative commission. Gilbert later designed the Capitols of Arkansas and West Virginia.

This is the third Capitol in St. Paul. The first was built in 1854. Prior to that year, the Minnesota Territorial Legislature had met in the Central House in St. Paul. The 1854 Capitol was destroyed by fire in 1881, and another building was completed in 1882 on the same site. In only eleven years it had become inadequate to house the State government, and it was then that the Legislature appointed a commission to find a site and to erect a new building.

The Capitol Commission of 1893 employed Edmund M. Wheelwright of Boston to select from the designs submitted by the architects, and it was he who chose the Cass Gilbert plan. Gilbert supervised construction and all details, including decoration and furnishings.

The Legislature appropriated $4.5 million for the land and building, and ground was broken on May 6, 1896. The cornerstone was laid on July 27, 1898, by Alexander Ramsey, the first Governor of the Minnesota Territory.

On the first floor are State administrative offices and the Governor's reception room, with gold-leaf ceiling, marble fireplace and several paintings of scenes from Minnesota's history.

The Capitol's "grand floor" is the second. Here are located the Senate and House, the Supreme Court and several legislative committee rooms and offices. Four paintings by John LaFarge appear in the Supreme Court Chamber. The adjacent Justices' Consultation Room is a scaled-down copy of the room in Independence Hall in which the Declaration of Independence was signed. The Senate Chamber features historical and allegorical murals as well as figures of Freedom, Courage, Justice and Equality. In the north, or House wing, ceiling decorations commemorate the explorers LaSalle, Hennepin, Perrot and Duluth.

The Capitol's third floor contains the House and Senate galleries, additional committee rooms, and the main part of the State Library. Other offices are on the ground floor.

The building measures 434 by 229 feet. It is 223 feet to the top of the large marble dome, which is 89 feet in diameter and topped by a columned lantern with a gold ball.

The virtues of Wisdom, Courage, Bounty, Truth, Integrity and Prudence are represented by six statues above the main entrance. These are the work of Daniel

A gilded quadriga representing Minnesota's progress since statehood stands at the base of the magnificent unsupported marble dome, said to be the world's largest.

Chester French, who collaborated with Edward C. Potter on the gilded quadriga, "The Progress of the State," which stands at the base of the dome. The figure of Prosperity rides the chariot, while two young women guide the horses. The sculpture is of copper-clad sheet metal over steel framing, overlaid with gold leaf.

Inside, limestone from Minnesota quarries was used for the walls and ceiling; the main staircases are marble. A large, eight-pointed glass star, set in the first floor at the center of the Rotunda, symbolizes the North Star State. Along the walls of the second floor balcony are statues of Civil War heroes from the State.

MISSISSIPPI

THE STATE CAPITOL *Jackson*

Mississippi actually has two State Capitol buildings in Jackson—the Old Capitol, built in 1839, which is now a historical museum, and the present Capitol, which was built in 1903 and has since served as the seat of government.

Toward the end of the nineteenth century, the Old Capitol was found to be inadequate to house all of the departments of the State government. Construction of the present building began in 1900 and was completed in 1903 at a cost of $1,093,641, which was financed without the necessity for a bond issue or extra tax levy. It was designed by architect Theodore C. Link of St. Louis, assisted by his son, Karl E. Link.

When the new Renaissance-style Capitol was completed, the Old Capitol was vacated and for a number of years was allowed to deteriorate. By 1916, however, the need for additional office space had grown to such an extent that the Old Capitol was renovated and used to house a number of departments of government until the Woolfolk State Office Building was completed in 1949. In 1959-1961 the Old Capitol was restored.

The present Capitol, which underwent extensive repairs in 1916 and again in 1934-35, is an impressive structure, standing with formal dignity on a commanding terrace in the center of downtown Jackson. Its architectural style is classical Renaissance, and its design is similar to that of the National Capitol.

The symmetrical, four-story building, constructed of Bedford limestone with a base of Georgia granite, is 402 feet long from east to west, 225 feet wide through the center pavilion. A high central dome and lantern which rises 180 feet above the entrance is topped by a copper eagle covered with genuine gold leaf. It stands eight feet high and has a wingspread of fifteen feet.

The interior features blue Vermont marble on a base of black Belgian; the main Rotunda is of Italian marble with trimmings of jet black marble from New York and friezes and columns of scagliola. Elsewhere in the building, other varieties of marble are used.

Only four kinds of wood are used in the building—maple, oak, walnut and mahogany. The two legislative halls, finished with marble and scagliola, have rich, domed ceilings of oxidized copper, stucco and colorful stained glass.

All three branches of the State government are housed in the Capitol, with the Governor's office located on the third floor midway between the two legislative halls. The Capitol also includes a Hall of Governors.

Mississippi has had two other sites of government as a member of the Federal Union. A small brick church in Washington, Mississippi, the Capitol when the State was admitted in 1817, served until Jackson became the capital city in 1822. A two-story brick structure served in Jackson until the "Old Capitol" was built in 1839. During the Civil War, the State government met in Columbus and Macon.

The classical Renaissance-style Capitol of Mississippi, built in 1903, is capped by an eight-foot copper eagle which is overlaid with gold leaf and has a wingspread of fifteen feet.

Missouri's white stone Capitol in Jefferson City is a relatively new building, completed in 1918. Limestone bluffs and the Missouri River form part of its impressive three-acre setting.

MISSOURI

THE STATE CAPITOL *Jefferson City*

The magnificent white stone Missouri State Capitol in Jefferson City covers three acres atop the limestone bluffs on the south bank of the Missouri River and overlooks a wide expanse of Cole and Callaway Counties.

Occupied on October 5, 1918, after more than four years under construction, it cost $4,215,000, including furnishings and site. The Capitol is five stories high, 437 feet long and 200 feet in the wings. The height is 238 feet to the top of the dome and 88 feet to the roof of the wings. It accommodates both branches of the Missouri Legislature, the offices of the elective State officials, and many boards and commissions.

The grand stairway, thirty feet across, is said to be the widest in the world. The front doors are of bronze, each thirteen by eighteen feet—largest cast since the Roman era. Considered especially outstanding are the legislative assembly rooms, the historic and resources museums, the legislative library, the Governor's reception room and the House and Senate lounges.

Colossal reclining bronze figures by Robert I. Aitken on either side of the steps leading to the south entrance symbolize Missouri's great rivers, the Missouri and the Mississippi, while atop the dome is a bronze figure of Ceres, the goddess of agriculture, by Sherry Fry.

On either hand at the top of the grand stairway leading from the principal entrance to the third floor are statues by James Earle Fraser of the explorers Meriwether Lewis and William Clark, whose expedition up the Missouri River played a prominent part in Missouri's early history.

Throughout the building are murals and decorative paintings telling the legend and history of Missouri, including the much-discussed murals on the walls of the House lounge by Thomas Hart Benton, Missouri artist and grandnephew of the distinguished Missouri statesman of the same name.

Jefferson City was established as the capital by the Missouri Legislature at the end of 1821, a few months after statehood was approved. That year the State government moved from St. Louis to St. Charles, which served as the capital until the first Capitol in Jefferson City was completed in 1827. This was destroyed by fire in 1837, and the Cole County Courthouse was then used until 1840 when another Capitol was completed on the present site. This Capitol, remodeled and expanded in 1888, burned in 1911. Other buildings were used until the present Capitol was completed.

MONTANA

THE STATE CAPITOL *Helena*

On a gentle slope, surrounded by ten acres of spacious lawns, native trees, and other State buildings, Montana's Capitol faces out over the beautiful Prickly Pear Valley. A mile west of the Capitol lies Last Chance Gulch, now the City of Helena's main street, where gold was discovered in 1864.

Native Columbus limestone was used in construction of the main section of the neoclassical Capitol, which was completed in 1902. The two large wings, faced with native granite, were finished in 1912, making the present structure 425 feet long and an average of 100 feet in width. The cost of construction was $1,650,000.

A statue representing liberty stands atop the Capitol's central copper dome, 165 feet from ground level. Visitors entering the Capitol see the bronze equestrian statue of General Thomas Francis Meagher, fiery Irish patriot and Civil War soldier, who was an acting Montana Territorial Governor in 1866. The Capitol's interior, done in French Renaissance style, features flaring staircases, wide corridors and large rooms, as well as many murals and statues.

On the main floor are the executive offices. Most impressive is the spacious Governor's reception room in the east wing, decorated in tan, ivory and brown, with marble fireplace mantels at both ends, silver chandeliers, paneled walls and eight massive columns of English oak. In the entrance room to the executive suite is the painting, "Scouting for Custer," by E. S. Paxson.

Tennessee marble and tones of deep green, brown and gold decorate the corridors extending east and west from the main-floor Rotunda. The dome rises to a height of one hundred feet over the Rotunda floor and is enhanced by stained glass windows and oil paintings. Embedded in the terrazzo floor of the Rotunda is the Great Seal of Montana, containing a central representation of a plow and a miner's pick and shovel, and surrounded by mountain scenery and the great falls of the Missouri River. "Driving of the Golden Spike," a mural depicting the coming of the railroads to Montana in the 1880's, appears above the grand staircase, which is of white marble with bronze decorations.

In the west wing of the third floor are the House of Representatives and Senate Chambers and their committee rooms and offices. The east wing houses the Supreme Court, State Law Library, and offices of the Justices of the Supreme Court.

Constituting the largest room in the Capitol, the rectangular House of Representatives Chamber also is the home of the largest and most valuable painting owned by the State of Montana: Charles M. Russell's historical depiction of Lewis and Clark meeting the Indians at Ross' Hole, September 5, 1805. Valued by critics at $250,000, the painting measures twenty-five by twelve feet and is in place directly over the Speaker's desk. Montanans generally consider the painting as priceless, because of the Statewide affinity with both the subject of the painting and their native-son artist.

Spacious lawns, neatly landscaped and bearing many varieties of trees native to the State of Montana, complement the spartan grandeur of the neoclassical Capitol at Helena, completed in 1902.

NEBRASKA

THE STATE CAPITOL *Lincoln*

The present Capitol, the fifth used by the Territory and the State, is known as "Tower on the Plains." A 1948 poll of five hundred of the Nation's best architects rated Nebraska's Capitol one of the five best buildings ever constructed in the United States.

The building, designed by Bertram Goodhue, drew upon elements of architectural styles of ancient Asia, Greece, Egypt, Spain and the American Southwest to produce a structure strikingly modern yet representative of the prairie and the people of the State.

Built of Indiana limestone, it is in the form of a cross in a square, with four interior courts. The base of the building, 437 feet square, is two stories high. From this base rises the tower, 400 feet high, crowned with Lee Lawrie's thirty-two-foot, eight-ton bronze figure of "The Sower."

The building, furnishings and landscaping cost over $10 million. The actual construction, begun in 1922, took ten years and was carried out under the direction of William Younkin. More than forty varieties of marble, granite, limestone and slate were used.

A particular attraction are the doors to the Senate and House Chambers. Plain on the inside but deeply carved on the outside, the "Indian" doors to the Senate represent the "Red Man's Tree of Life." Inlaid, tooled leather on the House doors depicts the "White Man's Tree of Life." They are boldly colored in the style of the prairie Indians.

When the Kansas-Nebraska Act of 1854 brought Territorial status to Nebraska, a dispute broke out between the North Platte and South Platte sections over the site of the permanent capital. Omaha was chosen by the acting Governor, but soon after statehood (March 1, 1867) the Legislature, with South Platte forces in the majority, voted to relocate the capital. The little village of Lancaster was chosen August 14, 1867, and renamed Lincoln.

The first Capitol built in Lincoln was used from 1869 to 1883. The present Capitol was built around the second, which was then torn down so that the tower section could be erected.

"Tower on the Plains" is the nickname of the striking skyscraper which serves as Nebraska's Capitol.

NEVADA

THE STATE CAPITOL BUILDING

Carson City

Carson City is the only capital city Nevada has known. From October 31, 1864, when President Lincoln proclaimed the new State, until 1870, the Legislature met in many places in the city. In January 1869, a bill to provide for the building of a State Capitol was introduced in the Nevada State Assembly. After a stormy passage through the Assembly, the "Capitol Bill" was passed by the Senate and, with a somewhat shaky hand, Governor Henry G. Blasdel signed it into law. The authorized construction was not to exceed $100,000 in cost. Subsequently, over an eighty-year period, the total cost amounted to $332,383.97.

The cornerstone of the Capitol was laid June 9, 1870. Construction moved rapidly, and within six months the Capitol building was ready for the fourth session of the Legislature.

Despite the speedy construction, Nevada had a handsome and imposing building—a two-story structure in the form of a Grecian cross featuring Corinthian, Ionic and Doric styles. The interior was both lavish and lasting. Windowpanes of twenty-six-ounce French Crystal, double-arched sashes, vaulted columns and chandeliers hanging from ornate, scrolled centerpieces were just some of the touches. Alaska marble was shipped to California in twenty-ton blocks where it was cut, polished and forwarded to Carson City to be inlaid into the wainscoting, arches and floors of the building.

Since those frontier days, the Statehouse has been expanded. The first addition came in 1905 when a State Library, octagonal in shape, was built as an annex to the east side. Currently housed in this section are the Division of Archives, part of the Legislative Council Bureau and legislative meeting rooms. The building was extended to the north and south in 1913, providing larger chambers for the State Assembly and the State Senate and additional office space for State agencies. The 1967 Legislature approved construction of a new Legislature Building to be situated immediately south of the Capitol.

The Nevada Capitol at Carson City is a handsome two-story structure with the basic form of a Greek cross.

NEW HAMPSHIRE

THE STATE HOUSE *Concord*

New Hampshire's State House, built in 1819, is constructed of granite blocks hewn from 20,000-year-old boulders.

New Hampshire's classic State House in Concord is the oldest in the Nation with the Legislature still occupying its original chambers. (Massachusetts and Maryland have older Capitols still standing, but their legislative bodies have long since spread into quarters of more modern vintage.)

Built in 1819 by Stuart J. Park for approximately $82,000, using prison labor, it has twice been doubled in size at forty-five year intervals—in 1864 and 1909. The first remodeling and enlargement was completed in 1866 at a cost of $200,000; the second, including fire-proofing, was a million-dollar project. On the eve of its sesquicentennial, the historic structure and its 2.6 acre site were given a $600,000 facelifting.

The Granite State's granite Capitol was originally a two-story parallelogram. It consisted of a center with a fifty-foot front and a depth of fifty-seven feet and two identical wings thirty-eight feet wide and forty-nine feet deep. It was surmounted by a silo-like dome upon which a hand-carved, seventy-eight-inch wooden "war" eagle was perched peering eastward toward possible European hostiles.

Time has engulfed the tiny wings, and the State House now has a handsome Doric-colonnaded frontage of 128 feet and a depth of 165 feet. It also boasts an enlarged dome and a "peace" eagle of metal composition, erected in 1955 when its predecessor's tail feathers had "molted" beyond further repair.

Granite for the original State House was hewn from giant boulders on nearby Rattlesnake Hill, said to have rolled into Concord twenty-thousand years earlier during a glacial period. Blocks for the two enlargements were blasted from the bowels of the same hill, said by geologists to be some twenty million years in age. A marked difference in texture is plainly visible to this day.

The State House Annex, completed in 1939, houses more than twenty State departments and is connected to the Capitol by an underground passage.

When the Senate Chamber was redone in 1942, a series of murals depicting New Hampshire's history were placed on the walls.

On the lawn around the State House are statues of famous sons of New Hampshire: Daniel Webster, renowned Senator and orator; General John Stark, Revolutionary War hero; John P. Hale, statesman during the Civil War; and Franklin Pierce, fourteenth President of the United States.

During the Revolutionary period and early statehood (New Hampshire became the ninth and deciding state to ratify the Constitution, at Concord on June 21, 1788), several towns served intermittently as the site of legislative sessions. Concord was first used in 1782 and has been the only capital since 1807.

NEW JERSEY

THE STATE CAPITOL *Trenton*

The New Jersey State Capitol, a massive structure erected in 1792 and added to at various times, is located in Trenton on West State Street, near Willow Street. The grounds now have a frontage of about 650 feet on State Street and extend south to the Delaware River. The present area of the State House grounds is about eight acres.

New Jersey's seat of government was first organized at Nassau Hall, Princeton, in August of 1776 and then alternated mainly between Burlington and Perth Amboy, as well as Trenton, until the Legislature fixed the capital at Trenton by an act approved November 25, 1790, almost three years after New Jersey ratified the Constitution. Commissioners were appointed to obtain land and to erect a suitable building. The old State House was a plain, bare-looking, rough-cast building, and was erected at a cost of less than four thousand pounds. Numerous alterations and additions were made later and new buildings were erected adjoining the main one. On March 21, 1885, the front portion was destroyed by fire, and the Legislature appropriated $275,000 for rebuilding it.

The new rectangular, Renaissance-style building was finished in 1889. It has a frontage of 160 feet on State Street and a depth of 67 feet. It is three and a half stories high, with a Rotunda 39 feet across, which connects the new section of the Capitol with the original part. The Rotunda is surmounted by a 145-foot dome.

The walls are constructed of solid, fireproof, brick masonry, faced with a light-colored stone from Indiana, known as Salem oolitic, with foundations and trimmings of New Jersey freestone from the Prallsville quarries in Hunterdon County. The portico, doorhead and trimmings about the door are of the same material. The portico, with balcony, is supported by massive pillars of polished granite and surmounted by the coat of arms of the State.

A new Assembly Chamber was constructed in 1891 and a new Senate Chamber in 1903. In 1907, an addition was built on to the Capitol. The west wing was extended in 1911 and the east wing was extended a year later. Many improvements were made in the Capitol between 1947 and 1962, including a new front entrance and main corridor. Both legislative chambers were enlarged in 1967 to accommodate the expanded 1968 Legislature.

A more attractive neoclassical State Capitol Annex was built in 1931. The four-story, H-shaped, limestone structure houses the courts and several departments and other offices.

The New Jersey State Capitol at Trenton rests on an eight-acre site.
The original portion of the building was completed in 1792, and
subsequent additions have added to the complexity of the massive structure.

New Mexico government is centered in a circular building adapting the Pueblo kiva design.

NEW MEXICO

THE STATE CAPITOL *Santa Fe*

One of the nation's newest, the New Mexico State Capitol also has one of the most unusual styles. Its circular design is an adaptation of the Pueblo Indian kiva and incorporates the Zia Pueblo sun symbol, which also appears in the State Flag. The Capitol's facade is in the modified New Mexico Territorial style.

The four-story building, costing $4,676,860 exclusive of furniture and accessories, was designed by W. C. Kruger and Associates of Santa Fe. It was dedicated in 1966. The Capitol's total area is 236,206 square feet.

The main floor of the Capitol is given over to the legislative chambers, spaced as segments of a circle. The Rotunda rising from this floor is twenty-five feet in diameter and sixty feet high, faced with marble quarried on the Laguna Indian Reservation and highlighted by the State Seal cast in its terrazzo floor.

Stairways, two public elevators and two private elevators for legislators and executive officials give access to the first floor offices, and to the upper two floors which contain offices for legislators and their committees, several executive agencies, the Governor, the Lieutenant Governor and the Secretary of State.

Construction began in June 1964 on the series of ever-widening circular structural elements consisting of rings and columns. Details include inner surfaces of marble quarried within the State, and movable partitions for future space requirements. The State Library, built during the same time, not only complements the Capitol but forms with it the first phase of a comprehensive Capitol expansion program authorized in 1963.

Santa Fe also contains the adobe brick Palace of the Governors, dating from 1610. It is said to be the oldest public building in the continental United States still in use, now serving as a unit of the Museum of New Mexico. For nearly three hundred years it housed the northern frontier governments under Spain and Mexico; the Provisional government set up by the United States in 1846; and the Territorial government after 1850.

The first Territorial Capitol was completed in 1886, but burned six years later. A second building was finished in 1900 and became the State Capitol when New Mexico was admitted into the Union on January 6, 1912. This Capitol was remodeled several times and expanded in 1952. It is now to be used as a State office building. With the new Capitol, it will form part of a Capitol complex.

New Mexico's written history spans over four hundred years, and in its buildings the tri-cultural course of that history is reflected. The new Capitol, while blending themes of the past, provides adequate facilities for New Mexico's future.

NEW YORK

THE STATE CAPITOL *Albany*

Started shortly after the Civil War, New York's Capitol took thirty years to build and today still ranks as one of the Nation's most unusual public buildings. Five stories high atop Albany's Capitol Hill, it commands a sweeping view of downtown Albany and the beautiful Hudson River Valley. The three-and-a-half-acre site, with almost as much ground area as the National Capitol, is beautifully landscaped.

The cost of the Renaissance and Romanesque building was $25 million, a figure almost unbelievable in those days. Chief among its distinctive features are the superbly finished executive and legislative chambers, swirling staircases and elaborate, carved stonework recreating dramatic moments in the State's history.

The building itself is a massive rectangle extending 400 feet from east to west and 300 feet from north to south, with walls 108 feet high and a large central court. The base of the outer walls, sixteen feet four inches thick, is reminiscent of a medieval fortress. The visitor immediately notices one of the world's largest staircases—100 feet wide at the bottom, it extends 166 feet eastward from the main building and rises to the main entrance on the second floor. Another superb stairway, the "million dollar" staircase inside the west end, rises 119 feet from the first to the fourth floor and is believed to have been inspired by the grand stairway of the Paris Opera.

Busts of famous Americans are sculpted into the Corsehill freestone. This work alone took many years to complete. Curiously included are some unrecognized heads, believed to be friends and relatives of the sculptors. The Albany Capitol has been in continuous use except for a few days in March 1911, when a fire forced the Legislature to meet in City Hall. The Senate and Assembly Chambers were spared destruction, suffering mainly water damage. Within three weeks, the legislators reconvened in the permanent Capitol.

The present Capitol is the second erected since Albany became the State's official seat of government in 1797. A stone tablet marks the spot where the first Capitol stood.

Until the move to Albany, New York City had been the capital since the break with Great Britain. However, the war forced the government to move to Fishkill, where the Provincial Congress met in a church; to White Plains, where the Declaration of Independence was approved July 9, 1776; to Kingston, where the first State Legislature convened in 1777, and to Poughkeepsie, where the U.S. Constitution was ratified in 1788.

The State Capitol in New York City, the old City Hall, which was torn down in 1812, had also served as the seat of government of the Province from 1699 to 1763, except for a few sessions of the Legislature held in private homes at various other locations. The last session of the Second Continental Congress was held there in 1788, followed by the First Congress of the United States of America in 1789, making it the first Federal Capitol under the Constitution. President Washington was inaugurated on its balcony. It was both the State Capitol and the U.S. Capitol from January 1785 to June 1790. The site on Wall Street is now marked by a statue of George Washington.

Opposite: The New York State Capitol in Albany is one of the Nation's most interesting and opulent public buildings.

NORTH CAROLINA

THE STATE CAPITOL *Raleigh*

The dominant feature of the heart of Raleigh is the North Carolina Capitol which is centered in Union Square, a delightful park-like area of over six acres.

When Raleigh was planned as a city, this portion was set aside as the site of the State Capitol. The first such structure was finished in 1794 in Union Square and was destroyed by fire in 1831. Construction on the current building was started two years later and it was finished in 1840. The architects were Ithiel Town and Alexander Jackson Davis.

Greek Revival was set as the architectural style and granite from a State-owned quarry near Raleigh was the main material used in construction. It is a cruciform shape, measuring 160 feet from north to south and 140 feet from east to west. The building is three stories high, and the top of its dome is 97.5 feet above the base of the Rotunda. The dome itself is copper that has attained a rich green gloss through the years of weathering.

The east and west facades have deep porticos. The Doric columns, five feet in diameter, and entablature are copied from the Parthenon in Athens.

Around the Rotunda are various historical tablets and busts of famous native sons. The circular, stone second-floor balcony is cantilevered over the Rotunda's first floor by nine feet. Massive stone stairways with wrought-iron railings lead to the second floor from the vestibules.

In the Capitol which burned in 1831 was a heroic-sized marble statue of George Washington by the Italian sculptor Antonio Canova. The designers of the present Capitol intended that a copy of this statue be placed in the Rotunda. Financial problems and disagreements about the appropriateness of the style of Canova's statue prevented this, but in 1967 the General Assembly authorized a private subscription of funds to execute a new copy, from the artist's original scale model, to be placed in this location.

Originally, the building housed all functions of State government: the offices of the Governor and Council of State were on the first floor, the Senate and House Chambers on the second, and the Supreme Court and library on the third. A separate building was constructed for the court and library later, and the new State Legislative Building, for the General Assembly, was occupied in 1963.

At present, the offices of the Governor, Secretary of State, Treasurer, and portions of their staffs are in the Capitol. The Senate and House Chambers have been restored to their original form and are kept as historic shrines by the Department of Archives and History.

Among the statuary on the well-landscaped lawns is Charles Keck's grouping of the three North Carolina-born Presidents: James K. Polk, Andrew Jackson, and Andrew Johnson.

Before Raleigh was chosen in 1792 to be North

North Carolina's Capitol is an outstanding example of the Grecian-style building often used in public architecture.

Carolina's permanent capital, the Legislature had been on the move since it first met in 1665—especially during North Carolina's first and third half-centuries. From 1723 to 1761, however, it settled down, first in Edenton and, from 1745, in New Bern, with only two sessions elsewhere. Most of the next nine years were spent in Wilmington. New Bern was used frequently thereafter until 1794, but from 1776 the early State General Assembly gathered also in Halifax, Hillsboro, Smithfield, Wake Court House, Salem, Tarboro and Fayetteville. It was in this last town that the U.S. Constitution was ratified on November 21, 1789.

NORTH DAKOTA

THE STATE CAPITOL *Bismarck*

The North Dakota State Capitol in Bismarck is a modern nineteen-story structure noted for its simplicity, practicability and usability. The towering administrative section is 241 feet, eight inches high and 95 feet square. The length of the entire building, east to west, is 389 feet, its width through the center line of the House and Senate 173 feet, eight inches.

The steel-framed "Skyscraper Capitol of the Plains" is faced with Wisconsin black granite base and white Indiana limestone. The main entrance doors are bronze. In the ground-floor lobby and the first-floor Memorial Hall, the walls are covered with Yellowstone travertine and the floor with Tennessee marble. The stairway leading to Memorial Hall has steps and risers of Tennessee marble and walls of Belgian black marble. Memorial Hall is forty feet high; its columns and large window frames are bronze.

Interior décor features woods of a variety of colors and sources. The dark wood in the Legislative Hall, for example, is rosewood from Asia and the light panel is curly maple; the walls in the House of Representatives are of American chestnut from the Appalachian area, while the Senate's are of English quarter-sawn oak. In the Governor's suite, the reception room walls are laurel wood from India. His conference room has wainscoting of Honduras mahogany and his private office has walls and ceiling covered with teakwood from Burma. American walnut and California walnut are used extensively in other offices.

In early Territorial days the Dakota capital was at Yanktown on the Nebraska border, but the Territorial Legislature of 1883 named a commission to relocate it. Citizens of Bismarck offered $100,000 in cash and 320 acres of land as an inducement.

Bismarck was selected due primarily to its location on the Missouri River, thus insuring an adequate water supply. Also the Northern Pacific Railroad was anxious to have the capital on its main line at Bismarck. The town's cash donation was used in 1883 to build the old Capitol's first section, which cost $97,600. After North Dakota was admitted to statehood, Bismarck was selected as the State Capitol. Jamestown also received serious consideration but lost out at the Constitutional Convention.

The old Capitol burned on December 28, 1930. For the 1931 session, the Legislature used the World War Memorial Building in Bismarck. The new Capitol was erected in 1933-1934 and occupied in 1935. W. F. Kurke and Joseph Bell DeRemer were the principal architects.

The functional Capitol building of North Dakota at Bismarck towers nineteen stories above the surrounding landscape. Granite and limestone faced, it is called "Skyscraper Capitol of the Plains."

OHIO

THE STATE HOUSE *Columbus*

The Ohio State House is considered one of the country's outstanding examples of Greek Revival architecture. However, for several years it appeared not only that the building would remain unfinished, but that the capital would be moved to another city.

The cornerstone was laid on July 4, 1839, and work continued on the twelve-foot-thick foundations. However, that winter, the Legislature repealed the State House act and for six years all construction stopped while the Legislature debated moving the capital from Columbus. Ultimately, in 1846, construction began again and was further spurred by the burning, in 1852, of the old State House.

The building was completed in 1861, twenty-three years after work had started. Meanwhile, eleven Governors had served in office, the State had had two Constitutions, six Boards of Commissioners had supervised the construction and five separate architects had been in charge at various times. In addition, Thomas U. Walter, one of the designers of the National Capitol, and Richard Upjohn, designer of New York City's famous Trinity Church, served as consulting architects.

The finished building was well worth the battle to overcome the controversy which beset the project from the start and lasted nearly to the finish. Eight Doric columns, each thirty-six feet high and six feet thick, are located along the main east and west entrances, with four similar columns at each of the north and south entrances. The cupola, which has a shallow conical roof, is 158 feet above ground level.

Double sets of massive bronze doors open onto the four foyers which lead to the Rotunda floor. A brightly lighted canvas, bearing the Great Seal of Ohio, looks down from the 120-foot dome. Circling the Seal are the names and inaugural dates of the eight Ohioans who served as President of the United States. The floor of the Rotunda is inlaid marble.

Four murals are set in recesses between the Rotunda arches: William Mark Young's "Freedom of Religion" and "Laws of Equity," and Arthur Crisp's "Education" and "Basic Laws of Justice and Authority." Below the murals are historical displays. Bronze tablets commemorating the deeds of Ohioans flank the foyer entries.

The Governor's office is along the north foyer. The south half of the second floor is occupied by the House of Representatives, while the Senate is to the north, as is the Legislative Library. A Lincoln Memorial by Sculptor T. D. Jones also is in this area, and the walls of the north and south foyers are hung with oil portraits of Ohio's past Governors.

The Judiciary Annex was constructed in 1899-1901. It stands to the east of the State House and complements it in style. Here are located the Supreme Court, the Court Library and the Attorney General's office.

Until the Legislature in 1812 accepted an offer of forest land on the "high bank east of the Scioto River" at what now is Columbus, Chillicothe had served as the capital except for two years when Zanesville held this honor. Ohio joined the Union in 1803, with the first legislative session being held in Chillicothe. Prior to statehood, when Ohio had been part of the Northwest Territory, Marietta, then Cincinnati, had been the Territorial capital.

Ohio had been a State fifty years before Congress set its official date of admission. The Statehood Enabling Act was signed in the spring of 1802 but a formal admission date was not designated. It was not until Ohio's Sesquicentennial in 1953 that Congress rectified this oversight and set March 1, 1803, as the official date of admission.

Opposite: Doric columns six feet thick and thirty-six feet high dominate the facade of Ohio's Greek Revival Capitol, completed in 1861.

OKLAHOMA

THE STATE CAPITOL *Oklahoma City*

As might be expected from the "Oil Capital of the World," the Oklahoma Statehouse is surrounded by oil derricks and oil has been produced for many years from pools beneath the Capitol grounds.

The design of the building is Gothic but many features of Greek and Roman architecture are also apparent. Standing guard atop the five-story structure are great statues of lions which seem to protect the building and the State itself. Unlike most Capitols, it has no dome, thus making the lions even more dominant. There are British features about the architecture, too, because one of the designers was S. Wemyss-Smith, a native of England. Working with him was American S. A. Layton.

They used many kinds of stone, primarily white Indiana limestone. The foundation is Oklahoma granite.

Construction of the building in the northeastern area of Oklahoma City was started July 20, 1914, and completed on June 30, 1917, at a total cost of $5 million. The cornerstone was laid November 16, 1915. A dome had been planned but the excessive cost of steel during World War I dictated a change in design.

The building faces south but has entrances on all four sides. Above the doors on the south entrance is a reproduction of the Great Seal of Oklahoma cast in bronze. This door opens to a grand staircase which leads to the fourth floor. The north and south facades have Corinthian porticos, and the east and west facades have Corinthian pilasters. In the center of the Rotunda ceiling is a colorful reproduction of the State Seal, surrounded by a sunburst of leaded glass artwork.

The five-story structure of 650 rooms houses the Governor's office, both Houses of the Legislature and numerous other offices of State government. The building has approximately eleven acres of floor space. Alabama marble was used for the floors, Vermont marble for the stairways.

The Governor's office is in the southeast wing of the second floor and adjoins the Blue Room, a reception room used by the Governor and other dignitaries for various business and social functions. This historical room has recently been renovated to reflect the original décor of the interior of the Capitol.

On the fourth floor are located the legislative halls.

The Senate Chamber is on the east side and is sixty-two feet long and fifty-one feet, four inches wide. The House Chamber, on the west side, is slightly larger. The galleries on the fifth floor overlook the House and Senate Chambers and provide seating for the public.

On the second floor in the west wing is the Supreme Court, the highest court in Oklahoma hearing civil cases. In the north wing on the second floor is located the Court of Criminal Appeals, the highest court in Oklahoma exclusively for criminal cases.

Oklahoma City was chosen as the capital city by vote of the people in 1910, but it required a decision by the

U.S. Supreme Court in 1911 to settle the question of legality of the move from Guthrie, which had been capital of the Territory since 1890 and of the State since its entry into the Union in 1907.

Before statehood, the eastern part of Oklahoma was known as the Indian Territory. The Indian nations had capitals in several places: the Creeks in Okmulgee, the Cherokees at Tahlequah, the Seminoles at Wewoka, the Choctaw in Tuskahoma, the Chickasaw at Tishomingo. The western "Panhandle" of the State was a portion of that area of the Republic of Texas which was ceded to the United States in 1850.

Oklahoma's Capitol combines Gothic, Greek and Roman styles. Two lions, which seem to stand guard over the building, flank the central pediment of the handsome structure.

Atop the white Vermont marble Oregon Capitol is Ulric Ellerhusen's statue of the "Pioneer."

OREGON
THE STATE CAPITOL *Salem*

The mastery of Ulric Ellerhusen, one of the West's greatest sculptors, is apparent throughout the four-story Oregon State Capitol, but the beauty of the building, its setting and its mountain vista share honors with the works of this distinguished craftsman.

The building of white Vermont marble is simple in design. It looks northward, with other State buildings on each side, over a beautifully landscaped mall toward the Cascade Mountains. Included on the Capitol grounds is Willson Park.

Atop the tower of the Statehouse, 128 feet high, is Ellerhusen's gilded eight-and-one-half ton, 42-foot statue of the "Pioneer," which can be seen for miles. At night, bathed in floodlight, it is especially outstanding. Other Ellerhusen decorations over the various entrances depict figures symbolic of Oregon's economy and history—the great eagle, salmon, wheat, a ship, a locomotive, a stagecoach, pack animals and a cow, sheep, horse, deer and buffalo. Ellerhusen also created the bronze of the State Seal which is set in the center of the Rotunda floor.

Marble, featured on the exterior, is also used extensively in the interior; rose travertine from Montana on the walls, Vermont black along the base and ramps of the great stairway, Napoleon grey from Missouri on the stairs and the Rotunda floor.

Among the Rotunda decorations is a sunburst with stars overhead, representing Oregon and the other States at the time of Oregon's entry into the Union in 1859. Four murals on the Rotunda walls show scenes from Oregon's history. Another four, on its industry, flank the stairs to the Senate and House.

Each legislative chamber also has a mural behind the rostrum, while friezes bear the names of 157 men and women prominent in Oregon history. Above the steps to the Senate Chamber on the east is the Provisional Seal (1834-1848); facing this is the Territorial Seal (1848-1859), which is atop the stairs to the House of Representatives. The seals were painted by Barry Faulkner and Frank H. Schwarz.

Specially designed furnishings are in the legislative chambers, the Governor's office, and the early American-style Board of Control Room, which is paneled in knotty ponderosa pine. The House Chamber's walls are of golden oak, while its carpet depicts the Douglas fir.

The Capitol grounds contain several statues—two large groups by sculptor Leo Friedlander are at the Capitol's main entrance, one showing the Lewis and Clark party led by Sacajawea and the other, a pioneer family on the Oregon Trail.

The present Capitol was begun in 1936, the year after fire had destroyed the preceding structure, and was completed in 1938. The first specially built Capitol in Salem was erected in 1854 but was destroyed by fire a year later. The Legislature met in the Holman Building during the twenty-one years before its next Capitol was ready. That Statehouse was completed in 1876 and occupied until destroyed by fire on April 25, 1935.

PENNSYLVANIA

THE STATE CAPITOL *Harrisburg*

The William Penn family is so much a part of the history of Pennsylvania that it is not surprising that the female figure atop the dome of the State Capitol at Harrisburg is nicknamed "Miss Penn"—but it is not true, as sometimes claimed, that it was modeled after Penn's daughter, Letitia. The bronze statue representing the Commonwealth holds a mace, symbolic of statehood, and also raises a hand in benediction. The Capitol was designed in Italian Renaissance and the dome is reminiscent of St. Peter's in Rome.

The building was dedicated on October 4, 1906, by President Theodore Roosevelt, and is the second Statehouse in Harrisburg. The first, which was built in 1821, was destroyed by fire on February 2, 1897.

In 1902, Architect Joseph M. Houston of Philadelphia was commissioned to design the present structure, which is 520 feet long and 254 feet wide. The dome rises to 272 feet. The exterior is of Vermont granite. Flanking the main entrance are two statuary groups by Pennsylvania-born George Grey Barnard. One represents man's spiritual burden, while the other depicts humanity advancing through work and brotherhood. Sculptured on the huge bronze doors at that entrance are the heads of the men responsible for the building of the Capitol.

Around the immense Rotunda are Penn's words:

> There may be room there for such a holy experiment. For the nations want a precedent. And my God will make it the seed of a nation. That an example may be set to the nations. That we may do the thing that is truly wise and just.

Paintings by the Pennsylvania artist Edwin Austin Abbey in the Rotunda's recessed arches and circular panels illustrate the spiritual, intellectual, and economic advances of the Commonwealth. They are entitled "The Spirit of Religious Liberty," "The Spirit of Light," "Science Revealing the Treasures of the Earth" and "The Spirit of Vulcan."

Other paintings in the wide south corridor represent the religious influences upon Pennsylvania's history. These are by W. B. Van Ingen, another noted artist of the State. Carvings on the gilded capitals along the corridors represent some of the State's most outstanding persons of different national origins.

Tile mosaics by Henry C. Mercer are interspersed along the richly colored floor of the Rotunda and corridors. A grand staircase leads to the legislative chambers, off the second floor balcony. In the Senate Chamber are several historical paintings by another native artist, Violet Oakley, while those in the House of Representatives are by Abbey. Both areas have stained glass windows by Van Ingen. Also on the second floor are the richly furnished Governor's Suite, with more Oakley paintings, and the rooms used by the Lieutenant Governor.

The Appellate Courtroom on the fourth floor is used by both the Supreme Court and the Superior Court. Sixteen panels by Oakley portray the evolution of law.

From 1683, the year after William Penn organized the colony's first Assembly in Upland (now Chester), until 1799, Philadelphia was Pennsylvania's capital. There, Independence Hall, then known as the State House, was used from 1736 by the Assembly. It was also the first National Capitol from May 10, 1775, to December 12, 1776, from March 4 to September 18, 1777, and from July 2, 1778, to June 21, 1783. Here were signed the Declaration of Independence and the Constitution of the United States.

The seat of government was moved to Lancaster in 1799, and, in 1812, Harrisburg became Pennsylvania's capital city. The General Assembly met at the Dauphin County Court House until the first Capitol there was authorized in 1816 and occupied in 1822.

The dome of Pennsylvania's Capitol is reminiscent of St. Peter's in Rome. The bronze statue at its peak represents the Commonwealth, but is nicknamed "Miss Penn" after William Penn's famous family.

RHODE ISLAND

THE STATE HOUSE *Providence*

Although Rhode Island was the first Colony to declare its independence from Great Britain, it was the last to decide on a single city to serve as the State capital. It was not until 1900 that the seat of government was permanently fixed at the present capital, Providence.

Legislative history goes back to May 19, 1647, when the first elected Legislature met at Portsmouth. Many cities served as the meeting site until about 1740. After that, most meetings of the Legislature alternated between the Old Colony House at Newport and the old Capitol at Providence until 1900.

The cornerstone for the present imposing Capitol was laid on October 15, 1896. The building was not officially delivered to the State until 1904 but the Secretary of State took occupany in 1900. Other State officials and the General Assembly moved in the following year.

The architects were McKim, Mead & White of New York, and the builders were Norcross Brothers of Worcester, Massachusetts. The grounds, buildings, furnishings and decorations cost $3,018,416.33. The City of Providence donated to the State 454,838 square feet of land adjacent to the land purchased by the State.

The length of the building is 333 feet and the depth of the wings is 133 feet. The diameter of the dome below the top of the gallery is 70 feet; the diameter of the dome proper is 50 feet. The height of the building to the top of the square base of the dome is 94 feet. The marble dome was the first in the United States and one of four in the world (Minnesota's Capitol in St. Paul, the Taj Mahal at Agra, India, and St. Peter's in Rome, the only one larger than this). At night, this dome is illuminated by a battery of floodlights.

Watching over the State from atop the dome at a height of 235 feet is a symbolic bronze statue of the "Independent Man." At the entrance are bronze statues of two great Rhode Island military leaders, General Nathanael Greene, of Revolutionary fame, and Commodore Oliver Hazard Perry, hero of the War of 1812.

A quotation from the Royal Charter of 1663 is carved in marble above the portico. Inscribed on the building's north side are the milestones of Rhode Island history: founding, incorporation, chartering, independence.

Around the inside of the dome is carved in Latin a quotation from Tacitus, which translated reads: "Rare felicity of the times when it is permitted to think as you like and to say what you think."

In the State Reception Room are four famous paintings. One is of General George Washington by Gilbert Stuart; the other paintings are of General Greene and Commodore Perry, both by Gari Melchers, and of Commodore John Barry by Wilfred I. Duphiney.

The State Library contains an excellent collection of books on Rhode Island, documents of the United States and the several States and books and pamphlets relating to history, political science and social science.

In the Governor's office and along the corridors are portraits of almost every Rhode Island Governor from colonial days to the present, while about the entrances are displayed battle flags and other relics and memorials.

Another historical relic in the State House is the original parchment charter granted by King Charles II, July 8, 1663, which continued in force (except for 1686-1689) until the present Constitution of the State became operative on May 2, 1843.

Opposite: Overlooking Rhode Island's capital city from a height of 235 feet is the bronze "Independent Man" on the dome of the State House.

SOUTH CAROLINA

THE STATE HOUSE *Columbia*

Just as Washington, D.C., was planned and built to serve as the Nation's capital, Columbia was established specifically to function as the capital of South Carolina, and the Carolina city even has claim to primacy because it was founded well ahead of the District of Columbia. In 1786, two years before the U.S. Constitution was ratified, the General Assembly chose a site "near Friday's Ferry on the Congaree River" to be the capital city. Later, the name Columbia was selected for the town and, in 1790, it became the seat of government, replacing Charleston, where an earlier State House had been in use since 1756.

Work on the present handsome Roman-Corinthian-style State House in Columbia got underway in 1855. The architect was Major John R. Niernsee. Five years later he reported that the project was nearing completion and would be ready within a year. Little did he realize that it would be nearly a half century before the building would be finished.

With the start of the Civil War, work came to a virtual standstill. However, to keep the quarry machinery and shortline railroad from deteriorating, the quarrying and transporting of the huge blocks of native granite continued and preparation of marble for the interior also proceeded.

When Union General William T. Sherman shelled Columbia on February 16, 1865, slight damage was done to the new State House. However, in the burning of the city the following day, the old State House, the existing seat of government, was demolished and much finished marble and granite at the site of the new edifice was ruined. So, too, were the architect's library and his drawings and plans for the new building.

After the war, it was decided to complete the building, but the advent of the Reconstruction period caused further delay, and not until 1869 was the roof installed and the unfinished building occupied.

Little additional work was done for some twenty years. Architect Niernsee returned in 1885 to resume work on the State House but died before the year ended. Finally, by the end of the century, the north and south porticos, with immense monolithic granite columns, and the copper-covered dome, a substitute for the originally designed soaring tower, were erected. Still later the great flights of steps were built.

In recent years, the interior has been renovated. The main lobby, its lofty embossed ceiling going up into the dome, features a bronzed statue of John C. Calhoun and real South Carolina palmetto trees, taken from the coast and preserved.

Above the triple doors leading to the State Library is a handsome stained glass window with the State Seal. The Library, to the rear of the main level, is centered with a Venetian glass chandelier, originally lighted by gas. Matching wrought-iron spiral staircases lead to the balcony.

In the east wing is the Senate Chamber, with its massive old desk of Honduras mahogany. The Sword of State hangs on the front of the desk when the Senate is in session. This was a personal gift of Lord Halifax, presented in 1951 to replace the original sword, which was made by a Charles Town silversmith and was in use from the beginning of statehood in 1776 until it was stolen in 1941.

Opposite is the Hall of the House of Representatives, also with its great desk and graceful proportions. It is paneled with Vermont verde antique marble. A lighted case displays the solid silver mace and gold burnishings, made in London in 1756. It is said to be the only mace now in use in this country which antedates the Revolutionary War.

On the lower level, with its vaulted ceilings and strong columns, are two recently renovated suites of offices, one for the Governor and one for the Supreme Court.

Construction on the Palmetto State's Capitol was begun in 1855, but the Civil War and Reconstruction period which followed delayed its completion until the end of the nineteenth century.

South Dakota's Capitol is built of raindrop sandstone and Bedford limestone in a modified Ionic style.

SOUTH DAKOTA

THE STATE CAPITOL *Pierre*

It is most appropriate that the South Dakota State Capitol should stand proudly on a bluff overlooking the storied Missouri River, famed as the highway to the frontier, because the State itself has been so much a part of the history of the frontier. Pierre, the capital city, is located on the site of what had been the capital of the Arikaka Indian nation for four hundred years.

South Dakota gained statehood in 1889 and Pierre was selected as the temporary capital. Fifteen years later, after much debate and two challenges by other cities, Pierre was named the permanent capital.

The first Capitol was a plain wooden structure just to the west of where the present building stands. The grounds around this building were prairie land with a deep gulch, but the gulch was filled and now is the handsome ten-acre Capitol Lake, fed by two warm water artesian wells. Visitors delight in this year-around haven for migratory waterfowl.

The exterior of the present State Capitol, started in 1907 and finished in 1910, is Marquette raindrop sandstone and Indiana Bedford limestone. The surrounding prairie furnished the boulder granite from which the basement was made. The original portion of the building was 292 feet by 124 feet and it is 161 feet from the ground to the top of lantern on the copper-covered dome.

The modified Ionic-style architecture, reminiscent of the National Capitol, is the work of Bell and Detweiler of Minneapolis. Including the art and furnishings, the total cost was only $944,000. The $400,000 annex on the north of the building was provided by the Legislature in 1931.

A wide sweep of gleaming white marble steps leads from the Rotunda and nearby Executive Suite to the legislative wings of the Capitol. The staircase, flanked by huge columns of concrete and marble, becomes an auditorium at Christmas and on other special occasions when programs are held in the Rotunda. The most impressive view in the Capitol is the dome as seen from the Rotunda, with sunlight filtering through stained glass panels in the circular walls of the dome.

The west wing of the legislative floor houses the Senate Chamber, patterned after that of the United States Senate. The South Dakota House of Representatives is in the shape of a rectangle, also patterned after the House Chamber in Washington. Galleries on the fourth floor provide excellent vantage points to view the proceedings. Supreme Court Chambers are located in the east wing of the second floor.

South Dakota's major governmental activities center in the Executive Department on the south side of the west wing of the Capitol. Here are the Governor's offices and conference room. One of the significant pieces of art among the Capitol's many murals and paintings depicting early-day history is the canvas "Spirit of the People" on the west wall of the conference room. It tells the story of the advance westward by the white settler and his family into what was then Dakota Territory.

Four adjacent State office buildings today complete the Capitol complex.

TENNESSEE

THE STATE CAPITOL *Nashville*

Tennessee's State Capitol, overlooking downtown Nashville's Memorial Square, is truly a Grecian edifice. It has a Doric base; four Ionic porticos, modeled after the Erectheum in Athens; and Corinthian pillars in the lantern of the tower which resemble the Choragic monument of Lysicrates, sometimes called the Lantern of Demosthenes. The design was by William Strickland of Philadelphia.

Despite the Grecian styling, the crystalline, fossilated limestone gives it a true Tennessee atmosphere, as this material was quarried near Nashville, then hewn into six- to ten-ton blocks for construction. Tennessee marble is also used extensively in the interior.

The structure's cornerstone was laid on July 4, 1845. It was first occupied in 1853 and completed in 1859 at a cost of approximately $1.5 million. Including the porticos, the building measures 270 by 140 feet. A terrace seventeen feet wide surrounds the Capitol. The height to the top of the rusticated-stone tower is 206 feet; the tower alone is 79 feet.

Extensive repairs on the exterior began in 1956. A new copper roof and new windows were installed, the terrace and steps were rebuilt, and columns, pediments, cornices and entablature were replaced. Some 90,000 cubic feet of Indiana limestone were used in this work.

Inside, a double flight of stairs leads to the House and Senate Chambers on the main floor. The Hall of Representatives, 100 by 70 feet, has a ceiling supported by sixteen fluted Ionic columns. In the smaller Senate Chamber, twelve Tennessee marble columns support a twelve-foot-wide gallery on three sides. The ceiling is formed in radiating panels of lacunaria.

The Capitol's interior also underwent a renovation in the late 1950's. Excavating and finishing the ground floor provided more office and committee space. Ceilings and floors were replaced. Other modifications included a tunnel and two elevators.

As North Carolina's "District of Washington," as the "State of Franklin" and as a Territory, Tennessee Legislatures met at Jonesboro, Greenville and Knoxville. Except for one day, Knoxville was the capital from 1796 to 1812, and the first State Legislature met there in a frame building after Tennessee was admitted to the Union on June 1, 1796. Nashville was Tennessee's capital from 1812 to 1815, Knoxville again from 1816 to 1819, Murfreesboro from 1819 through 1825, and Nashville again since 1826. The earlier Legislatures met in log cabins, frame homes, a school, the Presbyterian Church at Murfreesboro, and the Masonic Hall at Nashville before the Capitol in Nashville became the seat of government.

The popular Doric, Ionic and Corinthian styles are masterfully blended in the Tennessee Capitol.

TEXAS

THE STATE CAPITOL *Austin*

The Texas Capitol, which stands in magnificent splendor in the center of the City of Austin, is a symbol of the history and heritage of the Lone Star State.

Among the largest of the State Capitols, it was patterned after the National Capitol by architect E. E. Myers of Detroit in 1881. It is 566 feet, six inches long, 288 feet, ten inches wide, and towers 311 feet from the grade line to the top of the star held aloft by the "Goddess of Liberty." It is constructed of pink Texas granite donated to the State by the owners of Granite Mountain in Burnet County. Over fifteen thousand carloads were transported on a specially constructed railroad for the seventy-five-mile distance to Austin.

Ground was broken for the new building on February 1, 1882. It was dedicated on May 18, 1888, with the acceptance speech being made by State Senator Temple Houston, son of General Sam Houston, who was Commander of the Texas forces at San Jacinto, twice President of the Republic of Texas, United States Senator and then Governor of the State.

The House and Senate Chambers are located on the second floor on the west and east sides, respectively. On the same floor and between the legislative halls, the Governor's office is located in the front (south) center section and the Legislative Reference Library occupies the rear (north) center section. Offices and spacious living quarters for the Speaker of the House and the Lieutenant Governor are located to the rear of the House and Senate Chambers.

Originally the structure had 392 rooms and 18 vaults on the three floors and housed all branches and departments of the State government. Since then, eight buildings have been added to the Capitol complex for the Supreme Court and executive departments. Much of the first and third floors of the Capitol building has been partitioned into office space for legislators.

The history of the State under the six flags of Spain, France, Mexico, the Republic of Texas, the United States and the Confederacy is depicted in beautiful bright-colored seals inlaid in the terrazzo on the first floor Rotunda. These are flanked on each side by large inlaid names of the battles which were fought to win and maintain Texas' independence from Mexico.

Construction cost of the Capitol was $3,744,630, not counting the donated granite and the time of convict labor furnished by the State. However, the State paid only a small portion of the cost in cash. The basic bids were taken not on the lowest cost in dollars but on the lowest number of acres of public lands for which the contractors would complete the structure. The Constitution of 1875 provided that "Three million acres of the Public Domain are hereby appropriated and set apart for the purpose of erecting a new State Capitol and other necessary public buildings at the seat of government. . ."

The availability of these lands, upon which the building of this Capitol depended, results from an important circumstance relating to the annexation of the Republic of Texas to the United States. During its ten years as an independent nation, Texans voted twice in favor of joining the Union, but both of these early proposals were rejected by the United States. In the second of these offers, a treaty was signed in 1844 by which Texas agreed to cede all of its millions of acres of public domain if the United States would assume its $10 million public debt. This treaty was rejected by the United States Senate, with a major opposition argument being that the Texas lands were "worthless."

Thereupon, the Congress of the United States made a counterproposal that Texas pay its own debts and keep its public lands. This was accepted by the Congress of Texas, and Texas became annexed to the Union on December 29, 1845. This bad guess by the United States Congress enabled the State not only to pay for its fine Capitol with public lands but also to endow its Public Free School Fund with the remainder of its multimillion-dollar acreage.

The low bid of three million acres was submitted by a syndicate of individuals which included United States Senator Charles B. Farwell and his brother, John B. Farwell, Amos C. Babcock, Colonel Abner Taylor and Amos Taylor, all of Chicago. Amos Taylor served as the chief contractor. This land became the famous XIT Ranch located in ten Texas Panhandle counties.

Texas had earlier Capitols located at Columbia, Houston, Washington-on-the-Brazos and Austin. All were wooden construction except the immediate predecessor to the present Capitol, which was constructed in 1856 and burned in 1881, while plans for the present structure were being considered for approval.

The Lone Star State has one of the nation's largest Capitols,
a majestic pink granite structure which took six years to build.

The Utah State Capitol, situated on a natural terrace three hundred feet above the valley floor, provides an impressive view from every approach to Salt Lake City.

UTAH

THE STATE CAPITOL *Salt Lake City*

On a "bench," or natural terrace, of the Wasatch foothills three hundred feet above the valley floor, the Utah State Capitol can be seen from almost every approach to Salt Lake City. Although the site was granted by the city to the Territorial government in 1888, actual building did not begin until several years after Utah finally won statehood in 1896.

A Capitol Commission was created in 1909, and its members were appointed two years later. Architect Richard K. A. Kletting designed a mainly Corinthian-style structure, 404 by 240 feet, of Utah granite. Utah copper covers the 285-foot dome atop the four-story building, completed in 1915 at a cost of $2,739,528.54.

The two hundred rooms of the Capitol include chambers of the Senate, House of Representatives and Supreme Court. The Senate is in the north center section, with the Court in the east wing and the House in the west. The Governor's reception room—the "Gold Room"—is one of the costliest and most beautiful in the West. Offices of the Governor, Secretary of State, Attorney General, Auditor, Treasurer and the Departments of Health and Welfare, Development Services and Natural Resources are on the second floor.

Suspended by a 95-foot chain from the center of the dome, 165 feet above the Rotunda floor, is a 3,200-pound brass chandelier. A skyscape with huge seagulls is painted on the dome ceiling. The gull is referred to as Utah's "sacred bird" because a large flight of them once devoured vast numbers of crickets which endangered the settlers' crops.

The second-floor Rotunda also features larger-than-life statues of mining engineer Daniel Cowan Jackling, sculptured by Dr. Avard Fairbanks, and of Brigadier General Thomas L. Kane, by Ortho R. Fairbanks. Paintings by Gilbert White and Girard Hale, showing Utah pioneer scenes, are at each end of the Rotunda.

On the attractively landscaped grounds in front of the Capitol is a statue of Massasoit, the famous Indian of Massachusetts history, a copy of Cyrus E. Dallin's bronze original at Plymouth Bay. The Utah-born sculptor gave his State the original plaster cast from which the Capitol's bronze was later cast. Also on the Capitol grounds is Gilbert Griswold's Mormon Battalion Monument, commemorating the band of troops which marched two thousand miles from Iowa to California in 1846 during the Mexican War.

During the long wait for its present Capitol, the Utah State Legislature met from 1896 to 1916 in the City-County Building of Salt Lake City.

Salt Lake City has been the principal capital since Utah became a Territory in 1850. Fillmore, chosen in 1851 to be the capital, was used only sparingly in the latter 1850's by the Legislature, which preferred the Great Salt Lake City, as it was then called.

VERMONT

THE STATE CAPITOL *Montpelier*

The present State Capitol, dedicated in 1859, is Vermont's third in Montpelier, which was chosen as the capital in 1805. This majestic structure includes a central building with a Doric Greek Revival portico plus two wings that form a Greek cross. Appropriately, the exterior material is Vermont granite. The apex of the Doric portico rises sixty feet, and behind it, a gold-leaf dome and cupola add another fifty-six feet, nine inches. Topping this is a statue of Ceres, the goddess of agriculture, modeled after the work of Vermonter Larkin G. Mead.

Entered from the portico, the first story presents a striking appearance, with a black and white tessellated marble floor, deep double-sunk ceiling panels, and ornamented iron stairs. The columns in the lobby are Ionic.

Mead's bust of Lincoln faces the main entrance; his marble statue of Ethan Allen stands in the portico. Portraits of famous sons of Vermont line the walls.

On the first floor are the Hall of Inscriptions, various offices and the Legislative Reference Service. The second floor front houses the Governor's Chambers. In his office is an oaken chair carved from the timbers of the famed frigate *Constitution*—"Old Ironsides"—presented to the State in 1858.

On the second floor of the east wing, the elliptical Senate Chamber carries forward the Greek temple effect, with its fluted Corinthian columns and handsome ornamented ceiling.

The larger Representative's Hall is semicircular in shape, with fluted pilasters, Corinthian capitals, enriched entablature and paneled cove. Over the Speaker's desk is the State coat of arms, carved in wood by John A. Ellis. A raised platform in the curved rear of the hall accommodates the Senate during joint sessions.

Connecting with the west wing of the Statehouse is a rough-granite annex, used mainly for legislative committees. It was built in 1886 and remodeled in 1918.

Vermont's early history was one of turbulence. Although active in the Revolution, Vermont was not one of the original thirteen States but maintained an independent government for fourteen years. After it disposed of adverse claims against its territory by New York, New Hampshire and Massachusetts, it entered the Union as the fourteenth State on March 4, 1791.

At least ten different towns served as "capitals" from 1775 until 1805 as the legislators traveled from city to city for meetings. When Montpelier was finally selected as the permanent capital the first Statehouse was a wooden structure. This was used until 1836, when it was replaced by a granite building, which was destroyed by fire in 1857. At first, the Legislature appropriated only money for "repairs and improvements." However, the Governor's Commission decided that the State needed a new and larger building and consequently the present building was constructed.

Vermont's Capitol, following a Grecian motif throughout, is in the form of a Greek cross with a Doric Greek Revival portico and a majestic statue of Ceres, goddess of agriculture, on the dome.

VIRGINIA

THE STATE CAPITOL *Richmond*

Virginia has been the center of much of America's early history, and the State Capitol at Richmond has been the scene of many of these events.

The first representative assembly in the Western World convened at Jamestown on July 30, 1619. The elected Burgesses, the Council of State and Sir George Yeardley, the Governor, met in the simple frame church on Jamestown Island. This structure, about fifty feet by twenty feet, continued to be used for about twenty years for subsequent meetings of the General Assembly, a term still used for the Virginia Legislature. The National Park Service has established that four Statehouses were used until 1676. All were destroyed by fire, and in 1698 the General Assembly decided to remove the capital to Middle Plantation, which was renamed Williamsburg in honor of the reigning English King, William III.

During the construction of a new Capitol in Williamsburg, the legislators met in the Wren Building, the oldest academic building in English America. The foundations for the Capitol were laid in 1701, and the General Assembly first met in the new but unfinished building in 1704. This was gutted by a fire on January 30, 1747, and a second Capitol was completed on the same site in 1753. After the removal of the government to Richmond in 1780, the second building was destroyed by fire in 1832. Colonial Williamsburg, a nonprofit organization financed by Mr. John D. Rockefeller, reconstructed the first Capitol, and the building is one of the showpieces of the restoration of Williamsburg.

On May 15, 1776, the Virginia Convention meeting in the Williamsburg Capitol resolved that the Virginia delegates to the Continental Congress should have Congress "declare the United Colonies free and independent states," and that the Convention should "prepare a Declaration of Rights."

Under the Virginia Constitution of 1776, the House of Burgesses was renamed the House of Delegates, and at the meeting of the first General Assembly under the Constitution, Thomas Jefferson proposed that the seat of government be removed from Williamsburg. The bill failed of passage in this session but was revived in 1779 and Richmond City was designated as the new capital. The seat of government was moved the following year, the General Assembly occupying a temporary building until the necessary land could be acquired and plans prepared for a new Capitol.

In 1785, the Directors of the Public Buildings requested Thomas Jefferson, then Minister to France, for assistance in planning the Capitol, and he employed a French architect, Charles Clérisseau, to assist him. Plans were prepared based on the Maison Carrée, at Nimes, which Jefferson called "one of the most beautiful, if not the most beautiful and precious morsel of architecture left us by antiquity." In addition to plans for the new Capitol, Jefferson sent a plaster model of the Maison Carrée, still on exhibit in the Capitol.

The cornerstone for the structure was laid on August 18, 1785, and the General Assembly moved into the unfinished Capitol for the October 1788 session. The

The aristocratic Statehouse in Richmond, once the Capitol of the Confederacy, was designed by Thomas Jefferson with the aid of a French architect.

new building established the classic revival, and many plantation homes began to use the columned portico.

The old hall of the House of Delegates was the scene of many historic events. Here, in 1807, Chief Justice Marshall presided over the trial of Aaron Burr for treason. Various Constitutional Conventions were held here, and on April 23, 1861, in this historic chamber, Robert E. Lee was appointed commander of the armed forces of Virginia. Nine years later, on April 27, 1870, a spectacular disaster occurred when the floors of the Supreme Court of Appeals, located on the story above, collapsed. Hundreds of people had crowded into the courtroom to hear the arguments as to who was the rightful mayor of Richmond, and the weight of the spectators caused the tragedy which killed 62 persons and injured 251 others.

Between 1904 and 1906, two wings were added to the original building, and through the years various modern improvements have been made. The old chamber of the House of Delegates has been restored and contains numerous statues and busts, including those of Jefferson Davis and Alexander H. Stephens, which remind visitors that the Virginia Capitol was also once the Capitol of the Confederacy.

In the Rotunda is the famous statue by Houdon of George Washington, one of Virginia's most distinguished sons. In niches surrounding the Rotunda are busts of other Virginia-born Presidents as well as the Houdon bust of General Lafayette. Portraits and plaques of distinguished Virginians, including many former Governors, are hung in corridors and offices throughout the building. The Capitol is a monument to the strength and growth of representative government as nurtured in Virginia from 1619 to the present.

WASHINGTON

THE LEGISLATIVE BUILDING *Olympia*

Standing on a trim green knoll amid the Capitol group complex of State buildings, the imposing structure known as the Washington State Legislative Building looks out over the City of Olympia.

From the dome of the Legislative Building, Mt. Rainier, Mt. Baker, Mt. St. Helens and Mt. Adams can be seen on a clear day. The snow-capped Olympic Mountains are visible from the lower portico. Rising 287 feet from the base, the dome is encircled by Corinthian-capped columns more than 20 feet high and is topped by a lantern 31 feet in diameter and 47 feet high.

Modified Roman-Doric architecture and Wilkeson sandstone give strength and charm to the building. Outside decorations, such as the oxen skull and wreath frieze and the cornice fringings, are carved in sandstone. Simplified Doric columns enclose the building. The main entrance colonnade consists of eight Corinthian columns each more than thirty feet high.

On the large bronze doors at the main entrance are reproductions symbolic of the major industries of the State, along with a replica of the first Capitol and an early homestead cabin.

The Rotunda is located in the center of the building, covered with an inner dome rising 185 feet above the floor level. Suspended from this dome is a bronze chandelier weighing five tons. This chandelier, twenty-five feet in length, is beautifully carved between the open fretwork. It hangs fifty feet above the Rotunda floor directly over a bronze reproduction of the State Seal, which is embedded in the marble and encircled by a wreath of oak leaves and acorns. At the four corners of the marble-faced supporting columns of the Rotunda are tall bronze standards, elaborately carved and fluted, which are exact replicas of early Roman firepots. The top of each contains a powerful light for illuminating the Rotunda.

Around the four balconies running between the supporting columns of the Rotunda are ornamental bronze railings decorated on each side with three reproductions of the State Seal.

Opposite: On a clear day, Washington's highest mountains are visible from the dome of the Legislative Building.

On the second floor are the House and Senate Chambers, the former in Formosa marble, the latter in Escaletto marble. The Governor's Executive Chamber is finished in mahogany, maroon drapes and red tapestry. The chambers of the President of the Senate and the Speaker of the House are finished in walnut.

The State Reception Room is considered one of the most beautiful in the Western Hemisphere, with Bresche Violette marble from Italy, tapestried Martha Washington chairs and Tiffany chandeliers of Czechoslovakian crystal. Carpet and furnishings are in green, gold and red.

Foundations for the present Legislative Building were laid in 1893, but it was not until thirty years later that portions of that foundation were incorporated in the new building, which was finally completed in 1928 at a cost of $7,385,768.

Today, it is immediately surrounded by the Governor's Mansion, the Temple of Justice, the State Library and the General Administration, Archives, Insurance, Institutions, Public Lands and Public Health buildings. Close by are new State office structures.

When Washington became a Territory on March 2, 1853, Olympia was named its capital, retaining this honor when statehood was conferred on November 11, 1889. Originally, the State was to be known as Columbia, but Congress changed the name in honor of the first President of the United States.

A frame building—the Gold Bar Restaurant—near Capitol Way and Second Avenue was the first meeting place of the Territorial Legislature on February 27, 1854. The Olympia Masonic Hall was "home" to the Legislatures in late 1854 and 1855. A frame structure was then built on the present Capitol site and served as the Capitol until 1902.

In 1901 Washington State purchased the old stone Thurston County Courthouse and added a wing to house the Legislature. This building (now called the Old Capitol Building) housed all State departments from 1905 to 1919. Several departments still use it.

The West Virginia Capitol is located on a beautiful sixteen-acre esplanade facing the Kanawha River. The 333-room building is considered by many to be a prime example of fine Italian Renaissance architecture.

WEST VIRGINIA

THE STATE CAPITOL *Charleston*

Both the West Virginia State Capitol and its setting in Charleston are among the most attractive in the United States.

The main building and its two wings are on a sixteen-acre esplanade above the Kanawha River, with a fine view overlooking the river area. From Kanawha Boulevard below the Capitol, a majestic stone stairway leads down to the water.

Many architects have called the West Virginia Capitol one of the world's outstanding examples of Italian Renaissance architecture and one of the most beautiful of the State Capitols. More modestly, Cass Gilbert, its architect, described it as ". . . classic in style and what might correctly be termed as Renaissance; the architectural forms are Roman with the single exception of the Doric vestibule at the ground floor on the river side of the building."

One of the most recently built Capitols, it was completed in 1932 at a cost of nearly $10 million. With a total of 535,000 square feet of space, it has 333 rooms.

Its steel skeleton is covered by buff-colored Indiana limestone. Of its eighty-six columns, those on the main portico are Roman Corinthian, the others a modified Doric. The golden dome, three hundred feet high, is illuminated at night.

Bronze doors open onto marble-columned foyers. Marble is used extensively inside: Imperial Danby for the walls, Italian travertine and white Vermont for the floors. From a fifty-four-foot gold chain suspended from the center of the dome's ceiling, a two-ton chandelier, 180 feet above the floor, lights the Rotunda.

The House and Senate Chambers on the second floor of the main section also feature impressive chandeliers, using 10,000 separate pieces of rock crystal. In the Capitol's showpiece, the Governor's reception room, the standout attraction is the light turquoise rug, which measures twenty-seven by seventy-two feet, is two feet thick and weighs one ton. The State Museum is located beneath the Executive Suite.

Two previous Capitols in Charleston were destroyed by fire. One was in use from 1885, when Charleston became West Virginia's capital city the second time, until 1921, when it burned. A temporary wood and wallboard replacement was then erected in forty-two working days. When this "pasteboard capitol," as it was popularly known, burned in 1927, the Senate met in a church and the House used the Court House, the City Hall, and the YMCA building until the present Capitol was completed.

Charleston and Wheeling had alternated as capitals until 1885 when the Legislature finally settled on the former city. In 1861, a pro-Union State government representing Virginia in Congress was organized at Wheeling. The northwestern portion of Virginia was then separated and admitted to the Union on June 20, 1863, as the State of West Virginia. Wheeling remained the capital of this State until 1870, and Charleston until 1875. Wheeling again became the capital but, in 1885, Charleston was named the permanent capital city of West Virginia.

The cruciform-shaped Wisconsin Capitol rests in a landscaped garden park situated in the heart of Madison.

WISCONSIN

THE STATE CAPITOL *Madison*

Wisconsin is renowned for her lakes and the scenic beauty of her vacation lands, and the State's apitol exemplifies Wisconsin's tradition of beauty. ocated in the heart of Madison on an isthmus between wo lakes, the Capitol is set on a landscaped garden quare known as Capitol Park. Streets radiate from he square to all parts of the city including the nearby ee-studded campus of the University of Wisconsin.

The building, constructed in a cruciform, covers early two and a half acres. Each of the four wings xtends 157 feet from the center portion, for a total of 438 feet across the building either east to west or north to south. The architectural style is Roman Renaissance with Corinthian columns on each of the four porticos. The pediments over the porticos are covered with allegorical sculpture.

Atop the core is a great white dome, built of granite on a steel frame and floodlit at night. On it stands the figure of "Forward," symbol of the State's Motto, with the right arm outstretched and raised and the left hand holding a globe surmounted by an eagle. The work of the celebrated Daniel Chester French, the statue is done in bronze covered with gold leaf and measures fifteen feet, four inches in height. The distance of 285.9 feet from the esplanade to the top of the statue is, by design, a few inches shorter than that of the National Capitol.

The building, which was planned and designed by the New York architectural firm of George B. Post and Sons, cost $7.2 million with furnishings when completed in 1917, eleven years after construction began. Durable white Bethel Vermont granite was used on the exterior. A variety of marble from such faraway shores as France, Norway, Italy, Algeria, Greece and Germany was used inside. Granite in contrasting colors was used for the floors, panels and columns.

Two hundred feet above the large octagonal Rotunda, on the ceiling of the dome, is Edwin Howland Blashfield's painting, "Resources of Wisconsin," nearly thirty-four feet in diameter. In the artist's words, it "is a symbolization of Wisconsin enthroned upon clouds and wrapped in the folds of the American flag. She holds the escutcheon of the State with the coat of arms of Wisconsin upon it, and in her right hand a scepter of wheat."

Immense arches open from the Rotunda to the wings, each of which has a grand stairway.

The legislative chambers are on the second floor, with the Senate in the south wing and the Assembly in the west. Other principal areas are the reception room in the Executive Chambers, the Supreme Court Room and the Hearing Room. All five are decorated with large symbolic or historical murals. Offices of the Governor, Treasurer and Secretary of State are in the Capitol.

The first permanent Capitol in Madison was used from 1838 until 1857. When it was outgrown, it was replaced by another, built gradually between 1857 and 1869 and enlarged in 1883. This suffered heavy damage from fire in 1904, but was repaired and used until the present Capitol replaced it.

Madison has been the State's only capital city, although the Territorial Legislature first met in Belmont and in Burlington (now in Iowa) before settling on a permanent location in what was then wilderness.

Originally part of the Northwest Territory, Wisconsin became a separate Territory in 1836. Reduced to its present size a decade later, Wisconsin entered the Union on May 29, 1848.

WYOMING

THE CAPITOL BUILDING *Cheyenne*

The Corinthian-like architecture of the Wyoming Capitol in Cheyenne is reminiscent of the National Capitol. The building was completed in April 1890, about two months before Wyoming was granted statehood on July 10.

Unlike many States which have had several Capitols, Wyoming has had only the present structure, although early Legislative Assemblies met in various places in Cheyenne after the Territory was organized in 1869.

The building of the present structure was authorized in 1886 by the Ninth Territorial Legislative Assembly, which directed that it should be erected in Cheyenne at a cost not to exceed $150,000. Plans and specifications were drawn by David W. Gibbs & Co., architects, in 1886. The cornerstone was laid May 18, 1887. The Tenth Territorial Legislative Assembly convened in the building in 1888, shortly before the central portion was completed in March of that year. The first wings were finished in April 1890.

As the State grew, the building became overcrowded, and in 1915 the Legislature provided for new east and west wings, completed in 1917. Today, the Senate is housed in the west wing and the House in the east. Each of the chambers has four large murals, the work of Allen True, which depict industry, pioneer life, law and transportation. The ceiling in each chamber is of beautiful stained glass, with the Seal of the State of Wyoming in the center.

The entire building is 200 feet long by 120 feet wide, exclusive of approaches, and the tip of the dome is 146 feet above grade. The first two courses of the building (above the ground) are of stone from quarries at Ft. Collins, Colorado; the building proper is of sandstone from the quarries of Rawlins, Wyoming.

The Rotunda, which is the primary interior attraction, consists of a circular hall, thirty feet in diameter. The distance from the floor to the lantern above the Rotunda is fifty-four feet. Cathedral glass reflects a mellow light throughout the interior, which is richly ornamented with plaster and elaborately turned woodwork. Three wide halls lead off the Rotunda—one to the main entrance and the other two to the east and west wings. The hall floors are laid with alternate foot-square tiles of white and black marble.

Completed in 1890 and Corinthian in style, the Wyoming Capitol has as its main interior feature a Rotunda with cathedral glass windows which cast a mellow glow on the circular hall below.

AMERICAN SAMOA

THE TERRITORIAL CAPITOL *Pago Pago*

The immediate impression of the venerable Territorial Capitol at Pago Pago is almost paradoxical. First, the building itself is a stately, white, two-story structure reminiscent of an Old South home of the antebellum days. Yet the setting is as exotic and colorful as one would expect in the South Pacific. Second, it hardly strikes a visitor as a government building, with its large porches which provide comfortable visiting places for Samoans who have business to transact or who merely wish to meet with friends. Yet it is the center of government for the Territory and has been since 1904, when it was built at a cost of $46,000.

From 1904 until 1950 it was the headquarters of operations for the United States Naval Government which administered Samoa until 1950, when a civilian government took control. Since that time it has been the Territorial Capitol.

It is one of the oldest buildings on the main island of Tutuila and was built by Joseph Jewett, who came to American Samoa as naval builder in 1902.

The Territorial courtroom is on the ground floor, as are the offices of the Chief Justice, the Associate Justice and the Clerk of Court. A room housing the Territorial Archives is in the rear. Second-floor executive offices include those of the Governor, the Secretary (who also is Lieutenant Governor) and the Public Defender.

The Capitol is an old building for the South Seas, where humidity takes a heavy toll on wooden structures. It was enlarged and remodeled in 1929. Officials say that ultimately a new Capitol will have to be built. There are so many pressing needs for educational and health facilities, however, that available funds are necessarily being applied to these.

The Capitol stands on the main road of Fagatogo, the governmental center, and overlooks beautiful Pago Pago Bay, one of the finest harbors in the Pacific. Nearby is the Territorial market place, usually teeming with shoppers for native foodstuffs. Surrounding this are open-sided Samoan buildings which serve as shops, primarily selling curios and Samoan craft items.

The Territorial Capitol at Pago Pago is similar in design to the South's graceful antebellum homes.

The Legislature Building serving as Guam's Capitol was built during the United States Navy's administration of the Island.

GUAM

LEGISLATURE BUILDING *Agaña*

The Legislature Building in Agaña, Guam, is now completely occupied by the Guam Legislature. The courts, which were housed there for a few years after this Capitol was constructed in 1947-1948, during the U.S. Navy administration of the Island, are now located elsewhere.

Guam is a 225-square-mile island located at the southern end of the Marianas, five thousand miles from the U.S. mainland. It is used primarily as a naval and air base, and in 1966 it had 45,870 permanent residents and about 40,000 military members and dependents.

The Marianas are part of the U.S. Trust Territory of the Pacific Islands, along with the Carolines and the Marshalls. Guam itself, however, is not a part of the Trust Territory (under the United States since 1945) but is a separate, unincorporated Territory, ceded to the United States by Spain in the Treaty of Paris, December 10, 1898. Guamanians have U.S. citizenship.

The Legislature Building consists of one large assembly hall, one smaller hall and a number of offices and rooms. It was designed to house a bicameral Legislature, but the Organic Act of 1950 created a unicameral Legislature with a maximum of twenty-one members popularly elected for two-year terms. This act created an assembly with true law-making powers, a step in the evolution of government in Guam. For the first time a curb was put on the absolute power of the Governor and more responsibility given to the Territorial Congress, which had had little functional power.

With the completion of a new courthouse, all courts moved from the Legislature Building to new locations. The executive offices are in a two-story building between the Legislature Building and Government House.

The Governor has been appointed by the President, but effective in 1970, the office will be determined by popular election. The effort for an elected Chief Executive for Guam was begun by Governor Bill Daniel, who was also primarily responsible for the abolition, in 1961, of the naval security clearance, required since 1941, for anyone visiting the Island. With removal of this obsolete restriction, tourism is fast becoming a major industry in Guam.

Ferdinand Magellan, the Portuguese explorer, discovered Guam and the other Mariana Islands in 1521, but Guam was formally made a possession of Spain on January 26, 1655, and later colonized by Spanish missionaries.

During the Spanish-American War, the U.S. warship *Charleston* shelled the fort at Apra Harbor. The Spanish Governor then thanked the ship's captain for his "salute" and apologized for not returning it because the fort's guns were out of commission. Guam was so remote that the people did not know of the war. The Americans took the Island easily and held it until World War II.

The Japanese seized Guam on December 10, 1941, and it was retaken by the United States on July 21, 1944.

PUERTO RICO

THE COMMONWEALTH CAPITOL

San Juan

The harbor at San Juan is one of the most attractive in the Western Hemisphere and the Commonwealth Capitol, a three-story Italian Renaissance building, adds to the beauty of the harbor and city.

Located at the entrance to old San Juan, the Capitol faces the Atlantic to the north and offers a breathtaking view of the Bay to the south. The building itself is exquisite in design, faithfully following the Renaissance style. It has a shallow dome and cupola topped by an open lantern. A large building, it covers 51,814 square feet, and was designed by the architect Rafael Carmoega.

From Ponce de Leon Avenue on the south, a wide marble stairway ascends to one of two main entrances, each with eight Corinthian columns around seven doorways. Carved on the door's lintels are the names of the Island's seven districts before it became a Commonwealth.

The rectangular Rotunda, completed in 1958, has four Ionic columns in veined rose marble on each side. Centered on the marble-tiled floor is an urn containing the original of the Commonwealth Constitution, approved July 25, 1952. At the apex of the dome, eighty feet above, is the Puerto Rican coat of arms.

The Rotunda ceiling is richly ornamented with Venetian mosaic figures representing Justice, Freedom, Education, Health, Science, the Arts, Industry and Agriculture. In the corners beneath these curving panels are mosaics representing the discovery of the Island, its conquest and colonization, the autonomist movement of 1887 and the abolition of slavery. These are the work of Puerto Rican artists Rafael Ríos Rey, José R. Oliver, Jorge Rechani and Rafael Tufiño.

Above the white marble balustrade around the Rotunda at the third story, four great arches frame semicircular windows of brass and ground glass. Behind the columns at the second-story level are white Carrara marble friezes designed by Ríos Rey, Oliver and Rechani and executed by the Italian sculptor Tomassi. These tell the history of Puerto Rico from early Indian days to Commonwealth status.

On the first floor, marble columns veined in violet-black stand guard beside white marble staircases to the second story.

The second-floor House and Senate Chambers, with classic design, arched doorways and travertine-faced walls, have modern furnishings. A reception hall, rich in Renaissance ornamentation, is on the north.

Two modern buildings annexed to the Capitol serve as offices of the legislators and the Controller.

The cornerstone for the Capitol was laid on July 17, 1925. This date was most appropriate, as it was the birthday of Luis Muñoz Rivera, who had conceived the

Because of its meticulous Renaissance styling, the Capitol of Puerto Rico has an almost delicate appearance. The broad dome and cupola are capped by an open lantern.

idea of the building and had introduced enabling legislation in the House of Delegates. Also playing a vital role in the building of the Capitol was Antonio R. Barceló, his successor. Both men are honored with busts, in the House and Senate galleries respectively.

Puerto Rico became a possession of the United States under the 1898 treaty with Spain and was granted Commonwealth status by the Congress in 1952. In a 1967 referendum, the people chose to retain Commonwealth status rather than to seek either independence or statehood. But throughout Puerto Rico's varied political history, San Juan has always been the capital.

Government House in Charlotte Amalie serves as both office and residence for the Chief Executive. The three-story, brick-faced building also holds several government offices.

VIRGIN ISLANDS

GOVERNMENT HOUSE *Charlotte Amalie*

There are three separate major government buildings for the Virgin Islands, and residents like to say this is because they enjoy the excuses to move over the emerald-tinted waters and through the lush colors of the soft tropical forestlands.

It may seem that, in actuality, the Islands have two capital cities and two Capitol buildings, but officially the Capitol is Government House in Charlotte Amalie on the Island of St. Thomas. It is both office and residence for the Governor. However, there is another office and residence in another Government House, at Christiansted, St. Croix, which is described in this book under Executive Mansions. To add to the confusion, the Legislature meets for two months each year in a third structure, the two-story, green-colored Senate building on the Charlotte Amalie waterfront near Fort Christian.

The present Government House in St. Thomas came into existence when the city fathers of the 1860's—the Colonial Council of the Islands then under Danish rule—agreed that the existing Government Mansion had to be replaced. The latter was the official residence of the Vice Governor of the Danish West Indies (the Governor resided in St. Croix) and, since its construction in 1819, it had become dilapidated.

Here their agreement ended. They argued endlessly about whether or not they should build. One disgruntled townsman suggested the executive return to Fort Christian, the bastion of the Islands which was said to have quartered the Governors from early colonization days, beginning in 1665. Another possibility was to buy the beautiful residence and grounds of a former Vice Governor, which was for sale at $12,000.

In the end, the Council elected to build, a decision which has since caused their governmental heirs to shudder. Today the asking price for that same property is over one-half million dollars!

The present building cost $33,605 and was completed in September 1867. While it was being built, the Governor lived in Blackbeard's Castle in Charlotte Amalie.

The number of Governors residing in it and other Government Houses of the Islands have totalled twenty-five—nine Danish and sixteen American. Of the latter, seven were appointed by the Navy, as the Territory was under Navy jurisdiction from 1917 to 1931.

The brick-faced masonry building has three stories, the first of which consists of governmental offices. The Governor's office leads to an ever-blooming garden-patio, constructed in 1967. Thick red carpeting covers the foyer floor. On the walls are murals depicting scenes of historical significance in the Islands' development.

A fine, beautifully hand-molded mahogany handrail atop a wrought-iron stairway, and a recently installed elevator lead to a second story. Renovated in 1967, this floor has three rooms—a State Dining Room, often used for small conferences, a formal reception room and a kitchen-pantry.

The handmade dining room furniture is of English design, its rich, dark wood standing out against the gold brocade draperies and matching wallpaper. In particular, a Sheraton sideboard is outstanding for its fine workmanship.

The upholstered pieces of the reception room are of Victorian and French styling and are covered in silk, velvet and brocade. The high ceiling, ornate crowns and moldings are white, while the plaster-finished walls are in vibrant yellow-gold. Seven large baroque mirrors and original paintings by such artists as Camille Pissarro, Thomas Hart Benton, Gustave Courbet, Luciano Miori and Eduard Viullard hang on the walls. Three magnificent antique chandeliers of crystal are suspended from the ceiling.

The third floor is the residence of the Governor. This consists of a living room, study, three bedrooms with baths, dining room and kitchen-pantry. Throughout these rooms are a number of fine antique pieces, chests, cabinets and chairs, many of which were handmade by old West Indian craftsmen, acknowledged as among the finest of wood masters.

In addition, there is a glass-enclosed gallery, or solarium. This spacious room stands out in sharp contrast to its former state. Converted by Governor Ralph M. Paiewonsky, it had been an outdoor area for hanging laundry. It abounds in potted flora of all types.

Work has begun on a government center to accommodate the Virgin Islands' administrative agencies, commissions and boards.

III.
CHIEF EXECUTIVES

In preparing this book on *Executive Mansions and Capitols of America,* the authors found that there was no single complete and up-to-date publication listing the names of Chief Executives who have served the States, Commonwealths and Territories.

Believing that such a list would be a valuable reference for Federal officials, Governors and interested citizens, direct contacts were made with all Governors and many archivists in order to obtain complete and correct names and terms of those who have served within their respective jurisdictions. The lists supplied from these sources were then checked against official manuals of individual States, the *Encyclopedia Americana, White's Conspectus of American Biography,* and the publication of the Council of State Governments entitled *The Governors of the States, 1900-1966.* The result is a compilation from all of these original and published sources.

Except where otherwise indicated, the names of Governors prior to 1935 are the same as shown in *White's Conspectus of American Biography, Second Edition,* James T. White & Co., 1937. Those after 1935 are the same as shown by the Council of State Governments, unless otherwise noted.

The task of reconciling the various lists and compiling Part III of this book was performed by Mrs. Mary Pearl Williams under the supervision of the coauthor while he served as Assistant to the President for Federal-State Relations. In addition to Mrs. Williams, credit and appreciation are due to the Governors, many of the State Archivists and the Regional Directors and other staff members of the Office of Emergency Preparedness and Federal-State Relations, who cooperated and participated in this project. ——— Price Daniel

PRESIDENTS OF THE UNITED STATES

Term	
1789-1797	George Washington
1797-1801	John Adams
1801-1809	Thomas Jefferson
1809-1817	James Madison
1817-1825	James Monroe
1825-1829	John Quincy Adams
1829-1837	Andrew Jackson
1837-1841	Martin Van Buren
1841	William Henry Harrison
1841-1845	John Tyler
1845-1849	James K. Polk
1849-1850	Zachary Taylor
1850-1853	Millard Fillmore
1853-1857	Franklin Pierce
1857-1861	James Buchanan
1861-1865	Abraham Lincoln
1865-1869	Andrew Johnson
1869-1877	Ulysses S. Grant
1877-1881	Rutherford B. Hayes
1881	James A. Garfield
1881-1885	Chester A. Arthur
1885-1889	Grover Cleveland
1889-1893	Benjamin Harrison
1893-1897	Grover Cleveland
1897-1901	William McKinley
1901-1909	Theodore Roosevelt
1909-1913	William H. Taft
1913-1921	Woodrow Wilson
1921-1923	Warren G. Harding
1923-1929	Calvin Coolidge
1929-1933	Herbert C. Hoover
1933-1945	Franklin D. Roosevelt
1945-1953	Harry S. Truman
1953-1961	Dwight D. Eisenhower
1961-1963	John F. Kennedy
1963-1969	Lyndon B. Johnson
1969-	Richard M. Nixon

ALABAMA

Term	Mississippi Territorial Governors*
1798-1801	Winthrop Sargent
1801-1805	William C. C. Claiborne
1805-1809	Robert Williams
1809-1817	David Holmes
	Alabama Territorial Governor*
1817-1819	William Wyatt Bibb

	State Governors
1819-1820	William Wyatt Bibb
1820-1821	Thomas Bibb
1821-1825	Israel Pickens
1825-1829	John Murphy
1829-1831	Gabriel Moore
1831	Samuel B. Moore
1831-1835	John Gayle

1835-1837	Clement Comer Clay
1837-1841	Arthur P. Bagby
1841-1845	Benjamin Fitzpatrick
1845-1847	Joshua L. Martin
1847-1849	Reuben Chapman
1849-1853	Henry W. Collier
1853-1857	John A. Winston
1857-1861	Andrew B. Moore
1861-1863	John G. Shorter
1863-1865	Thomas Hill Watts
1865	Lewis E. Parsons
1865-1868	Robert Miller Patton
1868-1870	William Hugh Smith
1870-1872	Robert Burns Lindsay
1872-1874	David Peter Lewis
1874-1878	George Smith Houston
1878-1882	Rufus W. Cobb
1882-1886	Edward Asbury O'Neal
1886-1890	Thomas Seay
1890-1894	Thomas Goode Jones
1894-1896	William Calvin Oates
1896-1900	Joseph Forney Johnston
1900-1901	William James Samford
1901-1907	William Dorsey Jelks
1907-1911	Braxton Bragg Comer
1911-1915	Emmet O'Neal
1915-1919	Charles Henderson
1919-1923	Thomas Erby Kilby
1923-1927	William Woodward Brandon
1927-1931	David Bibb Graves
1931-1935	Benjamin Meek Miller
1935-1939	David Bibb Graves
1939-1943	Frank M. Dixon
1943-1947	Chauncey Sparks
1947-1951	James E. Folsom
1951-1955	Gordon Persons
1955-1959	James E. Folsom
1959-1963	John M. Patterson
1963-1967	George Corley Wallace
1967-1968	Lurleen Burns Wallace
1968-	Albert Preston Brewer

**Alabama Official and Statistical Register*, 1963, p. 30-31. The *Register* lists in addition Hugh McVay, 1837; William Dorsey Jelks (acting), in 1900; Russell McWhorter Cunningham (acting), 1904-1905.

ALASKA

TERM	DISTRICT GOVERNORS*
1884-1885	John H. Kinkead
1885-1889	A. P. Swineford
1889-1893	Lyman E. Knapp
1893-1897	James Sheakley
1897-1906	John G. Brady
1906-1909	Wilford B. Hoggatt
1909-1913	Walter E. Clark
	TERRITORIAL GOVERNORS*
1913-1918	John F. A. Strong
1918-1921	Thomas Riggs, Jr.
1921-1925	Scott C. Bone
1925-1933	George A. Parks
1933-1939	John W. Troy
1939-1953	Ernest Gruening
1953-1957	B. Frank Heintzelman
1957	Waino Hendrickson
1957-1958	Michael A. Stepovich
1958-1959	Waino Hendrickson
	STATE GOVERNORS
1959-1967	William A. Egan
1967-1969	Walter J. Hickel
1969-	Keith Miller

*The *Encyclopedia Americana*, Vol. 1, p. 320.

ARIZONA

TERM	TERRITORIAL GOVERNORS*
1863-1866	John N. Goodwin
1866-1869	Richard C. McCormick
1869-1877	A. P. K. Safford
1877-1878	John P. Hoyt
1878-1881	John C. Fremont
1881-1885	Frederick A. Tritle
1885-1889	C. Meyer Zulick
1889-1890	Lewis Wolfley
1890-1892	John N. Irwin
1892-1893	Nathan O. Murphy
1893-1896	Louis C. Hughes
1896-1897	Benjamin J. Franklin
1897-1898	Myron H. McCord
1898-1902	Nathan O. Murphy
1902-1905	Alexander O. Brodie
1905-1909	Joseph H. Kibbey
1909-1911	Richard E. Sloan
	STATE GOVERNORS
1912-1918	George W. P. Hunt
1919-1922	Thomas E. Campbell
1923-1928	George W. P. Hunt
1929-1930	John C. Phillips
1931-1932	George W. P. Hunt
1933-1936	Benjamin B. Moeur
1937-1938	Rawleigh C. Stanford
1939-1940	Robert T. Jones
1941-1948	Sidney P. Osborn
1948-1950	Dan E. Garvey
1951-1954	J. Howard Pyle
1955-1958	Ernest W. McFarland
1959-1964	Paul Fannin
1965-1967	Samuel P. Goddard, Jr.
1967-	John R. Williams

*The *Encyclopedia Americana*, Vol. 2, p. 256.

ARKANSAS

TERM TERRITORIAL GOVERNORS*

For earlier Territorial Governors, see Louisiana and Missouri.‡

TERM	TERRITORIAL GOVERNORS*
1819-1825	James Miller
1825-1829	George Izard
1829-1835	John Pope
1835-1836	William Fulton
	STATE GOVERNORS
1836-1840	James S. Conway
1840-1844	Archibald Yell
1844	Samuel Adams
1844-1848	Thomas S. Drew
1848-1852	John S. Roane
1852-1860	Elias N. Conway

1860-1862	Henry M. Rector
1862-1864	Harris Flanagin
1864-1868	Isaac Murphy
1868-1871	Powell Clayton
1871-1873	Ozro A. Hadley
1873-1874	Elisha Baxter
1874-1877	Augustus H. Garland
1877-1881	William R. Miller
1881-1883	Thomas J. Churchill
1883-1885	James H. Berry
1885-1889	Simon P. Hughes
1889-1893	James P. Eagle
1893-1895	William M. Fishback
1895-1897	James P. Clarke
1897-1901	Daniel W. Jones
1901-1907	Jefferson Davis
1907	John S. Little
1907-1909	X. O. Pindall
1909-1913	George W. Donaghey
1913	Joseph T. Robinson
1913-1917	George W. Hays
1917-1921	Charles H. Brough
1921-1925	Thomas C. McRae
1925-1927	Thomas J. Terrel†
1927-1929	John E. Martineau
1929-1933	Harvey Parnell
1933-1937	J. Marion Futrell
1937-1941	Carl E. Bailey
1941-1945	Homer M. Adkins
1945-1949	Benjamin T. Laney
1949-1953	Sidney S. McMath
1953-1955	Francis Cherry
1955-1967	Orval E. Faubus
1967-	Winthrop Rockefeller

*_Historical Report of the Secretary of State_ (Arkansas), 1958, p. 193. The _Report_ lists in addition John Williamson (acting), 1846; Richard C. Byrd (acting), 1849, John R. Hampton (acting), 1851; Thomas Fletcher (acting), 1862; Ben T. Embry (acting), 1883; John W. Stayton (acting), no date given but sometime between 1884 and 1886; D. E. Barker (acting), no date but sometime between 1886 and 1888; C. C. Hamby (acting), 1892; Clay Sloan (acting), 1893; J. C. Pinnix (acting); 1896; J. C. South (acting), 1897; J. C. Tappan (acting), between 1897 and 1898; R. L. Lawrence (acting), between 1898 and 1900; M. P. Huddleston (acting), between 1900 and 1902; O. N. Killough (acting), between 1902 and 1904; John P. Lee (acting), between 1904 and 1906; John S. Little, 1906; John I. Moore (acting), between 1906 and 1907; X. O. Pindall (acting), 1907; Allen H. Hamiter (acting), 1907; J. M. Martin (acting), sometime between 1907 and 1908; James T. Robertson (acting), sometime between 1908 and 1909; W. C. Rodgers (acting), sometime between 1911 and 1912; Wm. K. Oldham (acting), 1913; J. M. Futrell (acting), 1913.

†The _Report_ spells surname "Terral."

‡Prior to 1819, Arkansas was part of the Territory of Louisiana and then part of the Upper Louisiana and Missouri Territories.

CALIFORNIA*

Term	Spanish Governors
1769-1771	Gaspar de Portola
1771-1774	Felipe de Barri
1774-1782	Felipe de Neve
1782-1790	Pedro Fages
1790-1792	José Romeu
1792-1794	José Joaquín de Arrillaga
1794-1800	Diego de Borica
1800-1814	José Joaquín de Arrillaga
1814-1815	José Arguello
1815-1822	Pablo Vicente de Sola
	Mexican Governors
1823-1825	Luis Arguello
1825-1831	José María Echeandia
1831-1832	Manuel Victoria
1832-1833	Pío Pico
1833-1835	José Figueroa
1835-1836	José Castro
1836	Nicolás Gutierrez
1836	Mariano Chico
1836	Nicolás Gutierrez
1836-1842	Juan Bautista Alvarado
1842-1845	Manuel Micheltorena
1846	Pío Pico
	American Governors under Military Rule
1846	John D. Sloat
1846	Robert F. Stockton
1847	John C. Frémont
1847	Stephen W. Kearny
1847-1849	Richard B. Mason

Mexico ceded California to the United States on February 2, 1848, by the Treaty of Guadalupe Hidalgo.

1849	Persifor F. Smith
1849	Bennett Riley
	State Governors
1849-1851	Peter H. Burnett
1851-1852	John McDougall
1852-1856	John Bigler
1856-1858	James Neeley Johnson
1858-1860	John B. Weller
1860	Milton S. Latham
1860-1862	John G. Downey
1862-1863	Leland Stanford
1863-1867	Frederick F. Low
1867-1871	Henry H. Haight
1871-1875	Newton Booth
1875	Romualdo Pacheco
1875-1880	William Irwin
1880-1883	George C. Perkins
1883-1887	George Stoneman
1887	Washington Bartlett
1887-1891	Robert W. Waterman
1891-1895	Henry H. Markham
1895-1899	James H. Budd
1899-1903	Henry T. Gage
1903-1907	George C. Pardee
1907-1911	James N. Gillett
1911-1917	Hiram W. Johnson
1917-1923	William D. Stephens
1923-1927	Friend William Richardson
1927-1931	Clement C. Young
1931-1934	James Rolph, Jr.
1934-1939	Frank Finley Merriam
1939-1943	Culbert L. Olson
1943-1953	Earl Warren
1953-1959	Goodwin J. Knight
1959-1967	Edmund G. Brown
1967-	Ronald Reagan

*_California Almanac_, 1966 edition, pp. 68-69.

COLORADO

Term	Territorial Governors*
1861-1862	William Gilpin
1862-1865	John Evans
1865-1867	Alexander Cummings
1867-1869	A. C. Hunt
1869-1873	Edward McCook
1873-1874	Samuel H. Elbert
1874-1875	Edward McCook
1875-1876	John L. Routt
	State Governors
1876-1879	John L. Routt
1879-1883	Frederick W. Pitkin
1883-1885	James B. Grant

1885-1887	Benjamin H. Eaton
1887-1889	Alva Adams
1889-1891	Job A. Cooper
1891-1893	John L. Routt
1893-1895	Davis H. Waite
1895-1897	Albert W. McIntire
1897-1899	Alva Adams
1899-1901	Charles S. Thomas
1901-1903	James B. Orman
1903-1905	James H. Peabody
1905	Alva Adams
1905	James H. Peabody
1905-1907	Jesse F. McDonald
1907-1909	Henry A. Buchtel
1909-1913	John F. Shafroth
1913-1915	Elias M. Ammons
1915-1917	George A. Carlson
1917-1919	Julius C. Gunter
1919-1923	Oliver H. Shoup
1923-1925	William E. Sweet
1925-1929	Clarence J. Morley
1929-1933	William H. Adams
1933-1937	Edwin C. Johnson
1937	Ray H. Talbot
1937-1939	Teller Ammons
1939-1943	Ralph L. Carr
1943-1947	John C. Vivian
1947-1950	William Lee Knous
1950-1951	Walter Warren Johnson
1951-1955	Dan Thornton
1955-1957	Edwin C. Johnson
1957-1963	Stephen L. R. McNichols
1963-	John A. Love

**Colorado Yearbook*, 1959-61, p. 190.

CONNECTICUT

Term	Colonial Governors
1639-1640	John Haynes
1640-1641	Edward Hopkins
1641-1642	John Haynes
1642-1643	George Wyllys
1643-1644	John Haynes
1644-1645	Edward Hopkins
1645-1646	John Haynes
1646-1647	Edward Hopkins
1647-1648	John Haynes
1648-1649	Edward Hopkins
1649-1650	John Haynes
1650-1651	Edward Hopkins
1651-1652	John Haynes
1652-1653	Edward Hopkins
1653-1654	John Haynes
1654-1655	Edward Hopkins
1655-1656	Thomas Welles
1656-1657	John Webster
1657-1658	John Winthrop, Jr.
1658-1659	Thomas Welles
1659-1675	John Winthrop, Jr.
1675-1683	William Leete
1683-1687	Robert Treat
1687-1689	Edmund Andros
1689-1698	Robert Treat
1698-1707	Fitz-John Winthrop
1707-1724	Gurdon Saltonstall
1724-1741	Joseph Talcott
1741-1750	Jonathan Law
1750-1754	Roger Wolcott
1754-1766	Thomas Fitch
1766-1769	William Pitkin
1769-1776	Jonathan Trumbull
	State Governors
1776-1784	Jonathan Trumbull
1784-1786	Matthew Griswold
1786-1788	Samuel Huntington

Connecticut ratified U.S. Constitution on January 9, 1788.

1788-1796	Samuel Huntington
1796-1798	Oliver Wolcott
1798-1809	Jonathan Trumbull, II
1809-1811	John Treadwell
1811-1813	Roger Griswold
1813-1817	John Cotton Smith
1817-1827	Oliver Wolcott, Jr.
1827-1831	Gideon Tomlinson
1831-1833	John S. Peters
1833-1834	Henry W. Edwards
1834-1835	Samuel A. Foote*
1835-1838	Henry W. Edwards
1838-1842	William W. Ellsworth
1842-1844	Chauncey F. Cleveland
1844-1846	Roger S. Baldwin
1846-1847	Isaac Toucey
1847-1849	Clark Bissell
1849-1850	Joseph Trumbull
1850-1853	Thomas H. Seymour
1854-1855	Henry Dutton
1855-1857	William T. Minor
1857-1858	Alexander H. Holley
1858-1866	William A. Buckingham
1866-1867	Joseph R. Hawley
1867-1869	James E. English
1869-1870	Marshall Jewell
1870-1871	James E. English
1871-1873	Marshall Jewell
1873-1877	Charles R. Ingersoll
1877-1879	Richard D. Hubbard
1879-1881	Charles B. Andrews
1881-1883	Hobart B. Bigelow
1883-1885	Thomas M. Waller
1885-1887	Henry B. Harrison
1887-1889	Phineas C. Lounsbury
1889-1893	Morgan G. Bulkeley
1893-1895	Luzon B. Morris
1895-1897	Owen Vincent Coffin
1897-1899	Lorrin A. Cooke
1899-1901	George E. Lounsbury
1901-1903	George P. McLean
1903-1905	Abiram Chamberlain
1905-1907	Henry Roberts
1907-1909	Rollin S. Woodruff
1909	George L. Lilley
1909-1911	Frank B. Weeks
1911-1915	Simeon E. Baldwin
1915-1921	Marcus H. Holcomb
1921-1923	Everett J. Lake
1923-1925	Charles A. Templeton
1925-1931	John H. Trumbull
1931-1939	Wilbur L. Cross
1939-1941	Raymond E. Baldwin
1941-1943	Robert A. Hurley
1943-1945	Raymond E. Baldwin
1945-1947	Charles Wilbert Snow
1947-1948	James L. McConaughy
1948-1949	James C. Shannon
1949-1951	Chester Bowles
1951-1955	John Lodge
1955-1961	Abraham Ribicoff
1961-	John Dempsey

Note: *Register and Manual*, Connecticut, 1967, p. 86, adds Charles H. Pond, 1853-1854; Hiram Bingham, 1925 (one day).
*The *Manual* spells surname "Foot."

DELAWARE

Term	Governors of New Sweden*
1638	Peter Minuit†
1640-1643	Peter Hollandaer
1643-1653	Johan Printz
1653-1654	Johan Papegoja
1654-1655	Johan Classon Rising

For governors from 1655 to 1682, see New York; and from 1682 to 1776, Pennsylvania.

	Presidents of Delaware*
1777	John McKinly
1777	Thomas McKean (acting)
1777-1778	George Read (acting)
1778-1781	Caesar Rodney
1781-1782	John Dickinson
1782-1783	John Cook (acting)
1783-1786	Nicholas Van Dyke
1786-1787	Thomas Collins

Delaware ratified U.S. Constitution on December 7, 1787.

	State Governors‡
1787-1789	Thomas Collins
1789	Jehu Davis (acting)
1789-1796	Joshua Clayton
1796-1797	Gunning Bedford, Sr.
1797-1799	Daniel Rogers
1799-1801	Richard Bassett
1801-1802	James Sykes
1802-1805	David Hall
1805-1808	Nathaniel Mitchell
1808-1811	George Truitt
1811-1814	Joseph Haslet
1814-1817	Daniel Rodney
1817-1820	John Clark
1820-1822	John Collins
1822-1823	Caesar Rodney (acting)§
1823	Joseph Haslet
1823-1824	Charles Thomas (acting)
1824-1827	Samuel M. Paynter
1827-1830	Charles Polk
1830-1833	David Hazzard
1833-1837	Caleb P. Bennett
1837-1841	Cornelius P. Comegys
1841-1845	William B. Cooper
1845-1847	Thomas Stockton
1847-1851	William Tharp
1851-1855	William H. Ross
1855-1859	Peter F. Causey
1859-1863	William Burton
1863-1865	William Cannon
1865-1871	Gove Saulsbury
1871-1875	James Ponder
1875-1879	John P. Cochran
1879-1883	John W. Hall
1883-1887	Charles C. Stockley
1887-1891	Benjamin T. Biggs
1891-1895	Robert J. Reynolds
1895	Joshua H. Marvil§
1895-1897	William T. Watson (acting)
1897-1901	Ebe W. Tunnell
1901-1905	John Hunn
1905-1909	Preston Lea
1909-1913	Simeon S. Pennewill
1913-1917	Charles R. Miller
1917-1921	John G. Townsend, Jr.
1921-1925	William du H. Denney
1925-1929	Robert P. Robinson
1929-1937	C. Douglass Buck
1937-1941	Richard C. McMullen
1941-1949	Walter W. Bacon
1949-1953	Elbert N. Carvel
1953-1961	James Caleb Boggs
1961-1965	Elbert N. Carvel
1965-1969	Charles L. Terry, Jr.
1969-	Russell W. Peterson

*The *Encyclopedia Americana*, Vol. 8, p. 611.

†Peter Minuit was lost at sea in 1638, leaving the colony leaderless until 1640.

‡The *Encyclopedia Americana* also adds the following names to its list of State Governors: Jacob Stout (acting), 1820-1821; Charles Polk (acting), 1836-1837; Joseph Maull (acting), 1846; William Temple, 1846-1847.

§The *Encyclopedia Americana* lists names Caleb Rodney, Joshua H. Marvel.

FLORIDA

Term	Territorial Governors*
1822-1834	William P. DuVal
1834-1835	John H. Eaton
1835-1840	Richard K. Call
1840-1841	Robert Raymond Reid
1841-1844	Richard K. Call
1844-1845	John Branch

	State Governors
1845-1849	William D. Moseley
1849-1853	Thomas Brown
1853-1857	James E. Broome
1857-1861	Madison S. Perry
1861-1865	John Milton
1865	William Marvin
1865-1868	David S. Walker
1868-1873	Harrison Reed
1873-1874	Ossian B. Hart
1874-1877	Marcellus L. Stearns
1877-1881	George F. Drew
1881-1885	William D. Bloxham
1885-1889	Edward A. Perry
1889-1893	Francis P. Fleming
1893-1897	Henry L. Mitchell
1897-1901	William D. Bloxham
1901-1905	William Sherman Jennings
1905-1909	Napoleon B. Broward
1909-1913	Albert W. Gilchrist
1913-1917	Park Trammell
1917-1921	Sidney J. Catts
1921-1925	Cary A. Hardee
1925-1929	John W. Martin
1929-1933	Doyle E. Carlton
1933-1937	David Sholtz
1937-1941	Frederick P. Cone
1941-1945	Spessard L. Holland
1945-1949	Millard F. Caldwell
1949-1953	Fuller Warren
1953	Dan E. McCarty†
1953-1955	Charley E. Johns
1955-1961	LeRoy Collins
1961-1965	Farris Bryant
1965-1967	Haydon Burns
1967-	Claude R. Kirk, Jr.

*The *Florida Handbook*, 1967-1968, p. 56. The *Handbook* adds in addition Abram K. Allison (acting), 1865. Authority of both William H. Gleason, 1868, and Samuel T. Day, 1872, is disputed and neither is usually listed, according to the *Handbook*.

†The *Handbook* lists McCarty's middle initial as "T."

GEORGIA

Term	Colonial Governors*
1733-1743	James Edward Oglethorpe
1743-1750	William Stephens
1750-1754	Henry Parker
	Provincial Governors*
1754-1757	John Reynolds
1757-1760	Henry Ellis
1760-1776	James Wright
	Provisional Governors*
1776-1777	Archibald Bulloch
1777	Button Gwinnett
	State Governors
1777-1778	John Adam Treutlen
1778-1779	John Houston†
1779	George Walton
1779-1782	James Wright
1782-1783	John Martin
1783-1784	Lyman Hall
1784-1785	John Houston
1785-1786	Samuel Elbert
1786-1787	Edward Telfair
1787-1788	George Mathews
Georgia ratified U. S. Constitution on January 2, 1788.	
1788-1789	George Handley
1789-1791	George Walton
1791-1793	Edward Telfair
1794-1796	George Mathews
1796-1798	Jared Irwin
1798-1801	James Jackson
1801-1802	David Emanuel
1802-1803	Josiah Tattnall, Jr.
1803-1806	John Milledge
1806-1809	Jared Irwin
1809-1813	David Brydie Mitchell
1813-1815	Peter Early
1815-1817	David Brydie Mitchell
1817-1819	William Rabun
1819	Matthew Talbot
1819-1823	John Clarke†
1823-1827	George Michael Troup
1827-1829	John Forsyth
1829-1831	George Rockingham Gilmer
1831-1835	Wilson Lumpkin
1835-1837	William Schley
1837-1839	George Rockingham Gilmer
1839-1843	Charles James McDonald
1843-1847	George Walker Crawford
1847-1851	George Washington Towns
1851-1853	Howell Cobb
1853-1857	Herschel Vespasian Johnson
1857-1865	Joseph Emerson Brown
1865	James Johnson
1865-1868	Charles Jones Jenkins
1868	Thomas Howard Ruger
1868-1871	Rufus Brown Bullock
1871-1872	Benjamin Conley
1872-1876	Joseph Milton Smith†
1876-1882	Alfred Holt Colquitt
1882-1883	Alexander Hamilton Stephens
1883	James Stoddard Boynton
1883-1886	Henry Dickerson McDaniel
1886-1890	John Brown Gordon
1890-1895	William Jonathan Northern†
1895-1899	William Yates Atkinson
1899-1903	Allen Daniel Candler
1903-1907	Joseph Meriwether Terrell
1907-1909	Hoke Smith
1909-1911	Joseph Mackey Brown
1911	Hoke Smith
1911-1913	Joseph Mackey Brown
1913-1915	John Marshall Slaton
1915-1917	Nathaniel Edwin Harris
1917-1921	Hugh Manson Dorsey
1921-1923	Thomas William Hardwick
1923-1927	Clifford Walker
1927-1931	Lamartine Griffin Hardman
1931-1933	Richard Brevard Russell, Jr.
1933-1937	Eugene Talmadge
1937-1941	Eurith Dickinson Rivers
1941-1943	Eugene Talmadge
1943-1947	Ellis Gibbs Arnall
1947-1948	Melvin E. Thompson
1948-1955	Herman Eugene Talmadge
1955-1959	S. Marvin Griffin
1959-1963	Samuel Ernest Vandiver, Jr.
1963-1967	Carl Edward Sanders
1967-	Lester Maddox

**Georgia Official and Statistical Register*, 1959-1960, p. 1014. The *Register* adds the following names and terms: John Wereat, 1779-1780; Richard Howley, 1780 (one month); Stephen Heard, 1780-1781; Nathan Brownson, 1781-1782; John Marshall Slaton, 1911-1912.

†The *Register* lists name John "Houstoun," John "Clark," "James" Milton Smith, William Jonathan "Northen."

HAWAII

Term	Provisional Government*
	President
1893-1894	Sanford Ballard Dole
	Republic of Hawaii*
	President
1894-1900	Sanford Ballard Dole
	Territorial Governors*
1900-1903	Sanford Ballard Dole
1903-1907	George Robert Carter
1907-1913	Walter Francis Frear
1913-1918	Lucius Eugene Pinkham
1918-1921	Charles James McCarthy
1921-1929	Wallace Rider Farrington
1929-1934	Lawrence McCully Judd
1934-1942	Joseph Boyd Poindexter
1942-1951	Ingram Macklin Stainback
1951-1953	Oren Ethelbirt Long
1953-1957	Samuel Wilder King
1957-1959	William Francis Quinn
	State Governors
1959-1962	William F. Quinn
1962-	John Anthony Burns

**Thrum's Hawaiian Annual*, 78th Edition, 1953, pp. 319-322.

IDAHO

Term	Territorial Governors*
1863-1864	William H. Wallace
1864-1866	Caleb Lyon
1866-1870	David M. Ballard
1870	Samuel Bard
1870-1871	Gilman Marston
1871	Alexander H. Connor
1871	Thomas M. Bowen
1871-1875	Thomas W. Bennett
1875-1876	David P. Thompson
1876-1878	Mason Brayman
1878-1880	John P. Hoyt
1880-1883	John B. Neil
1883-1884	John N. Irwin
1884-1885	William M. Bunn
1885-1889	Edward A. Stevenson
1889	George L. Shoup
	State Governors
1889-1890	George L. Shoup
1890-1893	Norman B. Willey†
1893-1896	William J. McConnell
1896-1901	Frank Steunenberg
1901-1903	Frank W. Hunt
1903-1905	John T. Morrison
1905-1909	Frank R. Gooding
1909-1911	James H. Brady
1911-1913	James H. Hawley
1913-1915	John M. Haines
1915-1919	Moses Alexander
1919-1923	David W. Davis
1923-1927	Charles C. Moore
1927-1931	H. Clarence Baldridge
1931-1937	C. Ben Ross
1937-1939	Barzilla W. Clark
1939-1941	C. A. Bottolfsen
1941-1943	Chase A. Clark†
1943-1945	C. A. Bottolfsen
1945	Charles C. Gossett
1945-1947	Arnold Williams
1947-1951	Charles A. Robins
1951-1955	Leonard B. Jordan
1955-1967	Robert E. Smylie
1967-	Don W. Samuelson

*_Idaho Almanac_, Centennial Edition, 1863-1963. Published by Idaho Department of Commerce and Development, Boise, Idaho. 1963.
†Booklet entitled "Secretary of State of Idaho," 1963-1964, p. 20, lists surname "Wiley" (1890-1893) and Clark's first name (1941-1943) listed as "Charles."

ILLINOIS

Term	Territorial Governor*
1809-1818	Ninian Edwards
	State Governors
1818-1822	Shadrach Bond
1822-1826	Edward Coles
1826-1830	Ninian Edwards
1830-1834	John Reynolds
1834	William L. D. Ewing
1834-1838	Joseph Duncan
1838-1842	Thomas Carlin
1842-1846	Thomas Ford
1846-1853	Augustus C. French
1853-1857	Joel Aldrich Matteson
1857-1860	William H. Bissell
1860-1861	John Wood
1861-1865	Richard Yates
1865-1869	Richard J. Oglesby
1869-1873	John M. Palmer
1873	Richard J. Oglesby
1873-1877	John L. Beveridge
1877-1883	Shelby Moore Cullom
1883-1885	John M. Hamilton
1885-1889	Richard J. Oglesby
1889-1893	Joseph W. Fifer
1893-1897	John P. Altgeld
1897-1901	John R. Tanner
1901-1905	Richard Yates
1905-1913	Charles S. Deneen
1913-1917	Edward F. Dunne
1917-1921	Frank O. Lowden
1921-1929	Len Small
1929-1933	Louis L. Emmerson
1933-1937	Henry Horner
1937-1941	John H. Stelle
1941-1949	Dwight H. Green
1949-1953	Adlai E. Stevenson
1953-1961	William G. Stratton
1961-1968	Otto Kerner
1968-1969	Samuel H. Shapiro
1969-	Richard B. Ogilvie

*_Illinois Blue Book_, 1963-1964, p. 862 fn.

INDIANA

Term	Territorial Governors*
1800-1811	William Henry Harrison
1812-1813	John Gibson (acting)
1813-1816	Thomas Posey
	State Governors
1816-1822	Jonathan Jennings
1822	Ratliff Boon
1822-1825	William Hendricks
1825-1831	James Brown Ray
1831-1837	Noah Noble
1837-1840	David Wallace
1840-1843	Samuel Bigger
1843-1848	James Whitcomb
1848-1849	Paris C. Dunning
1849-1857	Joseph A. Wright
1857-1860	Ashbel P. Willard
1860-1861	Abram A. Hammond
1861	Henry S. Lane
1861-1867	Oliver P. Morton
1867-1873	Conrad Baker
1873-1877	Thomas A. Hendricks
1877-1880	James D. Williams
1880-1881	Isaac P. Gray
1881-1885	Albert G. Porter
1885-1889	Isaac P. Gray
1889-1891	Alvin P. Hovey
1891-1893	Ira J. Chase
1893-1897	Claude Matthews
1897-1901	James A. Mount
1901-1905	Winfield T. Durbin
1905-1909	J. Frank Hanly
1909-1913	Thomas R. Marshall
1913-1917	Samuel M. Ralston
1917-1921	James P. Goodrich
1921-1925	Warren T. McCray
1925-1929	Edward L. Jackson
1929-1933	Harry G. Leslie
1933-1937	Paul V. McNutt
1937-1941	M. Clifford Townsend
1941-1945	Henry F. Schricker

1945-1949	Ralph F. Gates
1949-1953	Henry F. Schricker
1953-1957	George N. Craig
1957-1961	Harold W. Handley
1961-1965	Matthew E. Welsh
1965-1969	Roger D. Branigin
1969-	Edgar D. Whitcomb

*Booklet entitled "Governors of Indiana" (reprinted from *The Indianapolis News*). The booklet lists in addition Emmett F. Branch, 1924-1925.

IOWA

Term	Territorial Governors*
1838-1841	Robert Lucas
1841-1845	John Chambers
1845-1846	James Clarke
	State Governors
1846-1850	Ansel Briggs
1850-1854	Stephen P. Hempstead
1854-1858	James W. Grimes
1858-1860	Ralph P. Lowe
1860-1864	Samuel J. Kirkwood
1864-1868	William M. Stone
1868-1872	Samuel Merrill
1872-1876	Cyrus C. Carpenter
1876-1877	Samuel J. Kirkwood
1877-1878	Joshua G. Newbold
1878-1882	John H. Gear
1882-1886	Buren R. Sherman
1886-1890	William Larrabee
1890-1894	Horace Boies
1894-1896	Frank D. Jackson
1896-1898	Francis M. Drake
1898-1902	Leslie M. Shaw
1902-1908	Albert Baird Cummins
1908-1909	Warren Garst†
1909-1913	Beryl F. Carroll
1913-1917	George W. Clarke
1917-1921	William L. Harding
1921-1925	Nathan E. Kendall
1925-1931	John Hammill
1931-1933	Daniel W. Turner
1933-1937	Clyde L. Herring
1937-1939	Nelson G. Kraschel
1939-1943	George A. Wilson
1943-1945	Bourke B. Hickenlooper
1945-1949	Robert D. Blue
1949-1954	William S. Beardsley
1954-1955	Leo Elthon
1955-1957	Leo A. Hoegh
1957-1961	Herschel C. Loveless
1961-1963	Norman A. Erbe
1963-1969	Harold E. Hughes
1969 (interim)	Robert D. Fulton
1969-	Robert D. Ray

**Iowa Official Register*, 1965-1966, p. 342.
†The *Register* lists Warren Garst, 1908-1909. This name is omitted from *White's Conspectus*.

KANSAS

Term	Territorial Governors*
1854-1855	Andrew H. Reeder
1855-1857	Daniel Woodson
1855-1856	Wilson Shannon
1856-1857	John White Geary
1857	Frederick P. Stanton
1857	Robert John Walker
1857-1858	James W. Denver
1858-1860	Hugh Sleight Walsh
1858-1860	Samuel Medary
1860-1861	George M. Beebe
	State Governors
1861-1863	Charles Robinson
1863-1865	Thomas Carney
1865-1868	Samuel J. Crawford
1869-1873	James M. Harvey
1873-1877	Thomas A. Osborn
1877-1879	George T. Anthony
1879-1883	John Pierce St. John
1883-1885	George W. Glick
1885-1889	John Alexander Martin
1889-1893	Lyman Underwood Humphrey
1893-1895	Lorenzo D. Lewelling
1895-1897	Edmund Needham Morill†
1897-1899	John W. Leedy
1899-1903	William Eugene Stanley
1903-1905	Willis Joshua Bailey
1905-1909	Edward Wallis Hoch
1909-1913	Walter Roscoe Stubbs
1913-1915	George Hartshorn Hodges
1915-1919	Arthur Capper
1919-1923	Henry J. Allen
1923-1925	Jonathan M. Davis
1925-1929	Ben S. Paulen
1929-1931	Clyde M. Reed
1931-1933	Harry H. Woodring
1933-1937	Alfred M. Landon
1937-1939	Walter A. Huxman
1939-1943	Payne Ratner
1943-1947	Andrew F. Schoeppel
1947-1950	Frank Carlson
1950-1951	Frank L. Hagaman
1951-1955	Edward F. Arn
1955-1957	Fred Hall
1957	John McCuish
1957-1961	George Docking
1961-1965	John Anderson, Jr.
1965-1967	William H. Avery
1967-	Robert B. Docking

**Kansas Directory*, 1967-1968, p. 26. Kansas Territorial Governors served short terms of a few months during years listed. The *Directory* adds Nehemiah Green, 1868-1869.
†The *Directory* lists surname "Morrill."

KENTUCKY

Term	State Governors
1792-1796	Isaac Shelby
1796-1804	James Garrard
1804-1808	Christopher Greenup
1808-1812	Charles Scott
1812-1816	Isaac Shelby
1816	George Madison
1816-1820	Gabriel Slaughter
1820-1824	John Adair
1824-1828	Joseph Desha
1828-1832	Thomas Metcalfe
1832-1834	John Breathitt
1834-1836	James T. Morehead
1836-1839	James Clark
1839-1840	Charles A. Wickliffe
1840-1844	Robert P. Letcher
1844-1848	William Owsley
1848-1850	John J. Crittenden
1850-1851	John L. Helm
1851-1855	Lazarus W. Powell
1855-1859	Charles S. Morehead
1859-1862	Beriah Magoffin
1862-1863	James F. Robinson

1863-1867	Thomas E. Bramlette
1867	John L. Helm
1867-1871	John W. Stevenson
1871-1875	Preston H. Leslie
1875-1879	James B. McCreary
1879-1883	Luke P. Blackburn
1883-1887	J. Proctor Knott
1887-1891	Simon Bolivar Buckner
1891-1895	John Young Brown
1895-1900	William O. Bradley
1900	William S. Taylor
1900	William Goebel
1900-1907	John Crepps Wickliffe Beckham
1907-1911	Augustus Everett Willson
1911-1915	James Bennett McCreary
1915-1919	Augustus Owsley Stanley
1919	James Dixon Black
1919-1923	Edwin Porch Morrow
1923-1927	William Jason Fields
1927-1931	Flem D. Sampson
1931-1935	Ruby Laffoon
1935-1939	Albert Benjamin Chandler
1939-1943	Keen Johnson
1943-1947	Simeon S. Willis
1947-1950	Earle C. Clements
1950-1955	Lawrence W. Wetherby
1955-1959	Albert Benjamin Chandler
1959-1963	Bert T. Combs
1963-1967	Edward T. Breathitt
1967-	Louie B. Nunn

LOUISIANA

Term	Governors Under French Rule*
1699	Pierre le Moyne, Sieur d'Iberville
1699-1701	Sieur de Sauvole
1701-1713	Jean Baptiste le Moyne, Sieur de Bienville
1713-1716	Antoine de la Mothe Cadillac
1716-1717	Jean Baptiste le Moyne, Sieur de Bienville
1717-1718	De l'Epinay
1718-1724	Jean Baptiste le Moyne, Sieur de Bienville
1724-1725	Pierre Dugue, Sieur de Boisbriant
1725-1733	Perier
1733-1743	Jean Baptiste le Moyne, Sieur de Bienville
1743-1753	Pierre Rigaud, Marquis de Vaudreuil
1753-1763	Louis Billouart, Chevalier de Kerlerec
1763-1765	D'Abbadie
1765-1769	Charles Phillippe Aubry (acting)
	Governors Under Spanish Rule*
1766-1768	Antonio de Ulloa (did not assume full power)
1768-1769	Alexandro O'Reilly
1769-1777	Luis de Unzaga
1777-1785	Bernardo de Galvez
1785-1791	Estevan Miró
1791-1797	Francois Louis Hector, Baron de Carondelet
1797-1799	Manual Gayoso de Lemos
1799	Francisco Bouligny
1799-1801	Sebastián, Marquis de Casa Calvo
1801-1803	Juan Manuel de Salcedo
1803	Pierre Clement de Laussat
	Territorial Governor*
	(Territory of Orleans)
1803-1812	William C. Claiborne
	State Governors
1812-1816	William C. Claiborne
1816-1820	Jacques P. Villeré
1820-1824	Thomas B. Robertson
1824	Henry S. Thibodeaux
1824-1828	Henry S. Johnson
1828-1829	Pierre Derbigny
1829-1830	Armand Beauvais
1830-1831	Jacques Dupré
1831-1835	André B. Roman
1835-1839	Edward D. White
1839-1843	André B. Roman
1843-1846	Alexandre Mouton
1846-1850	Isaac Johnson
1850-1853	Joseph M. Walker
1853-1856	Paul O. Hebert
1856-1860	Robert C. Wickliffe
1860-1864	Thomas O. Moore
1862-1864	George F. Shepley (Military Governor)
1864	Henry W. Allen
1864-1865	Michael Hahn
1865-1867	James Madison Wells
1867	Benjamin F. Flanders
1867-1868	Joshua Baker
1868-1872	Henry Clay Warmoth
1873	John McEnery†
1873-1877	William Pitt Kellogg
1877-1880	Francis T. Nicholls
1880-1881	Louis A. Wiltz
1881-1888	Samuel Douglas McEnery
1888-1892	Francis T. Nicholls
1892-1900	Murphy James Foster
1900-1904	William Wright Heard
1904-1908	Newton Crain Blanchard
1908-1912	Jared Young Sanders
1912-1916	Luther Egbert Hall
1916-1920	Ruffin Galson Pleasant
1920-1924	John Milliken Parker
1924-1926	Henry Luce Fuqua
1926-1928	Oramel Hinckley Simpson
1928-1932	Huey Pierce Long, Jr.
1932-1936	Oscar Kelly Allen
1936	James Albert Noe
1936-1939	Richard Webster Leche
1939-1940	Earl Kemp Long
1940-1944	Sam Houston Jones
1944-1948	James Houston Davis
1948-1952	Earl Kemp Long
1952-1956	Robert F. Kennon
1956-1960	Earl Kemp Long
1960-1964	James Houston Davis
1964-	John J. McKeithen

*"The Government of Louisiana," prepared by Louisiana Legislative Council, 1959, appendix No. 1. The handbook lists in addition P. B. S. Pinchback (acting), 1872-1873, and Alvin Olin King, 1932.

†The handbook above notes that John McEnery was elected in 1873 but ruled out.

MAINE

Term	State Governors

For governors prior to 1820, see Massachusetts.

1820-1821	William King
1821	William D. Williamson
1822-1827	Albion K. Parris
1827-1829	Enoch Lincoln
1829-1830	Nathan Cutler
1830-1831	Jonathan G. Hunton
1831-1834	Samuel E. Smith

1834-1838	Robert P. Dunlap
1838-1839	Edward Kent
1839-1840	John Fairfield
1840-1841	Edward Kent
1841-1843	John Fairfield
1843-1844	Edward Kavanagh
1844-1847	Hugh J. Anderson
1847-1850	John W. Dana
1850-1853	John Hubbard
1853-1855	William G. Crosby
1855-1856	Anson P. Morrill
1856-1857	Samuel E. Wells
1857	Hannibal Hamlin
1857-1858	Joseph H. Williams
1858-1861	Lot M. Morrill
1861-1863	Israel J. Washburn, Jr.
1863-1864	Abner Coburn
1864-1867	Samuel Cony
1867-1871	Joshua L. Chamberlain
1871-1874	Sidney Perham
1874-1876	Nelson Dingley, Jr.
1876-1879	Selden Connor
1879-1880	Alonzo Garcelon
1880-1881	Daniel F. Davis
1881-1883	Harris M. Plaisted
1883-1887	Frederick Robie
1887	Joseph R. Bodwell
1887-1889	Sebastian S. Marble
1889-1893	Edwin C. Burleigh
1893-1897	Henry B. Cleaves
1897-1901	Llewellyn Powers
1901-1905	John Fremont Hill
1905-1909	William T. Cobb
1909-1911	Bert M. Fernald
1911-1913	Frederick W. Plaisted
1913-1915	William T. Haines
1915-1917	Oakley C. Curtis
1917-1921	Carl E. Milliken*
1921	Frederick H. Parkhurst†
1921-1925	Percival P. Baxter
1925-1929	Ralph Owen Brewster
1929-1933	William Tudor Gardiner
1933-1937	Louis J. Brann
1937-1941	Lewis O. Barrows
1941-1945	Sumner Sewall
1945-1949	Horace A. Hildreth
1949-1952	Frederick G. Payne
1952-1955	Burton M. Cross
1955-1959	Edmund S. Muskie
1959	Robert N. Haskell
1959	Clinton A. Clauson
1959-1967	John H. Reed
1967-	Kenneth M. Curtis

Note: The *Encyclopedia Americana*, Vol. 18, p. 143c, lists, in addition, Benjamin Ames (acting), 1821; Joshua Hall (acting), 1830.
*Not listed in *White's Conspectus*.
†The *Encyclopedia Americana* spells first name "Frederic."

MARYLAND

Term	Barons of Baltimore and Lords Proprietary*
1580-1632	George Calvert
1605-1675	Cecilius Calvert
1637-1715	Charles Calvert
1679-1715	Benedict Leonard Calvert
1699-1751	Charles Calvert
1732-1771	Frederick Calvert
1760-1834	Henry Harford
	Colonial Governors*
1631	William Claiborne
1631	Leonard Calvert
	Proprietary Government
1634-1647	Leonard Calvert
1647-1649	Thomas Green
1649-1654	William Stone
1654-1657	Governed by Commissioners
1657-1660	Josias Fendall
1660-1661	Philip Calvert
1661-1676	Charles Calvert
1676-1679	Thomas Notley
1680-1684	Charles Calvert
1684-1688	William Joseph
	Royal Government
1688-1691	Governed by Protestant Associators
1691-1693	Lionel Copley
1694-1699	Francis Nicholson
1699-1701	Nathaniel Blackistone†
1701-1703	Thomas Tench
1703-1709	John Seymour
1709-1714	Edward Lloyd
1714-1715	John Hart
	Restoration of the Proprietary Government
1715-1720	John Hart
1720-1727	Charles Calvert
1727-1731	Benedict L. Calvert
1731-1732	Samuel Ogle
1732-1733	Charles Calvert
1733-1742	Samuel Ogle
1742-1747	Thomas Bladen
1747-1752	Samuel Ogle
1752-1753	Benjamin Tasker
1753-1769	Horatio Sharpe
1769-1776	Robert Eden
1776-1777	Governed by the Convention and Councils of Safety
	State Governors
1777-1779	Thomas Johnson
1779-1782	Thomas Sim Lee
1782-1785	William Paca
1785-1788	William Smallwood
Maryland ratified U. S. Constitution on April 28, 1788.	
1788-1791	John Eager Howard
1791-1792	George Plater
1792-1794	Thomas S. Lee
1794-1797	John H. Stone
1797-1798	John Henry
1798-1801	Benjamin Ogle
1801-1803	John Francis Mercer
1803-1806	Robert Bowie
1806-1809	Robert Wright
1809-1811	Edward Lloyd
1811-1812	Robert Bowie
1812-1815	Levin Winder
1815-1818	Charles Ridgely
1818-1819	Charles Goldsborough
1819-1822	Samuel Sprigg
1822-1825	Samuel Stevens, Jr.
1826-1828	Joseph Kent
1828-1829	Daniel Martin
1829-1830	Thomas King Carroll
1830-1831	Daniel Martin
1831-1833	George Howard
1833-1835	James Thomas

1835-1838	Thomas W. Veazey
1838-1841	William Grason
1841-1844	Francis Thomas
1844-1847	Thomas G. Pratt
1847-1850	Philip Francis Thomas
1850-1854	Enoch Louis Lowe
1854-1858	Thomas Watkins Ligon
1858-1862	Thomas Holliday Hicks
1862-1865	Augustus W. Bradford
1865-1869	Thomas Swann
1869-1872	Oden Bowie
1872-1874	William Pinkney Whyte
1874-1876	James Black Groome
1876-1880	John Lee Carroll
1880-1884	William T. Hamilton
1884-1885	Robert M. McLane
1885-1888	Henry Lloyd
1888-1892	Elihu E. Jackson
1892-1896	Frank Brown
1896-1900	Lloyd Lowndes
1900-1904	John Walter Smith
1904-1908	Edwin Warfield
1908-1912	Austin L. Crothers
1912-1916	Phillips Lee Goldsborough
1916-1920	Emerson C. Harrington
1920-1935	Albert C. Ritchie
1935-1939	Harry W. Nice
1939-1947	Herbert R. O'Conor
1947-1951	William Preston Lane, Jr.
1951-1959	Theodore R. McKeldin
1959-1967	J. Millard Tawes
1967-1969	Spiro T. Agnew
1969-	Marvin Mandel

*The *Maryland Manual*, 1965-1966. The *Manual* subdivides list as indicated and lists, in addition, Council of Deputy Governors, 1684-1688; Nehemiah Blackiston, 1690-1692; Thomas Lawrence, 1693, 1694; Edmund Andros, 1693, 1694; Nicholas Greenberry, 1693-1694; Thomas Brooke, 1720; James Brice, 1792; James Butcher, 1809.

†The *Manual* spells surname "Blackiston."

MASSACHUSETTS

Term	Plymouth Colony Governors
1620-1621	John Carver
1621-1633	William Bradford
1633-1634	Edward Winslow
1634-1635	Thomas Prince†
1635-1636	William Bradford
1636-1637	Edward Winslow
1637-1638	William Bradford
1638-1639	Thomas Prince
1639-1644	William Bradford
1644-1645	Edward Winslow
1645-1657	William Bradford
1657-1673	Thomas Prince
1673-1681	Josiah Winslow
1681-1686	Thomas Hinckley
1686-1689	Edmund Andros
1689-1692	Thomas Hinckley

MASSACHUSETTS BAY COLONY

1629-1630	John Endicott
1630-1634	John Winthrop
1634-1635	Thomas Dudley
1635-1636	John Haynes
1636-1637	Henry Vane
1637-1640	John Winthrop
1640-1641	Thomas Dudley
1641-1642	Richard Bellingham
1642-1644	John Winthrop
1644-1645	John Endicott
1645-1646	Thomas Dudley
1646-1649	John Winthrop
1649-1650	John Endicott
1650-1651	Thomas Dudley
1651-1654	John Endicott
1654-1655	Richard Bellingham
1655-1665	John Endicott
1665-1673	Richard Bellingham
1673-1679	John Leverett
1679-1686	Simon Bradstreet
1686-1687	Joseph Dudley
1687-1689	Edmund Andros
1689-1692	Simon Bradstreet
1692-1694	William Phips
1694-1699	William Stoughton
1699-1700	Richard Coote
1700-1701	William Stoughton
1701-1702	The Council
1702-1715	Joseph Dudley
1715-1716	William Tailer
1716-1723	Samuel Shute
1723-1728	William Dummer
1728-1729	William Burnet
1729-1730	William Dummer
1730	William Tailer
1730-1741	Jonathan Belcher
1741-1749	William Shirley
1749-1753	Spencer Phipps
1753-1756	William Shirley
1756-1757	Spencer Phipps
1757-1760	Thomas Pownal
1760-1769	Francis Bernard
1769-1774	Thomas Hutchinson
1774-1775	Thomas Gage
1775-1780	The Council

THE COMMONWEALTH

1780-1785	John Hancock
1785-1787	James Bowdoin
1787-1788	John Hancock

Massachusetts ratified U. S. Constitution on February 6, 1788.

STATE GOVERNORS

1788-1793	John Hancock
1793-1797	Samuel Adams
1797-1800	Increase Sumner
1800-1807	Caleb Strong
1807-1809	James Sullivan
1809	Levi Lincoln
1809-1810	Christopher Gore
1810-1812	Elbridge Gerry
1812-1816	Caleb Strong
1816-1823	John Brooks
1823-1825	William Eustis
1825	Marcus Morton
1825-1834	Levi Lincoln
1834-1835	John Davis
1835-1836	Samuel Armstrong
1836-1840	Edward Everett
1840-1841	Marcus Morton
1841-1843	John Davis
1843-1844	Marcus Morton
1844-1851	George N. Briggs
1851-1853	George S. Boutwell
1853-1854	John H. Clifford
1854-1855	Emory Washburn
1855-1858	Henry J. Gardner
1858-1861	Nathaniel P. Banks
1861-1866	John A. Andrew

1866-1869	Alexander H. Bullock
1869-1872	William Claflin
1872-1874	William B. Washburn
1874-1875	Thomas Talbott
1875-1876	William Gaston
1876-1879	Alexander H. Rice
1879-1880	Thomas Talbot
1880-1883	John D. Long
1883-1884	Benjamin F. Butler
1884-1887	George D. Robinson
1887-1890	Oliver Ames
1890-1891	John Q. A. Brackett
1891-1894	William E. Russell
1894-1896	Frederic T. Greenhalge
1896-1900	Roger Wolcott
1900-1903	Winthrop M. Crane
1903-1905	John L. Bates
1905-1906	William L. Douglas
1906-1909	Curtis Guild, Jr.
1909-1911	Eben S. Draper
1911-1914	Eugene N. Foss
1914-1916	David I. Walsh
1916-1919	Samuel W. McCall
1919-1921	Calvin Coolidge
1921-1925	Channing H. Cox
1925-1929	Alvan T. Fuller
1929-1931	Frank G. Allen
1931-1935	Joseph B. Ely
1935-1937	James M. Curley
1937-1939	Charles F. Hurley
1939-1945	Leverett Saltonstall
1945-1947	Maurice J. Tobin
1947-1949	Robert F. Bradford
1949-1953	Paul A. Dever
1953-1957	Christian A. Herter
1957-1961	Foster Furcolo
1961-1963	John A. Volpe
1963-1965	Endicott Peabody
1965-1969	John A. Volpe
1969-	Francis W. Sargent

Note: *The Manual for the General Court* (Mass.), 1965-1966, p. 305, lists, in addition, Matthew Cradock, 1629, and adds that he never came to New England; The Council, 1715, 1757; Thomas Hutchinson, 1760, 1771; a Provincial Congress, 1774.
†The *Manual* spells surname "Prence."

MICHIGAN

Term	French-Canadian Governors*
1603-1612	Aymar de Chastes and Sieur de Monts
1612-1619	Samuel de Champlain
1619-1629	Henry, Duke of Montmorenci

The English held possession of Canada from 1629-1632.

1633-1635	Samuel de Champlain
1636	Marc Antoine de Bras-de-Fer de Chateaufort
1636-1647	Charles Hualt de Montmagny
1648-1651	Louis d'Ailleboust Sieur de Coulonges
1651-1655	Jean de Lauson
1656-1657	Charles de Lauson-Charny
1657-1658	Louis d'Ailleboust Sieur de Coulonges
1658-1661	Pierre de Voyer, Viscount d'Argenson
1661-1663	Baron Dubois d'Avaugour
1663-1665	Augustin de Saffray-Mezy
1663	Alexandre de Prouville, Marquis de Tracy
1665-1672	Daniel Remy, Sieur de Courcelles
1672-1682	Louis de Buade, Count de Frontenac
1682-1685	Antoine Joseph Le Febvre de la Barre
1685-1689	Jacques Rene de Brisay, Marquis de Denonville
1689-1698	Louis de Buade, Count de Frontenac
1698-1702	Louis Hector de Callieres
1703	Philippe de Rigaud, Marquis de Vaudreuil
1725	Charles LeMoyne, Baron de Longueuil
1726-1747	Charles de la Boische, Marquis de Beauharnois
1747-1749	Rolland Michel Barrin, Marquis de la Galissonniere
1749-1752	Jacques Pierre de Taffanel, Marquis de la Jonquiere
1752	Charles LeMoyne, Baron de Longueuil
1752-1755	Michel Ange Duquesne, Marquis de Menneville
1755-1760	Pierre Rigaud, Marquis de Vaudreuil Cavagnal

	British-Canadian Governors*
1760-1763	Jeffrey Amherst
1763-1766	James Murray
1766	Palinus Emelius Irving
1766-1770	Guy Carleton
1770-1774	Hector Theophilus Cramahe
1774-1778	Guy Carleton
1778-1784	Frederick Haldimand
1784	Henry Hamilton
1785	Henry Hope
1785	Guy Carleton
1792	John Graves Simcoe

	Governors of the Northwest Territory*
1787-1800	Arthur St. Clair
1796	Winthrop Sargent (acting)

	Governor of Indiana Territory*
1800-1805	William Henry Harrison

	Territorial Governors*
1805-1806	William Hull
1806-1808	Stanley Griswold
1808-1811	William Hull
1811-1812	Reuben Atwatter
1813-1818	Lewis Cass
1818-1820	William Woodbridge
1820	Lewis Cass
1820-1822	William Woodbridge
1822-1823	Lewis Cass
1823-1825	William Woodbridge
1825-1826	Lewis Cass
1826-1827	William Woodbridge†
1828-1829	Lewis Cass
1830	James Witherell
1830-1831	John T. Mason†
1831	Stevens T. Mason
1831	George B. Porter
1831-1834	Stevens T. Mason†
1835	Charles Shaler
1835	John S. Horner

	State Governors
1837-1840	Stevens T. Mason
1840-1841	William Woodbridge
1841	James Wright Gordon
1842-1846	John S. Barry
1846-1847	Alpheus Felch
1847	William L. Greenly
1848-1850	Epaphroditus Ransom
1850-1851	John S. Barry
1852-1853	Robert McClelland
1853-1854	Andrew Parsons
1855-1858	Kinsley S. Bingham

1859-1860	Moses Wisner
1861-1864	Austin Blair
1865-1868	Henry H. Crapo
1869-1872	Henry P. Baldwin
1873-1876	John J. Bagley
1877-1880	Charles M. Croswell
1881-1882	David H. Jerome
1883-1884	Josiah W. Begole
1885-1886	Russell A. Alger
1887-1890	Cyrus G. Luce
1891-1892	Edwin B. Winans
1893-1896	John T. Rich
1897-1900	Hazen S. Pingree
1901-1904	Aaron T. Bliss
1905-1910	Fred M. Warner
1911-1912	Chase S. Osborn
1913-1916	Woodbridge N. Ferris
1917-1920	Albert E. Sleeper
1921-1926	Alexander J. Groesbeck
1927-1930	Fred W. Green
1931-1932	Wilber M. Brucker
1933-1934	William A. Comstock
1935-1936	Frank D. Fitzgerald
1937-1939	Frank Murphy
1939	Frank D. Fitzgerald
1939-1941	Luren D. Dickinson
1941-1943	Murray D. Van Wagoner
1943-1947	Harry F. Kelly
1947-1949	Kim Sigler
1949-1961	G. Mennen Williams
1961-1963	John B. Swainson
1963-1969	George Romney
1969-	William G. Milliken

**Michigan Manual,* 1967-1968, pp. 83-84.

†Territorial Governors served terms of a few months during years listed.

MINNESOTA

TERM	TERRITORIAL GOVERNORS*
1849-1853	Alexander Ramsey
1853-1857	Willis A. Gorman
1857-1858	Samuel Medary
	STATE GOVERNORS
1858-1860	Henry H. Sibley
1860-1863	Alexander Ramsey
1863-1864	Henry A. Swift
1864-1866	Stephen Miller
1866-1870	William R. Marshall
1870-1874	Horace Austin
1874-1876	Cushman K. Davis
1876-1882	John S. Pillsbury
1882-1887	Lucius F. Hubbard
1887-1889	Andrew R. McGill
1889-1893	William R. Merriam
1893-1895	Knute Nelson
1895-1899	David M. Clough
1899-1901	John Lind
1901-1905	Samuel R. Van Sant
1905-1909	John A. Johnson
1909-1915	Adolph O. Eberhart
1915	Winfield S. Hammond
1915-1921	Joseph A. A. Burnquist
1921-1925	Jacob A. O. Preus
1925-1931	Theodore Christianson
1931-1935	Floyd B. Olson
1935-1937	Hjalmar Petersen
1937-1939	Elmer A. Benson
1939-1943	Harold E. Stassen
1943-1947	Edward J. Thye
1947-1950	Luther W. Youngdahl
1950-1955	C. Elmer Anderson
1955-1961	Orville L. Freeman
1961-1963	Elmer L. Andersen
1963-1967	Karl F. Rolvaag
1967-	Harold L. LeVander

*The *Encyclopedia Americana,* Vol. 19, p. 192.

MISSISSIPPI

TERM	TERRITORIAL GOVERNORS*
1798-1801	Winthrop Sargent
1801-1805	William C. C. Claiborne
1805-1809	Robert Williams
1809-1817	David Holmes
	STATE GOVERNORS
1817-1820	David Holmes
1820-1822	George Poindexter
1822-1825	Walter Leake
1825-1826	Gerard C. Brandon
1826-1827	David Holmes
1827-1832	Gerard C. Brandon†
1832-1833	Abram M. Scott
1833	Charles Lynch
1833-1835	Hiram G. Runnels
1835-1836	John A. Quitman
1836-1838	Charles Lynch
1838-1842	Alexander G. McNutt
1842-1844	Tilgham M. Tucker
1844-1848	Albert G. Brown
1848-1850	Joseph W. Matthews†
1850-1851	John A. Quitman
1851	John I. Guion
1851-1852	James Whitfield
1852-1854	Henry S. Foote
1854-1857	John J. McRae
1858-1859	William McWillie
1860-1862	John J. Pettus
1862-1864	Jacob Thompson
1864-1865	Charles Clark
1865	William L. Sharkey
1865-1868	Benjamin G. Humphreys
1868-1870	Adelbert Ames
1870-1871	James L. Alcorn
1871-1874	Ridgley C. Powers
1874-1876	Adelbert Ames
1876-1882	John M. Stone
1882-1890	Robert Lowry
1890-1896	John M. Stone
1896-1900	Anselm J. McLaurin†
1900-1904	Andrew H. Longino†
1904-1908	James Kimble Vardaman
1908-1912	Edmund Favor Noel†
1912-1916	Earl LeRoy Brewer
1916-1920	Theodore Gilmore Bilbo
1920-1924	Lee Maurice Russell
1924-1927	Henry Lewis Whitfield
1927-1928	Dennis Murphree
1928-1932	Theodore Gilmore Bilbo
1932-1936	Martin Sennet Conner†
1936-1940	Hugh White
1940-1943	Paul B. Johnson
1943-1944	Dennis Murphree
1944-1946	Thomas L. Bailey
1946-1952	Fielding L. Wright
1952-1956	Hugh L. White
1956-1960	J. P. Coleman
1960-1964	Ross R. Barnett
1964-1968	Paul B. Johnson, Jr.
1968-	John Bell Williams

**Mississippi Official and Stastistical Register,* 1964-1968, p. 195. The *Register* lists, in addition, John J. Pettus, 1854 (five days).

†The *Register* lists Gerald C. Brandon, Joseph M. Matthews, Anslem J. McLaurin, Andrew W. Longino and Edmond Favor Noel and Martin Sennett Conner.

MISSOURI

Term	Territorial Governors*
1803-1804	William C. C. Claiborne
1804	Amos Stoddard
1804-1805	William Henry Harrison
1805-1807	James Wilkinson
1807	Joseph Browne
1807	Frederick Bates
1807-1809	Meriwether Lewis
1809-1810	Frederick Bates
1810-1812	Benjamin Howard
1812-1813	Frederick Bates
1813-1820	William Clark
	State Governors
1821-1824	Alexander McNair
1824-1825	Frederick Bates
1825-1826	Abraham J. Williams
1826-1832	John Miller
1832-1836	Daniel Dunklin
1836-1840	Lilburn W. Boggs
1840-1844	Thomas Reynolds
1844	Meredith Miles Marmaduke
1844-1848	John Cummins Edwards
1848-1852	Austin Augustus King
1853-1856	Sterling Price
1857	Trusten Polk
1857	Hancock Lee Jackson
1857-1861	Robert Marcellus Stewart†
1861	Claiborne Fox Jackson
1861-1864	Hamilton Rowan Gamble
1864-1865	Willard Preble Hall
1865-1869	Thomas Clement Fletcher
1869-1871	Joseph Washington McClurg
1871-1873	Benjamin Gratz Brown
1873-1875	Silas Woodson
1875-1877	Charles Henry Hardin
1877-1881	John Smith Phelps
1881-1885	Thomas Theodore Crittenden
1885-1887	John Sappington Marmaduke
1887-1889	Allen Pickett Morehouse†
1889-1893	David Rowland Francis
1893-1897	William Joel Stone
1897-1901	Lon Vest Stephens
1901-1905	Alexander Monroe Dockery
1905-1909	Joseph Wingate Folk
1909-1913	Herbert Spencer Hadley
1913-1917	Elliott Woolfolk Major
1917-1921	Frederick Dozier Gardner‡
1921-1925	Arthur Mastick Hyde
1925-1929	Sam Aaron Baker
1929-1933	Henry Stewart Caulfield
1933-1937	Guy Brasfield Park
1937-1941	Lloyd Crow Stark
1941-1945	Forrest C. Donnell
1945-1949	Phil M. Donnelly
1949-1953	Forrest Smith
1953-1957	Phil M. Donnelly
1957-1961	James T. Blair, Jr.
1961-1965	John M. Dalton
1965-	Warren E. Hearnes

*The *Encyclopedia Americana*, Vol. 19, p. 257.
†The *Official Manual*, State of Missouri, 1963-1964, p. 45, lists names as follows: Robert Marcellus Steward, Albert Pickett Morehouse.
‡Omitted in *White's Conspectus*, but shown in *Official Manual* and *Encyclopedia Americana*.

MONTANA

Term	Territorial Governors*
1856-1866	Sidney Edgerton
1866-1869	Green Clay Smith
1869-1870	James M. Ashley
1870-1883	Benjamin F. Potts
1883-1884	J. Schuyler Crosby
1884-1885	B. Platt Carpenter
1885-1887	Samuel T. Hauser
1887-1889	Preston H. Leslie
1889	Benjamin F. White
	State Governors
1889-1893	Joseph K. Toole
1893-1897	John E. Rickards
1897-1901	Robert B. Smith
1901-1908	Joseph K. Toole
1909-1913	Edwin L. Norris*
1913-1921	Samuel V. Stewart
1921-1925	Joseph M. Dixon
1925-1933	John E. Erickson
1933-1935	Frank H. Cooney
1935-1937	W. Elmer Holt
1937-1941	Roy E. Ayers
1941-1949	Sam C. Ford
1949-1953	John W. Bonner
1953-1961	J. Hugo Aronson
1961-1962	Donald G. Nutter
1962-1969	Tim M. Babcock
1969-	Forrest H. Anderson

*The *Montana Almanac*, 1959-1960, p. 148. The *Almanac* lists term for Edwin L. Norris, 1908-1913.

NEBRASKA

Term	Territorial Governors*
1854	Francis Burt
1854-1855	Thomas B. Cuming
1855-1857	Mark W. Izard
1857-1858	Thomas B. Cuming
1858	William A. Richardson
1858-1859	J. Sterling Morton
1859-1861	Samuel W. Black
1861	J. Sterling Morton
1861	Algernon S. Paddock
1861-1867	Alvin Saunders
	State Governors
1867-1871	David Butler
1871-1873	William H. James
1873-1875	Robert W. Furnas
1875-1879	Silas Garber
1879-1883	Albinus Nance
1883-1887	James W. Dawes
1887-1891	John M. Thayer
1891	James E. Boyd
1891-1892	John M. Thayer
1892-1893	James E. Boyd
1893-1895	Lorenzo Crounse
1895-1899	Silas A. Holcomb
1899-1901	William A. Poynter
1901	Charles H. Dietrich
1901-1903	Ezra P. Savage
1903-1907	John H. Mickey
1907-1909	George L. Sheldon
1909-1911	Ashton C. Shallenberger
1911-1913	Chester H. Aldrich
1913-1917	John H. Morehead
1917-1919	Keith Neville
1919-1923	Samuel R. McKelvie
1923-1925	Charles W. Bryan
1925-1929	Adam McMullen
1929-1931	Arthur J. Weaver
1931-1935	Charles W. Bryan
1935-1941	Robert Leroy Cochran
1941-1947	Dwight P. Griswold
1947-1953	Val Peterson
1953-1955	Robert B. Crosby

1955-1959	Victor E. Anderson
1959-1960	Ralph G. Brooks
1960-1961	Dwight W. Burney
1961-1967	Frank B. Morrison
1967-	Norbert T. Tiemann

*Nebraska Blue Book, 1966, p. 116.

NEVADA

TERM	TERRITORIAL GOVERNOR*
1861-1864	James W. Nye
	STATE GOVERNORS
1864-1871	Henry G. Blasdel
1871-1879	Lewis R. Bradley
1879-1883	John H. Kinkead
1883-1887	Jewett W. Adams
1887-1890	Charles C. Stevenson
1890-1891	Frank Bell
1891-1895	Roswell K. Colcord
1895-1896	John E. Jones
1896-1903	Reinhold Sadler
1903-1908	John Sparks
1908-1910	Denver S. Dickerson
1910-1915	Tasker L. Oddie
1915-1923	Emmet D. Boyle
1923-1927	James G. Scrugham
1927-1934	Frederick B. Balzar
1934-1935	Morley Griswold
1935-1939	Richard Kirman, Sr.
1939-1945	Edward P. Carville
1945-1951	Vail M. Pittman
1951-1958	Charles H. Russell*
1959-1967	Grant Sawyer
1967-	Paul D. Laxalt

*The *Encyclopedia Americana*, Vol. 20, p. 142. It lists term of Charles H. Russell, 1951-1959.

NEW HAMPSHIRE*

TERM	PROVINCIAL EXECUTIVES
1679-1681	John Cutt
1681-1682	Richard Waldron
1682-1685	Edward Cranfield
1685-1686	Walter Barefoote
1686-1687	Joseph Dudley
1687-1689	Edmund Andros
1689-1692	Simon Bradstreet
1692-1697	John Usher
1697-1698	William Partridge
1698-1699	Samuel Allen
1699-1701	Richard Coote
1702-1716	Joseph Dudley
1716-1723	Samuel Shute
1723-1727	John Wentworth
1727-1729	William Burnet
1730-1741	Jonathan Belcher
1741-1766	Benning Wentworth
1767-1775	John Wentworth
	REVOLUTIONARY EXECUTIVES
1775-1776	Matthew Thornton, President of Provincial Congress
1776-1784	Meshech Weare
	STATE GOVERNORS (Presidents until 1793)
1784-1785	Meshech Weare
1785-1786	John Langdon
1786-1787	John Sullivan

New Hampshire ratified U. S. Constitution on June 21, 1788.

1787-1788	John Sullivan
1788-1789	John Langdon
1789-1790	John Sullivan
1790-1794	Josiah Bartlett
1794-1805	John T. Gilman
1805-1809	John Langdon
1809-1810	Jeremiah Smith
1810-1812	John Langdon
1812-1813	William Plumer
1813-1816	John T. Gilman
1816-1819	William Plumer
1819-1823	Samuel Bell
1823-1824	Levi Woodbury
1824-1827	David L. Morrill
1827-1828	Benjamin Pierce
1828-1829	John Bell
1829-1830	Benjamin Pierce
1830-1831	Matthew Harvey
1831	Joseph M. Harper (acting)†
1831-1834	Samuel Dinsmoor
1834-1836	William Badger
1836-1839	Isaac Hill
1839-1842	John Page
1842-1844	Henry Hubbard
1844-1846	John H. Steele
1846-1847	Anthony Colby
1847-1849	Jared W. Williams
1849-1852	Samuel Dinsmoor, Jr.
1852-1854	Noah Martin
1854-1855	Nathaniel B. Baker
1855-1857	Ralph Metcalf
1857-1859	William Haile
1859-1861	Ichabod Goodwin
1861-1863	Nathaniel S. Berry
1863-1865	Joseph A. Gilmore
1865-1867	Frederick Smyth
1867-1869	Walter Harriman
1869-1871	Onslow Stearns
1871-1872	James A. Weston
1872-1874	Ezekiel A. Straw
1874-1875	James A. Weston
1875-1877	Person C. Cheney
1877-1879	Benjamin F. Prescott
1879-1881	Natt Head
1881-1883	Charles H. Bell
1883-1885	Samuel W. Hale
1885-1887	Moody Currier
1887-1889	Charles H. Sawyer
1889-1891	David H. Goodell
1891-1893	Hiram A. Tuttle
1893-1895	John B. Smith
1895-1897	Charles A. Busiel
1897-1899	George A. Ramsdell
1899-1901	Frank W. Rollins
1901-1903	Chester B. Jordan
1903-1905	Nahum J. Batchelder
1905-1907	John McLane
1907-1909	Charles M. Floyd
1909-1911	Henry B. Quinby
1911-1913	Robert P. Bass
1913-1915	Samuel D. Felker
1915-1917	Rolland H. Spaulding
1917-1919	Henry W. Keyes
1919	Jesse M. Barton (acting)†
1919-1921	John H. Bartlett
1921-1923	Albert O. Brown
1923-1925	Fred H. Brown

1925-1927	John G. Winant
1927-1929	Huntley N. Spaulding
1929-1931	Charles W. Tobey
1931-1935	John G. Winant
1935-1937	H. Styles Bridges
1937-1941	Francis P. Murphy
1941-1945	Robert O. Blood
1945-1949	Charles M. Dale
1949-1953	Sherman Adams
1953-1955	Hugh Gregg
1955-1959	Lane Dwinell
1959-1963	Wesley Powell
1963-1969	John W. King
1969-	Walter R. Peterson

**New Hampshire Manual for the General Court*, 1967, p. 172 is the general source for this list.

†The *Manual* omits these names, but they are shown as Acting Governors in *White's Conspectus* and *Encyclopedia Americana*.

NEW JERSEY

TERM	EARLY COLONIAL GOVERNORS*
1624	Cornelius Jacobsen Mey
1625	William Verhulst
1626-1631	Peter Minuit
1631-1633	Bastiaen Janssen Crol
1633-1637	Wouter Van Twiller
1637-1646	William Kleft
1642-1652	John Printz
1646-1664	Peter Stuyvesant
1664-1676	Philip Carteret
	GOVERNORS OF EAST NEW JERSEY*
1677-1682	Philip Carteret
1682-1690	Robert Barclay (England)
1682-1683	Thomas Rudyard
1683-1686	Gaven Lawrie
1686-1687	Neil Campbell
1687-1690	Andrew Hamilton
1688-1689	Edmund Andros (Royal Governor of New York)
1690	John Tatham
1692-1697	Joseph Dudley (Proprietary Governor —rejected by the Province)
1692-1697	Andrew Hamilton
1698-1699	Jeremiah Basse
1699	Andrew Bowne
1699-1702	Andrew Hamilton
	GOVERNORS OF WEST NEW JERSEY*
1676-1681	Board of Commissioners
1680-1687	Edward Byllinge
1681-1684	Samuel Jennings
1684-1685	Thomas Ollive
1685-1687	John Skene
1687-1692	Daniel Coxe
1688-1689	Edmund Andros
1690	Edward Hunloke
1691	West Jersey Society of Proprietors
1692-1697	Andrew Hamilton
1697-1699	Jeremiah Basse
1699-1702	Andrew Hamilton
	GOVERNORS OF EAST AND WEST JERSEY UNITED
1702-1708	Edward Hyde
1708-1710	John Lovelace
1710-1719	Robert Hunter
1720-1727	William Burnet
1728-1731	John Montgomerie
1731-1732	Lewis Morris
1732-1736	William Crosby†
1736-1738	John Hamilton
	GOVERNORS, SEPARATE FROM NEW YORK
1738-1746	Lewis Morris
1746	John Hamilton
1746-1747	John Reading
1747-1757	Jonathan Belcher
1757-1758	John Reading
1758-1760	Francis Bernard
1760-1761	Thomas Boone
1761-1762	Josiah Hardy
1763-1776	William Franklin
	GOVERNORS FROM THE ADOPTION OF THE STATE CONSTITUTION
1776-1787	William Livingston

New Jersey ratified U.S. Constitution on December 18, 1787.

1787-1790	William Livingston
1790-1792	William Paterson
1793-1801	Richard Howell
1801-1802	Joseph Bloomfield
1802-1803	John Lambert
1803-1812	Joseph Bloomfield
1812-1813	Aaron Ogden
1813-1815	William S. Pennington
1815-1817	Mahlon Dickerson
1817-1829	Isaac H. Williamson
1829-1832	Peter D. Vroom
1832-1833	Samuel L. Southard
1833	Elias P. Seeley
1833-1836	Peter D. Vroom
1836-1837	Philemon Dickerson
1837-1843	William Pennington
1843-1844	Daniel Haines
1844-1848	Charles C. Stratton
1848-1851	Daniel Haines
1851-1854	George F. Fort
1854-1857	Rodman M. Price
1857-1860	William A. Newell
1860-1863	Charles S. Olden
1863-1866	Joel Parker
1866-1869	Marcus L. Ward
1869-1872	Theodore F. Randolph
1872-1875	Joel Parker
1875-1878	Joseph D. Bedle
1878-1881	George B. McClellan
1881-1884	George C. Ludlow
1884-1887	Leon Abbett
1887-1890	Robert S. Green
1890-1893	Leon Abbett
1893-1896	George T. Werts
1896-1898	John W. Griggs
1898-1902	Foster M. Voorhees
1902-1905	Franklin Murphy
1905-1908	Edward C. Stokes
1908-1911	John Franklin Fort
1911-1913	Woodrow Wilson
1914-1917	James F. Fielder
1917-1919	Walter E. Edge
1920-1923	Edward I. Edwards
1923-1926	George S. Silzer
1926-1929	A. Harry Moore
1929-1932	Morgan F. Larson
1932-1935	A. Harry Moore
1935	Clifford R. Powell
1935	Horace G. Prall
1935-1938	Harold Giles Hoffman
1938-1941	A. Harry Moore
1941-1944	Charles Edison

1944-1947	Walter E. Edge
1947-1954	Alfred E. Driscoll
1954-1962	Robert B. Meyner
1962-	Richard J. Hughes

New Jersey Legislative Manual, 1967, p. 20. The *Manual* lists in addition Richard Ingoldsby (acting), 1709-1710; Lewis Morris, 1719-1720; John Anderson, 1736; Thomas Pownall (acting), 1757; Elisha Lawrence, 1790; Thomas Henderson, 1794; Charles Clark (acting), 1812; William Kennedy (acting), 1815; Garret D. Wall (declined), 1829; David O. Watkins, 1898-1899; Leon R. Taylor (acting), 1913-1914; William N. Runyon (acting), 1919-1920; Clarence E. Case (acting), 1920.

†The *Manual* spells surname "Cosby."

NEW MEXICO

Term	Governors Under Spanish Rule*
1598-1608	Don Juan de Oñate
1608-1610	Don Cristobal de Oñate
1610-1614	Don Pedro de Peralta
1614-1618	Don Bernadino de Ceballos
1618-1625	Don Juan de Eulate
1625-1630	Don Felipe Sotelo Ossorio
1630-1632	Don Francisco Manuel de Silva Nieto
1632-1635	Don Francisco de la Mora y Ceballos
1635-1637	Don Francisco Martínez de Baeza
1637-1641	Don Luis de Rosas
1641	Don Juan Flores de Sierra y Valdez
1641-1642	Francisco Gómez; Cabildo of Santa Fe
1642-1644	Don Alonzo Pacheco de Herédia
1644-1647	Don Fernando de Argüello Caravajál
1647-1649	Don Luis de Guzmán y Figueroa
1649-1653	Don Hernando de Ugarte y la Concha
1653-1656	Don Juan de Samaniego y Xaca
1656-1659	Don Juan Mansso de Contreras
1659-1661	Don Bernardo López de Mendizabal
1661-1664	Don Diego Dionisio de Peñalosa Briceño y Berdugo
1664-1665	Don Juan de Durán de Miranda
1665-1668	Don Fernando de Villanueva
1668-1671	Don Juan de Medrano y Mesia
1671-1675	Don Juan Durán de Miranda
1675-1677	Don Juan Francisco de Treviño
1677-1683	Don Antonio de Otermín
1683-1686	Don Domingo Jironza Pétriz de Cruzate
1686-1689	Pedro Reneros de Posada
1689-1691	Don Domingo Jironza Pétriz de Cruzate
1691-1697	Don Diego de Vargas Zapata Luan Ponce de León y Contreras
1697-1703	Don Pedro Rodriguez Cubero
1703-1704	Diego de Vargas Zapata Lujan Ponce de León y Contreras
1704-1705	Don Juan Paéz Hurtado
1705-1707	Don Francisco Cuervo y Valdez
1707-1712	Don Joseph Chacón Medina Salazar y Villaseñor
1712-1715	Don Juan Ignacio Flores Mogollón
1715-1717	Don Felipe Martínez
1717	Don Juan Paéz Hurtado
1717-1722	Don Antonio Valverde y Cossio
1722-1731	Don Juan Domingo de Bustamente
1731-1736	Don Gervasio Cruzat y Góngora
1736-1739	Don Henrique de Olavide y Micheleña
1739-1743	Don Gaspar Domingo de Mendoza
1743-1749	Don Joaquín Codallos y Rabal
1749-1754	Don Tomás Véles Cachupín
1754-1760	Don Francisco Antonio Marín de Valle
1760	Don Mateo Antonio de Mendoza
1760-1762	Don Manuel de Portillo y Urrisola
1762-1767	Don Tomás Véles Cachupín
1767-1778	Don Pedro Fermín de Mendinueta
1778	Don Francisco Trebol Navarro
1778-1788	Don Juan Bautista de Anza
1788-1794	Don Fernando de la Concha
1794-1805	Don Fernando Chacón
1805-1808	Don Joaquín del Real Alencaster
1808	Don Alberto Máynez
1808-1814	Don José Manrrique
1814-1816	Don Alberto Máynez
1816-1818	Don Pedro María de Allande
1818-1821	Don Facundo Mélgares
	Under Mexican Rule*
1821-1822	Don Facundo Mélgares
1822	Francisco Xavier Chavez
1822-1823	José Antonio Vizcarra
1823-1825	Bartolomé Baca
1825-1827	Antonio Narbona
1827-1829	Manuel Armijo
1829-1832	José Antonio Chavez
1832-1833	Santiago Abreú
1833-1835	Francisco Sarracino
1835-1837	Albino Perez
1837-1844	Manuel Armijo
1844	Mariano Chavez
1844	Felipe Sena
1844-1845	Mariano Martínez de Lejanza
1845	José Chavez y Castillo
1845-1846	Manuel Armijo
1846	Juan Bautista Vigil y Alaríd
	United States Occupation, 1846-1850*
1846	Brigadier Gen. Stephen Watts Kearny
1846-1847	Charles Bent (assassinated, January 19, 1847)
1847-1848	Donaciano Vigil (Civil) Col. Sterling Price (Military)
1848-1849	Col. John M. Washington
1849-1851	Col. John Munroe
	Territorial Governors*
1851-1852	James S. Calhoun
1852	John Greiner
1852-1853	William Carr Lane
1853	W. S. Messervy
1853-1856	David Meriwether
1856-1857	W. W. H. Davis
1857-1861	Abraham Rencher
1861-1866	Henry Connelley
1866	W. F. M. Arny
1866-1869	Robert B. Mitchell
1869-1871	William A. Pile
1871-1875	Marsh Giddings
1875	William G. Ritch
1875-1878	Samuel B. Axtell
1878-1881	Lew Wallace
1881-1885	Lionel A. Sheldon
1885-1889	Edmund G. Ross
1889-1893	L. Bradford Prince
1893-1897	William T. Thornton
1897-1906	Miguel A. Otero
1906-1907	Herbert J. Hagerman
1907	J. W. Raynolds
1907-1910	George Curry
1910-1912	William J. Mills
	State Governors
1912-1917	William C. McDonald
1917	Ezequiel C. de Baca
1917-1918	Washington E. Lindsey
1919-1921	Octaviano A. Larrazolo
1921-1923	Merritt C. Mechem

1923-1925	James F. Hinkle	1947-1950	Thomas J. Mabry
1925-1927	Arthur T. Hannett	1951-1954	Edwin L. Mechem
1927-1931	Richard C. Dillon	1955-1956	John F. Simms
1931-1933	Arthur Seligman	1957-1958	Edwin L. Mechem
1933-1935	A. W. Hockenhull	1959-1960	John Burroughs
1935-1938	Clyde Tingley	1961-1962	Edwin L. Mechem
1939-1942	John E. Miles	1962	Tom Bolack†
1943-1946	John J. Dempsey	1963-1966	Jack M. Campbell
		1967-	David F. Cargo

**New Mexico Blue Book*, 1965-1966, p. 39.
†"The Governors of the States, 1900-1966," published by the Council of State Governments lists date 1963.

NEW YORK

COLONIAL GOVERNORS*

TERM	FIRST DUTCH PERIOD
1623-1624	Adriaen Jorissen Tienpoint
1624-1625	Cornelis Jacobsen Mey
1625-1626	Willem Verhulst
1626-1632	Peter Minuit
1632-1633	Bastiaen Jansen Krol
1633-1638	Wouter Van Twiller
1638-1647	Willem Kieft
1647-1664	Peter Stuyvesant
	FIRST ENGLISH PERIOD
1664-1668	Richard Nicolls
1668-1673	Francis Lovelace
	SECOND DUTCH PERIOD
1673	Cornelis Evertsen
1673-1674	Anthony Colve
	SECOND ENGLISH PERIOD
1674-1677	Edmund Andros
1677-1678	Anthony Brockholls
1678-1681	Edmund Andros
1681-1683	Anthony Brockholls
1683-1688	Thomas Dongan
1688	Edmund Andros
1688-1689	Francis Nicholson
1689-1691	Jacob Leisler
1691	Henry Sloughter
1691-1692	Richard Ingoldsby
1692-1698	Benjamin Fletcher
1698-1699	Richard Coote
1699-1700	John Nanfan
1700-1701	Richard Coote
1701-1702	John Nanfan
1702-1708	Edward Hyde
1708-1709	John Lovelace
1709	Peter Schuyler
1709-1710	Richard Ingoldsby
1710	Gerardus Beekman
1710-1719	Robert Hunter
1719-1720	Peter Schuyler
1720-1728	William Burnet
1728-1731	John Montgomerie
1731-1732	Rip Van Dam
1732-1736	William Cosby
1736-1743	George Clarke
1743-1753	George Clinton
1753	Danvers Osborne
1753-1755	James De Lancey
1755-1757	Charles Hardy
1757-1760	James De Lancey
1760-1761	Cadwallader Colden
1761	Robert Monckton
1761-1762	Cadwallader Colden
1762-1763	Robert Monckton
1763-1765	Cadwallader Colden
1765-1769	Henry Moore
1769-1770	Cadwallader Colden
1770-1771	John Murray
1771-1774	William Tryon
1774-1775	Cadwallader Colden
1775-1778	William Tryon

STATE GOVERNORS

1777-1788	George Clinton

New York ratified U. S. Constitution on July 26, 1788.

1788-1795	George Clinton
1795-1801	John Jay
1801-1804	George Clinton
1804-1807	Morgan Lewis
1807-1817	Daniel D. Tompkins
1817-1822	De Witt Clinton
1823-1824	Joseph C. Yates
1825-1828	De Witt Clinton
1828	Nathaniel Pitcher
1829	Martin Van Buren
1829-1832	Enos T. Throop
1833-1838	William L. Marcy
1839-1842	William H. Seward
1843-1844	William C. Bouck
1845-1846	Silas Wright, Jr.
1847-1848	John Young
1849-1850	Hamilton Fish
1851-1852	Washington Hunt
1853-1854	Horatio Seymour
1855-1856	Myron H. Clark
1857-1858	John A. King
1859-1862	Edwin D. Morgan
1863-1864	Horatio Seymour
1865-1868	Reuben E. Fenton
1869-1872	John T. Hoffman
1873-1874	John A. Dix
1875-1876	Samuel J. Tilden
1877-1879	Lucius Robinson
1880-1882	Alonzo B. Cornell
1883-1885	Grover Cleveland
1885-1891	David B. Hill†
1892-1894	Roswell P. Flower
1895-1896	Levi P. Morton
1897-1898	Frank S. Black
1899-1900	Theodore Roosevelt
1901-1904	Benjamin B. Odell, Jr.
1905-1906	Frank W. Higgins
1907-1910	Charles E. Hughes
1910	Horace White
1911-1912	John A. Dix
1913	William Sulzer
1913-1914	Martin H. Glynn‡
1915-1918	Charles S. Whitman
1919-1920	Alfred E. Smith
1921-1922	Nathan L. Miller
1923-1928	Alfred E. Smith
1929-1932	Franklin D. Roosevelt
1933-1942	Herbert H. Lehman

1942	Charles Poletti	1955-1958	W. Averell Harriman
1943-1954	Thomas E. Dewey	1959-	Nelson A. Rockefeller

Note: The *Legislative Manual*, New York, 1967, lists, in addition, John Taylor (acting), 1817.
*The *Encyclopedia Americana*, Vol. 20, p. 204.
†*White's Conspectus* lists entry date for David B. Hill, 1884.
‡Not listed in *White's Conspectus*.

NORTH CAROLINA*

Term	Chief Executives Under the Proprietors
1663-1667	William Drummond
1667-1669	Samuel Stephens
1670-1673	Peter Carteret
1673-1676	John Jenkins
1676-1678	Thomas Eastchurch
1677	Thomas Miller
1677-1678	John Culpepper
1678	Seth Sothel
1679	John Harvey
1679-1681	John Jenkins
1682-1689	Seth Sothel
1689-1691	Philip Ludwell
1691-1694	Thomas Jarvis
1694	John Archdale
1694-1699	Thomas Harvey
1699-1704	Henderson Walker
1704-1705	Robert Daniel
1705-1706	Thomas Cary
1706-1708	William Glover
1708-1711	Thomas Cary
1710-1712	Edward Hyde
1712-1714	Thomas Pollock
1714-1722	Charles Eden
1722	Thomas Pollock
1722-1724	William Reed
1724-1725	George Burrington
1725-1728	Richard Everard
	Governors Under the Crown
1728-1731	Richard Everard
1731-1734	George Burrington
1734	Nathaniel Rice
1734-1752	Gabriel Johnston
1752-1754	Matthew Rowan
1754-1765	Arthur Dobbs
1765-1771	William Tryon
1771	James Hasell
1771-1775	Josiah Martin
	State Governors Elected by the Legislature
1776-1780	Richard Caswell
1780-1781	Abner Nash
1781-1782	Thomas Burke
1782-1785	Alexander Martin
1785-1787	Richard Caswell
1787-1789	Samuel Johnston

North Carolina ratified U.S. Constitution on November 21, 1789.

1789-1792	Alexander Martin
1792-1795	Richard D. Spaight
1795-1798	Samuel Ashe
1798-1799	William R. Davie
1799-1802	Benjamin Williams
1802-1805	James Turner
1805-1807	Nathaniel Alexander
1807-1808	Benjamin Williams
1808-1810	David Stone
1810-1811	Benjamin Smith
1811-1814	William Hawkins
1814-1817	William Miller
1817-1820	John Branch
1820-1821	Jesse Franklin
1821-1824	Gabriel Holmes
1824-1827	Hutchings G. Burton
1827-1828	James Iredell, Jr.
1828-1830	John Owen
1830-1832	Montfort Stokes
1832-1835	David L. Swain
1835-1836	Richard D. Spaight, Jr.
	State Governors Elected by the People
1836-1841	Edward B. Dudley
1841-1845	John M. Morehead
1845-1849	William A. Graham
1849-1851	Charles Manly
1851-1854	David S. Reid
1854-1855	Warren Winslow
1855-1859	Thomas Bragg
1859-1861	John W. Ellis
1861-1862	Henry T. Clark
1862-1865	Zebulon B. Vance
1865	William W. Holden
1865-1868	Jonathan Worth
1868-1870	William W. Holden
1871-1874	Tod R. Caldwell
1874-1877	Curtis H. Brogden
1877-1879	Zebulon B. Vance
1879-1885	Thomas J. Jarvis
1885-1889	Alfred M. Scales
1889-1891	Daniel G. Fowle
1891-1893	Thomas M. Holt
1893-1897	Elias Carr
1897-1901	Daniel L. Russell
1901-1905	Charles B. Aycock
1905-1909	Robert B. Glenn
1909-1913	William W. Kitchin
1913-1917	Locke Craig
1917-1921	Thomas W. Bickett
1921-1925	Cameron Morrison
1925-1929	Angus W. McLean
1929-1933	O. Max Gardner
1933-1937	John C. B. Ehringhaus
1937-1941	Clyde R. Hoey
1941-1945	Melville Broughton
1945-1949	R. Gregg Cherry
1949-1953	William Kerr Scott
1953-1954	William B. Umstead
1954-1961	Luther H. Hodges
1961-1965	Terry Sanford
1965-1969	Dan K. Moore
1969-	Robert W. Scott

*The *North Carolina Manual*, 1967, subdivides list as indicated and supplies closing year of terms. It also lists Ralph Lane, 1585-86; and John White, 1587; as Governors when North Carolina was part of "Virginia."

NORTH DAKOTA

TERM	TERRITORIAL GOVERNORS* (DAKOTA TERRITORY)
1861-1863	William Jayne
1863-1866	Newton Edmunds
1866-1869	Andrew J. Faulk
1869-1874	John A. Burbank
1874-1878	John L. Pennington
1878-1880	William A. Howard
1880-1884	Nehemiah G. Ordway
1884-1887	Gilbert A. Pierce
1887-1889	Louis K. Church
1889	Arthur C. Melette
	STATE GOVERNORS
1889-1890	John Miller
1891-1892	Andrew H. Burke
1893-1894	Edward C. D. Shortridge†
1895-1896	Roger Allin†
1897-1898	Frank A. Briggs
1899-1900	Frederick B. Fancher
1901-1904	Frank White
1905-1906	Elmore Y. Sarles
1907-1912	John Burke
1913-1916	Louis B. Hanna
1917-1921	Lynn J. Frazier
1921-1924	Ragnvald A. Nestos
1925-1928	Arthur G. Sorlie
1928	Walter Maddock
1929-1932	George F. Shafer
1933-1934	William Langer
1935-1936	Walter Welford
1937-1938	William Langer
1939-1944	John Moses
1945-1950	Fred G. Aandahl
1951-1956	C. Norman Brunsdale
1957-1960	John E. Davis
1961-	William L. Guy

**North Dakota Blue Book*, 1961, p. 122. The *Blue Book* lists, in addition, Joseph M. Devine, 1898; Ole H. Olson, 1934; Thomas H. Moodie, 1935. Closing date of terms is taken from *Blue Book*.

†The *Blue Book*, p. 130, lists as follows: Eli C. D. Shortridge, Roger Allen.

OHIO

TERM	TERRITORIAL GOVERNORS* (NORTHWEST TERRITORY)
1788-1802	Arthur St. Clair
1802-1803	Charles W. Byrd
	STATE GOVERNORS
1803-1807	Edward Tiffin
1807-1808	Thomas Kirker
1808-1810	Samuel Huntington
1810-1814	Return Jonathan Meigs, Jr.
1814	Othniel Looker†
1814-1818	Thomas Worthington
1819-1822	Ethan Allen Brown
1822	Allen Trimble
1822-1826	Jeremiah Morrow
1826-1830	Allen Trimble
1830-1832	Duncan McArthur
1832-1836	Robert Lucas
1836-1838	Joseph Vance
1838-1840	Wilson Shannon
1840-1842	Thomas Corwin
1842-1844	Wilson Shannon
1844-1846	Mordecai Bartley
1846-1848	William Bebb
1848-1850	Seabury Ford
1850-1853	Reuben Wood
1853-1856	William Medill
1856-1860	Salmon Portland Chase
1860-1862	William Dennison, Jr.
1862-1864	David Tod
1864-1865	John Brough
1866-1868	Jacob Dolson Cox
1868-1872	Rutherford Birchard Hayes
1872-1874	Edward Follansbee Noyes
1874-1876	William Allen
1876-1877	Rutherford Birchard Hayes
1877-1878	Thomas Lowry Young
1878-1880	Richard Moore Bishop
1880-1884	Charles Foster
1884-1886	George Hoadley†
1886-1890	Joseph Benson Foraker
1890-1892	James Edwin Campbell
1892-1896	William McKinley, Jr.
1896-1900	Asa Smith Bushnell
1900-1904	George Kilbon Nash
1904-1906	Myron Timothy Herrick
1906	John M. Pattison
1906-1909	Andrew Lintner Harris
1909-1913	Judson Harmon
1913-1915	James Middleton Cox
1915-1917	Frank Bartlett Willis
1917-1921	James Middleton Cox
1921-1923	Harry Lyman Davis
1923-1929	Alvin Victor Donahey
1929-1931	Myers Young Cooper
1931-1935	George White
1935-1939	Martin Luther Davey
1939-1945	John William Bricker
1945-1947	Frank John Lausche
1947-1949	Thomas John Herbert
1949-1957	Frank John Lausche
1957-1959	C. William O'Neill
1959-1963	Michael Vincent Di Salle
1963-	James Allen Rhodes

**Official Roster*, State of Ohio, Federal, State, County Officers, 1963-64, p. 104. The *Roster* lists in addition: Thomas W. Bartley (acting), 1844; Charles Anderson (acting), 1865-1866; John W. Brown, 1957.

†The *Roster* lists names as follows: Othneil Looker and George Hoadly.

OKLAHOMA

TERM	TERRITORIAL GOVERNORS*
1890-1891	George W. Steele
1891-1892	Robert Martin
1892-1893	Abraham Jefferson Seay
1893-1897	William Cary Renfrow
1897-1901	Cassius M. Barnes
1901	William M. Jenkins
1901	William C. Grimes
1901-1906	Thompson B. Ferguson
1906-1907	Frank Frantz
	STATE GOVERNORS
1907-1911	Charles N. Haskell
1911-1915	Lee Cruce
1915-1919	Robert L. Williams
1919-1923	James B. A. Robertson
1923	James C. Walton†
1923-1927	Martin E. Trapp

1927-1929	Henry S. Johnston
1929-1931	William J. Holloway
1931-1935	William H. Murray
1935-1939	Ernest Whitworth Marland
1939-1943	Leon C. Philipps
1943-1947	Robert S. Kerr
1947-1951	Roy J. Turner
1951-1955	Johnston Murray
1955-1959	Raymond Gary
1959-1963	J. Howard Edmondson
1963	George P. Nigh
1963-1967	Henry Bellmon
1967-	Dewey F. Bartlett

**Directory and Manual of the State of Oklahoma*, 1967, p. 26.
†*Manual* lists name Jack Callaway Walton.

OREGON

Term	Territorial Governors*
1849-1850	Joseph Lane
1850	Kintzing Prichette
1850-1853	John P. Gaines
1853	Joseph Lane
1853	George L. Curry
1853-1854	John W. Davis
1854-1859	George L. Curry
	State Governors
1859-1862	John Whiteaker
1862-1866	Addison C. Gibbs
1866-1870	George Lemuel Woods
1870-1877	LaFayette F. Grover
1877-1878	Stephen Fowler Chadwick
1878-1882	William Wallace Thayer
1882-1887	Zenas Ferry Moody
1887-1895	Sylvester Pennoyer
1895-1899	William Payne Lord
1899-1903	Theodore T. Geer
1903-1909	George E. Chamberlain
1909-1910	Frank W. Benson
1911-1915	Oswald West
1915-1919	James Withycombe
1919-1923	Ben W. Olcott
1923-1927	Walter M. Pierce
1927-1929	Isaac L. Patterson
1929-1931	Albin W. Norblad
1931-1935	Julius L. Meier
1935-1939	Charles Henry Martin
1939-1943	Charles A. Sprague
1943-1947	Earl Snell
1947-1949	John H. Hall
1949-1952	Douglas McKay
1952-1956	Paul L. Patterson
1956-1957	Elmo E. Smith
1957-1959	Robert D. Holmes
1959-1967	Mark O. Hatfield
1967-	Tom McCall

**Oregon Blue Book*, 1967-1968, p. 22. The *Blue Book* lists, in addition, Jay Bowerman (acting), 1910-1911.

PENNSYLVANIA

Term	Colonial Governors*
	New Sweden
1638	Peter Minuit
1640	Jost van Bogardt
1640-1643	Peter Hollandaer
1643-1653	Johan Björnsson Printz
1653-1654	Johan Papegoga
1654-1655	Johan Classon Rising
	First Dutch Period
1655-1664	Petrus Stuyvesant
	First English Period
1664-1667	Richard Nicolls
1667-1673	Francis Lovelace
	Second Dutch Period
1673-1674	Anthony Colve
	Second English Period
1674-1677	Edmund Andros
1677-1678	Anthony Brockholls
1678-1681	Edmund Andros
1681	Anthony Brockholls
	Province
1681-1693	William Penn, Proprietor
1681-1682	William Markham
1682-1684	William Penn
1684-1688	Thomas Lloyd
1688-1690	John Blackwell
1690-1691	Thomas Lloyd
1691-1693	Thomas Lloyd, Deputy Governor of the Province
1691-1693	William Markham, Deputy Governor of the Lower Counties
	Crown of England
1693-1695	Benjamin Fletcher, Governor of New York
1693-1695	William Markham, Lt. Governor
	Province
1694-1718	William Penn, Proprietor
1695-1699	William Markham
1699-1701	William Penn
1701-1703	Andrew Hamilton
1703-1704	Edward Shippen
1704-1709	John Evans
1709-1717	Charles Gookin
1717-1718	William Keith
1718-1746	John Penn, Richard Penn, and Thomas Penn, Proprietors
1718-1726	William Keith
1726-1736	Patrick Gordon
1736-1738	James Logan
1738-1746	George Thomas
1746-1771	Richard Penn and Thomas Penn, Proprietors
1746-1747	George Thomas
1747-1748	Anthony Palmer
1748-1754	James Hamilton
1754-1756	Robert Hunter Morris
1756-1759	William Denny
1759-1763	James Hamilton
1763-1771	John Penn
1771-1776	Thomas Penn and John Penn
1771	James Hamilton
1771-1773	Richard Penn
1773	James Hamilton
1773-1776	John Penn
1776-1777	Thomas Wharton, Jr.

	Presidents of the Executive Council
1777-1778	Thomas Wharton, Jr.
1778	George Bryan
1778-1781	Joseph Reed
1781-1782	William Moore
1782-1785	John Dickinson
1785-1787	Benjamin Franklin

Pennsylvania ratified U. S. Constitution on December 12, 1787.

1787-1788	Benjamin Franklin
1788-1790	Thomas Mifflin

	State Governors
1790-1799	Thomas Mifflin
1799-1808	Thomas McKean
1808-1817	Simon Snyder
1817-1820	William Findlay
1820-1823	Joseph Hiester
1823-1829	John A. Shulze
1829-1835	George Wolff†
1835-1839	Joseph Ritner
1839-1845	David R. Porter
1845-1848	Francis R. Shunk
1848-1852	William F. Johnston
1852-1855	William Bigler
1855-1858	James Pollock
1858-1861	William F. Packer
1861-1867	Andrew G. Curtin
1867-1873	John W. Geary
1873-1879	John F. Hartranft
1879-1883	Henry M. Hoyt
1883-1887	Robert E. Pattison
1887-1891	James A. Beaver
1891-1895	Robert E. Pattison
1895-1899	Daniel H. Hastings
1899-1903	William Alexis Stone
1903-1907	Samuel Whitaker Pennypacker
1907-1911	Edwin Sydney Stuart
1911-1915	John Kinley Tener
1915-1919	Martin Grove Brumbaugh
1919-1923	William Cameron Sproul
1923-1927	Gifford Pinchot
1927-1931	John Stuchell Fisher
1931-1935	Gifford Pinchot
1935-1939	George Howard Earle, III
1939-1943	Arthur Horace James
1943-1947	Edward Martin
1947	John C. Bell, Jr.
1947-1951	James H. Duff
1951-1955	John S. Fine
1955-1959	George M. Leader
1959-1963	David L. Lawrence
1963-1967	William W. Scranton
1967-	Raymond Philip Shafer

*The *Encyclopedia Americana*, Vol. 21, p. 523.
†The *Pennsylvania Manual*, 1967, pp. 402-403, lists name George Wolfe.

RHODE ISLAND*†

Term	Portsmouth Judges
1638-1639	William Coddington
1639-1640	William Hutchinson

	Newport Judge
1639-1640	William Coddington

	Portsmouth and Newport Governor
1640-1647	William Coddington

(In 1647 the four towns were united under Charter of 1643).

	Chief Officer Under the Charter of 1643
1645-1647	Roger Williams

	Presidents Under the Charter of 1643
1647-1648	John Coggeshall
1648-1649	Jeremy Clarke
1649-1650	John Smith
1650-1651	Nicholas Easton

(In 1651 Portsmouth and Newport broke away and set up jointly a new government).

	Providence and Warwick Presidents
1651-1652	Samuel Gorton
1652-1653	John Smith
1653-1654	Gregory Dexter

	Portsmouth and Newport Governor
1651-1653	William Coddington

	Portsmouth and Newport President
1653-1654	John Sanford

(In 1654 the union of the four towns was re-established).

	Presidents
1654	Nicholas Easton
1654-1657	Roger Williams
1657-1660	Benedict Arnold
1660-1662	William Brenton
1662-1663	Benedict Arnold

Term	Governors Under the Royal Charter
1663-1666	Benedict Arnold
1666-1669	William Brenton
1669-1672	Benedict Arnold
1672-1674	Nicholas Easton
1674-1676	William Coddington
1676-1677	Walter Clarke
1677-1678	Benedict Arnold
1678	William Coddington
1678-1680	John Cranston
1680-1683	Peleg Sanford
1683-1685	William Coddington, Jr.
1685-1686	Henry Bull
1686	Walter Clarke

(Charter suspended in 1686. The colony became a county of the Dominion of New England under Sir Edmund Andros until 1869).

1689-1690	John Coggeshall, Jr.
1690	Henry Bull
1690-1695	John Easton
1695	Caleb Carr
1696-1698	Walter Clarke
1698-1727	Samuel Cranston
1727-1732	Joseph Jencks
1732-1733	William Wanton
1734-1740	John Wanton
1740-1743	Richard Ward
1743-1745	William Greene
1745-1746	Gideon Wanton
1746-1747	William Greene

1747-1748	Gideon Wanton
1748-1755	William Greene
1755-1757	Stephen Hopkins
1757-1758	William Greene
1758-1762	Stephen Hopkins
1762-1763	Samuel Ward
1763-1765	Stephen Hopkins
1765-1767	Samuel Ward
1767-1768	Stephen Hopkins
1768-1769	Josias Lyndon
1769-1775	Joseph Wanton
1775-1778	Nicholas Cooke
1778-1786	William Greene
1786-1790	John Collins

Rhode Island ratified U.S. Constitution on May 29, 1790.

STATE GOVERNORS

1790-1805	Arthur Fenner
1805	Paul Mumford
1805-1806	Henry Smith
1806-1807	Isaac Wilbour
1807-1811	James Fenner
1811-1817	William Jones
1817-1821	Nehemiah R. Knight
1821-1824	William C. Gibbs
1824-1831	James Fenner
1831-1833	Lemuel H. Arnold
1833-1838	John Brown Francis
1838-1839	William Sprague
1840-1843	Samuel Ward King

GOVERNORS UNDER THE STATE CONSTITUTION ADOPTED IN 1842

1843-1845	James Fenner
1845-1846	Charles Jackson
1846-1847	Byron Diman
1847-1849	Elisha Harris
1849-1851	Henry B. Anthony
1851-1853	Philip Allen
1853-1854	Francis M. Dimond
1854-1857	William Warner Hoppin
1857-1859	Elisha Dyer
1859-1860	Thomas G. Turner
1860-1863	William Sprague
1863	William C. Cozzens
1863-1866	James Y. Smith
1866-1869	Ambrose E. Burnside
1869-1873	Seth Padelford
1873-1875	Henry Howard
1875-1877	Henry Lippitt
1877-1880	Charles C. Van Zandt
1880-1883	Alfred H. Littlefield
1883-1885	Augustus O. Bourn
1885-1887	George Peabody Wetmore
1887-1888	John W. Davis
1888-1889	Royal C. Taft
1889-1890	Herbert W. Ladd
1890-1891	John W. Davis
1891-1892	Herbert W. Ladd
1892-1895	D. Russell Brown
1895-1897	Charles Warren Lippitt
1897-1900	Elisha Dyer
1900-1901	William Gregory
1901-1903	Charles Dean Kimball
1903-1905	Lucius F. C. Garvin
1905-1907	George H. Utter
1907-1909	James H. Higgins
1909-1915	Aram J. Pothier
1915-1921	R. Livingston Beeckman
1921-1923	Emery J. San Souci
1923-1925	William S. Flynn
1925-1928	Aram J. Pothier
1928-1933	Norman S. Case
1933-1937	Theodore Francis Green
1937-1939	Robert E. Quinn
1939-1941	William H. Vanderbilt
1941-1945	J. Howard McGrath
1945-1950	John O. Pastore
1950-1951	John S. McKiernan
1951-1959	Dennis J. Roberts
1959-1961	Christopher Del Sesto
1961-1963	John A. Notte, Jr.
1963-1969	John H. Chafee
1969–	Frank Licht

*The *Rhode Island Manual*, 1965-1966, p. 184, subdivides list as indicated and is followed throughout. *White's Conspectus* also lists William B. Laurence as serving in 1852-1853 and John R. Bartlett in 1861-1863.

†The State originally consisted of four towns: Providence, settled in 1636; Portsmouth, in 1638; Newport, in 1639; and Warwick, in 1642. The executive heads of Portsmouth and Newport were entitled judges, until 1640, when these two towns were united, and the chief officer was thereafter called Governor. Providence and Warwick had no executive head until 1647.

SOUTH CAROLINA

TERM	GOVERNORS UNDER PROPRIETARY GOVERNMENT
1669-1671	William Sayle
1672-1674	John Yeamans
1674-1682	Joseph West
1682-1684	Joseph Morton
1684	Richard Kyrle
1684-1685	Robert Quarry*
1685	Joseph West
1685-1686	Joseph Morton
1686-1689	James Colleton
1689-1690	Thomas Smith
1690-1691	John Sothell*
1691-1693	Philip Ludwell
1693-1694	Thomas Smith
1694-1695	Joseph Blake
1695-1696	John Archdale
1696-1700	Joseph Blake
1700-1703	James Moore
1703-1708	Nathaniel Johnson
1708-1709	Edward Tynte
1709-1712	Robert Gibbes
1712-1716	Charles Craven
1716-1717	Robert Daniel
1717-1719	Robert Johnson

GOVERNORS UNDER ROYAL GOVERNMENT

1719-1721	James Moore
1721-1725	Francis Nicholson
1725-1730	Arthur Middleton
1731-1735	Robert Johnson
1735-1737	Thomas Broughton
1737-1743	William Bull
1743-1756	James Glen
1756-1760	William Henry Lyttleton*
1760-1761	William Bull, II
1761-1764	Thomas Boone
1764-1766	William Bull, II
1766-1768	Charles G. Montagu
1768	William Bull, II
1768-1769	Charles G. Montagu
1769-1771	William Bull, II
1771-1773	Charles G. Montagu
1773-1775	William Bull, II
1775	William Campbell

	REVOLUTIONARY PERIOD
	PRESIDENTS
1776-1778	John Rutledge
1778-1779	Rawlins Lowndes
	STATE GOVERNORS
1779-1782	John Rutledge
1782-1783	John Mathews
1783-1785	Benjamin Guerard
1785-1787	William Moultrie
1787-1788	Thomas Pinckney

South Carolina ratified U. S. Constitution on May 23, 1788.

1788-1789	Thomas Pinckney
1789-1792	Charles Pinckney
1792-1794	Arnoldus Vanderhorst†
1794-1796	William Moultrie†
1796-1798	Charles Pinckney
1798-1800	Edward Rutledge
1800-1802	John Drayton
1802-1804	James Burchill Richardson
1804-1806	Paul Hamilton
1806-1808	Charles Pinckney
1808-1810	John Drayton
1810-1812	Henry Middleton
1812-1814	Joseph Alston
1814-1816	David R. Williams
1816-1818	Andrew Pickens
1818-1820	John Geddes
1820-1822	Thomas Bennett
1822-1824	John Lyde Wilson
1824-1826	Richard Irvine Manning
1826-1828	John Taylor
1828-1830	Stephen D. Miller
1830-1832	James Hamilton, Jr.
1832-1834	Robert Y. Hayne
1834-1836	George McDuffie
1836-1838	Pierce Mason Butler
1838-1840	Patrick Noble
1840-1842	John Peter Richardson
1842-1844	James H. Hammond
1844-1846	William Aiken
1846-1848	David Johnson
1848-1850	Whitemarsh B. Seabrook
1850-1852	John Hugh Means
1852-1854	John Laurence Manning
1854-1856	James Hopkins Adams
1856-1858	Robert F. W. Allston
1858-1860	William H. Gist
1860-1862	Francis Wilkinson Pickens
1862-1864	Milledge Luke Bonham
1864-1865	Andrew Gordon Magrath
1865	Benjamin Franklin Perry
1866-1868	James Lawrence Orr
1868-1872	Robert K. Scott
1872-1874	Franklin J. Moses, Jr.
1874-1876	Daniel H. Chamberlain
1876-1878	Wade Hampton
1878-1880	William Dunlap Simpson
1880	Thomas B. Jeter
1880-1882	Johnson Hagood
1882-1886	Hugh Smith Thompson
1886	John C. Sheppard
1886-1890	John Peter Richardson
1890-1894	Benjamin Ryan Tillman
1894-1896	John Gary Evans
1896-1899	William H. Ellerbe
1899-1903	Miles B. McSweeney
1903-1907	Duncan Clinch Heyward
1907-1911	Martin F. Ansel
1911-1915	Coleman Livingston Blease
1915-1919	Richard Irvine Manning
1919-1922	Robert A. Cooper
1923-1927	Thomas G. McLeod
1927-1931	John G. Richards
1931-1935	Ibra C. Blackwood
1935-1939	Olin D. Johnston
1939-1941	Burnet R. Maybank
1941-1942	Joseph E. Harley
1942-1943	Richard M. Jeffries
1943-1945	Olin D. Johnston
1945-1947	Ransome J. Williams
1947-1951	J. Strom Thurmond
1951-1955	James F. Byrnes
1955-1959	George Bell Timmerman, Jr.
1959-1963	Ernest F. Hollings
1963-1965	Donald S. Russell
1965-	Robert E. McNair

*The *Encyclopedia Americana*, Vol. 25, p. 290, lists names Robert Quary, Seth Sothell, William Lyttelton. It adds the following names and terms: Joseph West, 1671-1672, 1684-1685; B. K. Henegan (acting), 1840; Charles A. Smith (acting), 1915; Wilson G. Harvey, 1922-1923.

†The *Americana* lists William Moultrie, 1792-1794, and Arnoldus Vanderhorst, 1794-1796.

SOUTH DAKOTA

TERM	TERRITORIAL GOVERNORS*
	(DAKOTA TERRITORY)
1861-1863	William Jayne
1863-1866	Newton Edmunds
1866-1869	Andrew J. Faulk
1869-1874	John A. Burbank
1874-1878	John L. Pennington
1878-1880	William A. Howard
1880-1884	Nehemiah G. Ordway
1884-1887	Gilbert A. Pierce
1887-1889	Louis K. Church
1889	Arthur C. Mellette
	STATE GOVERNORS
1889-1893	Arthur C. Mellette
1893-1897	Charles H. Sheldon
1897-1901	Andrew E. Lee
1901-1905	Charles N. Herreid
1905-1907	Samuel H. Elrod
1907-1909	Corie I. Crawford†
1909-1913	Robert S. Vessey
1913-1917	Frank M. Byrne‡
1917-1921	Peter Norbeck
1921-1925	William H. McMaster
1925-1927	Carl Gunderson
1927-1931	William J. Bulow
1931-1933	Warren E. Green
1933-1937	Tom Berry
1937-1939	Leslie Jensen
1939-1943	Harlan J. Bushfield
1943-1947	M. Q. Sharpe
1947-1951	George T. Mickelson
1951-1955	Sigurd Anderson
1955-1959	Joe Foss
1959-1961	Ralph Herseth
1961-1965	Archie Gubbrud
1965-1969	Nils A. Boe
1969-	Frank L. Farrar

**South Dakota Manual*, 1961, p. 408.

†The *Manual* lists name Coe I. Crawford.

‡*White's Conspectus* lists entering date of Frank M. Byrne as 1915.

TENNESSEE

Term	Territorial Governor*
1790-1796	William Blount
	State Governors
1796-1801	John Sevier
1801-1803	Archibald Roane
1803-1809	John Sevier
1809-1815	Willie Blount
1815-1821	Joseph McMinn
1821-1827	William Carroll
1827-1829	Samuel Houston
1829	William Hall
1829-1835	William Carroll
1835-1839	Newton Cannon
1839-1841	James K. Polk
1841-1845	James C. Jones
1845-1847	Aaron V. Brown
1847-1849	Neal S. Brown†
1849-1851	William Trousdale
1851-1853	William B. Campbell
1853-1857	Andrew Johnson
1857-1862	Isham G. Harris
1862-1865	Andrew Johnson
1865-1869	William G. Brownlow
1869-1871	DeWitt C. Senter
1871-1875	John C. Brown
1875-1879	James D. Porter
1879-1881	Albert S. Marks
1881-1883	Alvin Hawkins
1883-1887	William B. Bate
1887-1891	Robert L. Taylor
1891-1893	John P. Buchanan
1893-1897	Peter Turney
1897-1899	Robert L. Taylor
1899-1903	Benton McMillin
1903-1905	James B. Frazier
1905-1907	John I. Cox
1907-1911	Malcolm R. Patterson
1911-1915	Ben W. Hooper
1915-1919	Thomas C. Rye
1919-1921	Albert H. Roberts
1921-1923	Alfred A. Taylor
1923-1927	Austin Peay
1927-1933	Henry H. Horton
1933-1937	Hill McAlister
1937-1939	Gordon Browning
1939-1945	Prentice Cooper
1945-1949	Jim Nance McCord
1949-1953	Gordon Browning
1953-1959	Frank G. Clement
1959-1963	Buford Ellington
1963-1967	Frank G. Clement
1967-	Buford Ellington

**Tennessee Blue Book*, 1967-1968, p. 282.

†The *Blue Book* lists name Neill S. Brown.

TEXAS*†

Term	Spanish Royal Governors
1691-1692	Domingo Teran de los Rios
1692-1697	Gregorio de Salinas
1698-1702	Francisco Cuervo y Valdez
1703-1705	Mathias de Aguirre
1705-1708	Martín de Alarcón
1708-1712	Simón Padilla y Cordova
1712-1714	Pedro Fermín de Echevers y Subisa
1714-1716	Juan Valdez
1716-1719	Martín de Alarcón
1719-1722	Marquis de San Miguel de Aguayo
1722-1727	Fernando Perez de Almazán
1727-1730	Melchor Media Villa y Ascona
1730-1734	Juan Bustillos Zevallos
1734-1736	Manuel de Sandoval
1736-1737	Carlos Benites Franquis de Lugo
1737-1741	Prudencio de Orobio Bazterra
1741-1743	Tomás Felipe Wintuisen
1743-1744	Justo Boneo y Morales
1744-1748	Francisco Garcia Larios
1748-1751	Pedro del Barrio y Espriella
1751-1759	Jacinto de Barrios y Jauregui
1759-1766	Angel Matos y Navarete
1767-1770	Hugo Oconor
1770-1778	Baron of Ripperda
1778-1786	Domingo Cabello
1786	Bernardo Bonavia
1787-1788	Rafael Martinez Pacheco
1788-1789	(The office of Governor was ordered suppressed and the province put under a presidial captain.)
1790-1798	Manuel Muñoz
1798-1800	Josef Irigoyen
1800-1805	Juan Bautista de Elguezabal
1805-1810	Antonio Cordero y Bustamante
1811	Juan Bautista Casas
1811-1813	Manuel Salcedo
1814-1817	Cristobal Dominguez
1817	Ignacio Perez
1817	Manuel Pardo
1817-1822	Antonio Martinez
	Governors Under Mexican Rule‡
1822-1823	Felix Trespalacios
1823-1824	Luciano Garcia
1824-1826	Rafael Gonzalez
1826-1827	Victor Blanco
1827-1830	Jose Maria Viesca
1830-1831	Ramón Eca y Musquiz
1831-1832	Jose Maria Letona
1832	Ramón Eca y Musquiz
1832-1833	Juan Martin de Veramendi
1833-1834	Juan Jose de Vidauri y Villasenor
1834-1835	Juan Jose Elguezabal
1835	Jose Maria Cantu
1835	Agustín M. Viesca
1835	Marciel Borrego
1835	Ramón Eca y Musquiz
	Provisional Colonial Governors Before Independence
1835	Henry Smith
1836	James W. Robinson§
	Presidents of the Republic of Texas*
1836	David G. Burnet
1836-1838	Sam Houston
1838-1841	Mirabeau B. Lamar
1841-1844	Sam Houston
1844-1846	Anson Jones
	State Governors
1846-1847	James Pinckney Henderson
1847-1849	George T. Wood
1849-1853	Peter Hansbrough Bell
1853	J. W. Henderson
1853-1857	Elisha M. Pease
1857-1859	Hardin R. Runnels

1859-1861	Sam Houston
1861	Edward Clark
1861-1863	Francis R. Lubbock
1863-1865	Pendleton Murrah
1865-1866	Andrew J. Hamilton
1866-1867	James W. Throckmorton
1867-1869	Elisha M. Pease
1870-1874	Edmund J. Davis
1874-1876	Richard Coke
1876-1879	Richard B. Hubbard
1879-1883	Oran M. Roberts
1883-1887	John Ireland
1887-1891	Lawrence Sullivan Ross
1891-1895	James Stephen Hogg
1895-1899	Charles A. Culberson
1899-1903	Joseph D. Sayers
1903-1907	Samuel W. T. Lanham
1907-1911	Thomas Mitchell Campbell
1911-1915	Oscar Branch Colquitt
1915-1917	James E. Ferguson
1917-1921	William Pettus Hobby
1921-1925	Pat Morris Neff
1925-1927	Miriam A. Ferguson
1927-1931	Dan Moody
1931-1933	Ross S. Sterling
1933-1935	Miriam A. Ferguson
1935-1939	James V. Allred
1939-1941	W. Lee O'Daniel
1941-1947	Coke R. Stevenson
1947-1949	Beauford H. Jester
1949-1957	Allan Shivers
1957-1963	Price Daniel
1963-1969	John B. Connally
1969-	Preston Smith

**Texas Almanac*, 1964-1965, p. 514. The *Almanac* lists in addition Albert C. Horton (acting), 1847, and Fletcher S. Stockdale (acting), 1865.

†Some authorities would include Texas under administrations of several earlier Spanish Royal Governors. The late Dr. C. E. Castaneda, Latin-American librarian of University of Texas and authority on history of Texas and Southwestern region, would include the following four: Francisco de Garay, 1523-26; Panfilo de Narváez, 1526-28; Nuno de Guzmán, 1528-30; Hernando de Soto, 1538-43.

‡The first two Governors under Mexican rule, Trespalacios and Garcia, were of Texas only as Texas was then constituted. Beginning with Gonzales, 1824, the Governors were for the joint State of Coahuila-Texas.

§Served as acting Governor just prior to March 1836, after Smith was impeached.

UTAH

Term	State of Deseret*
1849-1851	Brigham Young
	Territorial Governors*
1851-1857	Brigham Young
1857-1861	Alfred Cumming
1861	Francis H. Wootten
1861	John W. Dawson
1861-1862	Frank Fuller
1862-1863	Stephen S. Harding
1863-1865	James Duane Doty
1865	Amos Reed
1865-1869	Charles Durkee
1869-1870	Edwin Higgins
1870	S. A. Mann
1870	J. Wilson Shaffer
1870-1871	Vernon H. Vaughan
1871	George A. Black
1871-1874	George L. Woods
1874-1875	S. B. Axtell
1875-1880	George B. Emery
1880-1886	Eli H. Murray
1886-1889	Caleb W. West
1889-1893	Arthur L. Thomas
1893-1896	Caleb W. West
	State Governors
1896-1905	Heber M. Wells
1905-1909	John C. Cutler
1909-1917	William Spry
1917-1921	Simon Bamberger
1921-1925	Charles R. Mabey
1925-1933	George H. Dern
1933-1941	Henry H. Blood
1941-1949	Herbert B. Maw
1949-1957	J. Bracken Lee
1957-1965	George Dewey Clyde
1965-	Calvin L. Rampton

*The *Encyclopedia Americana*, Vol. 27, p. 616.

VERMONT*

Term	"Independent State" Governors†
1778-1789	Thomas Chittenden
1789-1790	Moses Robinson
1790-1791	Thomas Chittenden
	State Governors
1791-1797	Thomas Chittenden
1797	Paul Brigham
1797-1807	Isaac Tichenor
1807-1808	Israel Smith
1808-1809	Isaac Tichenor
1809-1813	Jonas Galusha
1813-1815	Martin Chittenden
1815-1820	Jonas Galusha
1820-1823	Richard Skinner
1823-1826	Cornelius P. Van Ness
1826-1828	Ezra Butler
1828-1831	Samuel C. Crafts
1831-1835	William A. Palmer
1835-1841	Silas H. Jennison
1841-1843	Charles Paine
1843-1844	John Mattocks
1844-1846	William Slade
1846-1848	Horace Eaton
1848-1850	Carlos Coolidge
1850-1852	Charles K. Williams
1852-1853	Erastus Fairbanks
1853-1854	John S. Robinson
1854-1856	Stephen Royce
1856-1858	Ryland Fletcher
1858-1860	Hiland Hall
1860-1861	Erastus Fairbanks
1861-1863	Frederick Holbrook
1863-1865	John Gregory Smith
1865-1867	Paul Dillingham
1867-1869	John B. Page
1869-1870	Peter T. Washburn
1870	George W. Hendee
1870-1872	John W. Stewart
1872-1874	Julius Converse
1874-1876	Asahel Peck
1876-1878	Horace Fairbanks
1878-1880	Redfield Proctor
1880-1882	Roswell Farnham
1882-1884	John L. Barstow
1884-1886	Samuel E. Pingree
1886-1888	Ebenezer J. Ormsbee
1888-1890	William P. Dillingham
1890-1892	Carroll S. Page
1892-1894	Levi K. Fuller
1894-1896	Urban A. Woodbury
1896-1898	Josiah Grout

1898-1900	Edward C. Smith	1927-1931	John E. Weeks
1900-1902	William W. Stickney	1931-1935	Stanley C. Wilson
1902-1904	John G. McCullough	1935-1937	Charles M. Smith
1904-1906	Charles J. Bell	1937-1941	George D. Aiken
1906-1908	Fletcher D. Proctor	1941-1945	William H. Wills
1908-1910	George H. Prouty	1945-1947	Mortimer R. Proctor
1910-1912	John A. Mead	1947-1950	Ernest W. Gibson
1912-1915	Allen M. Fletcher	1950-1951	Harold J. Arthur
1915-1917	Charles W. Gates	1951-1955	Lee E. Emerson
1917-1919	Horace F. Graham	1955-1959	Joseph Blaine Johnson
1919-1921	Percival W. Clement	1959-1961	Robert T. Stafford
1921-1923	James Hartness	1961-1963	E. Ray Keyser, Jr.
1923-1925	Redfield Proctor	1963-1969	Philip H. Hoff
1925-1927	Franklin S. Billings	1969-	Deane C. Davis

**Vermont Legislative Directory and State Manual*, 1967, p. 370.

†In 1777, Vermont declared its independence and did not join the Union until 1791, as the fourteenth State.

VIRGINIA

Term	Chief Executives of Colony and State*
	In the Time of Elizabeth
1584-1603	Walter Raleigh, Lord Proprietor of Virginia
1585-1586	Ralph Lane, Governor of Raleigh's First Colony
1587-1590	John White, Governor of Raleigh's Second Colony
	Under the London Company
1606-1618	Thomas Smith (Smythe), President and Treasurer of the London Company, and the real Governor of Virginia, though resident in England
1607	Edward Maria Wingfield, President of the Council, resident in Virginia
1607-1608	John Ratcliffe, President of the Council, resident in Virginia
1608	Matthew Scrivener, President of the Council, resident in Virginia
1608-1609	John Smith, President of the Council, resident in Virginia
1609	Francis West, President of the Council, resident in Virginia
1609-1610	George Percy (Percie), President of the Council, resident in Virginia
1609-1618	Thomas West, Lord De La Warr (Delaware), Governor and Captain General
1610	Thomas Gates, Lieutenant and Deputy Governor
1610-1611	Thomas West, Lord De La Warr (Delaware), Governor, resident in Virginia
1611	George Percy (Percie), President of the Council and Deputy Governor
1611	Thomas Dale, High Marshal and Acting Governor
1611-1613	Thomas Gates, Lieutenant Governor
1613-1616	Thomas Dale, Acting Governor
1616-1617	George Yeardley, Deputy or Lieutenant Governor
1617-1619	Samuel Argall (Argoll), Deputy or Lieutenant Governor
1619-1624	Edwin Sandys, President and Treasurer of the London Company
1619	Nathaniel Powell, President of the Council in Virginia and Acting Governor
1619-1621	George Yeardley, Governor and Captain General
1621-1624	Francis Wyatt, Governor and Captain General
	Royal Province
1624-1626	Francis Wyatt, Governor and Captain General
1626-1627	George Yeardley, Governor and Captain General
1627-1628	Francis West, President of the Council and Acting Governor
1628-1639	John Harvey, Governor and Captain General
1628-1630	John Pott, President of the Council and Acting Governor
1630-1635	John Harvey, Governor and Captain General, resident in Virginia
1635-1636	John West, President of the Council and Acting Governor
1636-1639	John Harvey, Governor and Captain General, resident in Virginia
1639-1642	Francis Wyatt, Governor and Captain General
1642-1644	William Berkeley, Governor and Captain General
1644-1645	Richard Kemp (Kempe), President of the Council and Acting Governor
1645-1652	William Berkeley, Governor
	Under the Commonwealth (Cromwell)
1652-1655	Richard Bennett, Governor, elected by Assembly
1655-1658	Edward Diggs (Digges), President of the Council and Governor, elected by Assembly
1658-1660	Samuel Mathews (Matthews), Governor, elected by Assembly
1660	William Berkeley, Governor, elected by Assembly
	Royal Province
1660-1677	William Berkeley
1661-1662	Francis Morrison (Moryson), Deputy or Lieutenant Governor (acted in absence of Berkeley)
1677-1683	Thomas, Lord Culpeper, Governor
1677-1678	Herbert Jeffreys (Jeffries), Lieutenant Governor
1678-1680	Henry Chicheley, Deputy Governor
1680-1683	Thomas, Lord Culpeper, Governor, resident in Virginia
1683-1692	Francis, Lord Howard of Effingham, Governor
1683-1684	Nicholas Spencer, President of the Council and Acting Governor
1684-1689	Francis, Lord Howard of Effingham, Governor, resident in Virginia

1689-1690	Nathaniel Bacon, President of the Council
1690-1692	Francis Nicholson, Lieutenant Governor
1692-1698	Edmund Andros, Governor
1698-1705	Francis Nicholson, Governor
1705-1706	Edward Nott, Governor
1706-1710	Edmund Jennings, President of the Council and Acting Governor
1707	Robert Hunter, Governor, so commissioned but being captured by French, never reached Virginia
1710-1737	George Hamilton Douglas,† Earl of Orkney, Governor-in-Chief
1710-1722	Alexander Spotswood, Lieutenant Governor
1722-1726	Hugh Drysdale, Lieutenant Governor
1726-1727	Robert Carter, President of the Council and Acting Governor
1727-1737	William Gooch, Lieutenant Governor
1737-1754	William Anne Keppel,† Earl of Albermarle, Governor-in-Chief
1737-1740	William Gooch, Lieutenant Governor
1740-1741	James Blair, President of the Council and Acting Governor
1741-1749	William Gooch, Lieutenant Governor
1749	John Robinson, President of the Council and Acting Governor
1749-1751	Thomas Lee, President of the Council
1751	Lewis Burwell, President of the Council
1751-1756	Robert Dinwiddie, Lieutenant Governor
1756-1763	John Campbell,† Earl of Loudoun, Governor General of all the American Colonies
1756-1758	Robert Dinwiddie, Lieutenant Governor
1758	John Blair, President of the Council and Acting Governor
1758-1768	Francis Fauquier, Lieutenant Governor
1759-1768	Jeffrey Amherst,† Governor-in-Chief
1768	John Blair, President of the Council and Acting Governor
1768-1770	Norborne Berkeley, Lord Botetourt, Governor-in-Chief
1770-1771	William Nelson, President of the Council and Acting Governor
1771-1776	John Murray, Earl of Dunmore, Governor-in-Chief

THE CONVENTION PERIOD

1774-1775	Peyton Randolph, President of Virginia Convention of 1774, March, 1775, and July, 1775.
1775-1776	Edmund Pendleton, President of the Conventions of December, 1775, and May, 1776.

GOVERNORS OF INDEPENDENT COMMONWEALTH‡

1776-1779	Patrick Henry
1779-1781	Thomas Jefferson
1781	William Fleming, as only member of the Council present
1781	Thomas Nelson
1781-1784	Benjamin Harrison
1784-1786	Patrick Henry
1786-1788	Edmund Randolph

Virginia ratified U.S. Constitution on June 26, 1788.

STATE GOVERNORS

1788-1791	Beverley Randolph
1791-1794	Henry Lee
1794-1796	Robert Brook
1796-1799	James Wood
1799-1802	James Monroe
1802-1805	John Page
1805-1808	William H. Cabell
1808-1811	John Tyler, Sr.
1811	James Monroe,§ Governor, January to April
1811	George William Smith,§ Senior member of the Council of State, Acting Governor
1811-1812	Peyton Randolph,§ as Senior member of the Council of State, Acting Governor
1812-1814	James Barbour
1814-1816	Wilson Cary Nicholas
1816-1819	James P. Preston
1819-1822	Thomas Mann Randolph
1822-1825	James Pleasants
1825-1827	John Tyler, Jr.
1827-1830	William B. Giles
1830-1834	John Floyd
1834-1836	Littleton Waller Tazewell
1837	Wyndham Robertson, as Senior member of Council, Acting Governor
1837-1840	David Campbell
1840-1841	Thomas Walker Gilmer‖
1841	John Mercer Patton,‖ as Senior member of the Council, Acting Governor
1841-1842	John Rutherford,‖ as Senior member of the Council, Acting Governor
1843	John M. Gregory,‖ as Senior member of the Council, Acting Governor
1843-1846	James McDowell
1846-1849	William Smith
1849-1852	John Buchanan Floyd
1852-1856	Joseph Johnson
1856-1860	Henry Alexander Wise
1860-1864	John Letcher
1864-1865	William Smith

UNDER FEDERAL RULE

1865-1868	Francis H. Peirpont, Governor
1867-1869	Gen. J. M. Schofield, Military Commander
1868-1869	Henry H. Wells, Provisional Governor
1869-1870	Gen. E. R. S. Canby, Military Commander
1870	Gilbert C. Walker, Provisional Governor

AGAIN IN THE UNION—

STATE GOVERNORS

1870-1874	Gilbert C. Walker
1874-1878	James Lawson Kemper
1878-1882	Frederick W. M. Holliday
1882-1886	William Ewan Cameron
1886-1890	Fitzhugh Lee
1890-1894	Philip W. McKinney
1894-1898	Charles T. O'Ferrall
1898-1902	James Hoge Tyler
1902-1906	Andrew Jackson Montague
1906-1910	Claude A. Swanson
1910-1914	William Hodges Mann

1914-1918	Henry Carter Stuart	1942-1946	Colgate W. Darden, Jr.
1918-1922	Westmoreland Davis	1946-1950	William M. Tuck
1922-1926	E. Lee Trinkle	1950-1954	John Stewart Battle
1926-1930	Harry F. Byrd	1954-1958	Thos. B. Stanley
1930-1934	John Garland Pollard	1958-1962	J. Lindsay Almond, Jr.
1934-1938	George C. Peery	1962-1966	Albertis S. Harrison, Jr.
1938-1942	James H. Price	1966-	Mills E. Godwin, Jr.

Report of the Secretary of the Commonwealth of Virginia, 1966, pp. 312-316, subdivides the list as shown above, explaining that there is a difficulty in making a comprehensive list of the Colonial Governors, because many often resided in England, while "the real official head, residing in Virginia, was a deputy." Nevertheless, the *Report* appears to have the most comprehensive list available, and it has been used in preference to other sources.

†Never came to Virginia.

‡From 1776 to 1852, the Governors were elected by the Legislature and were assisted in their executive duties by a Council of State. On the resignation or death of a Governor, the senior councilor acted as Governor until the election of one by the Legislature.

§James Monroe resigned to become Secretary of State under President James Madison. George William Smith acted as Governor, but when he was burned to death in the Richmond Theatre, he was in turn succeeded by Peyton Randolph until the Legislature elected James Barbour.

||Governor Gilmer resigned because of a disagreement with the Legislature. The Legislature was unable to elect a Governor for twenty-one months, so senior councilors Patton, Rutherford, and Gregory were acting Governors.

WASHINGTON

Term	Territorial Governors*		State Governors
1853-1857	Isaac I. Stevens	1889-1893	Elisha P. Ferry
1857-1859	Fayette McMullen	1893-1897	John H. McGraw
1859-1861	R. D. Gholson	1897-1901	John Rankin Rogers
1861	William H. Wallace	1901-1905	Henry McBride
1862-1866	William Pickering	1905-1909	Albert Edward Mead
1866-1867	George E. Cole	1909	Samuel G. Cosgrove
1867-1869	Marshall F. Moore	1909-1913	Marion E. Hay
1869-1870	Alvan Flanders	1913-1919	Ernest Lister
1870-1872	Edward S. Salomon	1919-1925	Louis Folwell Hart†
1872-1880	Elisha P. Ferry	1925-1933	Roland Hill Hartley
1880-1884	W. A. Newell	1933-1941	Clarence Daniel Martin
1884-1887	Watson C. Squire	1941-1945	Arthur Bernard Langlie
1887-1889	Eugene Semple	1945-1949	Monrad Charles Wallgren
1889	Miles C. Moore	1949-1957	Arthur B. Langlie
		1957-1965	Albert D. Rosellini
		1965-	Daniel J. Evans

*"Facts to Help You Know Washington State," booklet published by Department of Commerce and Economic Development, State of Washington, p. 6.

†Omitted in *White's Conspectus*.

WEST VIRGINIA

Term	State Governors		
1863-1869	Arthur I. Boreman	1913-1917	Henry Drury Hatfield
1869	Daniel D. T. Farnsworth	1917-1921	John Jacob Cornwell
1869-1871	William E. Stevenson	1921-1925	Ephraim Franklin Morgan
1871-1877	John J. Jacob	1925-1929	Howard Mason Gore
1877-1881	Henry M. Mathews	1929-1933	William Gustavus Conley
1881-1885	Jacob B. Jackson	1933-1937	Herman Guy Kump
1885-1890	Emanuel W. Wilson	1937-1941	Homer Adams Holt
1890-1893	Aretas B. Fleming	1941-1945	Matthew Mansfield Neely
1893-1897	William A. MacCorkle	1945-1949	Clarence W. Meadows
1897-1901	George W. Atkinson	1949-1953	Okey L. Patteson
1901-1905	Albert Blakeslee White	1953-1957	William C. Marland
1905-1909	William M. O. Dawson	1957-1961	Cecil H. Underwood
1909-1913	William E. Glasscock	1961-1965	William W. Barron
		1965-1969	Hulett C. Smith
		1969-	Arch A. Moore, Jr.

WISCONSIN

Term	Territorial Governors*		
1836-1841	Henry Dodge	1874-1876	William R. Taylor
1841-1844	James Duane Doty	1876-1878	Harrison Ludington
1844-1845	Nathaniel P. Tallmadge	1878-1882	William E. Smith
1845-1848	Henry Dodge	1882-1889	Jeremiah McLain Rusk
		1889-1891	William D. Hoard
	State Governors	1891-1895	George W. Peck
		1895-1897	William H. Upham
1848-1852	Nelson Dewey	1897-1901	Edward Scofield
1852-1854	Leonard J. Farwell	1901-1906	Robert M. LaFollette
1854-1856	Wm. Augustus Barstow	1906-1911	James O. Davidson†
1856	Arthur MacArthur	1911-1915	Francis E. McGovern
1856-1858	Coles Bashford	1915-1921	Emanuel L. Philipp
1858-1862	Alexander W. Randall	1921-1927	John J. Blaine
1862	Louis P. Harvey	1927-1929	Fred R. Zimmerman
1862-1864	Edward Salomon	1929-1931	Walter J. Kohler
1864-1866	James T. Lewis	1931-1933	Philip F. LaFollette
1866-1872	Lucius Fairchild	1933-1935	Albert G. Schmedeman
1872-1874	Cadwallader C. Washburn	1935-1939	Philip F. LaFollette

1939-1943	Julius P. Heil
1943-1947	Walter S. Goodland
1947-1951	Oscar Rennebohm
1951-1957	Walter J. Kohler, Jr.
1957-1959	Vernon W. Thomson
1959-1963	Gaylord A. Nelson
1963-1965	John W. Reynolds
1965-	Warren P. Knowles

**Wisconsin Blue Book*, 1964, p. 300. The *Blue Book* also lists Orland S. Loomis, 1943, who died prior to inauguration.
†*White's Conspectus* lists entry date for James O. Davidson as 1905.

WYOMING

Term	Territorial Governors*
1869-1875	John A. Campbell
1875-1878	John M. Thayer
1878-1882	John W. Hoyt
1882-1885	William Hale
1885-1886	Francis E. Warren
1886	George W. Baxter
1887-1889	Thomas Moonlight
1889-1890	Francis E. Warren
	State Governors
1890	Francis E. Warren
1890-1893	Amos W. Barber
1893-1895	John E. Osborne
1895-1899	William A. Richards
1899-1903	De Forest Richards
1903-1905	Fennimore Chatterton†
1905-1911	Bryant B. Brooks
1911-1915	Joseph M. Carey
1915-1917	John B. Kendrick
1917-1919	Frank L. Houx
1919-1923	Robert D. Carey
1923-1924	William B. Ross
1924-1925	Frank E. Lucas‡
1925-1927	Nellie Tayloe Ross
1927-1931	Frank C. Emerson
1931-1933	Alonzo M. Clark
1933-1939	Leslie A. Miller
1939-1943	Nels H. Smith
1943-1949	Lester C. Hunt
1949-1951	Arthur Griswold Crane
1951-1953	Frank A. Barrett
1953-1955	C. J. Rogers
1955-1959	Milward L. Simpson
1959-1961	J. J. Hickey
1961-1963	Jack R. Gage
1963-1967	Clifford P. Hansen
1967-	Stanley K. Hathaway

*The *Encyclopedia Americana*, Vol. 29, p. 585.
†*Wyoming Official Directory*, 1965, p. 12, lists first name "Fenimore."
‡Not listed in *White's Conspectus*.

AMERICAN SAMOA*

American Samoa became U.S. Territory by a treaty with the United Kingdom and Germany in 1899 which was confirmed by local chiefs in 1900 and 1904.

Term	Military Governors
1900-1901	Commander B. F. Tilley, USN Comdt.
1901-1902	Captain U. Sebree, USN Comdt.
1902-1903	Lt. Comdr. H. Minett, USN Actg. Comdt.
1903-1905	Comdr. E.B. Underwood, USN Comdt.
1905-1908	Comdr. C. B. T. Moors, USN Comdt.
1908-1910	Captain John F. Parker, USN
1910-1913	Comdr. W. M. Crose, USN
1913	Lt. N. W. Post, USN
1913-1914	Comdr. C. D. Stearns, USN
1914	Lt. N. W. Post, USN
1914-1915	Lt. C. A. Woodruff, USN
1915-1919	Comdr. John M. Poyer, USN (Ret.)
1919-1920	Comdr. Warren J. Terhune, USN
1920-1922	Captain Waldo Evans, USN
1922-1923	Captain Edwin T. Pollock, USN
1923-1925	Captain Edward S. Kellogg, USN
1925-1927	Captain Henry F. Bryan, USN (Ret.)
1927-1929	Capt. Stephen V. Graham, USN (Ret.)
1929-1931	Capt. Gatewood S. Lincoln, USN (Ret.)
1931	Comdr. James S. Spore, USN
1931	Lt. Comdr. Arthur T. Emerson, USN
1931-1932	Capt. Gatewood S. Lincoln, USN (Ret.)
1932-1934	Capt. George B. Landenberger, USN
1934	Lt. Comdr. Thomas C. Latimore, USN
1934-1936	Captain Otto Dowling, USN
1936	Lt. Comdr. Thomas B. Fitzpatrick, USN
1936-1938	Captain MacGillvray Milne, USN
1938-1940	Captain Edward W. Hanson, USN
1940	Lt. Comdr. Jesse R. Wallace, USN
1940-1942	Captain Lawrence Wild, USN
1942-1944	Captain John G. Moyer, USN
1944-1945	Captain Allen Hobbs, USN
1945	Captain Ralph W. Hungerford, USN
1945	Comdr. Samuel W. Canan, USN
1945-1947	Captain Harold A. Houser, USN
1947-1949	Captain Vernon Huber, USN
1949-1951	Captain Thomas F. Darden, USN
	Civilian Governors
1951-1952	Phelps Phelps
1952	John C. Elliott
1952-1953	James Arthur Ewing
1953	Lawrence M. Judd
1953-1956	Richard Barrett Lowe
1956-1961	Peter Tali Coleman
1961-1967	H. Rex Lee
1967-	Owen S. Aspinall

Note: U. S. Territorial Governors of American Samoa are appointed.
*Source: The Honorable Owen S. Aspinall, Governor of American Samoa.

GUAM*

Term	Governors Under Spain Military Commanders
1668-1672	Capt. D. Juan de Santa Cruz
1672-1674	Capt. D. Juan de Santiago
1674-1676	Capt. D. Damián de Esplana
	Governors
1676-1678	Capt. D. Francisco de Irisarri
1678-1680	Capt. D. Juan Antonio de Salas
1680-1681	Major D. José Quiroga
1681-1683	Capt. D. Antonio Saravis
1683-1688	Major D. Damián de Esplana
1688-1690	Major D. José Quiroga
1690-1694	Lt. Gen. D. Damián de Esplana
1694-1696	Major D. José Quiroga
1696-1700	Gen. D. José Madraso

1700-1704	Major D. Francisco Madraso y Asiam
1704-1709	Major D. Antonio Villamor y Vadillo
1709-1720	Lt. Gen. D. Juan Antonio Pimentel
1720-1725	Capt. D. Luis Antonio Sanchez de Tagle
1725	Capt. D. Juan de Ojeda
1725-1730	Gen. D. Manuel Arguelles Valda
1730-1734	Major D. Pedro Laso de la Vega
1734-1740	General of the Fleet D. Francisco Cardenas Pacheco
1740-1746	Major D. Miguel For. de Cardenas
1746-1749	Capt. D. Domingo Gomez de la Sierra
1749-1756	Lt. (Navy) D. Enrique de Olavide y Michelena
1756-1759	Gen. D. Andrés del Barrio y Rábago
1759-1768	Lt. (Navy) D. José de Soroa
1768-1771	Lt. (Navy) D. Enrique de Olavide y Michelena
1771-1774	Major D. Mariano Tobias
1774-1776	Major D. Antonio Apodaca
1776-1786	Capt. D. Felipe de Cerain
1786-1794	Lt. Col. D. José Arlegue y Leon
1794-1802	Lt. Col. D. Manuel Muro
1802-1806	Capt. D. Vicente Blanco
1806-1812	Capt. D. Alexandro Parreno
1812-1822	Lt. D. José de Medinilla y Pineda
1822-1823	Capt. D. José Montilla
1823-1826	Capt. D. José Ganga Herrero
1826-1831	Lt. Col. D. José de Medinilla y Pineda
1831-1837	Capt. of Artillery D. Francisco Ramón de Villalobos
1837-1843	Lt. Col. D. José Casillas Salazar
1843-1848	Major D. Gregorio Sta. María
1848	D. Felix Calvo
1848-1855	Lt. Col. D. Pablo Perez
1855-1866	Capt. Engineers, rank of Lt. Col. D. Felipe María de la Corte
1866-1871	Lt. Col. D. Francisco Moscoso y Lara
1871-1873	Col. of Infantry D. Luis de Ybañez y Garcia
1873-1875	Lt. Col. of Infantry D. Eduardo Beaumont y Calafat
1875-1880	Lt. Col. of Cavalry D. Manuel Brado y Barrera
1880-1884	Lt. Col. of Infantry D. Francisco Brochero y Parreno
1884	Col. of Infantry D. Angel Pazos Vela-Hidalgo
1884	Capt. Comdt. of the Garrison D. Antonio Borreda
1884	Lt. Col. of Infantry D. Francisco Olive y Garcia
1884-1890	Lt. Col. of Infantry D. Enrique Solano
1890-1891	Lt. Col. of Infantry D. Joaquín Vera de Roy
1891-1892	Lt. Col. of Infantry D. Luis Santos
1892-1893	Lt. Col. of Infantry D. Vicente Gomez Hernandez
1893	Lt. of Infantry D. Juan Godoy
1893-1895	Lt. Col. of Infantry D. Emilio Galisteo Brunenque
1895-1897	Lt. Col. of Infantry Jacobo Marina
1897	Lt. of Infantry Angel Nieto
1897-1898	Lt. Col. of Infantry Juan Mariana
1898	Don José Sixto (acting)
1898-1899	Don Francisco Portusach (acting)
1899	Don José Sixto (acting)
1899	Don Joaquín Perez (acting)
1899	Mr. William Coe (acting)

Guam was ceded by Spain to the United States by the Treaty of Paris, December 10, 1898.

Under the United States*

Military Governors

1899-1900	Captain Richard P. Leary
1900-1901	Commander Seaton Schroeder
1901	Commander William Swift (acting)
1901-1903	Commander Seaton Schroeder
1903-1904	Commander William E. Sewell
1904	Lieutenant Frank H. Schofield (acting)
1904-1905	Lieutenant Raymond Stone (acting)
1905	Commander George L. Dyer
1905-1906	Lieutenant Luke McNamee (acting)
1906-1907	Commander Templin M. Potts
1907	Lt. Commander Luke McNamee (acting)
1907-1910	Captain Edward J. Dorn
1910-1911	Lieutenant Frank B. Freyer (acting)
1911-1912	Captain George R. Salisbury
1912-1913	Commander Robert E. Coontz
1913-1914	Lt. Commander Alfred W. Hinds
1914-1916	Captain William J. Maxwell
1916	Captain W. P. Cronan (acting)
1916	Captain Edward E. Simpson
1916-1918	Captain Roy C. Smith
1918-1920	Captain William W. Gilmer
1920	Captain Ivan C. Wettengel
1920-1921	Lt. Commander James S. Spore (acting)
1921	Captain Ivan C. Wettengel
1921-1922	Lt. Commander James S. Spore (acting)
1922	Captain A. Althouse
1922	Commander John P. Miller (acting)
1922-1923	Captain A. Althouse
1923	Captain H. B. Price
1923-1924	Commander A. W. Brown (acting)
1924-1926	Captain Henry B. Price
1926-1929	Captain Lloyd S. Shapley
1929-1931	Commander Willis W. Bradley, Jr.
1931-1933	Captain Edmund S. Root
1933-1936	Captain George A. Alexander
1936-1938	Cdr. Benjamin V. McCandlish
1938-1940	Captain James F. Alexander
1940-1944	Captain George McMillan
1944-1945	Admiral Chester E. Nimitz, Commander in Chief of Pacific Fleet
1945-1946	General Henry Larsen
1946-1949	Rear Admiral C. A. Pownall
1949	Admiral Leon Fiske

Civilian Governors

1949-1953	Carlton Skinner
1953	R. S. Herman (acting)
1953-1956	Ford Q. Elvidge
1956	William T. Corbett (acting)
1956-1960	Richard Barrett Lowe
1960-1961	Joseph Flores
1961-1963	Bill Daniel
1963-	Manuel F. L. Guerrero

Note: Up to September 27, 1949, (excepting World War II) the Governor of Guam was a naval officer appointed by the President of the United States. Thereafter, the Governor of the Territory has been a civilian appointed by the President. Governors Bill Daniel and Manuel F. L. Guerrero advocated election by the people, and on September 11, 1968, President Lyndon B. Johnson signed legislation providing for popular election of Governors beginning November 3, 1970.

*Source: The Honorable Manuel F. L. Guerrero, Governor of Guam.

PUERTO RICO*

Term	First and Last Spanish Governors
1508-1519	Juan Ponce de León
1898	Gen. Ricardo Ortega

Puerto Rico was ceded by Spain to the U.S. by the Treaty of Paris, December 10, 1898.

	U. S. Appointed Governors
1898	Gen. John R. Brooke
1898	Gen. Guy V. Henry
1899	Gen. George W. Davis
1900	Charles H. Allen†
1900-1904	William H. Hunt
1904-1907	Beekman Winthrop
1907-1909	Regis H. Post
1909-1913	George R. Colton
1913-1921	Arthur Yager
1921-1923	E. Montgomery Reilly
1923-1929	Horace Mann Towner
1929-1932	Theodore Roosevelt
1932-1933	James R. Beverly
1933-1934	Robert H. Gore
1934-1939	Blanton Winship
1939-1941	William D. Leahy
1941	Gay J. Swope
1941-1946	Rexford G. Tugwell
1946-1949	Jesús T. Piñeiro

	Elected Governors
1949-1965	Luis Muñoz Marín
1965-1969	Roberto Sánchez-Vilella
1969-	Luis A. Ferré

Note: President Truman signed an act on August 5, 1947, giving Puerto Rico the right to choose its Chief Executive by popular vote. Puerto Rico became a Commonwealth of the United States on July 25, 1952.

*Source: Col. Rafael Montilla, Director, Office of Emergency Planning, Commonwealth of Puerto Rico.

†Supplied by U. S. Department of Interior.

VIRGIN ISLANDS*

Term	Danish Governors
1672-1679	Joergen Eversen
1679-1682	Nicolai Esmit
1682	La Vigne
1682	Joergen Hansen
1682-1684	Adolph Esmit
1684-1687	Gabriel Milan
1687-1688	Adolph Esmit
1688-1690	Christopher Heins
1690-1702	Johan Lorentz
1702-1706	Claus Hansen
1706-1709	Joachim von Holten
1709-1716	Michel Krone
1716-1723	Eric Bredal
1723-1724	Otto Jacob Thambsen
1724-1728	Friderich Moth
1728-1732	Henrich Suhm
1732-1736	Philip Gardelin
1736-1740	Friderich Moth
1740-1744	Jacob Schonemann
1744-1749	Chr. Schweder
1749-1756	Chr. Suhm
1756-1766	Baron C. L. von Proeck
1766-1771	Major-General Peder Clausen
1771-1773	Lieutenant-Colonel U. W. Roepstorf
1773-1785	Major-General P. Clausen
1785-1787	Major-General H. C. E. Schimmelmann
1787-1796	Major-General E. F. von Walterstorff
1796-1799	Major-General T. von Malleville
1799-1802	Generalkrigskommissaer W. A. Lindemann
1802-1803	Major-General E. F. v. Waltersdorff
1803-1807	Major-General B. F. Muhlenfels
1807	Counsellor Lillienschiold

(1807-1815—The Islands were occupied by Great Britain)

1815-1816	Major-General v. Oxholm
1816-1820	Counsellor Bentzon
1820-1822	Commodore C. A. Rothe
1822-1827	Admiral J. F. Bardenfleth
1827-1848	Major-General P. C. F. v. Scholten
1848-1851	Counsellor of State P. Hansen
1851-1854	H. D. F. Feddersen
1854-1861	J. F. Schlegel
1861-1872	Wilhelm L. Birch
1872-1881	Rear Admiral J. A. Garde
1881-1893	General C. H. Arendrup
1893-1903	Colonel C. Hedeman
1903-1905	F. Nordlien
1905-1908	Commander C. M. T. Cold
1908-1912	P. C. Limpricht
1912-1916	L. C. Helweg-Larsen
1916-1917	Captain H. Konow

The Virgin Islands were purchased by the United States from Denmark for $25,000,000, effective March 31, 1917.

	American Governors
1917-1919	James Harrison Oliver
1919-1921	Joseph Wallace Oman
1921-1922	Sumner Ely Wetmore Kitelle
1922-1923	Henry Hughes Hough
1923-1925	Philip Williams
1925-1927	Martin Edward Trench
1927-1931	Waldo Evans
1931-1935	Paul M. Pearson
1935-1941	Lawrence William Cramer
1941-1946	Charles Harwood
1946-1949	William Henry Hastie
1950-1954	Morris Fidanque de Castro
1954-1955	Archie Alphonso Alexander
1955-1958	Walter Arthur Gordon
1958-1961	John David Merwin
1961-1969	Ralph M. Paiewonsky

Note: Since becoming a Territory of the United States, the Governors have been appointed. Popular election was recommended by Governor Paiewonsky, and on August 23, 1968, President Lyndon B. Johnson signed legislation providing for popular election of Governors beginning November 3, 1970.

*Source: Former Governor Ralph M. Paiewonsky and Mr. Leon A. Mawson, Emergency Planning Director, Virgin Islands.

IV. APPENDIX

EXECUTIVE MANSIONS (1968)

Listed alphabetically with approximate original cost and general style of architecture

	Date*	Cost and Method of Acquisition (Construction)	(Purchase or Gift)	Style of Architecture
The White House	1800	$400,000		Classical
Alabama	1950 (1907)		$100,000	Greek Revival
Alaska	1913	40,000		Colonial
Arkansas	1950	100,000		Georgian Colonial
California	1903 (1877)		32,500	Victorian
Colorado	1960 (1908)		Gift	Colonial
Connecticut	1945 (1909)		39,000	Georgian Colonial
Delaware	1965 (c. 1790)		65,000	Georgian
Florida	1957	360,000		Greek Revival
Georgia	1967	2,500,000		Greek Revival
Hawaii	1922 (1846)		55,000	Greek Revival
Idaho	1947 (1914)		25,000	Contemporary
Illinois	1855	45,794		Victorian
Indiana	1945 (1924)		72,500	Georgian
Iowa	1949 (1903)		27,200	Dutch Colonial
Kansas	1962 (1929)		Gift	Norman Château
Kentucky	1914	75,000		Renaissance
Louisiana	1963	1,000,000		Greek Revival
Maine	1919 (c. 1830)		Gift	Colonial
Maryland	1869	100,000		Georgian
Minnesota	1965 (1910)		Gift	English Tudor
Mississippi	1841	50,095		Greek Revival
Missouri	1871	50,000		French-Italian
Montana	1959	300,000		Modern
Nebraska	1957	200,000		Georgian Colonial
Nevada	1909	40,000		Georgian Colonial
New Jersey	1954 (1701)		Gift	Georgian
New Mexico	1955	201,234		Modified Territorial
New York	1877 (c. 1856)		45,000	Victorian
North Carolina	1890	25,000		Queen Anne
North Dakota	1960	250,000		Transitional
Ohio	1957 (1925)		Gift	Tudor-Norman
Oklahoma	1928	75,000		Dutch Colonial
Pennsylvania	1968	2,000,000		Georgian
South Carolina	1868 (1856)		Converted arsenal	Renaissance
South Dakota	1936	24,500		Modified Colonial
Tennessee	1949 (1927)		115,000	Georgian
Texas	1856	14,500		Greek Revival
Utah	1959	200,000		Contemporary
Virginia	1813	19,000		Georgian
Washington	1908	35,000		Georgian
West Virginia	1925	100,000		Georgian Colonial
Wisconsin	1949 (1927)		47,500	Georgian
Wyoming	1904	37,000		Georgian
Commonwealth and Territories				
American Samoa	1903	18,651		Island Colonial
Guam	1954	300,000		Modern
Puerto Rico	c. 1640 (1540)		Converted fort	Spanish
Virgin Islands-Christiansted	1775		14,000	Renaissance
Virgin Islands—St. Thomas	1867	33,605		Danish

*If acquired for Mansion use after construction, the year of construction is indicated in parenthesis.

STATE CAPITOLS

For each of the present Capitols—National, State, and Territorial—this table shows the year of completion of the original building (that of latest addition in parentheses), the approximate total cost of the present entire structure and the style of architecture generally ascribed to it. Some of the costs include land and furnishings.

	DATE	COST	ARCHITECTURE
United States	1800, 1811, 1829, 1859, 1863*	$50,000,000	Classical
Alabama	1851 (1911)	360,000	Classical (Corinthian)
Alaska	1931	1,000,000	Contemporary
Arizona	1900 (1939)	949,215	Spanish Classical
Arkansas	1914	2,205,779	Classical
California	1874 (1951)	10,204,000	Roman (Corinthian)
Colorado	1907	4,000,000	Classical (Corinthian)
Connecticut	1879	2,632,524	Gothic
Delaware	1933	750,000	Georgian
Florida	1845 (1947)	825,000	Greek (Doric)
Georgia	1889	999,882	Renaissance (Classical)
Hawaii	1969	20,000,000	Modern Hawaiian
Idaho	1912 (1920)	2,229,288	Classical
Illinois	1888	4,500,000	Classical
Indiana	1888	2,130,916	Classical (Corinthian)
Iowa	1886 (1904)	3,296,256	Romanesque (Corinthian)
Kansas	1873 (1903)	3,200,589	Classical
Kentucky	1910	1,820,000	Classical (Ionic)
Louisiana	1932	5,000,000	Modern (skyscraper)
Maine	1831 (1910)	489,000	Classical
Maryland	1779 (1906)	636,500	Georgian
Massachusetts	1798 (1960)	9,000,000	Classical
Michigan	1878	1,510,130	Renaissance (Classical)
Minnesota	1905	4,493,000	Italian Renaissance
Mississippi	1903	1,093,641	Renaissance (Classical)
Missouri	1917	4,215,000	Classical
Montana	1902	1,650,000	Neoclassical
Nebraska	1932	10,000,000	Modern (skyscraper)
Nevada	1870	332,384	Greek Classical
New Hampshire	1819 (1909)	1,282,000	Classical (Doric)
New Jersey	1889 (1912)	912,500	Renaissance
New Mexico	1966	4,676,860	Pueblo-Territorial
New York	1879 (1899)	25,000,000	Romanesque Renaissance
North Carolina	1840	531,674	Greek (Doric)
North Dakota	1934	2,000,000	Modern (skyscraper)
Ohio	1861	1,359,121	Greek (Doric)
Oklahoma	1917	5,000,000	Classical (Corinthian)
Oregon	1938	2,500,000	Greek Modern
Pennsylvania	1906	10,073,174	Italian Renaissance
Rhode Island	1904	3,018,416	Classical
South Carolina	1869 (1899)	3,540,000	Roman (Corinthian)
South Dakota	1910 (1931)	1,344,000	Classical (Ionic)
Tennessee	1859	1,500,000	Greek Classical
Texas	1888	3,744,630	Classical
Utah	1915	2,739,528	Classical (Corinthian)
Vermont	1859	252,077	Greek (Doric)
Virginia	1798 (1905)	244,753	Greek Classical
Washington	1928	7,385,768	Roman (Doric)
West Virginia	1932	4,807,861	Italian Renaissance
Wisconsin	1917	7,203,826	Italian Renaissance
Wyoming	1888 (1917)	400,500	Classical (Corinthian)
American Samoa	1904 (1929)	46,000	Island Colonial
Guam	1948	750,000	Modern
Puerto Rico	1929 (1958)	2,277,763	Italian Renaissance
Virgin Islands	1867 (1967)	33,605	Danish

*Completed in five sections involving a construction period of seventy years, not including terraces of 1884 and extension of east-central portion 1957-1962.

HISTORICAL LIST OF CAPITAL CITIES

The date after the name of the State indicates admission to the Union (in the case of the thirteen original States, ratification of the Constitution). Also listed are the sites of the Legislatures under Territorial status or, for the original thirteen, since independence. An asterisk indicates a temporary or provisional seat of government.

UNITED STATES
Philadelphia 1776
(The First Continental Congress had also met there, at Carpenter's Hall, in 1774. The Second Continental Congress convened in 1775 at the Pennsylvania State House, later named Independence Hall, after the Declaration of Independence, approved there in 1776.)
Baltimore* (December 20 to March 3) 1776-1777
Philadelphia (March 4 to September 18) 1777
Lancaster, Pennsylvania* (September 27) 1777
York, Pennsylvania* (September 30 to July 1) 1777-1778
Philadelphia 1778-1783
Princeton, New Jersey* (June 30 to November 20) 1783
Annapolis* 1783-1784
Trenton* 1784-1785
New York City 1785-1790
(First Capital under the Constitution—March 4, 1789)
Philadelphia* 1790-1800
Washington, D.C. 1800-

ALABAMA (December 14, 1819)
St. Stephens* 1817-1819
Huntsville* 1819-1820
Cahaba 1820-1826
Tuscaloosa 1826-1847
Montgomery 1847-

ALASKA (January 3, 1959)
Sitka 1867-1900
Juneau 1900-

ARIZONA (February 14, 1912)
(The Territorial Government was formally organized at Navajo Springs on December 29, 1863, then moved to Camp Whipple near Prescott in January and to Prescott itself in September 1864.)
Prescott 1864-1867
Tucson 1867-1877
Prescott 1877-1889
Phoenix 1889-

ARKANSAS (June 15, 1836)
Arkansas Post 1819-1821
Little Rock 1821-
(The Confederate State Capital was moved to Hot Springs for a few weeks in 1862 and to Washington in Hempstead County for four months in 1863.)

CALIFORNIA (September 9, 1850)
Monterey 1846-1849
(Under military Governors since 1846, California was ceded to the United States in 1848, but never officially had Territorial status prior to statehood.)
San Jose 1849-1851
Vallejo 1852
Sacramento 1852
Vallejo 1853
Benicia 1853-1854
Sacramento 1854-
(The Legislature met in San Francisco for part of 1862.)

COLORADO (August 1, 1876)
Colorado City 1861-1862
Golden 1862-1867
Denver 1867-

CONNECTICUT (January 9, 1788)
Hartford (Co-capital with New Haven until 1783) 1776-

DELAWARE (December 7, 1787)
New Castle 1776-1777
Dover 1777-

FLORIDA (March 3, 1845)
Pensacola* 1822-1823
Tallahassee 1824-

GEORGIA (January 2, 1788)
Savannah 1776-1785
(During the Revolutionary War, the seat of government was shifted to Augusta in 1778, to Heard's Fort in Wilkes County in 1779, to Ebenezer in Effingham County in 1780, to Augusta again in 1781, then back to Savannah in 1783.)
Augusta 1786-1795
Louisville 1796-1806
Milledgeville 1807-1868
(A special legislative session was held in Macon in 1865.)
Atlanta 1868-

HAWAII (August 21, 1959)
(The statehood act was signed on March 18; the citizens approved statehood in a plebiscite on June 27.)
Honolulu 1900-

IDAHO (July 3, 1890)
Lewiston 1863-1865
Boise 1865-

ILLINOIS (December 3, 1818)
Kaskaskia 1809-1820
Vandalia 1820-1839
Springfield 1839-

INDIANA (December 11, 1816)
Vincennes 1806-1816
Corydon 1816-1824
Indianapolis 1825-

IOWA (December 28, 1846)
Burlington 1838-1839
Iowa City 1839-1857
Des Moines 1857-

KANSAS (January 29, 1861)
(Beginning in 1855, the Territorial capital of Kansas was, in turn, Fort Leavenworth, Shawnee Mission, Pawnee, Shawnee Mission again, Minneola and Lecompton, which was also the first State capital.)
Lecompton 1857-1861
Topeka 1861-

KENTUCKY (June 1, 1792)
Lexington 1792
Frankfort 1792-

LOUISIANA (April 30, 1812)
New Orleans 1804-1828
Donaldsonville 1828-1831
New Orleans 1831-1849
Baton Rouge 1849-1862
Opelousas (Confederate only) 1863
Shreveport (Confederate only) 1864
New Orleans 1864-1882
Baton Rouge 1882-

MAINE (March 15, 1820)

Portland	1820-1827
Augusta	1827-

MARYLAND (April 28, 1788)

Annapolis	1776-

(The Legislature moved to Frederick briefly in 1861.)

MASSACHUSETTS (February 6, 1788)

Boston	1776-

MICHIGAN (January 26, 1837)

Detroit	1805-1848
Lansing	1848-

MINNESOTA (May 11, 1858)

St. Paul	1849-

MISSISSIPPI (December 10, 1817)

Natchez	1798-1802
Washington	1802-1820
Columbia*	1821
Jackson	1822-

(Columbus and Macon served as Confederate State capitals 1863-1864.)

MISSOURI (August 10, 1821)

St. Louis	1812-1821
St. Charles*	1821-1827
Jefferson City	1827-

MONTANA (November 8, 1889)

Bannack	1865
Virginia City	1866-1876
Helena	1876-

NEBRASKA (March 1, 1867)

Bellevue	1854
Omaha	1854-1867
Lincoln	1867-

NEVADA (October 31, 1864)

Carson City	1861-

NEW HAMPSHIRE (June 21, 1788)

Portsmouth	1775-1805
Concord	1782-

(Both of these cities, as well as Charlestown, Dover, Amherst, Hanover and Hopkinton, were used for legislative sessions. Concord has been the sole capital since 1807.)

NEW JERSEY (December 18, 1787)

Princeton	1776

(Legislative sessions were held thereafter at various locations, including Haddonfield in 1777, Princeton again in 1777 and 1778, Trenton, Burlington and Perth Amboy.)

Trenton	1790-

NEW MEXICO (January 6, 1912)

Santa Fe	1850-

NEW YORK (July 26, 1788)

New York City	1775-1776
White Plains*	1776
Kingston*	1777
Poughkeepsie*	1777-1784

(The Federal Constitution was ratified there in 1788.)

New York City	1784-1797
Albany	1797-

NORTH CAROLINA (November 21, 1789)

New Bern	1776-1794

(The Legislature also met in several other places during this period, including Halifax, Hillsboro, Smithfield, Wake Court House, Salem, Tarboro and Fayetteville.)

Raleigh	1794-

NORTH DAKOTA (November 2, 1889)

Yankton (South Dakota)	1861-1883
Bismarck	1883-

(These two were capitals of the Dakota Territory 1861-1889.)

OHIO (March 1, 1803)

(The first State General Assembly met on this date. The statehood enabling act was signed on April 30, 1802, and a Constitutional Convention met in November. Statehood was not officially designated, however. In 1953 Congress by resolution set March 1, 1803, as the date of admission.)

Marietta (Capital of the Northwest Territory. The General Assembly met in Cincinnati in 1799.)	1788-1800
Chillicothe*	1800-1809
Zanesville*	1810-1812
Chillicothe*	1812-1816
Columbus	1816-

OKLAHOMA (November 16, 1907)

Guthrie	1890-1911
Oklahoma City	1911-

OREGON (February 14, 1859)

Oregon City	1849-1851
Salem	1851-

(Salem was officially designated the Oregon Territory capital in 1852. The Legislature has remained there except for a few days at Corvallis in December 1855.)

PENNSYLVANIA (December 12, 1787)

Philadelphia	1776-1799

(Colonial capital since 1683. William Penn's first assembly met in nearby Upland—now Chester—in December 1682.)

Lancaster	1799-1812
Harrisburg	1812-

RHODE ISLAND (May 29, 1790)

(After independence, as before, the Rhode Island Legislature met in several towns during any year: Portsmouth, Providence, Warwick, Newport, Pawtucket, Kingstown, South Kingston, East Greenwich, Bristol, until 1854. A session was held almost every May in Newport, 1816-1900, and in October of odd years in South Kingston after 1824.)

Providence (alone)	1901-

SOUTH CAROLINA (May 23, 1788)

Charleston	1776-1789
Columbia	1790-

SOUTH DAKOTA (November 2, 1889)

Yankton	1861-1883
Bismarck (North Dakota)	1883-1889

(Above two cities were capitals of the Dakota Territory.)

Pierre	1889-

TENNESSEE (June 1, 1796)

(Settlers in North Carolina's "District of Washington" formed a Legislature which met at Jonesboro—where it petitioned Congress in 1784 for admission to the Union as the State of Franklin—and at Greeneville. Territorial status was granted in 1790.)

Knoxville	1790-1812

(Kingston was capital for one day—September 21, 1807.)

Nashville	1812-1815
Knoxville	1816-1819
Murfreesboro	1819-1825
Nashville	1826-

TEXAS (December 29, 1845)

Columbia (3 months)	1836
Houston	1837-1839
Austin	1839-1842
Houston (6 months)	1842
Washington-on-the-Brazos	1842
Austin	1843-

(These were all capitals of the Republic of Texas, 1836-1845. Independence from Mexico was declared in 1836 at Washington-on-the-Brazos.)

UTAH (January 4, 1896)

Salt Lake City (Then called Great Salt Lake City)	1850-1854
Fillmore	1855-1856
Salt Lake City	1856-1858
Fillmore	1858
Salt Lake City	1859-

VERMONT (March 4, 1791)

(In Westminster, in April 1775, the people proclaimed independence from New York and in January 1777, declared themselves the independent State of New Connecticut. Thereafter, various legislative sessions were held at Windsor, Bennington, Manchester, Westminster, Rutland, Norwich, Newbury and Castleton, before Vermont was admitted to the Union.)

Bennington	1791
Windsor (odd years)	1791-1799
Rutland (four sessions)	1792-1797
Vergennes	1798
Middlebury	1800
Newbury	1801
Burlington	1802
Westminster	1803
Windsor	1804
Rutland	1804
Danville	1805
Middlebury	1806
Woodstock	1807
Montpelier	1808-

VIRGINIA (June 25, 1788)

Jamestown	1607-1699
Williamsburg	1699-1780
Richmond	1780-

(Charlottesville and Staunton served as temporary homes for the Legislature in 1781.)

WASHINGTON (November 11, 1889)

Olympia	1854-

WEST VIRGINIA (June 20, 1863)

Wheeling	1861-1870
Charleston	1870-1875
Wheeling	1875-1885
Charleston	1885-

WISCONSIN (May 28, 1848)

Belmont	1836
Burlington (Iowa)	1837-1838
Madison	1838-

WYOMING (July 10, 1890)

Cheyenne	1869-

AMERICAN SAMOA

(Became a U.S. Territory by treaty with the United Kingdom and Germany on December 2, 1899, confirmed by local chiefs in 1900 and 1904. Pago Pago had been a U.S. Navy coaling station since 1872 under a commercial treaty.)

Pago Pago	1899-

GUAM

(Ceded by Spain by treaty of December 10, 1898.)

Agaña	1899-

PUERTO RICO

(Ceded by Spain by treaty of December 10, 1898; became a Commonwealth on July 25, 1952.)

San Juan	1898-

VIRGIN ISLANDS

(Purchased from Denmark January 25, 1917.)

Charlotte Amalie	1917-

BIBLIOGRAPHY

Aikman, Lonnelle. "Under the Dome of Freedom." *National Geographic*, vol. 125, no. 1 (January 1964).

ALABAMA: Alabama Department of Archives and History. *Alabama Official and Statistical Register, 1963.*

State of Alabama. *Capitol of Alabama.* (brochure).

ALASKA: State of Alaska. *Alaska, the 49th State.* (leaflet).

Alsberg, Henry G., ed. *The American Guide.* New York: Hastings House, 1949.

The American Heritage History of the Making of the Nation, 1783-1860. (Text by Francis Russell). New York: American Heritage Publishing Company, Inc., 1968.

The American Heritage History of the Thirteen Colonies. (Text by Louis B. Wright). New York: American Heritage Publishing Company, Inc., 1967.

AMERICAN SAMOA: *1967 Annual Report of the Governor of American Samoa to the Secretary of the Interior.* Washington: United States Government Printing Office, 1968.

ARIZONA: Arizona Secretary of State. *Arizona Blue Book, 1931-1932.*

State of Arizona Development Board, Travel Promotion Department. *Arizona State Capitol.* (pamphlet).

ARKANSAS: Arkansas Secretary of State. *Historical Report of the Secretary of State.* 1958.

Betts, Edwin Morris, and Bear, James Adam, Jr. *The Family Letters of Thomas Jefferson.* Columbia: University of Missouri Press, 1966.

Bryan, Wilhelmus Bogart. *A History of the National Capitol, 1790-1814.* vol. 1. New York: The Macmillan Company, 1914.

———. *A History of the National Capitol, 1815-1878.* vol. 2. New York: The Macmillan Company, 1916.

Burchard, John and Bush-Brown, Albert. *The Architecture of America.* Boston: Little, Brown and Company, 1966.

CALIFORNIA: *California Blue Book, 1967.* Office of State Printing.

Cleland, Robert Glass. *A History of California: The American Period.* New York: The Macmillan Company, 1930.

Salitore, Edward V., and Stone, Adolf. *California Information Almanac,* 1966 ed. Lakewood, California: California Almanac Company, 1965.

Carroll, John Alexander, and Ashworth, Mary Wells. *George Washington, First in Peace.* George Washington, a Biography, edited by Douglas Freeman, vol. 7. New York: Charles Scribner's Sons, 1957.

Churchill, Winston S. Our Buildings Shape Us. *New York Times Magazine.* (November 14, 1943).

Colonial Williamsburg Official Guidebook. 4th ed. Williamsburg, Virginia: Colonial Williamsburg, Inc., 1960.

COLORADO: State of Colorado, Department of Public Relations. *Colorado Capitol Building.* (booklet).

State of Colorado, Planning Division. *Colorado 1959-1961; Yearbook of the State of Colorado.*

Congress of the United States. *American State Papers.* Documents, Legislative and Executive, of the Congress of the United States, 1789-1809. Class X, Miscellaneous, vol. 1. Washington: Gales and Seaton, 1834.

Congress of the United States, 89th Congress, 1st Session. *The Capitol, Symbol of Freedom.* House Document no. 260, 4th ed. Washington: U.S. Government Printing Office, 1966.

Congress of the United States, 90th Congress, 2nd Session. *Dedication of the Bust of Constantino Brumidi.* House Document no. 321. Washington: U.S. Government Printing Office, 1968.

Congress of the United States, 89th Congress, 2nd Session. *Our Capitol.* Senate Document no. 105. Washington: U.S. G.P.O. 1966.

CONNECTICUT: Connecticut Secretary of State. *Register and Manual, 1967.*

State of Connecticut. *Welcome to the Connecticut State Capitol.* (pamphlet).

Council of State Governments. *Governors of the States, 1900-1966.* R.M. 377, rev. Chicago: 1966.

Country Beautiful Foundation, Inc. *America's Historic Houses: The Living Past.* New York: G.P. Putnam's Sons in association with Country Beautiful Foundation, Inc., 1967.

Cresson, W.P. *James Monroe.* Chapel Hill, North Carolina: The University of North Carolina Press, 1946.

Crothers, George D. *American History.* New York: Holt, Rinehart and Winston, Inc., 1964.

Davie, Emily, comp. *Profile of America.* New York: Thomas Y. Crowell Company, 1954.

DELAWARE: City of Dover. *Dover—the First Two Hundred and Fifty Years, 1717-1967.* Dover: City of Dover, 1967.

Delaware State Development Department. *Discover Wonderful Delaware.* (pamphlet).

Federal Writers' Program, Works Progress Administration. *Delaware, a Guide to the First State.* New York: The Viking Press, 1938.

Encyclopedia Americana. New York: Americana Corporation, 1962.

Encyclopedia Britannica. Chicago: Encyclopedia Britannica, Inc., 1967.

Fiske, John. *The Beginnings of New England.* New York: Houghton, Mifflin and Company, 1902.

FLORIDA: Morris, Allen, comp. *The Florida Handbook 1967-1968.* Tallahassee: The Peninsular Publishing Company, 1967.

Franzen, Marilyn D. *Capitol Capsules.* Pierpont, South Dakota: Rushmore, Inc., 1964.

Frary, I.T. *Thomas Jefferson: Architect and Builder.* Richmond: Garrett and Massie, 1950.

Furman, Bess. *White House Profile.* New York: The Bobbs-Merrill Company, 1951.

GEORGIA: Beeson, Leola (Selman). *The One Hundred Years of the Old Governor's Mansion, Milledgeville, Georgia, 1838-1938.* Macon, Georgia: The J. W. Burke Company, 1938.

State of Georgia, Department of Archives and History. *Georgia Official and Statistical Register 1959-1960.*

———. *The State of Georgia and Its Capitol.* (booklet).

Green, Constance McLaughlin. *Washington: Village and Capital, 1800-1878.* Princeton, New Jersey: Princeton University Press, 1962.

GUAM: Swan, Lt. T.O., USN, ed. *Glimpses of Guam 1967.* Published in conjunction with the 1967 Navy Relief Fund Drive, Guam.

HAWAII: Epstein, Moray, ed. and comp. *All about Hawaii.* 78th ed. Honolulu: The Honolulu Star Bulletin, Ltd., 1953.

Hitchcock, Henry-Russell. *Architecture: Nineteenth and Twentieth Centuries.* 2d ed. Baltimore: Penguin Books, 1963.

Holloway, Laura C. *The Ladies of the White House.* Philadelphia: Bradley, Garretson & Co., 1883.

Hurd, Charles. *The White House, A Biography.* New York: Harper & Brothers, 1940.

IDAHO: Donaldson, Thomas. *Idaho of Yesterday.* Caldwell, Idaho: The Caxton Printers Ltd., 1941.

Idaho Historical Society. *Idaho State Capitol.* Reference Series no. 133. (paper).

Idaho Secretary of State. *Secretary of State of Idaho 1963-1964, the 37th Biennial Report.*

State of Idaho. *Capitol Guide Book.* (brochure).

ILLINOIS: Illinois Secretary of State. *Capitol Guide.*

———. *Illinois Blue Book 1963-1964.*

INDIANA: Mannweiler, David. *Governors of Indiana.* Reprinted from the *Indianapolis News*

IOWA: *Iowa Official Register 1967-1968.* Des Moines: Superintendent of Printing.

Iowa Welcomes You. . . . Des Moines: Superintendent of Printing, 1963.

Jensen, Amy LaFollette. *The White House and Its Thirty-Three Families.* New York: McGraw-Hill Book Company, Inc., 1962.

KANSAS: Arnold, Anna E. *A History of Kansas.* Topeka: The State of Kansas, 1931.

Kansas Secretary of State. *Kansas Directory 1967-1968.*

KENTUCKY: Hardin, Bayless F. *The Capitols of Kentucky.* Reprinted from the Register of the Kentucky State Historical Society, July, 1947.

Kentucky Historical Society. *The Old State House.* (folder).

Kimball, Fiske. *American Architecture.* Indianapolis and New York: The Bobbs-Merrill Company, 1928.

———. *Domestic Architecture of the American Colonies and of the Early Republic.* New York: Dover Publications, Inc., 1966.

———. *Thomas Jefferson—Architect.* Cambridge: The Riverside Press, 1916.

Kocher, A. Lawrence, and Dearstyne, Howard. *Colonial Williamsburg: Its Buildings and Gardens.* rev. ed. Williamsburg, Virginia: Colonial Williamsburg, Inc., 1961.

Latrobe, Benjamin Henry. *The Journal of Latrobe.* New York: D. Appleton and Company, 1905.

Long, Luman H., ed. *The World Almanac and Book of Facts.* 1968 Centennial ed. Cleveland: Newspaper Enterprise Association, Inc., 1967.

LOUISIANA: Louisiana Legislative Council. *The Government of Louisiana.* Research Study no. 13. Baton Rouge: 1959.

Louisiana Tourist Development Commission. *Louisiana Capitol Guide.* (leaflet).

Wurzlow, Helen Emmelin. *Louisiana: Its Capitol.* 6th ed.

MAINE: State of Maine, Department of Economic Development. *Facts on Maine.* 1968.

———. *Maine, The Pine Tree State.* (folder).

Major, Howard. *The Domestic Architecture of the Early American Republic—The Greek Revival.* Philadelphia: J. B. Lippincott Company, 1926.

MARYLAND: Long, E. John. *A Walk in Old Annapolis.* Reprinted from the *New York Times.* Annapolis: Department of Economic Development, 1965.

Radoff, Morris L. *Buildings of the State of Maryland at Annapolis.* State of Maryland, 1954.

State of Maryland, Department of Economic Development. *Great Moments in Maryland's History.* (booklet).

———. *Maryland Statehouse Today.*

———. Hall of Records Commission. *Maryland Manual 1965-1966.*

MASSACHUSETTS: Massachusetts Clerk of the Senate and the Clerk of the House. *A Manual for the Use of the General Court for 1965-1966.* Boston: 1965.

McMaster, John Bach. *A History of the People of the United States.* vol. 1. New York: D. Appleton and Company, 1883.

MICHIGAN: Brown, David S. *A Governor's Residence in Michigan?* Papers in Public Administration no. 40. Ann Arbor: Institute of Public Administration, University of Michigan, 1961.

Michigan Secretary of State. *Michigan Manual 1967-1968.*

Welcome to Michigan's Capitol. (folder).

Miers, Earl Schenck. *The White House and the Presidency.* New York: Wonder Books, Division of Grossett & Dunlap, Inc., 1965.

Miller, Walter J. *The 49 Capitol Buildings of the United States.* Harrisburg, Pennsylvania: Capitol Publishing Company, Inc., 1938.

MINNESOTA: Federal Writers' Program, Works Progress Administration. *Minnesota, a State Guide.* New York: The Viking Press, 1938.

Minnesota Secretary of State. *Legislative Manual 1965-1966.*

State of Minnesota, Department of Administration. *The Minnesota Capitol, Official Guide and History.*

MISSISSIPPI: Holcomb, Gene. "The Mississippi Governor's Mansion." *The Journal of Mississippi History.* vol. 2, no. 1 (January 1940).

Mississippi Secretary of State. *Official and Statistical Register 1964-1968.*

MISSOURI: Missouri Secretary of State. *Official Manual, State of Missouri, 1963-1964.*

State of Missouri, Commerce and Industrial Development Commission. *Souvenir Guide to Missouri's Capitol.* (booklet).

MONTANA: Montana Highway Commission. *Welcome to Montana's State Capitol Building.* (brochure).

Montana State University. *The Montana Almanac.* 1959-1960 ed. Missoula: Montana State University Press, 1958.

Moore, Charles. *Washington Past and Present.* New York: The Century Co., 1929.

Morris, Edward Bateman, comp. *Report of the Commission on the Renovation of the Executive Mansion.* Washington: U.S. Government Printing Office, 1952.

Morris, Maud Burr, ed. *Records of the Columbia Historical Society.* vols. 33-34. Washington: Columbia Historical Society, 1932.

Morris, Richard B., ed. *Encyclopedia of American History.* New York: Harper & Brothers, 1953.

———. *Prehistory to 1774, The New World.* The *Life* History of the United States, edited by Henry F. Graff, vol. 1. New York: Time, Inc., 1963.

———. *1775-1789, The Making of a Nation.* The *Life* History of the United States, edited by HenryF. Graff, vol. 1. New York: Time, Inc., 1963.

The National Cyclopedia of American Biography, comp. *White's Conspectus of American Biography.* 2d ed. New York: James T. White and Company, 1937.

NEBRASKA: Nebraska Legislative Council. *Nebraska Blue Book 1966.*

NEVADA: Nevada State Archivist. *The History of the Capitol Building and Governor's Mansion.* Carson City: 1968.

NEW HAMPSHIRE: New Hampshire Department of State. *Manual for the General Court 1967.* no. 40.

NEW JERSEY: Bill, Alfred Hoyt. *A House Called Morven.* Princeton, New Jersey: Princeton University Press, 1954.

Gribbons, J. Joseph, ed. *New Jersey Legislative Manual 1967.* Trenton: J. Joseph Gribbons, 1967.

New Jersey Governor's Committee on Morven. *Morven as a Governor's Residence.* Trenton: 1955.

New Jersey Tercentenary Almanac. 1964.

NEW MEXICO: New Mexico Secretary of State. *New Mexico Blue Book 1965-1966.*

NEW YORK: *Civil List and Constitutional History of the State of New York.* Albany: Parsons and Company, 1889.

New York Red Book 1967-1968. Albany: Williams Press. 1967.

Roseberry, Cecil R. *Capitol Story.* State of New York, 1964.

New York Secretary of State. *Manual for the Use of the Legislature of the State of New York, 1967.*

Savell, Isabelle K. *The Executive Mansion in Albany.* Albany: 1960.

———. *The Governor's Mansion in Albany.* Albany: 1962.

State of New York, Office of General Services. *The New York State Capitol.* (booklet).

Nichols, Frederick Doveton, comp. *Thomas Jefferson's Architectural Drawings*. Charlottesville: University of Virginia Press, 1961.

NORTH CAROLINA: Executive Mansion Fine Arts Committee. *The Executive Mansion*. 1968.

North Carolina Secretary of State. *North Carolina Manual 1967*. Raleigh.

NORTH DAKOTA: North Dakota Secretary of State. *North Dakota Blue Book 1961*.

North Dakota State Board of Administration. *North Dakota State Capitol*. (booklet).

OHIO: Ohio Secretary of State. *Federal, State, County Officers and Departmental Information: the State of Ohio Official Roster, 1963-1964*. 1963.

———. *Ohio Capitals*. 1968.

Satterthwaite, Tina. "The Governor's 30-Room Home." *The (Toledo) Blade Sunday Magazine* (May 24, 1964).

OKLAHOMA: State Election Board of Oklahoma City. *Directory and Manual of the State of Oklahoma*. 1967.

OREGON: Oregon Secretary of State. *Oregon Blue Book 1967-1968*.

State of Oregon, Department of Finance and Administration. *Governor's Residence for Oregon*. Report to the 54th Legislative Assembly. 1966.

PENNSYLVANIA: Greene, LeRoy. *Shelter for His Excellency*. Harrisburg, Pennsylvania: Stackpole Books, 1951.

State of Pennsylvania, Department of Property and Supplies. *Pennsylvania Manual 1967*. vol. 98.

Pollack, Paul W. *The Capital Cities of the United States*. Phoenix, Arizona: Paul W Pollack, 1960.

PUERTO RICO: House of Representatives of the Commonwealth of Puerto Rico. *Puerto Rico's Capitol* or *Puerto Rico's House of Laws*. 1966.

Old San Juan, Puerto Rico. Boston: Colourpicture Publishers, Inc. (booklet).

RHODE ISLAND: Providence Journal. *1966 Providence Journal Almanac*.

Rhode Island Secretary of State. *Rhode Island Manual 1965-1966*.

Shankle, George Earlie. *State Names, Flags, Seals, Songs, Birds, Flowers, and Other Symbols*. New York: The H. W. Wilson Company, 1934.

Smelser, Marshall. *American Colonial and Revolutionary History*. New York: Barnes & Noble, 1950.

Smith, A. Robert, and Sevareid, Eric. *Washington: Magnificent Capital*. Garden City, New York: Doubleday & Company, Inc., 1965.

Smith, Margaret Bayard. *The First Forty Years of Washington Society*. New York: Charles Scribner's Sons, 1906.

SOUTH CAROLINA: Federal Writers' Program, Works Progress Administration. *South Carolina, a Guide to the Palmetto State*. New York: Oxford University Press, 1941.

Wallace, David Duncan. *South Carolina: A Short History, 1520-1948*. Chapel Hill, North Carolina: The University of North Carolina Press, 1951.

Watson, Inez, ed. *South Carolina Legislative Manual 1967*.

SOUTH DAKOTA: State of South Dakota, Department of Finance. *South Dakota Legislative Manual 1961*.

TENNESSEE: Tennessee Secretary of State. *Tennessee Blue Book 1967-1968*.

White, Robert H. Legislative Steps in the Purchase of a Mansion for the Governor of Tennessee. Address before the Tennessee Historical Society, October 10, 1969. Mimeographed.

TEXAS: The Dallas Morning News. *The Texas Almanac 1964-1965*. Dallas: A. H. Belo Corporation.

Daniel, Mrs. Price. *The Governor's Mansion of Texas*. Waco, Texas: Private printing, 1960.

Texas Legislative Council. *The Texas Capitol*. 1967.

Truett, Randle Bond. *The White House—Home of the Presidents*. New York: Hastings House, 1949.

The United States Capitol Historical Society. *We, the People—The Story of the United States Capitol*. 5th ed. (Text by Lonnelle Aikman). 1967.

United States Department of the Interior, National Park Service. *Thomas Jefferson and the National Capital*. Edited by Saul K. Padover. Washington: U.S. Government Printing Office, 1946.

UTAH: Federal Writers' Program, Works Progress Administration. *Utah, a Guide to the State*. New York: Hastings House, 1945.

Utah Secretary of State. *Utah Official Roster 1965-1967*.

VERMONT: State of Vermont, Board of Historic Sites and the Development Department. *The Official Guide to Historic Sites*.

Vermont Secretary of State. *Vermont Legislative Directory and State Manual 1967*.

VIRGIN ISLANDS: Harmon, Jeanne Perkins, ed. *Here's How: Your Guide to St. Thomas*. 17th ed. St. Thomas: *Here's How*, 1966.

United States Department of the Interior. *Our Caribbean Gems . . . the U.S. Virgin Islands*. Edited by Gladys Rafter. Washington: U.S. Government Printing Office, 1967.

VIRGINIA: *The Executive Mansion*. 1964. (booklet).

Secretary of the Commonwealth of Virginia. *Report of the Secretary of the Commonwealth to the Governor and the General Assembly of Virginia*. Department of Purchases and Supply, 1966.

Troubetzkoy, Ulrich. "The Governor's Mansion." *Virginia Cavalcade* (Summer 1961).

WASHINGTON: Bergem, Harold T. From Opera Hats to the Frug; An Intimate Glance at the Washington State Governor's Mansion. Mimeographed.

State of Washington, Department of Commerce and Economic Development. *The Capitol Group of Washington State*.

———. *Facts to Help You Know Washington*. (fact sheet).

Washington Society of Engineers. *Planning and Building the City of Washington*. Edited by Frederick Haynes Newell. Washington: Ransdell Inc., 1932.

WEST VIRGINIA: State of West Virginia, Department of Commerce. *West Virginia's Executive Mansion*. (booklet).

West Virginia Clerk of the Senate. *West Virginia Blue Book 1964*. Centennial ed.

White House Historical Association. *The Living White House*. (Text by Lonnelle Aikman). Washington: White House Historical Association with the cooperation of the National Geographic Society, 1966.

The White House. 1962.

Willets, Gibson. *Inside History of the White House*. New York: Christian Herald, 1908.

Williams, Henry Lionel, and Ottalie K. Williams, *Great Houses of America*. New York: G. P. Putnam's Sons, 1966.

WISCONSIN: Wisconsin Legislative Reference Bureau. *The Wisconsin Blue Book 1964*.

———. Wisconsin's State Capitol. LRB-WF63-1, rev. 1967.

Wolff, Perry. *A Tour of the White House with Mrs. John F. Kennedy*. Garden City, New York: Doubleday & Company, Inc., 1962.

WYOMING: Wyoming Secretary of State. *1967 Wyoming Official Directory*.

Zorn, Walter Lewis. *The Capitols of the United States*. Monroe, Michigan: Walter Lewis Zorn, 1955.

ACKNOWLEDGMENTS AND CREDITS

The Authors are indebted to the following persons for photographs, material, and other assistance without which this book could not have been completed:

The White House: former President and Mrs. Lyndon B. Johnson; Mrs. Elizabeth S. Carpenter; Mrs. Ashton Gonella; Mrs. Dorothy Territo; Mr. Joe Bruno; Mr. Robert L. Knudsen and Mr. Mike Geissinger, photographers.

Executive Office of the President, Office of Emergency Preparedness and Federal-State Relations: Honorable Mordecai M. Merker, Deputy Director; Mr. John C. Archer; Miss Alice B. Bandy; Mr. Donald J. Carbone; Miss Anne M. Dever; Miss Monica J. Douglass; Mr. Marion J. Forbes; Mr. Hubert R. Gallagher; Mr. James P. Greenstone; Mrs. Gloria Hill; Mr. Edward L. Keenan; Miss Margaret Legath; Mr. Walter L. Mazan; Miss Esther Robbins; Mr. Wayne Sherwin; Miss Linda Stonestreet; Miss Carol F. Wanner; Mrs. Mary Pearl Williams; Miss Mary L. Zajac; OEP Regional Directors Albert D. O'Connor, Robert J. Carmody, C. R. Bob Short, Frank P. Bourgin, George E. Hastings, Donald G. Eddy; Donal M. O'Callaghan, and Creath A. Tooley; and OEP Regional Representatives Philip D. Bassett, John L. Makey, Joseph J. Mastroianni, Harvey F. McPhail, Henry I. Molter, Richard A. Smith, John F. Sullivan, Jr., and William R. Swarm.

The U.S. Capitol: Lt. Col. M. W. Arps, Jr., USA (Ret.); Mr. Fred Bell, National Park Service, Department of the Interior; Miss Carol Smith, National Capital Region, National Park Service, Department of the Interior; Miss Mae Terrell, U.S. Capitol Historical Society; Mrs. Florian H. Thayn, Mr. Frederick W. Winkelman, Office of the Architect of the Capitol; photo—Courtesy of National Permanent Savings, by Glen Leach.

Alabama: Governor and Mrs. Albert P. Brewer; former Governor Lurleen B. Wallace; Mr. Peter A. Brannon; Mr. Milo B. Howard, Jr., Director, Department of Archives and History; Mr. Bob Ingram; Alabama Historical Commission.

Alaska: former Governor and Mrs. Walter J. Hickel; Governor Keith H. Miller; Miss Helen Dirtadian, State Librarian; Mrs. Phyllis Nottingham, Librarian, Alaska Historical Library; Travel Division, Department of Economic Development.

Arizona: Governor and Mrs. Jack Williams; Mrs. Sam Goddard, former First Lady; Mrs. Marguerite B. Cooley, Director, Department of Library and Archives; Department of Civil Defense and Emergency Planning; Travel Information Section, Department of Economic Planning and Development.

Arkansas: Governor and Mrs. Winthrop Rockefeller; Mr. John L. Ferguson, State Historian; Mr. Stanley Lucich; Public Relations Office.

California: Governor and Mrs. Ronald Reagan; Mrs. Helen Amick; Mr. William N. Davis, Jr., Chief of Archives; Mr. N. R. Hacken; Mrs. Adin D. Henderson; Mr. William Penn Mott, Jr.; Mr. Paul J. O'Brien; Division of Highways, Department of Public Works; McCurry Photo Company.

Colorado: Governor and Mrs. John A. Love; Mrs. Dolores C. Renze, State Archivist; Department of Public Relations; Colorado State Historical Society; Mr. George R. Dickson, Mansion photo.

Connecticut: Governor and Mrs. John Dempsey; Mr. Albert J. Ahern, Jr.; Miss Doris E. Cook; Mr. Ray Rosa; Mrs. Sylvie J. Turner, Archivist.

Delaware: former Governor and Mrs. Charles L. Terry, Jr.; Hon. Crawford J. Carroll, Mayor of Dover; Mr. Samuel T. W. Davidson; Mr. Leon deValinger, Jr., Archivist; Mr. Melvin C. Luff, Jr.; Col. James W. McCloskey; Delaware State Development Department.

Florida: Governor and Mrs. Claude R. Kirk, Jr.; Miss Dorothy Dodd; Mr. Horry Hair; Terry C. Lee; Mr. Robert Williams, Executive Director, Board of Archives and History; Florida Development Commission, photographs.

Georgia: Governor and Mrs. Lester G. Maddox; Miss Carroll Hart, State Archivist; Mr. Stanley Hathcock; Mr. Bill Birdsong, Mr. Bill Murphy, photographers.

Hawaii: Governor and Mrs. John A. Burns; Lt. Col. M. W. Arps, Jr., USA (Ret.); Brig. Gen. Francis R. Boyles; Col. John Butchart; Miss Agnes C. Conrad, Archivist; Mr. Myron Thompson.

Idaho: Governor and Mrs. Don Samuelson; Miss Judith Austin; Mr. H. J. Swinney; Mr. Mule Wells, Idaho State Historical Society; Idaho Department of Commerce and Development; Mr. Henri M. Gabel, photographer.

Illinois: former Governor and Mrs. Samuel H. Shapiro; Hon. Paul Powell, Secretary of State; Senator William Grindle; Mr. Theodore J. Cassady, Department Head (Archives); Mr. John D. Mellott, Illinois Region 8 Tourism Council; Mrs. Kathryn Tedrick, Vandalia Chamber of Commerce; Col. Fred H. Woick.

Indiana: former Governor and Mrs. Roger D. Branigin; Col. Robert S. Bates; Mrs. Hazel W. Hopper, Head, Indiana Division, State Library; Miss Dorothy E. Steinmeier; Mansion photo by State Police Dept.; Capitol photo by GAF Corp., USA.

Iowa: former Governor and Mrs. Harold E. Hughes; Mr. Peter Bralic; Mr. Jack W. Musgrove, Curator, Department of History and Archives; Miss Mildred E. Wilson; Iowa Development Commission.

Kansas: Governor and Mrs. Robert Docking; Mr. Nyle Miller, Secretary, Kansas State Historical Society; Miss Jessie Tucker; Miss Margaret Winchell; Capitol photo by GAF Corporation, USA.

Kentucky: Governor and Mrs. Louie B. Nunn; Mr. George Chinn, Director, Kentucky Historical Society; Mr. G. Glenn Clift; Mrs. Mary O'Hara; Office of Public Information; Mr. Kalman Papp, Old Mansion photo.

Louisiana: Governor and Mrs. John J. McKeithen; Mrs. Edith Atkinson, Librarian Louisiana Dept., State Library; Mr. Leon Gary; Mrs. Paul Pendley; photographs, Mr. Jim Lynch.

Maine: Governor and Mrs. Kenneth M. Curtis; Mrs. John H. Reed, former First Lady; Mrs. Esther L. Shaw; Mr. Samuel S. Silsby, State Archivist; Miss Margaret A. Whalen; Mr. Roy A. Whitcomb, Jr.; Maine Department of Economic Development; Mansion photo, Klebe painting by Norton.

Maryland: former Governor and Mrs. Spiro T. Agnew; Mrs. J. Millard Tawes, former First Lady; Dr. Morris L. Radoff, Archivist; Mr. John B. Richardson, Jr.; Mr. M. E. Warren, photographer.

Massachusetts: former Governor and Mrs. John A. Volpe; Col. Frederick J. Cooke; Mr. Richard W. Hale, Jr., Archivist; Mr. Ernest Ladeira; Mr. Barry M. Locke; Miss Grace M. MacEachern.

Michigan: former Governor and Mrs. George Romney; Hon. James S. Farnsworth, State Representative; Mr. Harry E. Kelsey, Jr., Director, Historical Commission; Capt. Edward Lenon; Mr. George T. Trumbull, Jr.; Michigan Tourist Council.

Minnesota: Governor and Mrs. Harold LeVander; Lt. Col. M. W. Arps, Jr., USA (Ret.); Mr. Roy V. Aune; Mr. Robert M. Brown, Archivist; Mr. Russell W. Fridley, Director, Historical Society; Mr. Wallace Hoaglund; Mr. Phillip A. Iverson.

Mississippi: Governor and Mrs. John Bell Williams; Mrs. Paul B. Johnson, former First Lady; Miss Charlotte Capers, Director, Department of Archives and History; Mr. Kenneth P. Phillips.

Missouri: Governor and Mrs. Warren E. Hearnes; Mr. Richard S. Brownlee, Director, State Historical Society; Mrs. Dorothy J. Caldwell; Missouri Division of Commerce and Industrial Development; Missouri Tourism Commission.

Montana: former Governor and Mrs. Tim Babcock; Mrs. Lucille Baker; Miss Mary Dempsey, Librarian, Historical Society; Mrs. Raymond T. Nagle; Advertising Department, Montana Highway Commission; Adjutant General's Office.

Nebraska: Governor and Mrs. Norbert T. Tiemann; Mr. W. D. Aeschbacher; Mr. Marvin F. Kivett, Director, State Historical Society; *Nebraska Farmer; Omaha World Herald;* Mr. Selmer Solheim, architect; Mr. Jack Riggle, photographer.

Nevada: Governor and Mrs. Paul Laxalt; Mrs. Grant Sawyer, former First Lady; Mr. Frederick C. Gale, Assistant State Archivist; Mrs. Patsy Hughes; Mrs. Marilyn Pochop; Highway Dept.

New Hampshire: former Governor and Mrs. John W. King; Mr. Edwin H. Hunt, Director, Division of Records Management and Archives; Mr. Arthur H. Fowler; Mr. Ralph H. Morse.

New Jersey: Governor and Mrs. Richard J. Hughes; Mr. Larry Bilder; Mr. Ronald A. Breslow; Mr. William M. Dwyer; Mr. Roger H. McDonough, Director, Division of the State Library, Archives and History; Mr. Kenneth W. Richards; Mr. John A. Leone, photographer.

New Mexico: Governor and Mrs. David F. Cargo; Mrs. Jack M. Campbell, former First Lady; Dr. Myra Ellen Jenkins, Deputy for Archives; Mr. Arthur L. Ortiz; Mrs. J. K. Shishkin, Research Librarian, Museum of New Mexico; Mr. Harvey Caplin, photographer.

New York: Governor and Mrs. Nelson A. Rockefeller; Hon. C. V. R. Schuyler, Commissioner of General Services; Mr. Herbert M. Koster; Miss Susan Lawrence, Assistant Librarian, New York State Library; Mrs. Isabelle K. Savell; Miss Juliet F. Wolohan, Associate Librarian, New York State Library.

North Carolina: former Governor and Mrs. Dan K. Moore; Mr. Christopher C. Crittenden, Director, Department of Archives and History; Mr. John R. Hampton; Mr. H. G. Jones, State Archivist, Department of Archives and History; Mrs. Joye E. Jordan, Museum Administrator, Department of Archives and History.

North Dakota: Governor and Mrs. William L. Guy; Mr. Ray H. Mattison, Superintendent, State Historical Society; Office of the Secretary of State; North Dakota Travel Department; Mr. Ernest Feland, photographer.

Ohio: Governor and Mrs. James A. Rhodes; Mr. James E. Douthitt; Mr. Louis Freeman; Mr. Daniel R. Porter, Director, Ohio Historical Society.

Oklahoma: Governor and Mrs. Dewey F. Bartlett; Mrs. Henry Bellmon, former First Lady; Mr. Ralph H. Funk, State Archivist; Mr. Mike McCarville; Mr. Ed Pritchett; Miss Anna A. Walls.

Oregon: Governor and Mrs. Tom McCall; Mrs. Mark O. Hatfield, former First Lady; Mr. Kessler R. Cannon; Mr. Victor Fryer; Mrs. Dorotha B. Kelsay, Oregon State Library; Mrs. Mary W. Thompson; Northwest Historical Section, Washington State Library; Travel Information Division, Oregon State Highway Department.

Pennsylvania: Governor and Mrs. Raymond P. Shafer; Mr. Robert K. Bloom; Mrs. Augusta Gale; Miss Evelyn Pletz; Mr. S. K. Stevens, Executive Director, Pennsylvania Historical and Museum Commission; Pennsylvania Department of Commerce; Pennsylvania Department of Property and Supplies; Mr. Fred R. Bell.

Rhode Island: former Governor and Mrs. John H. Chafee; Maj. Gen. John M. McGreevy; Miss Phyllis Peloquin; Miss Mary T. Quinn, Assistant for Archives; Alex Tvares Studios.

South Carolina: Governor and Mrs. Robert E. McNair; Dr. Everetta L. Blair; Mr. Fred C. Craft; Mrs. Joan R. Faunt, State Librarian; Dr. Charles E. Lee, Director, Department of Archives and History; Mr. Jack M. Scoville, A.I.D.; Miss Wylma Wates, Reference Archivist, Department of Archives and History; Mr. Philip B. Hill, photographer.

South Dakota: former Governor Nils A. Boe; Mr. Glenn L. Jorgenson, Director of Employment; Mrs. Starlene Mitchell; Mr. Will G. Robinson, Superintendent, Department of History; Mr. Joe McCully, Department of Highways, photographer.

Tennessee: Governor and Mrs. Buford Ellington; Mrs. Frank G. Clement, former First Lady; Mr. Hudley Crockett; Dr. Sam B. Smith, State Librarian and Archivist.

Texas: former Governor and Mrs. John Connally; Mrs. Bess Dunlavey, Research Associate, Mr. Robert E. Johnson, Executive Director, Texas Legislative Council; Mr. Tom H. Taylor, Director, Travel and Information Division, Texas Highway Department; Mr. Bill Malone, photographer.

Utah: Governor and Mrs. Calvin L. Rampton; Mr. Everett L. Cooley, Director, State Historical Society; Dept. of Highways.

Vermont: former Governor and Mrs. Philip H. Hoff; Mr. Charles T. Morrissey, Director, Vermont Historical Society; Mr. Arthur Ristau; Mr. John A. Williams, Editor of State Papers; Lizzari, Montpelier photographer.

Virginia: Governor and Mrs. Mills E. Godwin, Jr.; Mrs. Albertis S. Harrison, Jr., former First Lady; Mr. James Marshall Bradley; Mr. Minor Hawley; Mr. William J. Van Schreeven, State Archivist; Roger Shephardson, Dept. of Conservation and Economic Development, Dementi Studio; and Colonial Williamsburg photographs.

Washington: Governor and Mrs. Daniel J. Evans; Mr. Ron Allen; Mr. Sidney McAlpin, State Archivist; Mrs. Creath A. Tooley; Washington State Library; Tourist Promotion Division, Department of Commerce and Economic Development.

West Virginia: former Governor and Mrs. Hulett C. Smith; Mr. Con Hardman; Dr. James Lloyd Hupp, Historian and Archivist; West Virginia Department of Commerce, photographs.

Wisconsin: Governor Warren P. Knowles; Mr. Leslie H. Fishel, Jr., Director, State Historical Society; Mr. James Gruentzel; State Legislative Reference Bureau; Mr. Norvel R. Barger, photographer.

Wyoming: Governor and Mrs. Stanley K. Hathaway; Mrs. Clifford P. Hansen, former First Lady; Mr. Jack Fairweather; Miss Lola M. Homsher; Mr. Neal E. Miller, Director, Archives and History Department; Wyoming Travel Commission.

American Samoa: Governor and Mrs. Owen S. Aspinall; Mrs. Rex Lee, former First Lady; Office of Territories, U.S. Department of the Interior.

Guam: Governor and Mrs. Manuel F. L. Guerrero; former Governor and Mrs. Bill Daniel; Mr. Milton E. Garrison; Miss Magdalena S. Taitano, Librarian, N. M. Flores Memorial Library; Mr. A. B. Won Pat, Guam's Representative in Washington; Office of Territories, U.S. Department of the Interior; U.S. Naval Air Station, Agaña, photographs.

Puerto Rico: former Governor and Mrs. Roberto Sanchez-Vilella; Mr. Ricardo Alegria, Executive Director, Puerto Rican Institute of Culture; Miss Vicky Cobos; Col. Rafael Montilla; Mansion photograph, Colourpicture Publishers, Inc.; Capitol photograph, courtesy Puerto Rico Senate.

Virgin Islands: former Governor and Mrs. Ralph M. Paiewonsky; Miss Francesca Greve; Mr. Leon A. Mawson; Mrs. Gladys Rafter, Office of Territories, U.S. Department of the Interior; Mrs. Jo Costa and Miss Martha Olson, Farley Manning Associates, Inc., photographs.

Libraries: The Library of Congress; the libraries of the Office of Emergency Preparedness, the Bureau of the Budget, the Department of State, the Department of the Navy, the Smithsonian Institution; the District of Columbia Public Library; the libraries of the National Geographic Society, the American Institute of Architects, George Washington University, and the American Automobile Association.

INDEX

ALABAMA
Mansion 24
Capitol 144
Executives 250

ALASKA
Mansion 26
Capitol 146
Executives 251

ARIZONA
Capitol 148
Executives 251

ARKANSAS
Mansion 28
Capitol 150
Executives 251

CALIFORNIA
Mansion 30
Capitol 152
Executives 252

COLORADO
Mansion 32
Capitol 154
Executives 252

CONNECTICUT
Mansion 34
Capitol 156
Executives 253

DELAWARE
Mansion 36
Capitol 158
Executives 254

FLORIDA
Mansion 38
Capitol 160
Executives 254

GEORGIA
Mansion 40
Capitol 162
Executives 255

HAWAII
Mansion 44
Capitol 164
Executives 255

IDAHO
Mansion 46
Capitol 166
Executives 256

ILLINOIS
Mansion 48
Capitol 168
Executives 256

INDIANA
Mansion 50
Capitol 170
Executives 256

IOWA
Mansion 52
Capitol 172
Executives 257

KANSAS
Mansion 54
Capitol 174
Executives 257

KENTUCKY
Mansion 58
Capitol 176
Executives 257

LOUISIANA
Mansion 60
Capitol 178
Executives 258

MAINE
Mansion 62
Capitol 180
Executives 258

MARYLAND
Mansion 66
Capitol 182
Executives 259

MASSACHUSETTS
Capitol 184
Executives 260

MICHIGAN
Capitol 186
Executives 261

MINNESOTA
Mansion 68
Capitol 188
Executives 262

MISSISSIPPI
Mansion 70
Capitol 190
Executives 262

MISSOURI
Mansion 72
Capitol 192
Executives 263

MONTANA
Mansion 74
Capitol 194
Executives 263

NEBRASKA
Mansion 76
Capitol 196
Executives 263

NEVADA
Mansion 78
Capitol 198
Executives 264

NEW HAMPSHIRE
Capitol 200
Executives 264

NEW JERSEY
Mansion 80
Capitol 202
Executives 265

NEW MEXICO
Mansion 83
Capitol 204
Executives 266

NEW YORK
Mansion 86
Capitol 206
Executives 267

NORTH CAROLINA
Mansion 88
Capitol 208
Executives 268

NORTH DAKOTA
Mansion 90
Capitol 210
Executives 269

OHIO
Mansion 92
Capitol 212
Executives 269

OKLAHOMA
Mansion 94
Capitol 214
Executives 269

OREGON
Capitol 216
Executives 270

PENNSYLVANIA
Mansion 96
Capitol 218
Executives 270

RHODE ISLAND
Capitol 220
Executives 271

SOUTH CAROLINA
Mansion 98
Capitol 222
Executives 272

SOUTH DAKOTA
Mansion 100
Capitol 224
Executives 273

TENNESSEE
Mansion 102
Capitol 226
Executives 274

TEXAS
Mansion 104
Capitol 228
Executives 274

UTAH
Mansion 108
Capitol 230
Executives 275

VERMONT
Capitol 232
Executives 275

VIRGINIA
Mansion 110
Capitol 234
Executives 276

WASHINGTON
Mansion 114
Capitol 236
Executives 278

WEST VIRGINIA
Mansion 116
Capitol 238
Executives 278

WISCONSIN
Mansion 118
Capitol 240
Executives 278

WYOMING
Mansion 120
Capitol 242
Executives 279

AMERICAN SAMOA
Mansion 122
Capitol 244
Executives 279

GUAM
Mansion 124
Capitol 245
Executives 279

PUERTO RICO
Mansion 125
Capitol 246
Executives 281

VIRGIN ISLANDS
Mansion 128
Capitol 248
Executives 281